WILLIAM WORDSWORTH'S

The Prelude

WITH A SELECTION FROM THE

Shorter Poems, the Sonnets,
The Recluse, and The Excursion

AND THREE ESSAYS ON

The Art of Poetry

———— • ————

EDITED WITH AN INTRODUCTION BY
Carlos Baker

Holt, Rinehart and Wi

NEW YORK · CHICAGO · SAN FRAN
TORONTO · LONDON

*This volume of selections
is dedicated to the memory
of George McLean Harper.*

Sixteenth Printing, November, 1966

Introduction copyright, 1948, 1954, by Carlos Baker

Typography by Stefan Salter

Printed in the United States of America

Library of Congress Catalog Card Number: 54–7056

20775-0114

INTRODUCTION

For all those moderns to whom poetry matters, the continual re-examination of the poetry of the past is just as vital an obligation as the encouragement of good new poetry now. If we believe, as we are justified in doing, that there are literary giants on our earth today, it is well to remember that there were also giants in the earth in times past. And William Wordsworth, as John Crowe Ransom has recently reminded us, is one of the giants of English poetry.

Giantism, of course, has its embarrassments — for giants. When Captain Lemuel Gulliver visited the land of the Brobdingnagians, he discovered that the minor physical imperfections of his hulking hosts became unhappily visible. If Wordsworth is indeed a giant, the fact may help to explain why some of his faults are glaringly evident to those of us whose stature is lower than his own. That he shows imperfections, not even his hardiest admirers deny. As early as 1800, the poet warned prospective readers that they might "frequently have to struggle with feelings of strangeness and awkwardness" as they read the second edition of *Lyrical Ballads*. "They will look round for poetry and will be induced to inquire by what species of courtesy these attempts can be permitted to assume that title." In certain respects, readers have felt, looked, and inquired as Wordsworth predicted, not only in 1800, but ever since.

Among the earliest of these were his peers. Coleridge idolized him, even leaned upon him at times as a sturdy moral monolith, yet devoted some thousands of words in the *Biographia Literaria* to the errors of style, tone, and syntax into which he thought Wordsworth had been led by over-absorption in an indefensible theory of poetry. It seems to be a fact that Coleridge set the sights for what has been a continuing, though sporadic, critical barrage. Coleridge's list of the ineptitudes in Wordsworth has not been improved upon, nor has it been appreciably added to: inconstancy of style producing inadvertent bathos; occasional mental bombast; linguistic incongruities; a certain oversolemn matter-of-factness suggesting an underdeveloped sense of humor; and an eddying rather than a progression of thought, suggesting the muddy backwashes of a river rather than the clear, swift-running current of the main stream. Such errors of commission are scattered up and down the collected works like Brobdingnagian blemishes.

A few others have been observed. Byron found him dull, overmild, and flat, like a sauce into which the cook had forgotten to shake pepper. The bumptious young lord of *English Bards and Scotch Reviewers* called Wordsworth a "dull disciple" of Robert Southey's, and a "mild apostate" from the neoclassical rules. Homespun narratives like those of Martha Ray, the unwed mother of "The Thorn," or Betty Foy, "the idiot mother of the idiot boy," struck Byron (as they have since struck others) as "Christmas stories tortured into rhyme"; it was hardly to be expected, by anyone but Wordsworth, that they should "contain the essence of the true sublime." Keats approached the problem of sublimity from another angle. Having taken Shakespeare as his model for the poet's self-immolation in poetry, Keats was discomfited by the ever-recurrent "I" in Wordsworth; he spoke, not unkindly, of "the Wordsworthian, or egotistical sublime," and wondered, half-aloud, whether Wordsworth's grandeur was not in some respects contaminated and rendered obtrusive by the poet's sonorous ego. Shelley's latent satirical impulse was aroused by similar considerations. In his travesty, "Peter Bell the Third," he wrote of Wordsworth that

He had a mind which was somehow
At once circumference and centre
Of all he might or feel or know;
Nothing went ever out, although
Something did ever enter.
He had as much imagination
As a pint-pot; he never could
Fancy another situation,
From which to dart his contemplation,
Than that wherein he stood.

Yet that same group could not help admiring Wordsworth; as practicing poets they had the calipers to measure his stature. Coleridge in his conversation poems and Byron in *Childe Harold's Pilgrimage* paid him the compliment of imitation. Keats's letters are often punctuated with periods of praise for the master. And Shelley, whose *Alastor* sometimes reads as if Wordsworth had been guiding the pen, continues the "Peter Bell" poem with this astute comment:

Yet his was individual mind,
And new-created all he saw
In a new manner, and refined
Those new creations, and combined
Them, by a master-spirit's law.
Thus, though unimaginative,
An apprehension clear, intense,
Of his mind's work, had made alive
The things it wrought on; I believe
Wakening a sort of thought in sense.

Parody, however, is always more fun than balanced criticism. Whenever the giant nods, the caricaturists and parodists can be counted on to tiptoe out of the oven like mischievous small Jacks-of-the-Beanstalk, and to take up their stations behind his chair. Admirers of "We Are Seven" can never quite forget Max Beerbohm's acidulous portrait of a whey-faced old gentleman pontifically expostulating

with the little wench in the sunbonnet on the fact that seven
less two leaves five.   Laurence Housman, himself a skilled
parodist, was probably reflecting the Beerbohm influence
when he refused to reprint the poem in a recent Wordsworth
anthology because, he said, it annoyed him from end to end.
Almost anyone with a stiletto, an inkstand of vitriol, and a
groatsworth of wit can wreak wonderful havoc among the
more solemn poems.   Witness J. K. Stephen's manipulation
of Wordsworth's sonnet entitled "Thoughts of a Briton on
the Subjugation of Switzerland":

> Two voices are there; one is of the deep;
> It learns the storm-cloud's thunderous melody,
> Now roars, now murmurs with the changing sea,
> Now bird-like pipes, now closes soft in sleep;
> And one is of an old half-witted sheep
> Which bleats articulate monotony,
> And indicates that two and one are three,
> And grass is green, lakes damp, and mountains steep;
> And Wordsworth, both are thine; at certain times,
> Forth from the heart of thy melodious rhymes,
> The form and pressure of high thoughts will burst;
> At other times — Good Lord! I'd rather be
> Quite unacquainted with the ABC
> Than write such hopeless rubbish as thy worst.

The man the parodists call Wordswords or Worstworst is
occasionally (but not often) capable of being dull, homely,
flat, earth-bound, egotistical, humorless, obscure, and en-
tangled in prosaism.   At worst, his "incidents and agents
from common life" seem merely trite, his ultrasimplified
language merely silly — as if, say, we were being asked to
genuflect before Mother Goose as the patron saint of the Eng-
lish Lake District.   But his worst is infinitely less frequent
than the parodists would have us think.

The Victorians were wise enough to see what must be done
about it: they stressed the need of editing Wordsworth,

cracking off the common clay that disguised and obscured the durable gems. When Arnold made his own selection of the poems in 1879, he said unequivocally that "the poetical performance of Wordsworth is, after that of Shakespeare and Milton . . . undoubtedly the most considerable in our language from the Elizabethan age to the present time." The impression made by one of his fine poems was, however, "too often dulled and spoiled by a very inferior piece coming after it." Wordsworth had permitted "a great deal of poetical baggage" to encumber the collected works. What Arnold called baggage, Walter Pater thought of as débris. Few artists work quite cleanly, said Pater. They do not always cast off all débris and leave us only "what the heat of their imagination has wholly fused and transformed" into diamond-hard crystalline form. The critic, the editor, the anthologist must assume the obligation of carting off the débris, chucking out the baggage (Wordsworth at worst) in order to reveal what was there all the time — strong, clear, firm, deep, and lasting — Wordsworth at his best. For behind the shale in the valley, beyond the common lower hills, like Skiddaw in the Lake District or Snowdon in Wales, looms the old giant, a commanding presence.

II

If we ask what the particular virtue is which gives backbone to Wordsworth's giantism, Pater provides us with an excellent starting point. To expunge the worst and to concentrate on the best is, says he, to "trace the action of his unique incommunicable faculty, that strange, mystical sense of a life in natural things, and of man's life as a part of nature, drawing strength and color and character from local influences, from the hills and streams, and from natural sights and sounds. . . . That is the virtue, the active principle in

Wordsworth's poetry." An example would be those parts of "Michael" where this sense of the beneficial interaction of man and nature is projected — not the fable itself, not the story of Luke's going bad in the Big City, not even the memorable image of a father-son relationship in the unfinished sheepfold, but rather the portrait of old Michael himself, formed and strengthened by his mountainous environment and his enduring and durable will. *Levavi oculos meos in montes* runs the psalm; and this is part of Wordsworth's testament. Another instance, milder and less rugged, is the Lucy poem which begins, "Three years she grew" —

> The stars of midnight shall be dear
> To her; and she shall lean her ear
> In many a secret place
> Where rivulets dance their wayward round,
> And beauty born of murmuring sound
> Shall pass into her face.

Housman rightly believes that the last two lines could not have been written by any of the other major English poets: they are emphatically Wordsworth's. They display the essential quality and character of his poetical mind at its best. Wordsworth himself knew that this was so. As early as 1800 he set himself to oppose the widespread and degrading "thirst after outrageous stimulation" which resulted from the atmosphere of war and genocide, "the increasing accumulation of men in cities," the sensationalism of newspapers, and the deluge of cheap fiction. "Reflecting," he said, "upon the magnitude of the general evil, I should be oppressed with no dishonorable melancholy, had I not a deep impression of certain inherent and indestructible qualities of the human mind, and likewise of certain powers in the great and permanent objects that act upon it, which are equally inherent and indestructible." Out of this deep impression, long brooded over, arises the inherent and indestructible *virtue* of Wordsworth's poetry.

His dimensions are heightened also by his being (what Coleridge called him) a philosophical poet. Reading the neohumanist critics, one would gather that Wordsworth was some sort of blend of the hard-shelled naturalist Lucretius and the soft-shelled naturalist Rousseau. This view is false. It will never do to overstress the naturalistic element in his thought as over against the humanistic and theistic components. All three conspire to fructify in his belief in the motherhood of nature, the brotherhood of man, the fatherhood of God, and — it may be seriously added, the neighborhood of pain. If Wordsworth can write like a nature-mystic, a pantheist, or a pan-psychist, he can never be said to have forgotten the human figures in the foreground or the supreme Intelligence in the background. The Wordsworthian equivalent of the Miltonic "great argument" comes clear in the eloquent opening of his unfinished masterwork, *The Recluse*. Turning aside from the ancient epic theme of arms and the man, he chose to tell instead

> Of Truth, of Grandeur, Beauty, Love, and Hope,
> And melancholy Fear subdued by Faith;
> Of blessed consolations in distress;
> Of moral strength, and intellectual Power;
> Of joy in widest commonalty spread;
> Of the individual Mind that keeps her own
> Inviolate retirement, subject there
> To Conscience only, and the law supreme
> Of that Intelligence which governs all —
> I sing: — "Fit audience let me find though few!"

The individual mind of man, subject to the inner checks of conscience and of consciousness of the laws of God ("that Intelligence which governs all"), is surely a problem vast enough to preoccupy any poet. "Not Chaos," he wrote, still thinking of Milton, not

> The darkest pit of lowest Erebus,
> Nor aught of blinder vacancy, scooped out
> By help of dreams — can breed such fear and awe
> As fall upon us often when we look
> Into our Minds, into the Mind of Man —
> My haunt, and the main region of my song. . . .

If it was necessary for him to see "ill sights of madding passions mutally inflamed"; if in country and town alike he

> Must hear Humanity in fields and groves
> Pipe solitary anguish; or must hang
> Brooding above the fierce confederate storm
> Of sorrow, barricadoed evermore
> Within the walls of cities . . .

he had found means to encompass the sound of wailing into a symphony whose overtones were not ultimately tragic. One means was through the timely "utterance of numerous verse." Another, and anterior, means was to fix his contemplation upon the inherent and indestructible powers visible alike in nature and human nature. From that vantage point, it was possible to understand that moral evil ("what man has made of man") cannot finally cancel out the universal good. Under "nature's holy plan," by observing the myriad ways in which the mind is "fitted" to the external world, as well as the world to the mind, one could discover a sufficient justification of God's ways to men. "Nature is made to conspire with spirit to emancipate us." This was Emerson's cogent summary of the point Wordsworth made in a thousand ways throughout the course of his poetical career. Followed through all its ramifications, it is the point which permits us to claim for him the title of philosophical poet.

Emerson, the prophet of democratic vistas, helps to make us aware of yet another source of Wordsworth's strength and stature. It is that, like another giant named Antaeus, he believes that the poet must keep his feet on the ground, deriving substance and sustenance from his mother, the earth. The politics of Antaeus are unknown, but no one can read Wordsworth for very long without the conviction that at the deeper levels his democracy never wavers. In passages like those relating to Beaupuy in the ninth book of *The Prelude*, his political views come to the surface; later on, as we know, these views were subject to some adjustment in the direction of conservatism. Yet the readjustment does not affect the basic tenet of his democratic faith; few modern poets have embodied in their work, whether by statement or by implication, so firm a sense of the dignity or worth of the common individual man.

Whoever would read the famous preface of 1800 afresh and without preliminary prejudice can scarcely do better than to see it as a declaration of the need for democracy in poetry. Essentially the defence of a theory of poetry, it has long been a battleground for critics because of Wordsworth's espousal of a special doctrine of poetic diction. There is more to it than that. The preface makes a whole series of distinctions and connections whose importance to esthetic theory are not so much modern as timeless. He distinguishes true elevation of style from the false methods employed by certain eighteenth-century poetasters, noting especially the frozen artifice of perception and expression and the "curious elaboration" which beset that cult. In a searching passage he distinguishes the task of the poet from that of the scientist. He indicates the triple necessity of thought, feeling, and good sense in all good poetry. He compares the language of poetry to that of prose. He tries to show the relationship between poetry and the primary psychological laws of human nature, including the pleasure-pain principle as enunciated by Jeremy Bentham. His outline of the creative process is astute and valuable; like Coleridge he is a good psychologist because he is able to contemplate objectively the operations of his own mind. He is also enough of a proponent of the "low" and the "common" to insist throughout his essay on the remarriage of poetry to *things;* for to him democracy is not an abstraction but a way of life empirically learned.

It is, however, in his conception of the poet and of poetry itself that his democratic leanings are most apparent. This is not to say that he treats the subject exhaustively, but only to suggest from what quarter his winds of doctrine blow. The poet, he insists, is "a man speaking to men," not differing from them in kind but only in degree. Here is no vessel for the divine afflatus, set apart from his kind in lordly magnificence. Here is no frenzied enthusiast, no hierophant writing better than he knows, but rather one man, among men, speaking quietly to his fellows of what most moves his heart and what is most central to his deeper thoughts on the inter-relations of man, nature, and transcendental or immanent supernature. The poet's sensibility is livelier, of course. He is uncommonly imaginative, has more enthusiasm, tenderness, and knowledge than the common man. He is more articulate, and has a deeper capacity for delight in all he sees and knows. But he is only the uncommon common man, risen naturally from the ranks of the natural *aristoi*, coming of no diviner race than those to whom he speaks and writes.

Or take, on the same grounds, the question of what poetry is. It is, says Wordsworth, "the image of man and nature." It is also "the most philosophic" (that is, wisdom-loving, and the wisdom loved is that of the people) of all writing. "Its object is truth, not individual and local, but general and operative; not standing upon external testimony, but carried alive into the heart by passion." It is truth which "is its own testimony" because, having been proclaimed, it will immediately be recognized by other men as pertinent to the human situation in which they find themselves. It is thus a direct revelation of reality, or of the poet's considered version of the actual. Therefore Wordsworth is able to say that "in spite of difference of soil and climate, of language and manners, of laws and customs; in spite of things silently gone out of mind, and things violently destroyed; the poet binds together by passion and knowledge the vast empire of human society, as it is spread over the whole earth, and over all time." To do so, poetry must keep the reader "in the company of flesh and blood." It is not involved with the tears of angels, but with "natural and human tears." No celestial ichor distinguishes its language from that of prose: "the same human blood circulates through the veins of them both." The poetry of earth is never dead; but we may be best assured of this, thinks Wordsworth, if we assert the ultimate democracy of poetic language: the words of a man speaking to men in the tongue all men know because they are men.

The revolution Wordsworth led was not primarily a back-to-nature movement. It was rather a movement which called for a fresh and mutually fructifying reunion of reality and ideality. His special individual *virtue* as a poet comes from his preoccupation with the indestructibles in nature and in mind. His method is to combine the instruments and insights of the poet with the ideals of the philosopher whose bias is strongly humanistic. His continuing belief in the dignity and dependability of the common man brings his work into spiritual alignment with those democratic revolutions which in his time, both in Europe and America, were coming to the fore after the long years of the *ancien régime*.

III

Finally, there is the artist. As befits a giant, his most persistent theme is growth. Because, in a special sense, the child is father to the man, he becomes absorbed in the growth of children. The youngster may be Wordsworth himself passing through the three stages up the stairway towards maturity, as in "Tintern Abbey." It may be the child whose "progress" is detailed in the Great Ode. Gradually losing what Hazlitt called "the feeling of immortality in youth," he finds, somewhat reluctantly, that he must settle for "the faith which looks through death" rather than at it, and the "philosophic mind" of the Christian stoic who has kept watch over man's mortality and learned, in the end, what it takes to be a man. It may be his beloved sister Dorothy, or Coleridge, or the child called Lucy, or the small son of his friend Basil Montagu who appears charmingly in the "Anecdote for Fathers." The theme of such early lyrics as "Expostulation and Reply," "The Tables Turned," "Lines Written in Early Spring," and "To My Sister" is once again growth. He wishes to show how the mind develops through sense experience and reflection — John Locke's two great "fountains" of empirical knowledge. Or we may learn through the sudden leap of intuition, the unlooked-for epiphany by which one "impulse" (the word is a favorite of Locke's) from a springtime woodland *may* (Wordsworth does not say it necessarily *will*) teach the man of sensibility more about how men's minds work than a reading of all the sages. An overstatement used for shock value? Clearly it is. Yet what is an epiphany but a visionary overstatement which one hopes time will prove to have been approximately right? A perceptive and reflective observer of nature and its laws is provided with all sorts of emblems, analogies, and implications by the simple expedient of taking a walk and keeping his eyes open. Wordsworth, the perambulatory poet, well knew that the growth of our minds is controlled both by what we perceive and by "what we half-create." If we have imagination, together with a considered body of knowledge and conviction, we can "build up greatest things from least suggestions" — like the emblem writers of the Renaissance, or the Fathers of the medieval Church, or like any first-rate poet.

The subtitle of *The Prelude*, Wordsworth's most intricate exploration of the subject, is "Growth of a Poet's Mind." He undertook it partly as a practice poem, a way of learning to handle blank verse, but mainly as an exercise in understanding on the Socratic principle, "Know thyself." What were the formative forces which had been brought to bear upon that "stripling of the hills," that northern villager with whom, of all people, Wordsworth was most closely acquainted? His childhood luckily had been spent in Nature's lap. A nurse both stern and kindly, she had planted seeds of sympathy and understanding in that growing mind. "Fair seedtime had my soul," says Wordsworth. Its growth had been "fostered alike by beauty and by fear." The milder discipline of beauty informs such lines as those on the river Derwent, winding among its "grassy holms" with ceaseless calm music like a lullaby. The discipline of fear is embodied in the trap-robbing and boat-stealing episodes. The boy, troubled in conscience, seemed to hear low breathings coming after him in the woods. From a thwart of the stolen rowboat, he watched horror-struck the huge looming of the black peak from beyond the sheltering grove by the lakeside — something like the incarnation of a Mosaic commandment, which it was not, except as his conscience made it seem so. He is aware, of course, that Nature has no moral ideas. Natural scenes like the grassy Derwent riverbank or the monster shape of the night-shrouded mountain played a "needful part" in the development of his mind simply by having been there on occasions afterwards recognized as crucial. What gave them significance was the condition of mind with which they entered into permanent association.

There is a kind of "wise passiveness" (Keats called it "diligent indolence") in which Nature is a veritable treasure house of suggestion. Natural scenes, taken in their intricate totality, often awakened in Wordsworth what he called "the visionary power." Once he tells how he stood, for shelter from an approaching storm, under a brow of rock, listening all awake and aware to "the ghostly language of the ancient earth."

> Thence did I drink the visionary power;
> And deem not profitless those fleeting moods
> Of shadowy exultation: not for this
> That they are kindred to our purer mind
> And intellectual life; but that the soul,
> Remembering how she felt, but what she felt
> Remembering not, retains an obscure sense
> Of possible sublimity, whereto
> With growing faculties she doth aspire,
> With faculties still growing, feeling still
> That whatsoever point they gain, they yet
> Have something to pursue.

He records dozens of these natural scenes, not for themselves but for what his mind could learn through the stimuli they offered. This one provided a long vista or distant prospect up the way he knew he must go. Often, at such times, he seems to catch with his mind's eye "gleams like the flashing of a shield." The gleam is nearly always Merlin-like, magical, anticipating a period of epiphany when apprehensions hitherto disparate will suddenly coalesce to form another level of understanding. From there he can go on.

Since the structure of *The Prelude* is pyramidal, with a broad base in sense impressions and a capstone of semimystical insight into the ultimate unity of God's mighty plan, it is no accident, it is rather a triumph of the artistic intellect, that it should close with the Mount Snowdon episode. Once again the natural scene plays an emblematic part in what is essentially a religious intuition. Coming suddenly from the fog on the lower flanks of the mountain into bright clear moonlight; looking down on the cloud surface through which the backs of lesser peaks show like whales at sea; hearing, as from an abyss, the roar of mighty waters, the combined voices of innumerable streams, the poet has gained a symbol of such complexity as to be relatively inexhaustible to meditation. When he comes to recollect the scene's emotional impact in the tranquillity of a later time, he recognizes it, not for what it was, but for what, after rumination, it had become *for him:* a Gestalt pattern standing for the human mind at its highest stage of development, a mind sustained

> By recognitions of transcendent power,
> In sense conducting to ideal form.

Such minds are no longer the prisoners of sense impressions. Instead, the "quickening impulse" provided by sense stimuli prepares such minds all the better "to hold fit converse with the spiritual world" and to discover, as was never possible before, the true meanings of liberty and love. No wonder that Coleridge, having heard this poem read aloud, rose up at the end to find himself "in prayer."

Another way of watching the operation of the growth principle in Wordsworth is to see how and how often he uses it as an organizational device in the shorter poems. It may be called the double-exposure technique. Because he is interested in the stages of growth, he often juxtaposes two widely separated periods of time in such a way that we are made dramatically conscious of the degree of growth that has taken place between Stage One and Stage Two. It resembles the effect that might be produced by our seeing a double exposure on photographic film, where the same person appears in the same setting, except that ten years have elapsed between exposures.

The device is not uniquely Wordsworth's, though he has given to it his own special stamp and hallmark, as one of his ways of seeing. Shakespeare, for instance, uses the technique for dramatic effect in the two balcony scenes of *Romeo and Juliet.* The first of these is an almost perfect embodiment of romantic young love, untested in the alembic of mature experience, surrounded by danger, overstrewn with moonlight, punctuated with extravagant vows, compliments, and conceits. Between this and the second and far quieter balcony scene a process of accelerated maturation has set in. Mercutio and Tybalt have been killed, Romeo has been banished, a forced marriage for Juliet is in the offing, the lovers have made their secret matrimony and spent their wedding night together. The effect of the second balcony scene is then to remind us of the first, and to underscore dramatically how far adverse circumstances and their own responses to them have matured the youthful lovers in the meantime.

Something very like this is constantly happening in the poetry of Wordsworth. We have the picture which has long been held in memory; over against it is laid the picture of things as they are in the historical "now." Between the two exposures, subtle changes have always taken place. These may involve a simple translation of the protagonist from the conditions of the country to those of the city as in the early lyric, "The Reverie of Poor Susan." Here the song of the caged thrush at the corner of Wood Street in a poor part of London is the auditory image which, for a brief instant, opens the shutter in the camera obscura of Susan's mind. The film of memory still holds the impress of the rural scene, the "green pastures" where she happily spent the season of her childhood. Momentarily, and ironically, the drab present and the green past are juxtaposed. Then the vision fades and once more the prison house of the city closes round her.

The technique which gives "The Reverie" whatever distinction it possesses is used far more subtly in many of the better lyrics. In "Tintern Abbey," for example, the light in the eyes of his sister seems to reflect for Wordsworth the very set of mind with which, five years before, he had exulted over the beauties of this quiet rural panorama beside the river Wye. "I behold in thee what I was once." As he overlooks the scene once more, with the mental landscape of the past still in his purview, he is made doubly aware of a sense of loss (the past will not return) and a sense of compensation greater than the loss (the new maturity and insight which the advancing years have brought). Again, however, it is the collocation of two separate "spots of time" which dramatizes for him (and for us) the degree and kind of his growth in the intervening period. Again it is the technique of double exposure, this odd co-presence in the mind of the then and the now, which gives dramatic life to his reflective lyric.

The great ode, "Intimations of Immortality," abounds, of course, in a complexity of metaphorical activity that differentiates it markedly from "Tintern Abbey." Yet its broad strategy of deployment strikingly resembles that of the earlier poem. For its vitality once more depends upon a dialectical interplay between ideas of innocence and ideas of experience. Here is the picture of the true innocent, trailing his clouds of glory, clothed with the sun. Yet here beside it is also the voice of experience, neither harsh nor grating, though deeply informed with the knowledge of the possibilities of good and evil. The two voices make a sort of antiphonal chant which runs throughout this wonderful poem, accounting, perhaps, for the incantational quality it has for the ear when read aloud. The visual aspects, however, are more important than the auditory. Through the mind's eye we are made to see the two states of being in the sharpest contrast, but with the one overlying though not obscuring the other, as in a palimpsest. Thereby the interior drama of the poem — a parable, essentially, of experience and innocence — is made to transpire; and with what effect only the reader of the poem can truly know.

The same principle is at work in "The Two April Mornings," "She was a phantom of delight," and the "Ode to Duty." It gives special dramatic impact to a number of the best sonnets, including such triumphs as "Composed upon

Westminster Bridge" and that moving sonnet of bereavement which begins, ironically, with the phrase, "Surprised by joy." A very clear manifestation appears in the "Elegiac Stanzas Suggested by a Picture of Peele Castle." Here one finds, still, the two pictures. One is in memory: a calm summer Wordsworth spent long ago by the seaside in the vicinity of the castle. The second is an actual canvas painted by the poet's friend and sometime patron, Sir George Beaumont. It shows the same castle in a season of storm and stress, ruggedly fronting the fierce onslaughts of waves and wind. Between these two moralized landscapes stretches the poem. The first eight stanzas set up the poet's dream of human life through the sunsmitten image of the castle "sleeping in a glassy sea." Recantation comes in the last seven stanzas with a farewell to the youthful dream and a willing acceptance of the actual as the passage of time has discovered it to be.

The examination of these poems leads at last to an explanation of the elegiac tone which overlies or penetrates so much of the work of this lyricist of human growth. Regret, a certain kind of lamentation, does battle with joy, a certain kind of paean for the blessings of this life, and the joy tends, on the whole, to win out. The regret is for things lost: a vision of immortality in youth, an absolute sense of nature's ultimate beneficence, an unchartered freedom, or (it may be) a daughter, or the "phantom of delight" one's wife was when first she gleamed upon the sight. At the same time Wordsworth accepts, not only without demur or sentimental self-pity but also with positive joy, those substitutes which life makes for the early raptures. These may be a faith that looks through death, a sense of the value of the "pageantry of fear" in natural scenes, a responsible pleasure in following the dictates of duty, a beautiful child to be admired though not owned, and (with all that means) a woman in place of a phantom loveliness that could never be real.

Maturity for Wordsworth is not, of course, a state in which

peace or happiness are guaranteed. A number of the shorter poems — "Resolution and Independence" is a good example — offer "frequent sights of what is to be borne" by all men, everywhere, at some time or other. Ills of the spirit, like those of the body, must be endured and if possible overcome. The road the mature man travels may have its detours through the seasons of hell, unreasoning despairs, despondencies that will not be denied. This is mainly what *The Excursion* is about: an eloquent "morality" in the form of quasi-dramatic dialogue. The heart of its meaning is in the titles of Books III and IV — "Despondency" and "Despondency Corrected." Wordsworth knows what human life is, and what is required of us if we are to learn how to live in it. He is gigantic in the final sense that he is a moral realist.

Too much has probably been made of the alleged shrinkage of power in Wordsworth, as if, after forty, his stature had suddenly declined to that of a dwarf. We read of how his genius decays, of how "tragically" he is carried off the stage on the double shield of religious orthodoxy and political conservatism. This is a "despondency" about Wordsworth that needs to be corrected, and a number of modern critics have undertaken the task of correction. "Some think," wrote the poet, "I have lost that poetic ardour and fire 'tis said I once had — the fact is perhaps I have: but instead of that I hope I shall substitute a more thoughtful and quiet power." The poet speaking here is not Wordsworth; the sentences come from a letter by John Keats. Yet it is a clear statement of what happened to Wordsworth. His powers ripened gradually, reached a peak in his middle and late thirties, and thereafter very gradually declined. In that development and decline, as in so many other respects, the giant Wordsworth is one of us: the epitome of the normal man.

C. B.

Princeton, New Jersey
February 12, 1954

A Brief Chronology of the Life of Wordsworth

1770 William Wordsworth born April 7, Cockermouth, Cumberland, second son of John Wordsworth, lawyer, and Anne Crackanthorp. Elder brother Richard born 1768.

1771–1774 Birth of only sister Dorothy (1771), and younger brothers John (1772) and Christopher (1774).

1778–1783 Mother dies (1778) and William enters Hawkshead Grammar School. See *Prelude*, Bks. I–II. Father dies (1783) and children placed in guardianship of uncles.

1787 William enters St. John's College, Cambridge. See *Prelude*, Bk. III.

1790 Walking tour with Robert Jones, France and Switzerland (summer vacation). See *Prelude*, Bk. VI, lines 342 ff.

1791 B. A. degree, Cambridge. Residence in London. See *Prelude*, Bk. VII. Goes to France.

1792 At Orleans and Blois. Meets Michael Beaupuy. See *Prelude*, Bk. IX. Love affair with Annette Vallon. Birth of illegitimate daughter Caroline. William returns temporarily to England.

1793 England declares war on France. William publishes *An Evening Walk* and *Descriptive Sketches*. Walking tour includes visit to Tintern Abbey. Visits Jones in Wales. See *Prelude*, Bk. XIV.

1795 Partly as result of legacy from dead friend Raisley Calvert, William enabled to settle with sister Dorothy at Racedown Farm, Dorset. First meeting with Samuel Taylor Coleridge at Bristol.

1797 William and Dorothy visit Coleridge at Nether Stowey; soon move to Alfoxden to be near William's future collaborator.

1798 First edition of *Lyrical Ballads*, mostly by Wordsworth, but including Coleridge's *Ancient Mariner*. William, Dorothy, and Coleridge winter in Germany.

1799 William and Dorothy settle in the Lake District at Dove Cottage, Grasmere, the poet's chief residence until 1808. Serious beginning on early books of *Prelude*.

1800–1801 Prepares for press the much enlarged two-volume second edition of *Lyrical Ballads*, published, with the important preface, in January, 1801.

1802–1807 Remarkable series of miscellaneous sonnets; visit to Annette Vallon to settle affairs; marriage to Mary Hutchinson (1802). Brother John drowned at sea (1805). Finishes *Prelude* (spring, 1805). Beginning October, 1806, spends ten months at Coleorton farm, lent by friend Sir George Beaumont. Publishes *Poems in Two Volumes* (1807).

1808–1812 Lives at Allan Bank. Six children born to Wordsworths since birth of eldest in 1803. Two children die in 1812.

1813 Moves to Rydal Mount, his residence until death. Becomes Stamp Distributor for Westmorland, an appointive office which he holds for nearly thirty years.

1814–1815 Publishes *The Excursion*, part of projected poem *The Recluse* (1814); publishes *The White Doe of Rylstone* (1815) and first collected edition of his poems (1815), including a valuable new preface.

1816–1827 Meeting with Keats in London (1817). Publishes *Peter Bell* and *The Waggoner* (1819); *The River Duddon* (sonnets) and the four-volume *Miscellaneous Poems* (1820); *Ecclesiastical Sketches* (sonnets) and *Memorials of a Tour on the Continent* (1822); and the third collected edition, in five volumes (1827).

1832–1843 Fourth collected edition of the poems (1832). Death of Coleridge (1834). Insanity of sister Dorothy (1835). Publishes *Yarrow Revisited and other poems* (1835) followed by the fifth collected edition (1836–

1837), and a collection of the sonnets in one volume (1838). Honorary D.C.L. from Durham University (1838). Publishes *Poems, Chiefly of Early and Late Years* (1842). Resigns as Stamp Distributor and is pensioned (1842). Succeeds Robert Southey as Poet Laureate (1843).

1849–1850 Publishes a sixth collected edition of the poems, with his final revisions.

1850 William Wordsworth dies April 23. Burial by Grasmere church. In this year *The Prelude* was posthumously published.

Selected Bibliography

The modern standard biography is by George McLean Harper, *William Wordsworth: His Life, Works, and Influence*, 2 vols., 1916, abridged and otherwise revised in 1929. Other biographical studies of first importance include Emile Legouis, *The Early Life of Wordsworth*, 1897; Mary E. Burton, *The One Wordsworth*, 1942; and G. W. Meyer, *Wordsworth's Formative Years*, 1943. James V. Logan's *Wordsworthian Criticism: A Guide and Anthology*, 1947, is indispensable. A good working bibliography is in Ernest Bernbaum, *Guide through the Romantic Movement*, second edition, 1949. Lane Cooper compiled the concordance, 1911. *The Letters of William and Dorothy Wordsworth* were edited in six volumes, 1935–1939, by E. de Selincourt, who also edited *The Journals of Dorothy Wordsworth*, 2 vols., 1941; the parallel text edition of *The Prelude*, 1926; and (with Helen Darbishire) *The Poetical Works*, 5 vols., 1941–1949.

Among the innumerable critiques and special studies, the following are of great use: on *The Prelude*, R. D. Havens, *The Mind of a Poet*, 1941, and N. P. Stallknecht, *Strange*

Seas of Thought, 1945; on *The Excursion*, Judson S. Lyon's
study, 1950; on Wordsworth and Hartley, Arthur Beatty,
William Wordsworth, 1922, rev. 1927; on his metaphysic,
M. M. Rader, *Presiding Ideas in Wordsworth's Poetry*, 1931;
Norman Lacey, *Wordsworth's View of Nature*, 1948;
S. G. Dunn, "Wordsworth's Metaphysical System," *Essays
and Studies*, 1933; A. D. Martin, *The Religion of Wordsworth*,
1936. Among useful short treatments, see Matthew Arnold,
Essays in Criticism, 1888; A. V. Dicey, *The Statesmanship of
Wordsworth*, 1917; J. W. Beach, *The Concept of Nature in
Nineteenth-Century English Poetry*, 1936; Basil Willey, *The
Eighteenth Century Background*, 1940; F. R. Leavis, *Revalua-
tion*, 1936; Josephine Miles, *Wordsworth and the Vocabulary
of Emotion*, 1942; Douglas Bush, *Mythology and the Romantic
Tradition*, 1937; Z. S. Fink, "Wordsworth and the English
Republican Tradition," *JEGP*, 1948; and G. T. Dunklin,
ed., *Wordsworth Centenary Studies*, 1951.

A NOTE ON THE TEXT

As is customary in modern selections from Wordsworth,
the basic text followed in this volume is that of the standard
edition of 1849–1850, the last to pass under Wordsworth's
scrutiny, and therefore the one most likely to carry his
stamp of final approval. In a very few instances, silent
corrections of punctuation have been introduced, partly on
the authority of Dowden's Aldine edition of 1892, and partly
on the authority of E. de Selincourt and Helen Darbishire,
to whom modern scholarship is indebted for the Clarendon
Press edition of *The Poetical Works of William Wordsworth*

CONTENTS

PART THREE: Thirty-Five Sonnets

PART FOUR: Long Poems

PREFACE TO LYRICAL BALLADS (*1800*)

The first volume of these poems has already been submitted to general perusal. It was published as an experiment, which I hoped might be of some use to ascertain how far, by fitting to metrical arrangement a selection of the real language of men in a state of vivid sensation, that sort of pleasure and that quantity of pleasure may be imparted, which a poet may rationally endeavor to impart.

I had formed no very inaccurate estimate of the probable effect of those poems: I flattered myself that they who should be pleased with them would read them with more than common pleasure: and, on the other hand, I was well aware that by those who should dislike them they would be read with more than common dislike. The result has differed from my expectation in this only, that a greater number have been pleased than I ventured to hope I should please.

Several of my friends are anxious for the success of these poems, from a belief that, if the views with which they were composed were indeed realized, a class of poetry would be produced, well adapted to interest mankind permanently, and not unimportant in the quality and in the multiplicity of its moral relations: and on this account they have advised me to prefix a systematic

defence of the theory upon which the poems were
written. But I was unwilling to undertake the task,
knowing that on this occasion the reader would look
coldly upon my arguments, since I might be suspected
of having been principally influenced by the selfish and
foolish hope of *reasoning* him into an approbation of
these particular poems; and I was still more unwilling
to undertake the task, because adequately to display
the opinions, and fully to enforce the arguments, would
require a space wholly disproportionate to a preface.
For to treat the subject with the clearness and coher-
ence of which it is susceptible, it would be necessary to
give a full account of the present state of the public
taste in this country, and to determine how far this taste
is healthy or depraved; which, again, could not be
determined, without pointing out in what manner lan-
guage and the human mind act and re-act on each
other, and without retracing the revolutions, not of
literature alone, but likewise of society itself. I have
therefore altogether declined to enter regularly upon
this defence; yet I am sensible that there would be
something like impropriety in abruptly obtruding upon
the public, without a few words of introduction, poems
so materially different from those upon which general
approbation is at present bestowed.

It is supposed that by the act of writing in verse an
author makes a formal engagement that he will gratify
certain known habits of association; that he not only
thus apprises the reader that certain classes of ideas and
expressions will be found in his book, but that others
will be carefully excluded. This exponent or symbol
held forth by metrical language must in different eras

of literature have excited very different expectations: for example, in the age of Catullus, Terence, and Lucretius, and that of Statius or Claudian; and in our own country, in the age of Shakespeare and Beaumont and Fletcher, and that of Donne and Cowley, or Dryden, or Pope. I will not take upon me to determine the exact import of the promise which, by the act of writing in verse, an author in the present day makes to his reader; but it will undoubtedly appear to many persons that I have not fulfilled the terms of an engagement thus voluntarily contracted. They who have been accustomed to the gaudiness and inane phraseology of many modern writers, if they persist in reading this book to its conclusion, will, no doubt, frequently have to struggle with feelings of strangeness and awkwardness: they will look round for poetry, and will be induced to inquire by what species of courtesy these attempts can be permitted to assume that title. I hope, therefore, the reader will not censure me for attempting to state what I have proposed to myself to perform; and also (as far as the limits of a preface will permit) to explain some of the chief reasons which have determined me in the choice of my purpose: that at least he may be spared any unpleasant feeling of disappointment, and that I myself may be protected from one of the most dishonorable accusations which can be brought against an author; namely, that of an indolence which prevents him from endeavoring to ascertain what is his duty, or, when his duty is ascertained, prevents him from performing it.

The principal object, then, proposed in these poems was to choose incidents and situations from common life, and to relate or describe them, throughout, as far as was possible in a selection of language really used by men, and, at the same time, to throw over them a certain coloring of imagination, whereby ordinary things should be presented to the mind in an unusual aspect; and further, and above all, to make these incidents and situations interesting by tracing in them, truly though not ostentatiously, the primary laws of our nature: chiefly, as far as regards the manner in which we associate ideas in a state of excitement. Humble and rustic life was generally chosen, because in that condition the essential passions of the heart find a better soil in which they can attain their maturity, are less under restraint, and speak a plainer and more emphatic language; because in that condition of life our elementary feelings coëxist in a state of greater simplicity, and consequently may be more accurately contemplated and more forcibly communicated; because the manners of rural life germinate from those elementary feelings, and, from the necessary character of rural occupations, are more easily comprehended, and are more durable; and, lastly, because in that condition the passions of men are incorporated with the beautiful and permanent forms of nature. The language, too, of these men has been adopted (purified indeed from what appear to be its real defects, from all lasting and rational causes of dislike or disgust) because such men hourly communicate with the best objects from which the best part of language is originally derived; and because, from their rank in society and the sameness and narrow circle of their intercourse, being less under the influence of social vanity, they convey their feelings and notions in simple and unelaborated expressions. Accordingly, such a language, arising out of repeated experience and regular feelings, is a more permanent and a far more philosophical language than that which is frequently substituted for it by poets, who think that they are conferring honor upon themselves and their art, in proportion as they separate themselves from the sympathies of men, and indulge in arbitrary and capricious habits of expression, in order to furnish food for fickle tastes, and fickle appetites, of their own creation.

I cannot, however, be insensible to the present outcry against the triviality and meanness, both of thought and language, which some of my contemporaries have occasionally introduced into their metrical compositions; and I acknowledge that this defect, where it exists, is more dishonorable to the writer's own character than false refinement or arbitrary innovation, though I should contend at the same time that it is far less pernicious in the sum of its consequences. From such verses the poems in these volumes will be found distinguished at least by one mark of difference, that each of them has a worthy *purpose*. Not that I always began to write with a distinct purpose formally conceived; but habits of meditation have, I trust, so prompted and regulated my feelings, that my descriptions of such objects as strongly excite those feelings will be found to carry along with them a *purpose*. If this opinion be erroneous, I can have little right to the name of a poet. For all good poetry is the spontaneous overflow of powerful feelings: and though this be true, poems to which any value can be attached were never produced on any variety of subjects but by a man who, being possessed of more than usual organic sensibility, had also thought long and deeply. For our continued influxes of feeling are modified and directed by our thoughts, which are indeed the representatives of all our past feelings; and, as by contemplating the relation of these general representatives to each other, we discover what is really important to men, so, by the repetition and continuance of this act, our feelings will be connected with important subjects, till at length, if we be originally possessed of much sensibility, such habits of mind will be produced that, by obeying blindly and mechanically the impulses of those habits, we shall describe objects, and utter sentiments, of such a nature, and in such connection with each other, that the understanding of the reader must necessarily be in some degree enlightened, and his affections strengthened and purified.

It has been said that each of these poems has a purpose. Another circumstance must be mentioned which distinguishes these poems from the popular poetry of the day; it is this, that the feeling therein developed gives importance to the action and situation, and not the action and situation to the feeling.

A sense of false modesty shall not prevent me from asserting that the reader's attention is pointed to this mark of distinction, far less for the sake of these particular poems than from the general importance of the subject. The subject is indeed important! For the human mind is capable of being excited without the application of gross and violent stimulants; and he must have a very faint perception of its beauty and dignity who does not know this, and who does not further know that one being is elevated above another in proportion as he possesses this capability. It has therefore appeared to me that to endeavor to produce or enlarge this capability is one of the best services in which, at any period, a writer can be engaged; but this service, excellent at all times, is especially so at the present day. For a multitude of causes, unknown to former times, are now acting with a combined force to blunt the discriminating powers of the mind, and, unfitting it for all voluntary exertion, to reduce it to a state of almost savage torpor. The most effective of these causes are the great national events which are daily taking place, and the increasing accumulation of men in cities, where the uniformity of their occupations produces a craving for extraordinary incident, which the rapid communication of intelligence hourly gratifies. To this tendency of life and manners the literature and theatrical exhibitions of the country have conformed themselves. The invaluable works of our elder writers, I had almost said the works of Shakespeare and Milton, are driven into neglect by frantic novels, sickly and stupid German tragedies, and deluges of idle and extravagant stories in verse. When I think upon this degrading thirst after outrageous stimulation, I am almost ashamed to have spoken of the feeble endeavor made in these volumes to counteract it; and, reflecting upon the magnitude of the general evil, I should be oppressed with no dishonorable melancholy, had I not a deep impression of certain inherent and indestructible qualities of the human mind, and likewise of certain powers in the great and permanent objects that act upon it, which are equally inherent and indestructible; and were there not added to this impression a belief that the time is approaching when the evil will be systematically opposed, by men of greater powers, and with far more distinguished success.

Having dwelt thus long on the subjects and aim of these poems, I shall request the reader's permission to apprise him of a few circumstances relating to their *style*, in order, among other reasons, that he may not censure me for not having performed what I never attempted. The reader will find that personifications of abstract ideas rarely occur in these volumes, and are utterly rejected, as an ordinary device to elevate the style, and raise it above prose. My purpose was to imitate, and, as far as possible, to adopt the very language of men; and assuredly such personifications do not make any natural or regular part of that language. They are, indeed, a figure of speech occasionally prompted by passion, and I have made use of them as such; but have endeavored utterly to reject them as a mechanical device of style, or as a family language which writers in meter seem to lay claim to by prescription. I have wished to keep the reader in the company of flesh and blood, persuaded that by so doing I shall interest him. Others who pursue a different track will interest him likewise; I do not interfere with their claim, but wish to prefer a claim of my own. There will also be found in these volumes little of what is usually called poetic diction; as much pains has been taken to avoid it as is ordinarily taken to produce it; this has been done for the reason already alleged, to bring my language near to the language of men; and further, because the pleasure which I have proposed to

myself to impart is of a kind very different from that
which is supposed by many persons to be the proper
object of poetry. Without being culpably particular, I
do not know how to give my reader a more exact notion
of the style in which it was my wish and intention to
write, than by informing him that I have at all times
endeavored to look steadily at my subject; conse-
quently there is, I hope, in these poems little falsehood
of description, and my ideas are expressed in language
fitted to their respective importance. Something must
have been gained by this practice, as it is friendly to
one property of all good poetry, namely, good sense:
but it has necessarily cut me off from a large portion of
phrases and figures of speech which from father to son
have long been regarded as the common inheritance of
poets. I have also thought it expedient to restrict
myself still further, having abstained from the use of
many expressions, in themselves proper and beautiful,
but which have been foolishly repeated by bad poets,
till such feelings of disgust are connected with them as
it is scarcely possible by any art of association to
overpower.

If in a poem there should be found a series of lines, or
even a single line, in which the language, though natu-
rally arranged, and according to the strict laws of meter,
does not differ from that of prose, there is a numerous
class of critics, who, when they stumble upon these
prosaisms, as they call them, imagine that they have
made a notable discovery, and exult over the poet as
over a man ignorant of his own profession. Now these
men would establish a canon of criticism which the
reader will conclude he must utterly reject, if he wishes

to be pleased with these volumes. And it would be a most easy task to prove to him that not only the language of a large portion of every good poem, even of the most elevated character, must necessarily, except with reference to the meter, in no respect differ from that of good prose, but likewise that some of the most interesting parts of the best poems will be found to be strictly the language of prose when prose is well written. The truth of this assertion might be demonstrated by innumerable passages from almost all the poetical writings, even of Milton himself. To illustrate the subject in a general manner, I will here adduce a short composition of Gray, who was at the head of those who, by their reasonings, have attempted to widen the space of separation betwixt prose and metrical composition, and was more than any other man curiously elaborate in the structure of his own poetic diction.

> In vain to me the smiling mornings shine,
> And reddening Phoebus lifts his golden fire:
> The birds in vain their amorous descant join,
> Or cheerful fields resume their green attire.
> These ears, alas! for other notes repine;
> *A different object do these eyes require;*
> *My lonely anguish melts no heart but mine;*
> *And in my breast the imperfect joys expire;*
> Yet morning smiles the busy race to cheer,
> And new-born pleasure brings to happier men;
> The fields to all their wonted tribute bear;
> To warm their little loves the birds complain.
> *I fruitless mourn to him that cannot hear,*
> *And weep the more because I weep in vain.*

It will easily be perceived, that the only part of this sonnet which is of any value is the lines printed in italics; it is equally obvious that, except in the rhyme, and in the use of the single word "fruitless" for fruit-lessly, which is so far a defect, the language of these lines does in no respect differ from that of prose.

By the foregoing quotation it has been shown that the language of prose may yet be well adapted to poetry; and it was previously asserted that a large portion of the language of every good poem can in no respect differ from that of good prose. We will go further. It may be safely affirmed that there neither is, nor can be, any *essential* difference between the language of prose and metrical composition. We are fond of tracing the resemblance between poetry and painting, and, accordingly, we call them sisters: but where shall we find bonds of connection sufficiently strict to typify the affinity betwixt metrical and prose composition? They both speak by and to the same organs; the bodies in which both of them are clothed may be said to be of the same substance, their affections are kindred, and almost identical, not necessarily differ-ing even in degree; poetry sheds no tears "such as angels weep," but natural and human tears; she can boast of no celestial ichor that distinguishes her vital juices from those of prose; the same human blood cir-culates through the veins of them both.

If it be affirmed that rhyme and metrical arrangement of themselves constitute a distinction which overturns what has just been said on the strict affinity of metrical language with that of prose, and paves the way for other artificial distinctions which the mind voluntarily ad-mits, I answer that the language of such poetry as is here recommended is, as far as is possible, a selection of the language really spoken by men; that this selection, wherever it is made with true taste and feeling, will of itself form a distinction far greater than would at first be imagined, and will entirely separate the composition from the vulgarity and meanness of ordinary life; and, if meter be superadded thereto, I believe that a dissimilitude will be produced altogether sufficient for the gratification of a rational mind. What other distinction would we have? Whence is it to come? And where is it to exist? Not, surely, where the poet speaks through the mouths of his characters: it cannot be necessary here, either for elevation of style, or any of its supposed ornaments: for, if the poet's subject be judiciously chosen, it will naturally, and upon fit occasion, lead him to passions the language of which, if selected truly and judiciously, must necessarily be dignified and variegated, and alive with metaphors and figures. I forbear to speak of an incongruity which would shock the intelligent reader, should the poet interweave any foreign splendor of his own with that which the passion naturally suggests: it is sufficient to say that such addition is unnecessary. And surely it is more probable that those passages which with propriety abound with metaphors and figures will have their due effect, if, upon other occasions where the passions are of a milder character, the style also be subdued and temperate.

But as the pleasure which I hope to give by the poems now presented to the reader must depend entirely on just notions upon this subject, and as it is in itself of high importance to our taste and moral feelings, I cannot content myself with these detached remarks.

And if, in what I am about to say, it shall appear to some that my labor is unnecessary, and that I am like a man fighting a battle without enemies, such persons may be reminded that, whatever be the language outwardly holden by men, a practical faith in the opinions which I am wishing to establish is almost unknown. If my conclusions are admitted, and carried as far as they must be carried if admitted at all, our judgments concerning the works of the greatest poets both ancient and modern will be far different from what they are at present, both when we praise, and when we censure; and our moral feelings influencing and influenced by these judgments will, I believe, be corrected and purified.

Taking up the subject, then, upon general grounds, let me ask, what is meant by the word Poet? What is a poet? To whom does he address himself? And what language is to be expected from him?—He is a man speaking to men: a man, it is true, endowed with more lively sensibility, more enthusiasm and tenderness, who has a greater knowledge of human nature, and a more comprehensive soul, than are supposed to be common among mankind; a man pleased with his own passions and volitions, and who rejoices more than other men in the spirit of life that is in him; delighting to contemplate similar volitions and passions as manifested in the goings-on of the universe, and habitually impelled to create them where he does not find them. To these qualities he has added a disposition to be affected more than other men by absent things as if they were present; an ability of conjuring up in himself passions which are indeed far from being the same as those produced by real events, yet (especially in those parts of the general sympathy which are pleasing and delightful) do more nearly resemble the passions produced by real events than anything which, from the motions of their own minds merely, other men are accustomed to feel in themselves: — whence, and from practice, he has acquired a greater readiness and power in expressing what he thinks and feels, and especially those thoughts and feelings which, by his own choice, or from the structure of his own mind, arise in him without immediate external excitement.

But whatever portion of this faculty we may suppose even the greatest poet to possess, there cannot be a doubt that the language which it will suggest to him must often, in liveliness and truth, fall short of that which is uttered by men in real life under the actual pressure of those passions, certain shadows of which the poet thus produces, or feels to be produced, in himself.

However exalted a notion we would wish to cherish of the character of a poet, it is obvious that while he describes and imitates passions, his employment is in some degree mechanical, compared with the freedom and power of real and substantial action and suffering. So that it will be the wish of the poet to bring his feelings near to those of the persons whose feelings he describes, — nay, for short spaces of time, perhaps, to let himself slip into an entire delusion, and even confound and identify his own feelings with theirs; modifying only the language which is thus suggested to him by a consideration that he describes for a particular purpose, that of giving pleasure. Here, then, he will

apply the principle of selection which has been already
insisted upon. He will depend upon this for removing
what would otherwise be painful or disgusting in the
passion; he will feel that there is no necessity to trick
out or to elevate nature: and, the more industriously
he applies this principle, the deeper will be his faith that
no words which *his* fancy or imagination can suggest
will be to be compared with those which are the emana-
tions of reality and truth.

But it may be said by those who do not object to the
general spirit of these remarks, that, as it is impossible
for the poet to produce upon all occasions language as
exquisitely fitted for the passion as that which the real
passion itself suggests, it is proper that he should con-
sider himself as in the situation of a translator, who does
not scruple to substitute excellencies of another kind
for those which are unattainable by him, and endeavors
occasionally to surpass his original, in order to make
some amends for the general inferiority to which he
feels that he must submit. But this would be to en-
courage idleness and unmanly despair. Further, it is
the language of men who speak of what they do not
understand; who talk of poetry as of a matter of amuse-
ment and idle pleasure; who will converse with us as
gravely about a *taste* for poetry, as they express it,
as if it were a thing as indifferent as a taste for rope-
dancing, or Frontiniac or Sherry. Aristotle, I have
been told, has said that poetry is the most philosophic
of all writing: it is so: its object is truth, not individual
and local, but general, and operative; not standing
upon external testimony, but carried alive into the
heart by passion; truth which is its own testimony,

which gives competence and confidence to the tribunal
to which it appeals, and receives them from the same
tribunal. Poetry is the image of man and nature.
The obstacles which stand in the way of the fidelity
of the biographer and historian, and of their conse-
quent utility, are incalculably greater than those which
are to be encountered by the poet who comprehends the
dignity of his art. The poet writes under one restric-
tion only, namely, the necessity of giving immediate
pleasure to a human being possessed of that informa-
tion which may be expected from him, not as a lawyer,
a physician, a mariner, an astronomer, or a natural
philosopher, but as a man. Except this one restriction,
there is no object standing between the poet and the
image of things; between this, and the biographer and
historian, there are a thousand.

Nor let this necessity of producing immediate pleas-
ure be considered as a degradation of the poet's art.
It is far otherwise. It is an acknowledgment of the
beauty of the universe, an acknowledgment the more
sincere, because not formal, but indirect; it is a task
light and easy to him who looks at the world in the
spirit of love: further, it is a homage paid to the native
and naked dignity of man, to the grand elementary
principle of pleasure, by which he knows, and feels, and
lives, and moves. We have no sympathy but what is
propagated by pleasure: I would not be misunderstood;
but wherever we sympathize with pain, it will be found
that the sympathy is produced and carried on by subtle
combinations with pleasure. We have no knowledge,
that is, no general principles drawn from the con-
templation of particular facts, but what has been built

up by pleasure, and exists in us by pleasure alone.
The man of science, the chemist and mathematician,
whatever difficulties and disgusts they may have had
to struggle with, know and feel this. However pain-
ful may be the objects with which the anatomist's
knowledge is connected, he feels that his knowledge is
pleasure; and where he has no pleasure he has no
knowledge. What then does the poet? He considers
man and the objects that surround him as acting and
reacting upon each other, so as to produce an infinite
complexity of pain and pleasure; he considers man in
his own nature and in his ordinary life as contemplating
this with a certain quantity of immediate knowledge,
with certain convictions, intuitions, and deductions,
which from habit acquire the quality of intuitions; he
considers him as looking upon this complex scene of
ideas and sensations, and finding everywhere objects
that immediately excite in him sympathies which,
from the necessities of his nature, are accompanied by
an over-balance of enjoyment.

To this knowledge which all men carry about with
them, and to these sympathies in which, without any
other discipline than that of our daily life, we are fitted
to take delight, the poet principally directs his atten-
tion. He considers man and nature as essentially
adapted to each other, and the mind of man as naturally
the mirror of the fairest and most interesting properties
of nature. And thus the poet, prompted by this feeling
of pleasure, which accompanies him through the whole
course of his studies, converses with general nature,
with affections akin to those which, through labor and
length of time, the man of science has raised up in him-

self, by conversing with those particular parts of nature which are the objects of his studies. The knowledge both of the poet and the man of science is pleasure; but the knowledge of the one cleaves to us as a necessary part of our existence, our natural and unalienable inheritance; the other is a personal and individual acquisition, slow to come to us, and by no habitual and direct sympathy connecting us with our fellow-beings. The man of science seeks truth as a remote and unknown benefactor; he cherishes and loves it in his solitude: the poet, singing a song in which all human beings join with him, rejoices in the presence of truth as our visible friend and hourly companion. Poetry is the breath and finer spirit of all knowledge; it is the impassioned expression which is in the countenance of all science. Emphatically may it be said of the poet, as Shakespeare hath said of man, that "he looks before and after." He is the rock of defence for human nature; an upholder and preserver, carrying everywhere with him relationship and love. In spite of difference of soil and climate, of language and manners, of laws and customs; in spite of things silently gone out of mind, and things violently destroyed; the poet binds together by passion and knowledge the vast empire of human society, as it is spread over the whole earth, and over all time. The objects of the poet's thoughts are everywhere; though the eyes and senses of man are, it is true, his favorite guides, yet he will follow wheresoever he can find an atmosphere of sensation in which to move his wings. Poetry is the first and last of all knowledge — it is as immortal as the heart of man. If the labors of men of science should ever create any material revolution, direct or indirect, in our condition, and in the impressions which we habitually receive, the poet will sleep then no more than at present; he will be ready to follow the steps of the man of science, not only in those general indirect effects, but he will be at his side, carrying sensation into the midst of the objects of the science itself. The remotest discoveries of the chemist, the botanist, or mineralogist, will be as proper objects of the poet's art as any upon which it can be employed, if the time should ever come when these things shall be familiar to us, and the relations under which they are contemplated by the followers of these respective sciences shall be manifestly and palpably material to us as enjoying and suffering beings. If the time should ever come when what is now called science, thus familiarized to men, shall be ready to put on, as it were, a form of flesh and blood, the poet will lend his divine spirit to aid the transfiguration, and will welcome the being thus produced, as a dear and genuine inmate of the household of man. — It is not, then, to be supposed that any one who holds that sublime notion of poetry which I have attempted to convey, will break in upon the sanctity and truth of his pictures by transitory and accidental ornaments, and endeavor to excite admiration of himself by arts the necessity of which must manifestly depend upon the assumed meanness of his subject.

What has been thus far said applies to poetry in general, but especially to those parts of composition where the poet speaks through the mouths of his characters; and upon this point it appears to authorize the conclusion that there are few persons of good sense who would not allow that the dramatic parts of composition are defective, in proportion as they deviate from the real language of nature, and are colored by a diction of the poet's own, either peculiar to him as an individual poet or belonging simply to poets in general, — to a body of men who, from the circumstance of their compositions being in meter, it is expected will employ a particular language.

It is not, then, in the dramatic parts of composition that we look for this distinction of language; but still it may be proper and necessary where the poet speaks to us in his own person and character. To this I answer by referring the reader to the description before given of a poet. Among the qualities there enumerated as principally conducing to form a poet, is implied nothing differing in kind from other men, but only in degree. The sum of what was said is, that the poet is chiefly distinguished from other men by a greater promptness to think and feel without immediate external excitement, and a greater power in expressing such thoughts and feelings as are produced in him in that manner. But these passions and thoughts and feelings are the general passions and thoughts and feelings of men. And with what are they connected? Undoubtedly with our moral sentiments and animal sensations, and with the causes which excite these; with the operations of the elements, and the appearances of the visible universe; with storm and sunshine, with the revolutions of the seasons, with cold and heat, with loss of friends and kindred, with injuries and resentments, gratitude and hope, with fear and sorrow. These, and the like, are the sensations and objects which the poet describes, as

they are the sensations of other men, and the objects
which interest them. The poet thinks and feels in the
spirit of human passions. How, then, can his language
differ in any material degree from that of all other men
who feel vividly and see clearly? It might be *proved*
that it is impossible. But supposing that this were not
the case, the poet might then be allowed to use a pecul-
iar language when expressing his feelings for his own
gratification, or that of men like himself. But poets do
not write for poets alone, but for men. Unless, there-
fore, we are advocates for that admiration which sub-
sists upon ignorance, and that pleasure which arises
from hearing what we do not understand, the poet must
descend from this supposed height; and, in order to
excite rational sympathy, he must express himself as
other men express themselves. To this it may be added
that while he is only selecting from the real language of
men, or, which amounts to the same thing, composing
accurately in the spirit of such selection, he is treading
upon safe ground, and we know what we are to expect
from him. Our feelings are the same with respect to
meter; for, as it may be proper to remind the reader,
the distinction of meter is regular and uniform, and
not, like that which is produced by what is usually
called POETIC DICTION, arbitrary, and subject to in-
finite caprices upon which no calculation whatever
can be made. In the one case, the reader is utterly at
the mercy of the poet, respecting what imagery or
diction he may choose to connect with the passion;
whereas in the other, the meter obeys certain laws, to
which the poet and reader both willingly submit be-
cause they are certain, and because no interference is

made by them with the passion, but such as the concurring testimony of ages has shown to heighten and improve the pleasure which co-exists with it.

It will now be proper to answer an obvious question, namely, Why, professing these opinions, have I written in verse? To this, in addition to such answer as is included in what has been already said, I reply, in the first place, Because, however I may have restricted myself, there is still left open to me what confessedly constitutes the most valuable object of all writing, whether in prose or verse — the great and universal passions of men, the most general and interesting of their occupations, and the entire world of nature before me — to supply endless combinations of forms and imagery. Now, supposing for a moment that whatever is interesting in these objects may be as vividly described in prose, why should I be condemned for attempting to superadd to such description the charm which, by the consent of all nations, is acknowledged to exist in metrical language? To this, by such as are yet unconvinced, it may be answered that a very small part of the pleasure given by poetry depends upon the meter, and that it is injudicious to write in meter, unless it be accompanied with the other artificial distinctions of style with which meter is usually accompanied, and that, by such deviation, more will be lost from the shock which will thereby be given to the reader's associations than will be counterbalanced by any pleasure which he can derive from the general power of numbers. In answer to those who still contend for the necessity of accompanying meter with certain appropriate colors of style in order to the accomplishment of its appropriate end, and who also, in my opinion, greatly underrate the power of meter in itself, it might, perhaps, as far as relates to these volumes, have been almost sufficient to observe that poems are extant, written upon more humble subjects, and in a still more naked and simple style, which have continued to give pleasure from generation to generation. Now if nakedness and simplicity be a defect, the fact here mentioned affords a strong presumption that poems somewhat less naked and simple are capable of affording pleasure at the present day; and what I wished *chiefly* to attempt, at present, was to justify myself for having written under the impression of this belief.

But various causes might be pointed out why, when the style is manly, and the subject of some importance, words metrically arranged will long continue to impart such a pleasure to mankind as he who proves the extent of that pleasure will be desirous to impart. The end of poetry is to produce excitement in co-existence with an overbalance of pleasure; but, by the supposition, excitement is an unusual and irregular state of the mind; ideas and feelings do not, in that state, succeed each other in accustomed order. If the words, however, by which this excitement is produced be in themselves powerful, or the images and feelings have an undue proportion of pain connected with them, there is some danger that the excitement may be carried beyond its proper bounds. Now the co-presence of something regular, something to which the mind has been accustomed in various moods and in a less excited state, cannot but have great efficacy in tempering and restraining the passion by an intertexture of ordinary feeling, and of feeling not strictly and necessarily connected with the passion. This is unquestionably true; and hence, though the opinion will at first appear paradoxical, from the tendency of meter to divest language, in a certain degree, of its reality, and thus to throw a sort of half-consciousness of unsubstantial existence over the whole composition, there can be little doubt but that more pathetic situations and sentiments, that is, those which have a greater proportion of pain connected with them, may be endured in metrical composition, especially in rhyme, than in prose. The meter of the old ballads is very artless, yet they contain many passages which would illustrate this opinion; and, I hope, if the following poems be attentively perused, similar instances will be found in them. This opinion may be further illustrated by appealing to the reader's own experience of the reluctance with which he comes to the reperusal of the distressful parts of *Clarissa Harlowe*, or *The Gamester*, while Shakespeare's writings, in the most pathetic scenes, never act upon us, as pathetic, beyond the bounds of pleasure — an effect which, in a much greater degree than might at first be imagined, is to be ascribed to small but continual and regular impulses of pleasurable surprise from the metrical arrangement. — On the other hand (what it must be allowed will much more frequently happen), if the poet's words should be incommensurate with the passion, and inadequate to raise the reader to a height of desirable excitement, then (unless the poet's choice of his meter has been grossly injudicious) in the feelings of pleasure which the reader has been accustomed to connect with meter in general, and in the feeling, whether cheerful or melancholy, which he has been accustomed to connect with that particular movement of meter, there will be found something which will greatly contribute to impart passion to the words, and to effect the complex end which the poet proposes to himself.

If I had undertaken a SYSTEMATIC defence of the theory here maintained, it would have been my duty to develop the various causes upon which the pleasure received from metrical language depends. Among the chief of these causes is to be reckoned a principle which must be well known to those who have made any of the arts the object of accurate reflection; namely, the pleasure which the mind derives from the perception of similitude in dissimilitude. This principle is the great spring of the activity of our minds, and their chief feeder. From this principle the direction of the sexual appetite, and all the passions connected with it, take their origin: it is the life of our ordinary conversation; and upon the accuracy with which similitude in dissimilitude, and dissimilitude in similitude are perceived, depend our taste and our moral feelings. It would not be a useless employment to apply this principle to the consideration of meter, and to show that meter is hence enabled to afford much pleasure, and to point out in what manner that pleasure is produced. But my limits will not permit me to enter upon this subject, and I must content myself with a general summary.

I have said that poetry is the spontaneous overflow of powerful feelings; it takes its origin from emotion recollected in tranquillity: the emotion is contemplated till, by a species of reaction, the tranquillity gradually disappears, and an emotion, kindred to that which was before the subject of contemplation, is gradually produced, and does itself actually exist in the mind. In this mood successful composition generally begins, and in a mood similar to this it is carried on; but the emotion, of whatever kind, and in whatever degree, from various causes, is qualified by various pleasures, so that in describing any passions whatsoever, which are voluntarily described, the mind will, upon the whole, be in a state of enjoyment. If Nature be thus cautious to preserve in a state of enjoyment a being so employed, the poet ought to profit by the lesson held forth to him, and ought especially to take care that, whatever passions he communicates to his reader, those passions, if his reader's mind be sound and vigorous, should always be accompanied with an over-balance of pleasure. Now the music of harmonious metrical language, the sense of difficulty overcome, and the blind association of pleasure which has been previously received from works of rhyme or meter of the same or similar construction, an indistinct perception perpetually renewed of language closely resembling that of real life, and yet, in the circumstance of meter, differing from it so widely—all these imperceptibly make up a complex feeling of delight, which is of the most important use in tempering the painful feeling always found intermingled with powerful descriptions of the deeper passions. This effect is always produced in pathetic and impassioned poetry; while in lighter compositions the ease and gracefulness with which the poet manages his numbers are themselves confessedly a principal source of the gratification of the reader. All that it is *necessary* to say, however, upon this subject, may be effected by affirming, what few persons will deny, that of two descriptions, either of passions, manners, or characters each of them equally well executed, the one in prose and the other in verse, the verse will be read a hundred times where the prose is read once.

Having thus explained a few of my reasons for writing in verse, and why I have chosen subjects from common life, and endeavored to bring my language near to the real language of men, if I have been too minute in pleading my own cause, I have at the same time been treating a subject of general interest; and for this reason a few words shall be added with reference solely to these particular poems, and to some defects which will probably be found in them. I am sensible that my associations must have sometimes been particular instead of general, and that, consequently, giving to things a false importance, I may have sometimes written upon unworthy subjects; but I am less apprehensive on this account, than that my language may frequently have suffered from those arbitrary connections of feelings and ideas with particular words and phrases, from which no man can altogether protect himself. Hence I have no doubt that, in some instances, feelings, even of the ludicrous, may be given to my readers by expressions which appeared to me tender and pathetic. Such faulty expressions, were I convinced they were faulty at present, and that they must necessarily continue to be so, I would willingly take all reasonable pains to correct. But it is dangerous to make these alterations on the simple authority of a few individuals, or even of certain classes of men; for where the understanding of an author is not convinced, or his feelings altered, this cannot be done without great injury to himself: for his own feelings are his stay and support; and, if he set them aside in one instance, he may be induced to repeat this act till his mind shall lose all confidence in itself, and become utterly debilitated. To this it may be added that the critic ought never to forget that he is himself exposed to the same errors as the poet, and perhaps in a much greater degree: for there can be no presumption in saying of most readers that it is not probable they will be so well acquainted with the various stages of meaning through which words have passed, or with the fickleness or stability of the relations of particular ideas to each other; and, above all, since they are so much less interested in the subject, they may decide lightly and carelessly.

Long as the reader has been detained, I hope he will permit me to caution him against a mode of false criticism which has been applied to poetry, in which the language closely resembles that of life and nature. Such verses have been triumphed over in parodies, of which Dr. Johnson's stanza is a fair specimen: —

> I put my hat upon my head
> And walked into the Strand,
> And there I met another man
> Whose hat was in his hand.

Immediately under these lines let us place one of the most justly admired stanzas of the "Babes in the Woods."

> These pretty babes with hand in hand
> Went wandering up and down;
> But never more they saw the man
> Approaching from the town.

In both these stanzas the words, and the order of the words, in no respect differ from the most unimpassioned conversation. There are words in both, for example, "the Strand," and "the town," connected with none but the most familiar ideas; yet the one stanza we admit as admirable, and the other as a fair example of the superlatively contemptible. Whence arises this difference? Not from the meter, not from the language, not from the order of the words; but the *matter* expressed in Dr. Johnson's stanza is contemptible. The proper method of treating trivial and simple verses to which Dr. Johnson's stanza would be a fair parallelism, is not to say, This is a bad kind of poetry, or This is not poetry; but, This wants sense; it is neither interesting in itself, nor can *lead* to anything interesting; the images neither originate in that sane state of feeling which arises out of thought, nor can excite thought or feeling in the reader. This is the only sensible manner of dealing with such verses. Why trouble yourself about the species till you have previously decided upon the genus? Why take pains to prove that an ape is not a Newton, when it is self-evident that he is not a man?

One request I must make of my reader, which is, that in judging these poems he would decide by his own feelings genuinely, and not by reflection upon what will probably be the judgment of others. How common is it to hear a person say, I myself do not object to this style of composition, or this or that expression, but to such and such classes of people it will appear mean or ludicrous! This mode of criticism, so destructive of all sound unadulterated judgment, is almost universal:

let the reader then abide, independently, by his own feelings, and, if he finds himself affected, let him not suffer such conjectures to interfere with his pleasure.

If an author, by any single composition, has impressed us with respect for his talents, it is useful to consider this as affording a presumption that on other occasions, where we have been displeased, he nevertheless may not have written ill or absurdly; and further, to give him so much credit for this one composition as may induce us to review what has displeased us with more care than we should otherwise have bestowed upon it. This is not only an act of justice, but, in our decisions upon poetry especially, may conduce in a high degree to the improvement of our own taste; for an *accurate* taste in poetry, and in all the other arts, as Sir Joshua Reynolds has observed, is an *acquired* talent, which can only be produced by thought and a long-continued intercourse with the best models of composition. This is mentioned, not with so ridiculous a purpose as to prevent the most inexperienced reader from judging for himself (I have already said that I wish him to judge for himself), but merely to temper the rashness of decision, and to suggest that, if poetry be a subject on which much time has not been bestowed, the judgment may be erroneous; and that, in many cases, it necessarily will be so.

Nothing would, I know, have so effectually contributed to further the end which I have in view, as to have shown of what kind the pleasure is, and how that pleasure is produced, which is confessedly produced by metrical composition essentially different from that which I have here endeavored to recommend: for the

reader will say that he has been pleased by such com-
position; and what more can be done for him? The
power of any art is limited; and he will suspect that, if
it be proposed to furnish him with new friends, that can
be only upon condition of his abandoning his old friends.
Besides, as I have said, the reader is himself conscious
of the pleasure which he has received from such com-
position, composition to which he has peculiarly at-
tached the endearing name of poetry; and all men feel
an habitual gratitude, and something of an honorable
bigotry, for the objects which have long continued to
please them: we not only wish to be pleased, but to be
pleased in that particular way in which we have been
accustomed to be pleased. There is in these feelings
enough to resist a host of arguments; and I should be
the less able to combat them successfully, as I am will-
ing to allow that, in order entirely to enjoy the poetry
which I am recommending, it would be necessary to
give up much of what is ordinarily enjoyed. But,
would my limits have permitted me to point out how
this pleasure is produced, many obstacles might have
been removed, and the reader assisted in perceiving that
the powers of language are not so limited as he may
suppose; and that it is possible for poetry to give other
enjoyments, of a purer, more lasting, and more ex-
quisite nature. This part of the subject has not been
altogether neglected, but it has not been so much my
present aim to prove that the interest excited by some
other kinds of poetry is less vivid, and less worthy of
the nobler powers of the mind, as to offer reasons for
presuming that, if my purpose were fulfilled, a species
of poetry would be produced which is genuine poetry,

adoption of these figures of speech, and made use of them, sometimes with propriety, but much more frequently applied them to feelings and thoughts with which they had no natural connection whatsoever. A language was thus insensibly produced, differing materially from the real language of men in *any situation*. The Reader or Hearer of this distorted language found himself in a perturbed and unusual state of mind: when affected by the genuine language of passion he had been in a perturbed and unusual state of mind also: in both cases he was willing that his common judgment and understanding should be laid asleep, and he had no instinctive and infallible perception of the true to make him reject the false; the one served as a passport for the other. The emotion was in both cases delightful, and no wonder if he confounded the one with the other, and believed them both to be produced by the same, or similar causes. Besides, the Poet spake to him in the character of a man to be looked up to, a man of genius and authority. Thus, and from a variety of other causes, this distorted language was received with admiration; and Poets, it is probable, who had before contented themselves for the most part with misapplying only expressions which at first had been dictated by real passion, carried the abuse still further, and introduced phrases composed apparently in the spirit of the original figurative language of passion, yet altogether of their own invention, and characterised by various degrees of wanton deviation from good sense and nature.

It is indeed true, that the language of the earliest Poets was felt to differ materially from ordinary lan-

guage, because it was the language of extraordinary
occasions; but it was really spoken by men, language
which the Poet himself had uttered when he had been
affected by the events which he described, or which he
had heard uttered by those around him. To this lan-
guage it is probable that metre of some sort or other
was early superadded. This separated the genuine
language of Poetry still further from common life, so
that whoever read or heard the poems of these earliest
Poets felt himself moved in a way in which he had not
been accustomed to be moved in real life, and by causes
manifestly different from whose which acted upon him
in real life. This was the great temptation to all the
corruptions which have followed: under the protection
of this feeling succeeding Poets constructed a phrase-
ology which had one thing, it is true, in common with
the genuine language of poetry, namely, that it was
not heard in ordinary conversation; that it was unusual.
But the first Poets, as I have said, spake a language
which, though unusual, was still the language of men.
This circumstance, however, was disregarded by their
successors; they found that they could please by easier
means: they became proud of modes of expression
which they themselves had invented, and which were
uttered only by themselves. In process of time metre
became a symbol or promise of this unusual language,
and whoever took upon him to write in metre, according
as he possessed more or less of true poetic genius, intro-
duced less or more of this adulterated phraseology into
his compositions, and the true and the false were insep-
arably interwoven until, the taste of men becoming
gradually perverted, this language was received as a

natural language: and at length, by the influence of books upon men, did to a certain degree really become so. Abuses of this kind were imported from one nation to another, and with the progress of refinement this diction became daily more and more corrupt, thrusting out of sight the plain humanities of nature by a motley masquerade of tricks, quaintnesses, hieroglyphics, and enigmas.

It would not be uninteresting to point out the causes of the pleasure given by this extravagant and absurd diction. It depends upon a great variety of causes, but upon none, perhaps, more than its influence in impressing a notion of the peculiarity and exaltation of the Poet's character, and in flattering the Reader's self-love by bringing him nearer to a sympathy with that character; an effect which is accomplished by unsettling ordinary habits of thinking, and thus assisting the Reader to approach to that perturbed and dizzy state of mind in which if he does not find himself, he imagines that he is *balked* of a peculiar enjoyment which poetry can and ought to bestow.

The sonnet quoted from Gray, in the Preface, except the lines printed in Italics, consists of little else but this diction, though not of the worst kind; and indeed, if one may be permitted to say so, it is far too common in the best writers both ancient and modern. Perhaps in no way, by positive example, could more easily be given a notion of what I mean by the phrase *poetic diction* than by referring to a comparison between the metrical paraphrase which we have of passages in the Old and New Testament, and those passages as they exist in our common Translation. See Pope's "Messiah" throughout; Prior's "Did sweeter sounds adorn my flowing tongue," &c. &c. "Though I speak with the tongues of men and of angels," &c. &c. 1st Corinthians, chap. xiii. By way of immediate example take the following of Dr. Johnson:—

> "Turn on the prudent Ant thy heedless eyes,
> Observe her labours, Sluggard, and be wise;
> No stern command, no monitory voice,
> Prescribes her duties, or directs her choice;
> Yet, timely provident, she hastes away
> To snatch the blessings of a plenteous day;
> When fruitful Summer loads the teeming plain,
> She crops the harvest, and she stores the grain.
> How long shall sloth usurp thy useless hours,
> Unnerve thy vigour, and enchain thy powers?
> While artful shades thy downy couch enclose,
> And soft solicitation courts repose,
> Amidst the drowsy charms of dull delight,
> Year chases year with unremitted flight,
> Till Want now following, fraudulent and slow,
> Shall spring to seize thee, like an ambush'd foe."

From this hubbub of words pass to the original. "Go to the Ant, thou Sluggard, consider her ways, and be wise: which having no guide, overseer, or ruler, provideth her meat in the summer, and gathereth her food in the harvest. How long wilt thou sleep, O Sluggard? when wilt thou arise out of thy sleep? Yet a little sleep, a little slumber, a little folding of the hands to sleep. So shall thy poverty come as one that travelleth, and thy want as an armed man." Proverbs, chap. vi.

One more quotation, and I have done. It is from Cowper's Verses supposed to be written by Alexander Selkirk:—

"Religion! what treasure untold
Resides in that heavenly word!
More precious than silver and gold,
Or all that this earth can afford.
But the sound of the church-going bell
These valleys and rocks never heard,
Ne'er sighed at the sound of a knell,
Or smiled when a sabbath appeared.

"Ye winds, that have made me your sport
Convey to this desolate shore
Some cordial endearing report
Of a land I must visit no more.
My Friends, do they now and then send
A wish or a thought after me?
O tell me I yet have a friend,
Though a friend I am never to see."

This passage is quoted as an instance of three different styles of composition. The first four lines are poorly expressed; some Critics would call the language prosaic; the fact is, it would be bad prose, so bad, that it is scarcely worse in metre. The epithet "church-going" applied to a bell, and that by so chaste a writer as Cowper, is an instance of the strange abuses which Poets have introduced into their language, till they and their Readers take them as matters of course, if they do not single them out expressly as objects of admiration. The two lines "Ne'er sighed at the sound," &c., are, in my opinion, an instance of the language of passion wrested from its proper use, and, from the mere circumstance of the composition being in metre, applied upon an occasion that does not justify such violent expressions; and I should condemn the passage, though perhaps few Readers will agree with me, as vicious poetic diction. The last stanza is throughout admirably expressed: it would be equally good whether in prose or verse, except that the Reader has an exquisite pleasure in seeing such natural language so naturally connected with metre. The beauty of this stanza tempts me to conclude with a principle which ought never to be lost sight of, and which has been my chief guide in all I have said,—namely, that in works of *imagination and sentiment*, for of these only have I been treating, in proportion as ideas and feelings are valuable, whether the composition be in prose or in verse, they require and exact one and the same language. Metre is but adventitious to composition, and the phraseology for which that passport is necessary, even where it may be graceful at all, will be little valued by the judicious.

1802

ESSAY SUPPLEMENTARY TO THE PREFACE OF 1815

With the young of both sexes, Poetry is, like love, a passion; but, for much the greater part of those who have been proud of its power over their minds, a necessity soon arises of breaking the pleasing bondage; or it relaxes of itself; — the thoughts being occupied in domestic cares, or the time engrossed by business. Poetry then becomes only an occasional recreation; while to those whose existence passes away in a course of fashionable pleasure, it is a species of luxurious amusement. In middle and declining age, a scattered number of serious persons resort to poetry, as to religion, for a protection against the pressure of trivial employments, and as a consolation for the afflictions of life. And, lastly, there are many, who, having been enamoured of this art in their youth, have found leisure, after youth was spent, to cultivate general literature; in which poetry has continued to be comprehended *as a study*.

Into the above classes the Readers of poetry may be divided; Critics abound in them all; but from the last only can opinions be collected of absolute value, and worthy to be depended upon, as prophetic of the destiny of a new work. The young, who in nothing can escape delusion, are especially subject to it in their intercourse with Poetry. The cause, not so obvious as the fact is unquestionable, is the same as that from which erroneous judgments in this art, in the minds of men of all ages, chiefly proceed; but upon Youth it operates with peculiar force. The appropriate business of poetry, (which, nevertheless, if genuine, is as permanent as pure science,) her appropriate employment, her privilege and her *duty*, is to treat of things not as they *are*, but as they *appear;* not as they exist in themselves, but as they *seem* to exist to the *senses*, and to the *passions*. What a world of delusion does this acknowledged obligation prepare for the inexperienced! what temptations to go astray are here held forth for them whose thoughts have been little disciplined by the understanding, and whose feelings revolt from the sway of reason! — When a juvenile Reader is in the height of his rapture with some vicious passage, should experience throw in doubts, or common-sense suggest suspicions, a lurking consciousness that the realities of the Muse are but shows, and that her liveliest excitements are raised by transient shocks of conflicting feeling and successive assemblages of contradictory thoughts — is ever at hand to justify extravagance, and to sanction absurdity. But, it may be asked, as these illusions are unavoidable, and, no doubt, eminently useful to the mind as a process, what good can be gained by making observations, the tendency of which is to diminish the confidence of youth in its feelings, and thus to abridge its innocent and even profitable pleasures? The reproach implied in the question could not be warded off, if Youth were incapable of being delighted with what is truly excellent; or, if these errors always terminated of themselves in due season. But, with the majority, though their force be abated, they continue through life. Moreover, the fire of youth is too vivacious an element to be extinguished or damped by a philosophical remark; and, while there is no danger that what has been said will be injurious or painful to the ardent and the confident, it may prove beneficial to those who, being enthusiastic, are, at the same time, modest and ingenuous. The intimation may unite with their own misgivings to regulate their sensibility, and to bring in, sooner than it would otherwise have arrived, a more discreet and sound judgment.

If it should excite wonder that men of ability, in later life, whose understandings have been rendered acute by practice in affairs, should be so easily and so far imposed upon when they happen to take up a new work in verse, this appears to be the cause; — that, having discontinued their attention to poetry, whatever progress may have been made in other departments of knowledge, they have not, as to this art, advanced in true discernment beyond the age of youth. If, then, a new poem fall in their way, whose attractions are of that kind which would have enraptured them during the heat of youth, the judgment not being improved to a degree that they shall be disgusted, they are dazzled; and prize and cherish the faults for having had power to make the present time vanish before them, and to throw the mind back, as by enchantment, into the happiest season of life. As they read, powers seem to be revived, passions are regenerated, and pleasures restored. The Book was probably taken up after an escape from the burden of business, and with a wish to forget the world, and all its vexations and anxieties. Having obtained this wish, and so much more, it is natural that they should make report as they have felt.

If Men of mature age, through want of practice, be thus easily beguiled into admiration of absurdities, extravagances, and misplaced ornaments, thinking it proper that their understandings should enjoy a holiday, while they are unbending their minds with verse, it may be expected that such Readers will resemble their former selves also in strength of prejudice, and an inaptitude to be moved by the unostentatious beauties of a pure style. In the higher poetry, an enlightened Critic chiefly looks for a reflection of the wisdom of the heart and the grandeur of the imagination. Wherever these appear, simplicity accompanies them; Magnificence herself when legitimate, depending upon a simplicity of her own, to regulate her ornaments. But it is a well-known property of human nature, that our estimates are ever governed by comparisons, of which we are conscious with various degrees of distinctness. Is it not, then, inevitable (confining these observations to the effects of style merely) that an eye, accustomed to the glaring hues of diction by which such Readers are caught and excited, will for the most part be rather repelled than attracted by an original Work, the colouring of which is disposed according to a pure and refined scheme of harmony? It is in the fine arts as in the affairs of life, no man can *serve* (*i.e.* obey with zeal and fidelity) two Masters.

As Poetry is most just to its own divine origin when it administers the comforts and breathes the spirit of religion, they who have learned to perceive this truth, and who betake themselves to reading verse for sacred purposes, must be preserved from numerous illusions to which the two Classes of Readers, whom we have been considering, are liable. But, as the mind grows serious from the weight of life, the range of its passions is contracted accordingly; and its sympathies become so exclusive, that many species of high excellence wholly escape, or but languidly excite, its notice. Besides, men who read from religious or moral inclinations, even when the subject is of that kind which they approve, are beset with misconceptions and mistakes peculiar to themselves. Attaching so much importance to the truths which interest them, they are prone to overrate the Authors by whom those truths are expressed and enforced. They come prepared to impart so much passion to the Poet's language, that they remain unconscious how little, in fact, they receive from it. And, on the other hand, religious faith is to him who holds it so momentous a thing, and error appears to be attended with such tremendous consequences, that, if opinions touching upon religion occur which the Reader condemns, he not only cannot sympathise with them, however animated the expression, but there is, for the most part, an end put to all satisfaction and enjoyment. Love, if it before existed, is converted into dislike; and the heart of the Reader is set against the Author and his book. — To these excesses, they, who from their professions ought to be the most guarded against them, are perhaps the most liable; I mean those sects whose religion, being from the calculating understanding, is cold and formal. For when Christianity, the religion of humility, is founded upon the proudest faculty of our nature, what can be expected but contradictions? Accordingly, believers of this cast are at one time contemptuous; at another, being troubled, as they are and must be, with inward misgivings, they are jealous and suspicious; — and at all seasons, they are under temptation to supply by the heat with which they defend their tenets, the animation which is wanting to the constitution of the religion itself.

Faith was given to man that his affections, detached from the treasures of time, might be inclined to settle upon those of eternity; — the elevation of his nature, which this habit produces on earth, being to him a presumptive evidence of a future state of existence; and giving him a title to partake of its holiness. The religious man values what he sees chiefly as an "imperfect shadowing forth" of what he is incapable of seeing. The concerns of religion refer to indefinite objects, and are too weighty for the mind to support them without relieving itself by resting a great part of the burthen upon words and symbols. The commerce between Man and his Maker cannot be carried on but by a process where much is represented in little, and the Infinite Being accommodates himself to a finite capacity. In all this may be perceived the affinity between religion and poetry; between religion — making up the deficiencies of reason by faith; and poetry — passionate for the instruction of reason; between religion — whose element is infinitude, and whose ultimate trust is the supreme of things, submitting herself to circumscription, and reconciled to substitutions; and poetry — ethereal and transcendent, yet incapable to sustain her existence without sensuous incarnation. In this community of nature may be perceived also the lurking incitements of kindred error; — so that we shall find that no poetry has been more subject to distortion, than that species, the argument and scope of which is religious; and no lovers of the art have gone farther astray than the pious and the devout.

Whither then shall we turn for that union of qualifications which must necessarily exist before the decisions of a critic can be of absolute value? For a mind at once poetical and philosophical; for a critic whose affections are as free and kindly as the spirit of society, and whose understanding is severe as that of dispassionate government? Where are we to look for that initiatory composure of mind which no selfishness can disturb? For a natural sensibility that has been tutored into correctness without losing anything of its quickness; and for active faculties, capable of answering the demands which an Author of original imagination shall make upon them, associated with a judgment that cannot be duped into admiration by aught that is unworthy of it? — among those and those only, who, never having suffered their youthful love of poetry to remit much of its force, have applied to the consideration of the laws of this art the best power of their understandings. At the same time it must be observed — that, as this Class comprehends the only judgments which are trust-worthy, so does it include the most erroneous and perverse. For to be mistaught is worse than to be untaught; and no perverseness equals that which is supported by system, no errors are so difficult to root out as those which the understanding has pledged its credit to uphold. In this Class are contained censors, who, if they be pleased with what is good, are pleased with it only by imperfect glimpses, and upon false principles; who, should they generalise rightly, to a certain point, are sure to suffer for it in the end; who, if they stumble upon a sound rule, are fettered by misapplying it, or by straining it too far; being incapable of perceiving when it ought to yield to one of higher order. In it are found critics too petulant to be passive to a genuine poet, and too feeble to grapple with him; men, who take upon them to report of the course which *he* holds whom they are utterly unable to accompany, — confounded if he turn quick upon the wing, dismayed if he soar steadily "into the region;" — men of palsied imaginations and indurated hearts; in whose minds all healthy action is languid, who therefore feed as the many direct them, or, with the many, are greedy after vicious provocatives; — judges, whose censure is auspicious, and whose praise ominous! In this class meet together the two extremes of best and worst.

The observations presented in the foregoing series are of too ungracious a nature to have been made without reluctance; and, were it only on this account, I would invite the reader to try them by the test of comprehensive experience. If the number of judges who can be confidently relied upon be in reality so small, it ought to follow that partial notice only, or neglect, perhaps long continued, or attention wholly inadequate to their merits — must have been the fate of most works in the higher departments of poetry; and that, on the other hand, numerous productions have blazed into popularity, and have passed away, leaving scarcely a trace behind them: it will be further found, that when Authors shall have at length raised themselves into general admiration and maintained their ground, errors and prejudices have prevailed concerning their genius and their works, which the few who are conscious of those errors and prejudices would deplore; if they were not recompensed by perceiving that there are select Spirits for whom it is ordained that their fame shall be in the world an existence like that of Virtue, which owes its being to the struggles it makes, and its vigour to the enemies whom it provokes; — a vivacious quality, ever doomed to meet with opposition, and still triumphing over it; and, from the nature of its dominion, incapable of being brought to

the sad conclusion of Alexander, when he wept that
there were no more worlds for him to conquer.

Let us take a hasty retrospect of the poetical litera-
ture of this Country for the greater part of the last
two centuries, and see if the facts support these infer-
ences.

Who is there that now reads the "Creation" of
Dubartas? Yet all Europe once resounded with his
praise; he was caressed by kings; and, when his
Poem was translated into our language, the "Faery
Queen" faded before it. The name of Spenser, whose
genius is of a higher order than even that of Ariosto, is
at this day scarcely known beyond the limits of the
British Isles. And if the value of his works is to be
estimated from the attention now paid to them by his
countrymen, compared with that which they bestow
on those of some other writers, it must be pronounced
small indeed.

> "The laurel, meed of mighty conquerors
> And poets *sage*" —

are his own words; but his wisdom has, in this par-
ticular, been his worst enemy: while its opposite, whether
in the shape of folly or madness, has been *their* best
friend. But he was a great power, and bears a high
name: the laurel has been awarded to him.

A dramatic Author, if he write for the stage, must
adapt himself to the taste of the audience, or they will
not endure him; accordingly the mighty genius of
Shakspeare was listened to. The people were delighted:
but I am not sufficiently versed in stage antiquities to
determine whether they did not flock as eagerly to the

representation of many pieces of contemporary Authors, wholly undeserving to appear upon the same boards. Had there been a formal contest for superiority among dramatic writers, that Shakspeare, like his predecessors Sophocles and Euripides, would have often been subject to the mortification of seeing the prize adjudged to sorry competitors, becomes too probable, when we reflect that the admirers of Settle and Shadwell were, in a later age, as numerous, and reckoned as respectable in point of talent, as those of Dryden. At all events, that Shakspeare stooped to accommodate himself to the People, is sufficiently apparent; and one of the most striking proofs of his almost omnipotent genius, is, that he could turn to such glorious purpose those materials which the prepossessions of the age compelled him to make use of. Yet even this marvellous skill appears not to have been enough to prevent his rivals from having some advantage over him in public estimation; else how can we account for passages and scenes that exist in his works, unless upon a supposition that some of the grossest of them, a fact which in my own mind I have no doubt of, were foisted in by the Players, for the gratification of the many?

But that his Works, whatever might be their reception upon the stage, made but little impression upon the ruling Intellects of the time, may be inferred from the fact that Lord Bacon, in his multifarious writings, nowhere either quotes or alludes to him. His dramatic excellence enabled him to resume possession of the stage after the Restoration; but Dryden tells us that in his time two of the plays of Beaumont and Fletcher were acted for one of Shakspeare's. And so faint and limited was the perception of the poetic beauties of his dramas in the time of Pope, that, in his Edition of the Plays, with a view of rendering to the general reader a necessary service, he printed between inverted commas those passages which he thought most worthy of notice.

At this day, the French Critics have abated nothing of their aversion to this darling of our Nation: "the English, with their bouffon de Shakspeare," is as familiar an expression among them as in the time of Voltaire. Baron Grimm is the only French writer who seems to have perceived his infinite superiority to the first names of the French Theatre; an advantage which the Parisian Critic owed to his German blood and German education. The most enlightened Italians, though well acquainted with our language, are wholly incompetent to measure the proportions of Shakspeare. The Germans only, of foreign nations, are approaching towards a knowledge and feeling of what he is. In some respects they have acquired a superiority over the fellow-countrymen of the Poet: for among us it is a current, I might say, an established opinion, that Shakspeare is justly praised when he is pronounced to be "a wild irregular genius, in whom great faults are compensated by great beauties." How long may it be before this misconception passes away, and it becomes universally acknowledged that the judgment of Shakspeare in the selection of his materials, and in the manner in which he has made them, heterogeneous as they often are, constitute a unity of their own, and contribute all to one great end, is not less admirable than his imagination, his invention, and his intuitive knowledge of human Nature?

There is extant a small Volume of miscellaneous poems, in which Shakspeare expresses his own feelings in his own person. It is not difficult to conceive that

the Editor, George Steevens, should have been insensible
to the beauties of one portion of that Volume, the
Sonnets; though in no part of the writings of this Poet
is found, in an equal compass, a greater number of ex-
quisite feelings felicitously expressed. But, from regard
to the Critic's own credit, he would not have ventured
to talk of an act of parliament not being strong enough
to compel the perusal of those little pieces, if he had
not known that the people of England were ignorant of
the treasures contained in them: and if he had not,
moreover, shared the too common propensity of human
nature to exult over a supposed fall into the mire of a
genius whom he had been compelled to regard with
admiration, as an inmate of the celestial regions —
"there sitting where he durst not soar."

Nine years before the death of Shakspeare, Milton
was born; and early in life he published several small
poems, which, though on their first appearance they
were praised by a few of the judicious, were afterwards
neglected to that degree, that Pope in his youth could
borrow from them without risk of its being known.
Whether these poems are at this day justly appreciated,
I will not undertake to decide: nor would it imply a
severe reflection upon the mass of readers to suppose
the contrary; seeing that a man of the acknowledged
genius of Voss, the German poet, could suffer their
spirit to evaporate; and could change their character, as
is done in the translation made by him of the most
popular of those pieces. At all events, it is certain that
these Poems of Milton are now much read, and loudly
praised; yet were they little heard of till more than 150
years after their publication; and of the Sonnets, Dr.

Johnson, as appears from Boswell's Life of him, was in the habit of thinking and speaking as contemptuously as Steevens wrote upon those of Shakspeare.

About the time when the Pindaric odes of Cowley and his imitators, and the productions of that class of curious thinkers whom Dr. Johnson has strangely styled metaphysical Poets, were beginning to lose something of that extravagant admiration which they had excited, the "Paradise Lost" made its appearance. "Fit audience find though few," was the petition addressed by the Poet to his inspiring Muse. I have said elsewhere that he gained more than he asked; this I believe to be true; but Dr. Johnson has fallen into a gross mistake when he attempts to prove, by the sale of the work, that Milton's Countrymen were "*just* to it" upon its first appearance. Thirteen hundred Copies were sold in two years; an uncommon example, he asserts, of the prevalence of genius in opposition to so much recent enmity as Milton's public conduct had excited. But, be it remembered that, if Milton's political and religious opinions, and the manner in which he announced them, had raised him many enemies, they had procured him numerous friends; who, as all personal danger was passed away at the time of publication, would be eager to procure the master-work of a man whom they revered, and whom they would be proud of praising. Take, from the number of purchasers, persons of this class, and also those who wished to possess the Poem as a religious work, and but few I fear would be left who sought for it on account of its poetical merits. The demand did not immediately increase; "for," says Dr. Johnson, "many more readers" (he means persons in the habit of reading poetry) "than were supplied at first the Nation did not afford." How careless must a writer be who can make this assertion in the face of so many existing title-pages to belie it! Turning to my own shelves, I find the folio of Cowley, seventh edition, 1681. A book near it is Flatman's Poems, fourth edition, 1686; Waller, fifth edition, same date. The Poems of Norris of Bemerton not long after went, I believe, through nine editions. What further demand there might be for these works I do not know; but I well remember, that, twenty-five years ago, the booksellers' stalls in London swarmed with the folios of Cowley. This is not mentioned in disparagement of that able writer and amiable man; but merely to show — that, if Milton's work were not more read, it was not because readers did not exist at the time. The early editions of the "Paradise Lost" were printed in a shape which allowed them to be sold at a low price, yet only three thousand copies of the Work were sold in eleven years; and the Nation, says Dr. Johnson, had been satisfied from 1623 to 1664, that is, forty-one years, with only two editions of the Works of Shakspeare; which probably did not together make one thousand Copies; facts adduced by the critic to prove the "paucity of Readers." — There were readers in multitudes; but their money went for other purposes, as their admiration was fixed elsewhere. We are authorised, then, to affirm, that the reception of the "Paradise Lost," and the slow progress of its fame, are proofs as striking as can be desired that the positions which I am attempting to establish are not erroneous. — How amusing to shape to one's self such a critique as a Wit of Charles's days, or a Lord of the Miscellanies or trading Journalist of

King William's time, would have brought forth, if he had set his faculties industriously to work upon this Poem, everywhere impregnated with *original* excellence.

So strange indeed are the obliquities of admiration, that they whose opinions are much influenced by authority will often be tempted to think that there are no fixed principles in human nature for this art to rest upon. I have been honoured by being permitted to peruse in MS. a tract composed between the period of the Revolution and the close of that century. It is the Work of an English Peer of high accomplishments, its object to form the character and direct the studies of his son. Perhaps nowhere does a more beautiful treatise of the kind exist. The good sense and wisdom of the thoughts, the delicacy of the feelings, and the charm of the style, are, throughout, equally conspicuous. Yet the Author, selecting among the Poets of his own country those whom he deems most worthy of his son's perusal, particularises only Lord Rochester, Sir John Denham, and Cowley. Writing about the same time, Shaftesbury, an author at present unjustly depreciated, describes the English Muses as only yet lisping in their cradles.

The arts by which Pope, soon afterwards, contrived to procure to himself a more general and a higher reputation than perhaps any English Poet ever attained during his life-time, are known to the judicious. And as well known is it to them, that the undue exertion of those arts is the cause why Pope has for some time held a rank in literature, to which, if he had not been seduced by an over-love of immediate popularity, and had confided more in his native genius, he never could have descended. He bewitched the nation by his melody, and dazzled it by his polished style, and was himself blinded by his own success. Having wandered from humanity in his Eclogues with boyish inexperience, the praise, which these compositions obtained, tempted him into a belief that Nature was not to be trusted, at least in pastoral Poetry. To prove this by example, he put his friend Gay upon writing those Eclogues which their author intended to be burlesque. The instigator of the work, and his admirers, could perceive in them nothing but what was ridiculous. Nevertheless, though these Poems contain some detestable passages, the effect, as Dr. Johnson well observes, " of reality and truth became conspicuous even when the intention was to show them grovelling and degraded." The Pastorals, ludicrous to such as prided themselves upon their refinement, in spite of those disgusting passages, "became popular, and were read with delight, as just representations of rural manners and occupations."

Something less than sixty years after the publication of the "Paradise Lost" appeared Thomson's "Winter;" which was speedily followed by his other Seasons. It is a work of inspiration; much of it is written from himself, and nobly from himself. How was it received? "It was no sooner read," says one of his contemporary biographers, "than universally admired: those only excepted who had not been used to feel, or to look for anything in poetry, beyond a *point* of satirical or epigrammatic wit, a smart *antithesis* richly trimmed with rhyme, or the softness of an *elegiac* complaint. To such his manly classical spirit could not readily commend itself; till, after a more attentive perusal, they had got the better of their prejudices, and either acquired or affected a truer taste. A few others stood aloof, merely because they had long before fixed the articles of their poetical creed, and resigned themselves to an absolute despair of ever seeing anything new and original. These were somewhat mortified to find their notions disturbed by the appearance of a poet, who seemed to owe nothing but to nature and his own genius. But, in a short time, the applause became unanimous; every one wondering how so many pictures, and pictures so familiar, should have moved them but faintly to what they felt in his descriptions. His digressions too, the overflowings of a tender benevolent heart, charmed the reader no less; leaving him in doubt, whether he should more admire the Poet or love the Man."

This case appears to bear strongly against us: — but we must distinguish between wonder and legitimate admiration. The subject of the work is the changes produced in the appearances of nature by the revolution of the year: and, by undertaking to write in verse, Thomson pledged himself to treat his subject as became a Poet. Now, it is remarkable that, excepting the nocturnal Reverie of Lady Winchilsea, and a passage or two in the "Windsor Forest" of Pope, the poetry of the period intervening between the publication of the "Paradise Lost" and the "Seasons" does not contain a single new image of external nature; and scarcely presents a familiar one from which it can be inferred that the eye of the Poet had been steadily fixed upon his object, much less that his feelings had urged him to work upon it in the spirit of genuine imagination. To what a low state knowledge of the most obvious and important phe-

nomena had sunk, is evident from the style in which
Dryden has executed a description of Night in one of his
Tragedies, and Pope his translation of the celebrated
moonlight scene in the "Iliad." A blind man, in the
habit of attending accurately to descriptions casually
dropped from the lips of those around him, might easily
depict these appearances with more truth. Dryden's
lines are vague, bombastic, and senseless; those of Pope,
though he had Homer to guide him, are throughout false
and contradictory. The verses of Dryden, once highly
celebrated, are forgotten; those of Pope still retain their
hold upon public estimation, — nay, there is not a pas-
sage of descriptive poetry, which at this day finds so
many and such ardent admirers. Strange to think of
an enthusiast, as may have been the case with thousands,
reciting those verses under the cope of a moonlight sky,
without having his raptures in the least disturbed by a
suspicion of their absurdity! — If these two distin-
guished writers could habitually think that the visible
universe was of so little consequence to a poet, that it
was scarcely necessary for him to cast his eyes upon it,
we may be assured that those passages of the elder
poets which faithfully and poetically describe the
phenomena of nature, were not at that time holden in
much estimation, and that there was little accurate
attention paid to those appearances.

Wonder is the natural product of Ignorance; and as
the soil was *in such good condition* at the time of the
publication of the "Seasons," the crop was doubtless
abundant. Neither individuals nor nations become cor-
rupt all at once, nor are they enlightened in a moment.
Thomson was an inspired poet, but he could not work

miracles; in cases where the art of seeing had in some
degree been learned, the teacher would further the pro-
ficiency of his pupils, but he could do little *more;* though
so far does vanity assist men in acts of self-deception,
that many would often fancy they recognized a likeness
when they knew nothing of the original. Having shown
that much of what his biographer deemed genuine ad-
miration must in fact have been blind wonderment —
how is the rest to be accounted for? — Thomson was
fortunate in the very title of his poem, which seemed to
bring it home to the prepared sympathies of every one:
in the next place, notwithstanding his high powers, he
writes a vicious style; and his false ornaments are
exactly of that kind which would be most likely to
strike the undiscerning. He likewise abounds with
sentimental common-places, that, from the manner in
which they were brought forward, bore an imposing air
of novelty. In any well-used copy of the "Seasons"
the book generally opens of itself with the rhapsody on
love, or with one of the stories (perhaps "Damon and
Musidora"); these also are prominent in our collections
of Extracts, and are the parts of his Work which, after
all, were probably most efficient in first recommending
the author to general notice. Pope, repaying praises
which he had received, and wishing to extol him to the
highest, only styles him "an elegant and philosophical
Poet;" nor are we able to collect any unquestionable
proofs that the true characteristics of Thomson's genius
as an imaginative poet were perceived, till the elder
Warton, almost forty years after the publication of the
"Seasons," pointed them out by a note in his Essay on
the "Life and Writings of Pope." In the "Castle of

Indolence" (of which Gray speaks so coldly) these characteristics were almost as conspicuously displayed, and in verse more harmonious, and diction more pure. Yet that fine poem was neglected on its appearance, and is at this day the delight only of a few!

When Thomson died, Collins breathed forth his regrets in an Elegiac Poem, in which he pronounces a poetical curse upon *him* who should regard with insensibility the place where the Poet's remains were deposited. The Poems of the mourner himself have now passed through innumerable editions, and are universally known; but if, when Collins died, the same kind of imprecation had been pronounced by a surviving admirer, small is the number whom it would not have comprehended. The notice which his poems attained during his lifetime was so small, and of course the sale so insignificant, that not long before his death he deemed it right to repay to the bookseller the sum which he had advanced for them, and threw the edition into the fire.

Next in importance to the "Seasons" of Thomson, though at considerable distance from that work in order of time, come the "Reliques of Ancient English Poetry;" collected, new-modelled, and in many instances (if such a contradiction in terms may be used) composed by the Editor, Dr. Percy. This work did not steal silently into the world, as is evident from the number of legendary tales, that appeared not long after its publication; and had been modelled, as the authors persuaded themselves, after the old Ballad. The Compilation was however ill suited to the then existing taste of city society; and Dr. Johnson, 'mid the little senate to which he gave laws, was not sparing in his exertions to make it an object of contempt. The critic triumphed, the legendary imitators were deservedly disregarded, and, as undeservedly, their ill-imitated models sank, in this country, into temporary neglect; while Bürger, and other able writers of Germany, were translating or imitating these Reliques, and composing, with the aid of inspiration thence derived, poems which are the delight of the German nation. Dr. Percy was so abashed by the ridicule flung upon his labours from the ignorance and insensibility of the persons with whom he lived, that, though while he was writing under a mask he had not wanted resolution to follow his genius into the regions of true simplicity and genuine pathos (as is evinced by the exquisite ballad of "Sir Cauline" and by many other pieces), yet when he appeared in his own person and character as a poetical writer, he adopted, as in the tale of the "Hermit of Warkworth," a diction scarcely in any one of its features distinguishable from the vague, the glossy, and unfeeling language of his day. I mention this remarkable fact with regret, esteeming the genius of Dr. Percy in this kind of writing superior to that of any other man by whom in modern times it has been cultivated. That even Bürger (to whom Klopstock gave, in my hearing, a commendation which he denied to Goethe and Schiller, pronouncing him to be a genuine poet, and one of the few among the Germans whose works would last) had not the fine sensibility of Percy, might be shown from many passages, in which he has deserted his original only to go astray. For example,

> "Now daye was gone, and night was come,
> And all were fast asleepe,
> All save the Lady Emeline,
> Who sate in her bowre to weepe:

> "And soone she heard her true Love's voice
> Low whispering at the walle,
> Awake, awake, my dear Ladye,
> 'Tis I thy true-love call."

Which is thus tricked out and dilated:

> "Als nun die Nacht Gebirg' und Thal
> Vermummt in Rabenschatten,
> Und Hochburgs Lampen überall
> Schon ausgeflimmert hatten,
> Und alles tief entschlafen war;
> Doch nur das Fräulein immerdar,
> Voll Fieberangst, noch wachte,
> Und seinen Ritter dachte:
> Da horch! Ein süsser Liebeston
> Kam leis' empor geflogen.
> 'Ho, Trudchen, ho! Da bin ich schon!
> Frisch auf! Dich angezogen!'"

But from humble ballads we must ascend to heroics. All hail, Macpherson! hail to thee, Sire of Ossian! The Phantom was begotten by the snug embrace of an impudent Highlander upon a cloud of tradition — it travelled southward, where it was greeted with acclamation, and the thin Consistence took its course through Europe, upon the breath of popular applause. The Editor of the "Reliques" had indirectly preferred a claim to the praise of invention, by not concealing that his supplementary labours were considerable! how selfish his conduct, contrasted with that of the disinterested Gael, who, like Lear, gives his kingdom away, and is content to become a pensioner upon his own issue for a beggarly pittance! — Open this far-famed Book! — I have done so at random, and the beginning of the "Epic Poem Temora," in eight Books, presents itself. "The

blue waves of Ullin roll in light. The green hills are
covered with day. Trees shake their dusky heads in
the breeze. Grey torrents pour their noisy streams.
Two green hills with aged oaks surround a narrow
plain. The blue course of a stream is there. On its
banks stood Cairbar of Atha. His spear supports the
king; the red eyes of his fear are sad. Cormac rises on
his soul with all his ghastly wounds." Precious memo-
randums from the pocket-book of the blind Ossian!

If it be unbecoming, as I acknowledge that for the
most part it is, to speak disrespectfully of Works that
have enjoyed for a length of time a widely-spread repu-
tation, without at the same time producing irrefragable
proofs of their unworthiness, let me be forgiven upon
this occasion. — Having had the good fortune to be born
and reared in a mountainous country, from my very
childhood I have felt the falsehood that pervades the
volumes imposed upon the world under the name of
Ossian. From what I saw with my own eyes, I knew
that the imagery was spurious. In nature everything is
distinct, yet nothing defined into absolute independent
singleness. In Macpherson's work, it is exactly the
reverse; everything (that is not stolen) is in this manner
defined, insulated, dislocated, deadened, — yet nothing
distinct. It will always be so when words are sub-
stituted for things. To say that the characters never
could exist, that the manners are impossible, and that
a dream has more substance than the whole state of
society, as there depicted, is doing nothing more than
pronouncing a censure which Macpherson defied; when,
with the steeps of Morven before his eyes, he could
talk so familiarly of his Car-borne heroes; — of Morven,

which, if one may judge from its appearance at the dis-
tance of a few miles, contains scarcely an acre of ground
sufficiently accommodating for a sledge to be trailed
along its surface. — Mr. Malcolm Laing has ably shown
that the diction of this pretended translation is a motley
assemblage from all quarters; but he is so fond of making
out parallel passages as to call poor Macpherson to ac-
count for his "*ands*" and his "*buts!*" and he has weak-
ened his argument by conducting it as if he thought that
every striking resemblance was a *conscious* plagiarism.
It is enough that the coincidences are too remarkable
for its being probable or possible that they could arise
in different minds without communication between
them. Now as the Translators of the Bible, and Shak-
speare, Milton, and Pope, could not be indebted to
Macpherson, it follows that he must have owed his fine
feathers to them; unless we are prepared gravely to
assert, with Madame de Staël, that many of the charac-
teristic beauties of our most celebrated English Poets
are derived from the ancient Fingallian; in which case the
modern translator would have been but giving back to
Ossian his own. — It is consistent that Lucien Buona-
parte, who could censure Milton for having surrounded
Satan in the infernal regions with courtly and regal
splendour, should pronounce the modern Ossian to be
the glory of Scotland; — a country that has produced a
Dunbar, a Buchanan, a Thomson, and a Burns! These
opinions are of ill omen for the Epic ambition of him
who has given them to the world.

Yet, much as those pretended treasures of antiquity
have been admired, they have been wholly uninfluential
upon the literature of the Country. No succeeding
writer appears to have caught from them a ray of in-

spiration; no author, in the least distinguished, has ventured formally to imitate them — except the boy, Chatterton, on their first appearance. He had perceived, from the successful trials which he himself had made in literary forgery, how few critics were able to distinguish between a real ancient medal and a counterfeit of modern manufacture; and he set himself to the work of filling a magazine with *Saxon Poems*, counterparts of those of Ossian, as like his as one of his misty stars is to another. This incapability to amalgamate with the literature of the Island, is, in my estimation, a decisive proof that the book is essentially unnatural; nor should I require any other to demonstrate it to be a forgery, audacious as worthless. — Contrast, in this respect, the effect of Macpherson's publication with the "Reliques" of Percy, so unassuming, so modest in their pretensions! — I have already stated how much Germany is indebted to this latter work; and for our own country, its poetry has been absolutely redeemed by it. I do not think that there is an able writer in verse of the present day who would not be proud to acknowledge his obligations to the "Reliques;" I know that it is so with my friends; and, for myself, I am happy in this occasion to make a public avowal of my own.

Dr. Johnson, more fortunate in his contempt of the labours of Macpherson than those of his modest friend, was solicited not long after to furnish Prefaces biographical and critical for the works of some of the most eminent English Poets. The booksellers took upon themselves to make the collection; they referred probably to the most popular miscellanies, and, unquestionably, to their books of accounts; and decided upon the claim of authors to be admitted into a body of the most eminent, from the familiarity of their names with the readers of that day, and by the profits, which, from the sale of his works, each had brought and was bringing to the Trade. The Editor was allowed a limited exercise of discretion, and the Authors whom he recommended are scarcely to be mentioned without a smile. We open the volume of Prefatory Lives, and to our astonishment the *first* name we find is that of Cowley! — What is become of the morning-star of English Poetry? Where is the bright Elizabethan constellation? Or, if names be more acceptable than images, where is the ever-to-be-honoured Chaucer? where is Spenser? where Sidney? and, lastly, where he, whose rights as a poet, contra-distinguished from those which he is universally allowed to possess as a dramatist, we have vindicated, — where Shakspeare? — These, and a multitude of others not unworthy to be placed near them, their contemporaries and successors, we have *not*. But in their stead, we have (could better be expected when precedence was to be settled by an abstract of reputation at any given period made, as in this case before us?) Roscommon, and Stepney, and Phillips, and Walsh, and Smith, and Duke, and King, and Spratt — Halifax, Granville, Sheffield, Congreve, Broome, and other reputed Magnates — metrical writers utterly worthless and useless, except for occasions like the present, when their productions are referred to as evidence what a small quantity of brain is necessary to procure a considerable stock of admiration, provided the aspirant will accommodate himself to the likings and fashions of his day.

As I do not mean to bring down this retrospect to our own times, it may with propriety be closed at the era of this distinguished event. From the literature of other ages and countries, proofs equally cogent might have been adduced, that the opinions announced in the former part of this Essay are founded upon truth. It was not an agreeable office, nor a prudent undertaking, to declare them; but their importance seemed to render it a duty. It may still be asked, where lies the particular relation of what has been said to these Volumes? — The question will be easily answered by the discerning Reader who is old enough to remember the taste that prevailed when some of these poems were first published, seventeen years ago; who has also observed to what degree the poetry of this Island has since that period been coloured by them; and who is further aware of the unremitting hostility with which, upon some principle or other, they have each and all been opposed. A sketch of my own notion of the constitution of Fame has been given; and, as far as concerns myself, I have cause to be satisfied. The love, the admiration, the indifference, the slight, the aversion, and even the contempt, with which these Poems have been received, knowing, as I do, the source within my own mind, from which they have proceeded, and the labour and pains, which, when labour and pains appeared needful, have been bestowed upon them, must all, if I think consistently, be received as pledges and tokens, bearing the same general impression, though widely different in value; — they are all proofs that for the present time I have not laboured in vain; and afford assurances, more or less authentic, that the products of my industry will endure.

If there be one conclusion more forcibly pressed upon us than another by the review which has been given of the fortunes and fate of poetical Works, it is this, — that every author, as far as he is great and at the same time *original*, has had the task of *creating* the taste by which he is to be enjoyed: so has it been, so will it continue to be. This remark was long since made to me by the philosophical Friend for the separation of whose poems from my own I have previously expressed my regret. The predecessors of an original Genius of a high order will have smoothed the way for all that he has in common with them; — and much he will have in common; but, for what is peculiarly his own, he will be called upon to clear and often to shape his own road: — he will be in the condition of Hannibal among the Alps.

And where lies the real difficulty of creating that taste by which a truly original poet is to be relished? Is it in breaking the bonds of custom, in overcoming the prejudices of false refinement, and displacing the aversions of inexperience? Or, if he labour for an object which here and elsewhere I have proposed to myself, does it consist in divesting the reader of the pride that induces him to dwell upon those points wherein men differ from each other, to the exclusion of those in which all men are alike, or the same; and in making him ashamed of the vanity that renders him insensible of the appropriate excellence which civil arrangements, less unjust than might appear, and Nature illimitable in her bounty, have conferred on men who may stand below him in the scale of society? Finally, does it lie in establishing that dominion over the spirits of readers by which they are to be humbled and humanised, in order that they may be purified and exalted?

If these ends are to be attained by the mere communication of *knowledge*, it does *not* lie here. — TASTE,

I would remind the reader, like IMAGINATION, is a word
which has been forced to extend its services far beyond
the point to which philosophy would have confined
them. It is a metaphor, taken from a *passive* sense of the
human body, and transferred to things which are in
their essence *not* passive, — to intellectual *acts* and
operations. The word, Imagination, has been over-
strained, from impulses honourable to mankind, to meet
the demands of the faculty which is perhaps the noblest
of our nature. In the instance of Taste, the process
has been reversed; and from the prevalence of disposi-
tions at once injurious and discreditable, being no other
than that selfishness which is the child of apathy, —
which, as Nations decline in productive and creative
power, makes them value themselves upon a presumed
refinement of judging. Poverty of language is the
primary cause of the use which we make of the word,
Imagination; but the word, Taste, has been stretched
to the sense which it bears in modern Europe by habits
of self-conceit, inducing that inversion in the order of
things whereby a passive faculty is made paramount
among the faculties conversant with the fine arts. Pro-
portion and congruity, the requisite knowledge being
supposed, are subjects upon which taste may be trusted;
it is competent to this office; — for in its intercourse
with these the mind is *passive*, and is affected painfully
or pleasurably as by an instinct. But the profound and
the exquisite in feeling, the lofty and universal in thought
and imagination; or, in ordinary language, the pathetic
and the sublime; — are neither of them, accurately
speaking, objects of a faculty which could ever without
a sinking in the spirit of Nations have been designated

element into the intellectual universe: or, if that be not allowed, it is the application of powers to objects on which they had not before been exercised, or the employment of them in such a manner as to produce effects hitherto unknown. What is all this but an advance, or a conquest, made by the soul of the poet? Is it to be supposed that the reader can make progress of this kind, like an Indian prince or general — stretched on his palanquin, and borne by his slaves? No; he is invigorated and inspirited by his leader, in order that he may exert himself; for he cannot proceed in quiescence, he cannot be carried like a dead weight. Therefore to create taste is to call forth and bestow power, of which knowledge is the effect; and *there* lies the true difficulty.

As the pathetic participates of an *animal* sensation, it might seem — that, if the springs of this emotion were genuine, all men, possessed of competent knowledge of the facts and circumstances, would be instantaneously affected. And, doubtless, in the works of every true poet will be found passages of that species of excellence, which is proved by effects immediate and universal. But there are emotions of the pathetic that are simple and direct, and others — that are complex and revolutionary; some — to which the heart yields with gentleness; others — against which it struggles with pride; these varieties are infinite as the combinations of circumstance and the constitutions of character. Remember, also, that the medium through which, in poetry, the heart is to be affected, is language; a thing subject to endless fluctuations and arbitrary associations. The genius of the poet melts these down for his purpose; but they retain their shape and quality to him who is not capable of exerting, within his own mind, a corresponding energy. There is also a meditative, as well as a human, pathos; an enthusiastic, as well as an ordinary, sorrow; a sadness that has its seat in the depths of reason, to which the mind cannot sink gently of itself — but to which it must descend by treading the steps of thought. And for the sublime, — if we consider what are the cares that occupy the passing day, and how remote is the practice and the course of life from the sources of sublimity, in the soul of Man, can it be wondered that there is little existing preparation for a poet charged with a new mission to extend its kingdom, and to augment and spread its enjoyments?

Away, then, with the senseless iteration of the word, *popular*, applied to new works in poetry, as if there were no test of excellence in this first of the fine arts but that all men should run after its productions, as if urged by an appetite, or constrained by a spell! — The qualities of writing best fitted for eager reception are either such as startle the world into attention by their audacity and extravagance; or they are chiefly of a superficial kind, lying upon the surfaces of manners; or arising out of a selection and arrangement of incidents, by which the mind is kept upon the stretch of curiosity, and the fancy amused without the trouble of thought. But in everything which is to send the soul into herself, to be admonished of her weakness, or to be made conscious of her power; — wherever life and nature are described as operated upon by the creative or abstracting virtue of the imagination; wherever the instinctive wisdom of antiquity and her heroic passions uniting, in the heart of the poet, with the meditative wisdom of later ages, have

produced that accord of sublimated humanity, which is
at once a history of the remote past and a prophetic
enunciation of the remotest future, *there*, the poet must
reconcile himself for a season to few and scattered hear-
ers. — Grand thoughts (and Shakspeare must often
have sighed over this truth), as they are most naturally
and most fitly conceived in solitude, so can they not be
brought forth in the midst of plaudits, without some
violation of their sanctity. Go to a silent exhibition
of the productions of the sister Art, and be convinced
that the qualities which dazzle at first sight, and kindle
the admiration of the multitude, are essentially different
from those by which permanent influence is secured.
Let us not shrink from following up these principles as
far as they will carry us, and conclude with observing
— that there never has been a period, and perhaps never
will be, in which vicious poetry, of some kind or other,
has not excited more zealous admiration, and been far
more generally read, than good; but this advantage
attends the good, that the *individual*, as well as the
species, survives from age to age; whereas, of the de-
praved, though the species be immortal, the individual
quickly *perishes;* the object of present admiration van-
ishes, being supplanted by some other as easily pro-
duced; which, though no better, brings with it at least
the irritation of novelty, — with adaptation, more or
less skilful, to the changing humours of the majority
of those who are most at leisure to regard poetical works
when they first solicit their attention.

Is it the result of the whole, that, in the opinion of the
Writer, the judgment of the People is not to be re-
spected? The thought is most injurious; and, could

the charge be brought against him, he would repel it
with indignation. The People have already been justi-
fied, and their eulogium pronounced by implication,
when it was said, above — that, of *good* poetry, the
individual, as well as the species, *survives*. And how does
it survive but through the People? What preserves it
but their intellect and their wisdom?

> "— Past and future, are the wings
> On whose support, harmoniously conjoined,
> Moves the great Spirit of human knowledge —"
>
> *MS.*

The voice that issues from this Spirit, is that Vox
Populi which the Deity inspires. Foolish must he be
who can mistake for this a local acclamation, or a transi-
tory outcry — transitory though it be for years, local
though from a Nation. Still more lamentable is his error
who can believe that there is anything of divine infalli-
bility in the clamour of that small though loud portion of
the community, ever governed by factitious influence,
which, under the name of the Public, passes itself, upon
the unthinking, for the People. Towards the Public,
the Writer hopes that he feels as much deference as it is
entitled to: but to the People, philosophically charac-
terised, and to the embodied spirit of their knowledge,
so far as it exists and moves, at the present, faithfully
supported by its two wings, the past and the future, his
devout respect, his reverence, is due. He offers it will-
ingly and readily; and, this done, takes leave of his
Readers, by assuring them — that, if he were not per-
suaded that the contents of these Volumes, and the
Work to which they are subsidiary, evince something of

the "Vision and the Faculty divine;" and that, both in words and things, they will operate in their degree, to extend the domain of sensibility for the delight, the honour, and the benefit of human nature, notwithstanding the many happy hours which he has employed in their composition, and the manifold comforts and enjoyments they have procured to him, he would not, if a wish could do it, save them from immediate destruction; — from becoming at this moment, to the world, as a thing that had never been.

1815

Part Two

A SELECTION FROM THE SHORTER POEMS

LINES

Left upon a Seat in a Yew-tree, which stands near the lake of Esthwaite, on a desolate part of the shore, commanding a beautiful prospect.

NAY, Traveller! rest. This lonely Yew-tree stands
Far from all human dwelling: what if here
No sparkling rivulet spread the verdant herb?
What if the bee love not these barren boughs?
Yet, if the wind breathe soft, the curling waves,
That break against the shore, shall lull thy mind
By one soft impulse saved from vacancy.
———————————Who he was
That piled these stones and with the mossy sod
First covered, and here taught this aged Tree
With its dark arms to form a circling bower,
I well remember. — He was one who owned
No common soul. In youth by science nursed,
And led by nature into a wild scene
Of lofty hopes, he to the world went forth
A favoured Being, knowing no desire
Which genius did not hallow; 'gainst the taint
Of dissolute tongues, and jealousy, and hate,
And scorn, — against all enemies prepared,

All but neglect. The world, for so it thought,
Owed him no service; wherefore he at once
With indignation turned himself away,
And with the food of pride sustained his soul
In solitude. — Stranger! these gloomy boughs
Had charms for him; and here he loved to sit,
His only visitants a straggling sheep,
The stone-chat, or the glancing sandpiper:
And on these barren rocks, with fern and heath,
And juniper and thistle, sprinkled o'er,
Fixing his downcast eye, he many an hour
A morbid pleasure nourished, tracing here
An emblem of his own unfruitful life:
And, lifting up his head, he then would gaze
On the more distant scene, — how lovely 'tis
Thou seest, — and he would gaze till it became
Far lovelier, and his heart could not sustain
The beauty, still more beauteous! Nor, that time,
When nature had subdued him to herself,
Would he forget those Beings to whose minds
Warm from the labours of benevolence
The world, and human life, appeared a scene
Of kindred loveliness: then he would sigh,
Inly disturbed, to think that others felt
What he must never feel: and so, lost Man!
On visionary views would fancy feed,
Till his eye streamed with tears. In this deep vale
He died, — this seat his only monument.

If Thou be one whose heart the holy forms
Of young imagination have kept pure,
Stranger! henceforth be warned; and know that pride,
Howe'er disguised in its own majesty,
Is littleness; that he who feels contempt
For any living thing, hath faculties

Which he has never used; that thought with him
Is in its infancy. The man whose eye
Is ever on himself doth look on one,
The least of Nature's works, one who might move
The wise man to that scorn which wisdom holds
Unlawful, ever. O be wiser, Thou!
Instructed that true knowledge leads to love;
True dignity abides with him alone
Who, in the silent hour of inward thought,
Can still suspect, and still revere himself,
In lowliness of heart.

1787–1797   *1798*

THE REVERIE OF POOR SUSAN

At the corner of Wood Street, when daylight appears,
Hangs a Thrush that sings loud, it has sung for three
          years:
Poor Susan has passed by the spot, and has heard
In the silence of morning the song of the Bird.

'Tis a note of enchantment; what ails her? She sees
A mountain ascending, a vision of trees;
Bright volumes of vapour through Lothbury glide,
And a river flows on through the vale of Cheapside.

Green pastures she views in the midst of the dale,
Down which she so often has tripped with her pail;
And a single small cottage, a nest like a dove's,
The one only dwelling on earth that she loves.

She looks, and her heart is in heaven: but they fade,
The mist and the river, the hill and the shade:
The stream will not flow, and the hill will not rise,
And the colours have all passed away from her eyes!

1797   *1800*

EXPOSTULATION AND REPLY

"WHY, William, on that old grey stone,
Thus for the length of half a day,
Why, William, sit you thus alone,
And dream your time away?

"Where are your books? — that light bequeathed
To Beings else forlorn and blind!
Up! up! and drink the spirit breathed
From dead men to their kind.

"You look round on your Mother Earth,
As if she for no purpose bore you;
As if you were her first-born birth,
And none had lived before you!"

One morning thus, by Esthwaite lake,
When life was sweet, I knew not why,
To me my good friend Matthew spake,
And thus I made reply:

"The eye — it cannot choose but see;
We cannot bid the ear be still;
Our bodies feel, where'er they be,
Against or with our will.

"Nor less I deem that there are Powers
Which of themselves our minds impress;
That we can feed this mind of ours
In a wise passiveness.

"Think you, 'mid all this mighty sum
Of things for ever speaking,
That nothing of itself will come,
But we must still be seeking?

"— Then ask not wherefore, here, alone,
Conversing as I may,
I sit upon this old grey stone,
And dream my time away."

1798   *1798*

THE TABLES TURNED

AN EVENING SCENE ON THE SAME SUBJECT

Up! up! my Friend, and quit your books;
Or surely you'll grow double:
Up! up! my Friend, and clear your looks;
Why all this toil and trouble?

The sun, above the mountain's head,
A freshening lustre mellow
Through all the long green fields has spread,
His first sweet evening yellow.

Books! 'tis a dull and endless strife:
Come, hear the woodland linnet,
How sweet his music! on my life,
There's more of wisdom in it.

And hark! how blithe the throstle sings!
He, too, is no mean preacher:
Come forth into the light of things,
Let Nature be your Teacher.

She has a world of ready wealth,
Our minds and hearts to bless —
Spontaneous wisdom breathed by health,
Truth breathed by cheerfulness.

One impulse from a vernal wood
May teach you more of man,
Of moral evil and of good,
Than all the sages can.

Sweet is the lore which Nature brings;
Our meddling intellect
Mis-shapes the beauteous forms of things: —
We murder to dissect.

Enough of Science and of Art;
Close up those barren leaves;
Come forth, and bring with you a heart
That watches and receives.

1798   *1798*

LINES WRITTEN IN EARLY SPRING

I HEARD a thousand blended notes,
While in a grove I sate reclined,
In that sweet mood when pleasant thoughts
Bring sad thoughts to the mind.

To her fair works did Nature link
The human soul that through me ran;
And much it grieved my heart to think
What man has made of man.

Through primrose tufts, in that green bower;
The periwinkle trailed its wreaths;
And 'tis my faith that every flower
Enjoys the air it breathes.

The birds around me hopped and played,
Their thoughts I cannot measure: —
But the least motion which they made,
It seemed a thrill of pleasure.

The budding twigs spread out their fan,
To catch the breezy air;
And I must think, do all I can,
That there was pleasure there.

If this belief from heaven be sent,
If such be Nature's holy plan,
Have I not reason to lament
What man has made of man?

1798　　　　　　　　　　　　　　*1798*

TO MY SISTER

IT is the first mild day of March;
Each minute sweeter than before,
The redbreast sings from the tall larch
That stands beside our door.

There is a blessing in the air,
Which seems a sense of joy to yield
To the bare trees, and mountains bare,
And grass in the green field.

My sister! ('tis a wish of mine)
Now that our morning meal is done,
Make haste, your morning task resign;
Come forth and feel the sun.

Edward will come with you; — and, pray,
Put on with speed your woodland dress;
And bring no book: for this one day
We'll give to idleness.

No joyless forms shall regulate
Our living calendar:
We from to-day, my Friend, will date
The opening of the year.

Love, now a universal birth,
From heart to heart is stealing.
From earth to man, from man to earth:
— It is the hour of feeling.

One moment now may give us more
Than years of toiling reason:
Our minds shall drink at every pore
The spirit of the season.

Some silent laws our hearts will make,
Which they shall long obey:
We for the year to come may take
Our temper from to-day.

And from the blessed power that rolls
About, below, above,
We'll frame the measure of our souls:
They shall be tuned to love.

Then come, my Sister! come, I pray,
With speed put on your woodland dress;
And bring no book: for this one day
We'll give to idleness.

1798   *1798*

"MY HEART LEAPS UP..."

My heart leaps up when I behold
    A rainbow in the sky:
So was it when my life began;
So is it now I am a man;
So be it when I shall grow old,
    Or let me die!
The Child is father of the Man;
And I could wish my days to be
Bound each to each by natural piety.

March 26, 1802   *1807*

WE ARE SEVEN

A simple Child,
That lightly draws its breath,
And feels its life in every limb,
What should it know of death?

I met a little cottage Girl:
She was eight years old, she said;
Her hair was thick with many a curl
That clustered round her head.

She had a rustic, woodland air,
And she was wildly clad:
Her eyes were fair, and very fair;
— Her beauty made me glad.

"Sisters and brothers, little maid,
How many may you be?"
"How many? Seven in all," she said,
And wondering looked at me.

"And where are they? I pray you tell."
She answered, "Seven are we;
And two of us at Conway dwell,
And two are gone to sea.

"Two of us in the church-yard lie,
My sister and my brother;
And, in the church-yard cottage, I
Dwell near them with my mother."

"You say that two at Conway dwell,
And two are gone to sea,
Yet ye are seven! I pray you tell,
Sweet Maid, how this may be."

Then did the little Maid reply,
"Seven boys and girls are we;
Two of us in the church-yard lie,
Beneath the church-yard tree."

"You run about, my little Maid,
Your limbs they are alive;
If two are in the church-yard laid,
Then ye are only five."

"Their graves are green, they may be seen,"
The little Maid replied,
"Twelve steps or more from my mother's door,
And they are side by side.

"My stockings there I often knit,
My kerchief there I hem;
And there upon the ground I sit,
And sing a song to them.

"And often after sun-set, Sir,
When it is light and fair,
I take my little porringer,
And eat my supper there.

"The first that died was sister Jane;
In bed she moaning lay,
Till God released her of her pain;
And then she went away.

"So in the church-yard she was laid;
And, when the grass was dry,
Together round her grave we played,
My brother John and I.

"And when the ground was white with snow,
And I could run and slide,
My brother John was forced to go,
And he lies by her side."

"How many are you, then," said I,
"If they two are in heaven?"
Quick was the little Maid's reply,
"O Master! we are seven."

"But they are dead; those two are dead!
Their spirits are in heaven!"
'Twas throwing words away; for still
The little Maid would have her will,
And said, "Nay, we are seven!"

1798   *1800*

ANECDOTE FOR FATHERS

"Retine vim istam, falsa enim dicam, si coges."

EUSEBIUS

I HAVE a boy of five years old;
His face is fair and fresh to see;
His limbs are cast in beauty's mould,
And dearly he loves me.

One morn we strolled on our dry walk,
Our quiet home all full in view,
And held such intermitted talk
As we are wont to do.

My thoughts on former pleasures ran;
I thought of Kilve's delightful shore,
Our pleasant home when spring began,
A long, long year before.

A day it was when I could bear
Some fond regrets to entertain;
With so much happiness to spare,
I could not feel a pain.

The green earth echoed to the feet
Of lambs that bounded through the glade,
From shade to sunshine, and as fleet
From sunshine back to shade.

Birds warbled round me — and each trace
Of inward sadness had its charm;
Kilve, thought I, was a favoured place,
And so is Liswyn farm.

My boy beside me tripped, so slim
And graceful in his rustic dress!
And, as we talked, I questioned him,
In very idleness.

"Now tell me, had you rather be,"
I said, and took him by the arm,
"On Kilve's smooth shore, by the green sea,
Or here at Liswyn farm?"

In careless mood he looked at me,
While still I held him by the arm,
And said, "At Kilve I'd rather be
Than here at Liswyn farm."

"Now, little Edward, say why so:
My little Edward, tell me why." —
"I cannot tell, I do not know." —
"Why, this is strange," said I;

"For here are woods, hills smooth and warm:
There surely must some reason be
Why you would change sweet Liswyn farm
For Kilve by the green sea."

At this my boy hung down his head,
He blushed with shame, nor made reply;
And three times to the child I said,
"Why, Edward, tell me why?"

His head he raised — there was in sight,
It caught his eye, he saw it plain —
Upon the house-top, glittering bright,
A broad and gilded vane.

Then did the boy his tongue unlock,
And eased his mind with this reply:
"At Kilve there was no weather-cock;
And that's the reason why."

O dearest, dearest boy! my heart
For better lore would seldom yearn,
Could I but teach the hundredth part
Of what from thee I learn.

1798   1798

THE THORN

I

"THERE is a Thorn — it looks so old,
In truth, you'd find it hard to say
How it could ever have been young,
It looks so old and grey.
Not higher than a two years' child
It stands erect, this aged Thorn;
No leaves it has, no prickly points;
It is a mass of knotted joints,
A wretched thing forlorn.
It stands erect, and like a stone
With lichens is it overgrown.

II

"Like rock or stone, it is o'ergrown,
With lichens to the very top,
And hung with heavy tufts of moss,
A melancholy crop:

Up from the earth these mosses creep,
And this poor Thorn they clasp it round
So close, you'd say that they are bent
With plain and manifest intent
To drag it to the ground;
And all have joined in one endeavour
To bury this poor Thorn for ever.

III

"High on a mountain's highest ridge,
Where oft the stormy winter gale
Cuts like a scythe, while through the clouds
It sweeps from vale to vale;
Not five yards from the mountain path,
This Thorn you on your left espy;
And to the left, three yards beyond,
You see a little muddy pond
Of water — never dry,
Though but of compass small, and bare
To thirsty suns and parching air.

IV

"And, close beside this aged Thorn,
There is a fresh and lovely sight,
A beauteous heap, a hill of moss,
Just half a foot in height.
All lovely colours there you see,
All colours that were even seen;
And mossy network too is there,
As if by hand of lady fair
The work had woven been;
And cups, the darlings of the eye,
So deep is their vermilion dye.

V

"Ah me! what lovely tints are there
Of olive green and scarlet bright,
In spikes, in branches, and in stars,
Green, red, and pearly white!
This heap of earth o'ergrown with moss,
Which close beside the Thorn you see,
So fresh in all its beauteous dyes,
Is like an infant's grave in size,
As like as like can be:
But never, never any where,
An infant's grave was half so fair.

VI

"Now would you see this aged Thorn,
This pond, and beauteous hill of moss,
You must take care and choose your time
The mountain when to cross.
For oft there sits between the heap,
So like an infant's grave in size,
And that same pond of which I spoke,
A Woman in a scarlet cloak,
And to herself she cries,
'Oh misery! oh misery!
Oh woe is me! oh misery!'

VII

"At all times of the day and night
This wretched Woman thither goes;
And she is known to every star,
And every wind that blows;

And there, beside the Thorn, she sits
When the blue daylight's in the skies,
And when the whirlwind's on the hill,
Or frosty air is keen and still,
And to herself she cries,
'O misery! oh misery!
Oh woe is me! oh misery!'"

VIII

"Now wherefore, thus, by day and night,
In rain, in tempest, and in snow,
Thus to the dreary mountain-top
Does this poor Woman go?
And why sits she beside the Thorn
When the blue daylight's in the sky
Or when the whirlwind's on the hill,
Or frosty air is keen and still,
And wherefore does she cry? —
O wherefore? wherefore? tell me why
Does she repeat that doleful cry?"

IX

"I cannot tell; I wish I could;
For the true reason no one knows:
But would you gladly view the spot,
The spot to which she goes;
The hillock like an infant's grave,
The pond — and Thorn, so old and grey;
Pass by her door — 'tis seldom shut —
And if you see her in her hut —
Then to the spot away!
I never heard of such as dare
Approach the spot when she is there."

X

"But wherefore to the mountain-top
Can this unhappy Woman go,
Whatever star is in the skies,
Whatever wind may blow?"
"Full twenty years are past and gone
Since she (her name is Martha Ray)
Gave with a maiden's true good-will
Her company to Stephen Hill;
And she was blithe and gay,
While friends and kindred all approved
Of him whom tenderly she loved.

XI

"And they had fixed the wedding day,
The morning that must wed them both.
But Stephen to another Maid
Had sworn another oath;
And, with this other Maid, to church
Unthinking Stephen went —
Poor Martha! on that woeful day
A pang of pitiless dismay
Into her soul was sent;
A fire was kindled in her breast,
Which might not burn itself to rest.

XII

"They say, full six months after this,
While yet the summer leaves were green,
She to the mountain-top would go,
And there was often seen.

What could she seek? — or wish to hide?
Her state to any eye was plain;
She was with child, and she was mad;
Yet often was she sober sad
From her exceeding pain.
O guilty Father — would that death
Had saved him from that breach of faith!

XIII

"Sad case for such a brain to hold
Communion with a stirring child!
Sad case, as you may think, for one
Who had a brain so wild!
Last Christmas-eve we talked of this,
And grey-haired Wilfred of the glen
Held that the unborn infant wrought
About its mother's heart, and brought
Her senses back again:
And, when at last her time drew near,
Her looks were calm, her senses clear.

XIV

"More know I not, I wish I did,
And it should all be told to you;
For what became of this poor child
No mortal ever knew;
Nay — if a child to her was born
No earthly tongue could ever tell;
And if 'twas born alive or dead,
Far less could this with proof be said;
But some remember well
That Martha Ray about this time
Would up the mountain often climb.

XV

"And all that winter, when at night
The wind blew from the mountain-peak,
'Twas worth your while, though in the dark,
The churchyard path to seek:
For many a time and oft were heard
Cries coming from the mountain head:
Some plainly living voices were;
And others, I've heard many swear,
Were voices of the dead:
I cannot think, whate'er they say,
They had to do with Martha Ray.

XVI

"But that she goes to this old Thorn,
The Thorn which I described to you,
And there sits in a scarlet cloak,
I will be sworn is true.
For one day with my telescope,
To view the ocean wide and bright,
When to this country first I came,
Ere I had heard of Martha's name,
I climbed the mountain's height: —
A storm came on, and I could see
No object higher than my knee.

XVII

"'Twas mist and rain, and storm and rain:
No screen, no fence could I discover;
And then the wind! in sooth, it was
A wind full ten times over.

I looked around, I thought I saw
A jutting crag, — and off I ran,
Head-foremost, through the driving rain,
The shelter of the crag to gain;
And, as I am a man,
Instead of jutting crag I found
A Woman seated on the ground.

XVIII

"I did not speak — I saw her face;
Her face! — it was enough for me;
I turned about and heard her cry,
'Oh misery! oh misery!'
And there she sits, until the moon
Through half the clear blue sky will go;
And when the little breezes make
The waters of the pond to shake,
As all the country know,
She shudders, and you hear her cry,
'Oh misery! oh misery!'"

XIX

"But what's the·Thorn? and what the pond?
And what the hill of moss to her?
And what the creeping breeze that comes
The little pond to stir?"
"I cannot tell; but some will say
She hanged her baby on the tree;
Some say she drowned it in the pond,
Which is a little step beyond:
But all and each agree,
The little Babe was buried there,
Beneath that hill of moss so fair.

XX

"I've heard, the moss is spotted red
With drops of that poor infant's blood;
But kill a new-born infant thus,
I do not think she could!
Some say if to the pond you go,
And fix on it a steady view,
The shadow of a babe you trace,
A baby and a baby's face,
And that it looks at you;
Whene'er you look on it, 'tis plain
The baby looks at you again.

XXI

"And some had sworn an oath that she
Should be to public justice brought;
And for the little infant's bones
With spades they would have sought.
But instantly the hill of moss
Before their eyes began to stir!
And, for full fifty yards around,
The grass — it shook upon the ground!
Yet all do still aver
The little Babe lies buried there,
Beneath that hill of moss so fair.

XXII

"I cannot tell how this may be,
But plain it is the Thorn is bound
With heavy tufts of moss that strive
To drag it to the ground;

And this I know, full many a time,
When she was on the mountain high,
By day, and in the silent night,
When all the stars shone clear and bright,
That I have heard her cry,
'Oh misery! oh misery!
Oh woe is me! oh misery!'"

March–April, 1798   *1798*

LINES

Composed a few miles above Tintern Abbey, on revisiting the banks of the Wye during a tour.   July 13, 1798.

FIVE years have past; five summers, with the length
Of five long winters! and again I hear
These waters, rolling from their mountain-springs
With a soft inland murmur. — Once again
Do I behold these steep and lofty cliffs,
That on a wild secluded scene impress
Thoughts of more deep seclusion; and connect
The landscape with the quiet of the sky.
The day is come when I again repose
Here, under this dark sycamore, and view
These plots of cottage-ground, these orchard-tufts,
Which at this season, with their unripe fruits,
Are clad in one green hue, and lose themselves
'Mid groves and copses. Once again I see
These hedge-rows, hardly hedge-rows, little lines
Of sportive wood run wild: these pastoral farms,
Green to the very door; and wreaths of smoke
Sent up, in silence, from among the trees!
With some uncertain notice, as might seem
Of vagrant dwellers in the houseless woods,
Or of some Hermit's cave, where by his fire
The Hermit sits alone.

These beauteous forms,
Through a long absence, have not been to me
As is a landscape to a blind man's eye:
But oft, in lonely rooms, and 'mid the din
Of towns and cities, I have owed to them,
In hours of weariness, sensations sweet,
Felt in the blood, and felt along the heart;
And passing even into my purer mind,
With tranquil restoration: — feelings too
Of unremembered pleasure: such, perhaps,
As have no slight or trivial influence
On that best portion of a good man's life,
His little, nameless, unremembered, acts
Of kindness and of love. Nor less, I trust,
To them I may have owed another gift,
Of aspect more sublime; that blessed mood,
In which the burthen of the mystery,
In which the heavy and the weary weight
Of all this unintelligible world,
Is lightened: — that serene and blessed mood,
In which the affections gently lead us on, —
Until, the breath of this corporeal frame
And even the motion of our human blood
Almost suspended, we are laid asleep
In body, and become a living soul:
While with an eye made quiet by the power
Of harmony, and the deep power of joy,
We see into the life of things.

If this
Be but a vain belief, yet, oh! how oft —
In darkness and amid the many shapes
Of joyless daylight; when the fretful stir
Unprofitable, and the fever of the world,

Have hung upon the beatings of my heart —
How oft, in spirit, have I turned to thee,
O sylvan Wye! thou wanderer thro' the woods,
How often has my spirit turned to thee!

And now, with gleams of half-extinguished thought
With many recognitions dim and faint,
And somewhat of a sad perplexity,
The picture of the mind revives again:
While here I stand, not only with the sense
Of present pleasure, but with pleasing thoughts
That in this moment there is life and food
For future years. And so I dare to hope,
Though changed, no doubt, from what I was when first
I came among these hills; when like a roe
I bounded o'er the mountains, by the sides
Of the deep rivers, and the lonely streams,
Wherever nature led: more like a man
Flying from something that he dreads than one
Who sought the thing he loved. For nature then
(The coarser pleasures of my boyish days,
And their glad animal movements all gone by)
To me was all in all. — I cannot paint
What then I was. The sounding cataract
Haunted me like a passion: the tall rock,
The mountain, and the deep and gloomy wood,
Their colours and their forms, were then to me
An appetite; a feeling and a love,
That had no need for a remoter charm,
By thought supplied, nor any interest
Unborrowed from the eye. — That time is past,
And all its aching joys are now no more,
And all its dizzy raptures. Not for this
Faint I, nor mourn nor murmur; other gifts

Have followed; for such loss, I would believe,
Abundant recompense. For I have learned
To look on nature, not as in the hour
Of thoughtless youth; but hearing oftentimes
The still, sad music of humanity,
Nor harsh nor grating, though of ample power
To chasten and subdue. And I have felt
A presence that disturbs me with the joy
Of elevated thoughts; a sense sublime
Of something far more deeply interfused,
Whose dwelling is the light of setting suns,
And the round ocean and the living air,
And the blue sky, and in the mind of man:
A motion and a spirit, that impels
All thinking things, all objects of all thought,
And rolls through all things. Therefore am I still
A lover of the meadows and the woods,
And mountains; and of all that we behold
From this green earth; of all the mighty world
Of eye, and ear, — both what they half create,
And what perceive; well pleased to recognise
In nature and the language of the sense
The anchor of my purest thoughts, the nurse,
The guide, the guardian of my heart, and soul
Of all my moral being.

                          Nor perchance,
If I were not thus taught, should I the more
Suffer my genial spirits to decay:
For thou art with me here upon the banks
Of this fair river; thou my dearest Friend,
My dear, dear Friend; and in thy voice I catch
The language of my former heart, and read
My former pleasures in the shooting lights

Of thy wild eyes. Oh! yet a little while
May I behold in thee what I was once,
My dear, dear Sister! and this prayer I make,
Knowing that Nature never did betray
The heart that loved her; 'tis her privilege,
Through all the years of this our life, to lead
From joy to joy: for she can so inform
The mind that is within us, so impress
With quietness and beauty, and so feed
With lofty thoughts, that neither evil tongues,
Rash judgments, nor the sneers of selfish men,
Nor greetings where no kindness is, nor all
The dreary intercourse of daily life,
Shall e'er prevail against us, or disturb
Our cheerful faith, that all which we behold
Is full of blessings. Therefore let the moon
Shine on thee in thy solitary walk;
And let the misty mountain-winds be free
To blow against thee: and, in after years,
When these wild ecstasies shall be matured
Into a sober pleasure; when thy mind
Shall be a mansion for all lovely forms,
Thy memory be as a dwelling-place
For all sweet sounds and harmonies; oh! then,
If solitude, or fear, or pain, or grief
Should be thy portion, with what healing thoughts
Of tender joy wilt thou remember me,
And these my exhortations! Nor, perchance —
If I should be where I no more can hear
Thy voice, nor catch from thy wild eyes these gleams
Of past existence — wilt thou then forget
That on the banks of this delightful stream
We stood together; and that I, so long
A worshipper of Nature, hither came
Unwearied in that service: rather say

With warmer love — oh! with far deeper zeal
Of holier love.   Nor wilt thou then forget
That after many wanderings, many years
Of absence, these steep woods and lofty cliffs,
And this green pastoral landscape, were to me
More dear, both for themselves and for thy sake!

July 13, 1798   *1798*

LUCY GRAY

OR, SOLITUDE

Oft I had heard of Lucy Gray:
And, when I crossed the wild,
I chanced to see at break of day
The solitary child.

No mate, no comrade Lucy knew;
She dwelt on a wide moor,
— The sweetest thing that ever grew
Beside a human door!

You yet may spy the fawn at play,
The hare upon the green;
But the sweet face of Lucy Gray
Will never more be seen.

"To-night will be a stormy night —
You to the town must go;
And take a lantern, Child, to light
Your mother through the snow."

"That, Father! will I gladly do:
'Tis scarcely afternoon —
The minster-clock has just struck two,
And yonder is the moon!"

At this the Father raised his hook,
And snapped a faggot-band;
He plied his work; — and Lucy took
The lantern in her hand.

Not blither is the mountain roe:
With many a wanton stroke
Her feet disperse the powdery snow,
That rises up like smoke.

The storm came on before its time:
She wandered up and down;
And many a hill did Lucy climb:
But never reached the town.

The wretched parents all that night
Went shouting far and wide;
But there was neither sound nor sight
To serve them for a guide.

At day-break on a hill they stood
That overlooked the moor;
And thence they saw the bridge of wood,
A furlong from their door.

They wept — and, turning homeward, cried,
"In heaven we all shall meet;"
— When in the snow the mother spied
The print of Lucy's feet.

Then downwards from the steep hill's edge
They tracked the footmarks small;
And through the broken hawthorn hedge,
And by the long stone-wall;

And then an open field they crossed;
The marks were still the same;
They tracked them on, nor ever lost;
And to the bridge they came.

They followed from the snowy bank
Those footmarks, one by one,
Into the middle of the plank;
And further there were none!

— Yet some maintain that to this day
She is a living child;
That you may see sweet Lucy Gray
Upon the lonesome wild.

O'er rough and smooth she trips along,
And never looks behind;
And sings a solitary song
That whistles in the wind.

1799   *1800*

THE TWO APRIL MORNINGS

WE walked along, while bright and red
Uprose the morning sun;
And Matthew stopped, he looked, and said,
"The will of God be done!"

A village schoolmaster was he,
With hair of glittering grey;
As blithe a man as you could see
On a spring holiday.

And on that morning, through the grass,
And by the steaming rills,
We travelled merrily, to pass
A day among the hills.

"Our work," said I, "was well begun,
Then from thy breast what thought,
Beneath so beautiful a sun,
So sad a sigh has brought?"

A second time did Matthew stop;
And fixing still his eye
Upon the eastern mountain-top,
To me he made reply:

"Yon cloud with that long purple cleft
Brings fresh into my mind
A day like this which I have left
Full thirty years behind.

"And just above yon slope of corn
Such colours, and no other,
Were in the sky, that April morn,
Of this the very brother.

"With rod and line I sued the sport
Which that sweet season gave,
And, to the churchyard come, stopped short
Beside my daughter's grave.

"Nine summers had she scarcely seen,
The pride of all the vale;
And then she sang; — she would have been
A very nightingale.

"Six feet in earth my Emma lay;
And yet I loved her more,
For so it seemed, than till that day
I e'er had loved before.

"And, turning from her grave, I met,
Beside the churchyard yew,
A blooming Girl, whose hair was wet
With points of morning dew.

"A basket on her head she bare;
Her brow was smooth and white:
To see a child so very fair,
It was a pure delight!

"No fountain from its rocky cave
E'er tripped with foot so free;
She seemed as happy as a wave
That dances on the sea.

"There came from me a sigh of pain
Which I could ill confine;
I looked at her, and looked again:
And did not wish her mine!"

Matthew is in his grave, yet now,
Methinks, I see him stand,
As at that moment, with a bough
Of wilding in his hand.

1799   *1800*

THE FOUNTAIN

A CONVERSATION

WE talked with open heart, and tongue
Affectionate and true,
A pair of friends, though I was young,
And Matthew seventy-two.

We lay beneath a spreading oak,
Beside a mossy seat;
And from the turf a fountain broke,
And gurgled at our feet.

"Now, Matthew!" said I, "let us match
This water's pleasant tune
With some old border-song, or catch
That suits a summer's noon;

"Or of the church-clock and the chimes
Sing here beneath the shade,
That half-mad thing of witty rhymes
Which you last April made!"

In silence Matthew lay, and eyed
The spring beneath the tree;
And thus the dear old Man replied,
The grey-haired man of glee:

"No check, no stay, this Streamlet fears;
How merrily it goes!
'Twill murmur on a thousand years,
And flow as now it flows.

"And here, on this delightful day,
I cannot choose but think
How oft, a vigorous man, I lay
Beside this fountain's brink.

"My eyes are dim with childish tears,
My heart is idly stirred,
For the same sound is in my ears
Which in those days I heard.

"Thus fares it still in our decay:
And yet the wiser mind
Mourns less for what age takes away
Than what it leaves behind.

"The blackbird amid leafy trees,
The lark above the hill,
Let loose their carols when they please,
Are quiet when they will.

"With Nature never do *they* wage
A foolish strife; they see
A happy youth, and their old age
Is beautiful and free:

"But we are pressed by heavy laws;
And often, glad no more,
We wear a face of joy, because
We have been glad of yore.

"If there be one who need bemoan
His kindred laid in earth,
The household hearts that were his own;
It is the man of mirth.

"My days, my Friend, are almost gone,
My life has been approved,
And many love me! but by none
Am I enough beloved."

"Now both himself and me he wrongs,
The man who thus complains!
I live and sing my idle songs
Upon these happy plains;

"And, Matthew, for thy children dead
I'll be a son to thee!"
At this he grasped my hand, and said,
"Alas! that cannot be."

We rose up from the fountain-side;
And down the smooth descent
Of the green sheep-track did we glide;
And through the wood we went;

And, ere we came to Leonard's rock,
He sang those witty rhymes
About the crazy old church-clock,
And the bewildered chimes.

1799   *1800*

THE LUCY POEMS

I

STRANGE fits of passion have I known:
And I will dare to tell,
But in the Lover's ear alone,
What once to me befell.

When she I loved looked every day
Fresh as a rose in June,
I to her cottage bent my way,
Beneath an evening-moon.

Upon the moon I fixed my eye,
All over the wide lea;
With quickening pace my horse drew nigh
Those paths so dear to me.

And now we reached the orchard-plot;
And, as we climbed the hill,
The sinking moon to Lucy's cot
Came near, and nearer still.

In one of those sweet dreams I slept,
Kind Nature's gentlest boon!
And all the while my eyes I kept
On the descending moon.

My horse moved on; hoof after hoof
He raised, and never stopped:
When down behind the cottage roof,
At once, the bright moon dropped.

What fond and wayward thoughts will slide
Into a Lover's head!
"O mercy!" to myself I cried,
"If Lucy should be dead!"

1799   *1800*

II

SHE dwelt among the untrodden ways
   Beside the springs of Dove,
A Maid whom there were none to praise
   And very few to love:

A violet by a mossy stone
   Half hidden from the eye!
— Fair as a star, when only one
   Is shining in the sky.

She lived unknown, and few could know
  When Lucy ceased to be;
But she is in her grave, and, oh,
  The difference to me!

1799   *1800*

III

THREE years she grew in sun and shower,
Then Nature said, "A lovelier flower
On earth was never sown;
This Child I to myself will take;
She shall be mine, and I will make
A Lady of my own.

"Myself will to my darling be
Both law and impulse: and with me
The Girl, in rock and plain,
In earth and heaven, in glade and bower,
Shall feel an overseeing power
To kindle or restrain.

"She shall be sportive as the fawn
That wild with glee across the lawn
Or up the mountain springs;
And hers shall be the breathing balm,
And hers the silence and the calm
Of mute insensate things.

"The floating clouds their state shall lend
To her; for her the willow bend;
Nor shall she fail to see
Even in the motions of the Storm
Grace that shall mould the Maiden's form
By silent sympathy.

"The stars of midnight shall be dear
To her; and she shall lean her ear
In many a secret place
Where rivulets dance their wayward round,
And beauty born of murmuring sound
Shall pass into her face.

  And vital feelings of delight
Shall rear her form to stately height,
Her virgin bosom swell;
Such thoughts to Lucy I will give
While she and I together live
Here in this happy dell."

Thus Nature spake — The work was done —
How soon my Lucy's race was run!
She died, and left to me
This heath, this calm, and quiet scene;
The memory of what has been,
And never more will be.

1799   *1800*

IV

A SLUMBER did my spirit seal;
  I had no human fears:
She seemed a thing that could not feel
  The touch of earthly years.

No motion has she now, no force;
  She neither hears nor sees;
Rolled round in earth's diurnal course,
  With rocks, and stones, and trees.

1799   *1800*

V

I TRAVELLED among unknown men,
    In lands beyond the sea;
Nor, England! did I know till then
    What love I bore to thee.

'Tis past, that melancholy dream!
    Nor will I quit thy shore
A second time; for still I seem
    To love thee more and more.

Among thy mountains did I feel
    The joy of my desire;
And she I cherished turned her wheel
    Beside an English fire.

Thy mornings showed, thy nights concealed,
    The bowers where Lucy played;
And thine too is the last green field
    That Lucy's eyes surveyed.

1801   *1807*

A POET'S EPITAPH

ART thou a Statist in the van
Of public conflicts trained and bred?
— First learn to love one living man;
Then may'st thou think upon the dead.

A Lawyer art thou? — draw not nigh!
Go, carry to some fitter place
The keenness of that practised eye,
The hardness of that sallow face.

Art thou a Man of purple cheer?
A rosy Man, right plump to see?
Approach; yet, Doctor, not too near,
This grave no cushion is for thee.

Or art thou one of gallant pride,
A Soldier and no man of chaff?
Welcome! — but lay thy sword aside,
And lean upon a peasant's staff.

Physician art thou? — one, all eyes,
Philosopher! — a fingering slave,
One that would peep and botanize
Upon his mother's grave?

Wrapt closely in thy sensual fleece,
O turn aside, — and take, I pray,
That he below may rest in peace,
Thy ever-dwindling soul, away!

A Moralist perchance appears;
Led, Heaven knows how! to this poor sod:
And he has neither eyes nor ears;
Himself his world, and his own God;

One to whose smooth-rubbed soul can cling
Nor form, nor feeling, great or small;
A reasoning, self-sufficing thing,
An intellectual All-in-all!

Shut close the door; press down the latch;
Sleep in thy intellectual crust;
Nor lose ten tickings of thy watch
Near this unprofitable dust.

But who is He, with modest looks,
And clad in homely russet brown?
He murmurs near the running brooks
A music sweeter than their own.

He is retired as noontide dew,
Or fountain in a noon-day grove;
And you must love him, ere to you
He will seem worthy of your love.

The outward shows of sky and earth,
Of hill and valley, he has viewed;
And impulses of deeper birth
Have come to him in solitude.

In common things that round us lie
Some random truths he can impart, —
The harvest of a quiet eye
That broods and sleeps on his own heart.

But he is weak; both Man and Boy,
Hath been an idler in the land;
Contented if he might enjoy
The things which others understand.

— Come hither in thy hour of strength;
Come, weak as is a breaking wave!
Here stretch thy body at full length;
Or build thy house upon this grave.

1799   *1800*

THE OLD CUMBERLAND BEGGAR

I saw an aged Beggar in my walk;
And he was seated, by the highway side,
On a low structure of rude masonry
Built at the foot of a huge hill, that they
Who lead their horses down the steep rough road
May thence remount at ease. The aged Man
Had placed his staff across the broad smooth stone
That overlays the pile; and, from a bag
All white with flour, the dole of village dames,
He drew his scraps and fragments, one by one;
And scanned them with a fixed and serious look
Of idle computation. In the sun,
Upon the second step of that small pile,
Surrounded by those wild unpeopled hills,
He sat, and ate his food in solitude:
And ever, scattered from his palsied hand,
That, still attempting to prevent the waste,
Was baffled still, the crumbs in little showers
Fell on the ground; and the small mountain birds,
Not venturing yet to peck their destined meal,
Approached within the length of half his staff.

Him from my childhood have I known; and then
He was so old, he seems not older now;
He travels on, a solitary Man,
So helpless in appearance, that for him
The sauntering Horseman throws not with a slack
And careless hand his alms upon the ground,
But stops, — that he may safely lodge the coin
Within the old Man's hat; nor quits him so,

But still, when he has given his horse the rein,
Watches the aged Beggar with a look
Sidelong, and half-reverted. She who tends
The toll-gate, when in summer at her door
She turns her wheel, if on the road she sees
The aged Beggar coming, quits her work,
And lifts the latch for him that he may pass.
The post-boy, when his rattling wheels o'ertake
The aged Beggar in the woody lane,
Shouts to him from behind; and, if thus warned
The old man does not change his course, the boy
Turns with less noisy wheels to the roadside,
And passes gently by, without a curse
Upon his lips or anger at his heart.

　　He travels on, a solitary Man;
His age has no companion. On the ground
His eyes are turned, and, as he moves along,
They move along the ground; and, evermore,
Instead of common and habitual sight
Of fields with rural works, of hill and dale,
And the blue sky, one little span of earth
Is all his prospect. Thus, from day to day,
Bow-bent, his eyes for ever on the ground,
He plies his weary journey; seeing still,
And seldom knowing that he sees, some straw,
Some scattered leaf, or marks which, in one track,
The nails of cart or chariot-wheel have left
Impressed on the white road, — in the same line,
At distance still the same. Poor Traveller!
His staff trails with him; scarcely do his feet
Disturb the summer dust; he is so still
In look and motion, that the cottage curs,
Ere he has passed the door, will turn away,
Weary of barking at him. Boys and girls,
The vacant and the busy, maids and youths,

And urchins newly breeched — all pass him by:
Him even the slow-paced waggon leaves behind.

But deem not this Man useless. — Statesmen!   ye
Who are so restless in your wisdom, ye
Who have a broom still ready in your hands
To rid the world of nuisances; ye proud,
Heart-swoln, while in your pride ye contemplate
Your talents, power, or wisdom, deem him not
A burthen of the earth! 'Tis Nature's law
That none, the meanest of created things,
Of forms created the most vile and brute,
The dullest or most noxious, should exist
Divorced from good — a spirit and pulse of good,
A life and soul, to every mode of being
Inseparably linked. Then be assured
That least of all can aught — the ever owned
The heaven-regarding eye and front sublime
Which man is born to — sink, howe'er depressed,
So low as to be scorned without a sin;
Without offence to God cast out of view;
Like the dry remnant of a garden-flower
Whose seeds are shed, or an implement
Worn out and worthless. While from door to door,
This old Man creeps, the villagers in him
Behold a record which together binds
Past deeds and offices of charity,
Else unremembered, and so keeps alive
The kindly mood in hearts which lapse of years,
And that half-wisdom half-experience gives,
Make slow to feel, and by sure steps resign
To selfishness and cold oblivious cares.
Among the farms and solitary huts,
Hamlets and thinly-scattered villages,
Where'er the aged Beggar takes his rounds,
The mild necessity of use compels

To acts of love; and habit does the work
Of reason; yet prepares that after-joy
Which reason cherishes. And thus the soul,
By that sweet taste of pleasure unpursued,
Doth find herself insensibly disposed
To virtue and true goodness.

                 Some there are,
By their good works exalted, lofty minds,
And meditative, authors of delight
And happiness, which to the end of time
Will live, and spread, and kindle: even such minds
In childhood, from this solitary Being,
Or from like wanderer, haply have received
(A thing more precious far than all that books
Or the solicitudes of love can do!)
That first mild touch of sympathy and thought,
In which they found their kindred with a world
Where want and sorrow were. The easy man
Who sits at his own door, — and, like the pear
That overhangs his head from the green wall,
Feeds in the sunshine; the robust and young,
The prosperous and unthinking, they who live
Sheltered, and flourish in a little grove
Of their own kindred; — all behold in him
A silent monitor, which on their minds
Must needs impress a transitory thought
Of self-congratulation, to the heart
Of each recalling his peculiar boons,
His charters and exemptions; and, perchance,
Though he to no one give the fortitude
And circumspection needful to preserve
His present blessings, and to husband up
The respite of the season, he, at least,
And 'tis no vulgar service, makes them felt.

Yet further. —— Many, I believe, there are
Who live a life of virtuous decency,
Men who can hear the Decalogue and feel
No self-reproach; who of the moral law
Established in the land where they abide
Are strict observers; and not negligent
In acts of love to those with whom they dwell,
Their kindred, and the children of their blood.
Praise be to such, and to their slumbers peace!
— But of the poor man ask, the abject poor;
Go, and demand of him, if there be here
In this cold abstinence from evil deeds,
And these inevitable charities,
Wherewith to satisfy the human soul?
No — man is dear to man; the poorest poor
Long for some moments in a weary life
When they can know and feel that they have been,
Themselves, the fathers and the dealers-out
Of some small blessings; have been kind to such
As needed kindness, for this single cause,
That we have all of us one human heart.
— Such pleasure is to one kind Being known,
My neighbour, when with punctual care, each week,
Duly as Friday comes, though pressed herself
By her own wants, she from her store of meal
Takes one unsparing handful for the scrip
Of this old Mendicant, and, from her door
Returning with exhilarated heart,
Sits by her fire, and builds her hope in heaven.

Then let him pass, a blessing on his head!
And while in that vast solitude to which
The tide of things has borne him, he appears
To breathe and live but for himself alone,

Unblamed, uninjured, let him bear about
The good which the benignant law of Heaven
Has hung around him: and, while life is his,
Still let him prompt the unlettered villagers
To tender offices and pensive thoughts.
— Then let him pass, a blessing on his head!
And, long as he can wander, let him breathe
The freshness of the valleys; let his blood
Struggle with frosty air and winter snows;
And let the chartered wind that sweeps the heath
Beat his grey locks against his withered face.
Reverence the hope whose vital anxiousness
Gives the last human interest to his heart.
May never HOUSE, misnamed of INDUSTRY,
Make him a captive! — for that pent-up din,
Those life-consuming sounds that clog the air,
Be his the natural silence of old age!
Let him be free of mountain solitudes;
And have around him, whether heard or not,
The pleasant melody of woodland birds.
Few are his pleasures: if his eyes have now
Been doomed so long to settle upon earth
That not without some effort they behold
The countenance of the horizontal sun,
Rising or setting, let the light at least
Find a free entrance to their languid orbs,
And let him, *where* and *when* he will, sit down
Beneath the trees, or on a grassy bank
Of highway side, and with the little birds
Share his chance-gathered meal; and, finally,
As in the eye of Nature he has lived,
So in the eye of Nature let him die!

1797 *1800*

MICHAEL

A PASTORAL POEM

If from the public way you turn your steps
Up the tumultuous brook of Green-head Ghyll,
You will suppose that with an upright path
Your feet must struggle; in such bold ascent
The pastoral mountains front you, face to face.
But, courage! for around that boisterous brook
The mountains have all opened out themselves,
And made a hidden valley of their own.
No habitation can be seen; but they
Who journey thither find themselves alone
With a few sheep, with rocks and stones, and kites
That overhead are sailing in the sky.
It is in truth an utter solitude;
Nor should I have made mention of this Dell
But for one object which you might pass by,
Might see and notice not. Beside the brook
Appears a straggling heap of unhewn stones!
And to that simple object appertains
A story — unenriched with strange events,
Yet not unfit, I deem, for the fireside,
Or for the summer shade. It was the first
Of those domestic tales that spake to me
Of Shepherds, dwellers in the valleys, men
Whom I already loved; — not verily
For their own sakes, but for the fields and hills
Where was their occupation and abode.
And hence this Tale, while I was yet a Boy
Careless of books, yet having felt the power
Of Nature, by the gentle agency
Of natural objects, led me on to feel

For passions that were not my own, and think
(At random and imperfectly indeed)
On man, the heart of man, and human life.
Therefore, although it be a history
Homely and rude, I will relate the same
For the delight of a few natural hearts;
And, with yet fonder feeling, for the sake
Of youthful Poets, who among these hills
Will be my second self when I am gone.

   Upon the forest-side in Grasmere Vale
There dwelt a Shepherd, Michael was his name;
An old man, stout of heart, and strong of limb.
His bodily frame had been from youth to age
Of an unusual strength: his mind was keen,
Intense, and frugal, apt for all affairs,
And in his shepherd's calling he was prompt
And watchful more than ordinary men.
Hence had he learned the meaning of all winds,
Of blasts of every tone; and oftentimes,
When others heeded not, he heard the South
Make subterraneous music, like the noise
Of bagpipers on distant Highland hills.
The Shepherd, at such warning, of his flock
Bethought him, and he to himself would say,
"The winds are now devising work for me!"
And, truly, at all times, the storm, that drives
The traveller to a shelter, summoned him
Up to the mountains: he had been alone
Amid the heart of many thousand mists,
That came to him, and left him, on the heights.
So lived he till his eightieth year was past.
And grossly that man errs, who should suppose
That the green valleys, and the streams and rocks,
Were things indifferent to the Shepherd's thoughts.

Fields, where with cheerful spirits he had breathed
The common air; hills, which with vigorous step
He had so often climbed; which had impressed
So many incidents upon his mind
Of hardship, skill or courage, joy or fear;
Which, like a book, preserved the memory
Of the dumb animals, whom he had saved,
Had fed or sheltered, linking to such acts
The certainty of honourable gain;
Those fields, those hills — what could they less? had
    laid
Strong hold on his affections, were to him
A pleasurable feeling of blind love,
The pleasure which there is in life itself.

His days had not been passed in singleness.
His Helpmate was a comely matron, old —
Though younger than himself full twenty years.
She was a woman of a stirring life,
Whose heart was in her house: two wheels she had
Of antique form, this large, for spinning wool;
That small, for flax; and, if one wheel had rest,
It was because the other was at work.
The Pair had but one inmate in their house,
An only Child, who had been born to them
When Michael, telling o'er his years, began
To deem that he was old, — in shepherd's phrase,
With one foot in the grave. This only Son,
With two brave sheep-dogs tried in many a storm,
The one of an inestimable worth,
Made all their household. I may truly say,
That they were as a proverb in the vale
For endless industry. When day was gone,
And from their occupations out of doors
The Son and Father were come home, even then,

Their labour did not cease; unless when all
Turned to the cleanly supper-board, and there,
Each with a mess of pottage and skimmed milk,
Sat round the basket piled with oaten cakes,
And their plain home-made cheese. Yet when the meal
Was ended, Luke (for so the Son was named)
And his old Father both betook themselves
To such convenient work as might employ
Their hands by the fire-side; perhaps to card
Wool for the Housewife's spindle, or repair
Some injury done to sickle, flail, or scythe,
Or other implement of house or field.

Down from the ceiling, by the chimney's edge,
That in our ancient uncouth country style
With huge and black projection overbrowed
Large space beneath, as duly as the light
Of day grew dim the Housewife hung a lamp;
An aged utensil, which had performed
Service beyond all others of its kind.
Early at evening did it burn — and late,
Surviving comrade of uncounted hours,
Which, going by from year to year, had found,
And left, the couple neither gay perhaps
Nor cheerful, yet with objects and with hopes,
Living a life of eager industry.
And now, when Luke had reached his eighteenth year,
There by the light of this old lamp they sate,
Father and Son, while far into the night
The Housewife plied her own peculiar work,
Making the cottage through the silent hours
Murmur as with the sound of summer flies.
This light was famous in its neighbourhood,
And was a public symbol of the life
That thrifty Pair had lived. For, as it chanced,

Their cottage on a plot of rising ground
Stood single, with large prospect, north and south,
High into Easedale, up to Dunmail-Raise,
And westward to the village near the lake;
And from this constant light, so regular,
And so far seen, the House itself, by all
Who dwelt within the limits of the vale,
Both old and young, was named THE EVENING STAR.

Thus living on through such a length of years,
The Shepherd, if he loved himself, must needs
Have loved his Helpmate; but to Michael's heart
This son of his old age was yet more dear —
Less from instinctive tenderness, the same
Fond spirit that blindly works in the blood of all —
Than that a child, more than all other gifts
That earth can offer to declining man,
Brings hope with it, and forward-looking thoughts,
And stirrings of inquietude, when they
By tendency of nature needs must fail.
Exceeding was the love he bare to him,
His heart and his heart's joy! For oftentimes
Old Michael, while he was a babe in arms,
Had done him female service, not alone
For pastime and delight, as is the use
Of fathers, but with patient mind enforced
To acts of tenderness; and he had rocked
His cradle, as with a woman's gentle hand.

And in a later time, ere yet the Boy
Had put on boy's attire, did Michael love,
Albeit of a stern unbending mind,
To have the Young-one in his sight, when he
Wrought in the field, or on his shepherd's stool
Sate with a fettered sheep before him stretched

Under the large old oak, that near his door
Stood single, and, from matchless depth of shade,
Chosen for the Shearer's covert from the sun,
Thence in our rustic dialect was called
The CLIPPING TREE, a name which yet it bears.
There, while they two were sitting in the shade,
With others round them, earnest all and blithe,
Would Michael exercise his heart with looks
Of fond correction and reproof bestowed
Upon the Child, if he disturbed the sheep
By catching at their legs, or with his shouts
Scared them, while they lay still beneath the shears.

And when by Heaven's good grace the boy grew up
A healthy Lad, and carried in his cheek
Two steady roses that were five years old;
Then Michael from a winter coppice cut
With his own hand a sapling, which he hooped
With iron, making it throughout in all
Due requisites a perfect shepherd's staff,
And gave it to the Boy; wherewith equipt
He as a watchman oftentimes was placed
At gate or gap, to stem or turn the flock;
And, to his office prematurely called,
There stood the urchin, as you will divine,
Something between a hindrance and a help;
And for this cause not always, I believe,
Receiving from his Father hire of praise;
Though nought was left undone which staff, or voice,
Or looks, or threatening gestures, could perform.

But soon as Luke, full ten years old, could stand
Against the mountain blasts; and to the heights,
Not fearing toil, nor length of weary ways,
He with his Father daily went, and they

Were as companions, why should I relate
That objects which the Shepherd loved before
Were dearer now? that from the Boy there came
Feelings and emanations — things which were
Light to the sun and music to the wind;
And that the old Man's heart seemed born again?

Thus in his Father's sight the Boy grew up:
And now, when he had reached his eighteenth year,
He was his comfort and his daily hope.

While in this sort the simple household lived
From day to day, to Michael's ear there came
Distressful tidings. Long before the time
Of which I speak, the Shepherd had been bound
In surety for his brother's son, a man
Of an industrious life, and ample means;
But unforeseen misfortunes suddenly
Had prest upon him; and old Michael now
Was summoned to discharge the forfeiture,
A grievous penalty, but little less
Than half his substance. This unlooked-for claim,
At the first hearing, for a moment took
More hope out of his life than he supposed
That any old man ever could have lost.
As soon as he had armed himself with strength
To look his trouble in the face, it seemed
The Shepherd's sole resource to sell at once
A portion of his patrimonial fields.
Such was his first resolve; he thought again,
And his heart failed him. "Isabel," said he,
Two evenings after he had heard the news,
"I have been toiling more than seventy years,
And in the open sunshine of God's love
Have we all lived; yet, if these fields of ours

Should pass into a stranger's hand, I think
That I could not lie quiet in my grave.
Our lot is a hard lot; the sun himself
Has scarcely been more diligent than I;
And I have lived to be a fool at last
To my own family.   An evil man
That was, and made an evil choice, if he
Were false to us; and, if he were not false,
There are ten thousand to whom loss like this
Had been no sorrow.   I forgive him; — but
'Twere better to be dumb than to talk thus.

When I began, my purpose was to speak
Of remedies and of a cheerful hope.
Our Luke shall leave us, Isabel; the land
Shall not go from us, and it shall be free;
He shall possess it, free as is the wind
That passes over it.   We have, thou know'st,
Another kinsman — he will be our friend
In this distress.   He is a prosperous man,
Thriving in trade — and Luke to him shall go,
And with his kinsman's help and his own thrift
He quickly will repair this loss, and then
He may return to us.   If here he stay,
What can be done?   Where every one is poor,
What can be gained?"

                  At this the old Man paused,
And Isabel sat silent, for her mind
Was busy, looking back into past times.
There's Richard Bateman, thought she to herself,
He was a parish-boy — at the church-door
They made a gathering for him, shillings, pence,
And halfpennies, wherewith the neighbours bought
A basket, which they filled with pedlar's wares;
And, with this basket on his arm, the lad
Went up to London, found a master there,

Who, out of many, chose the trusty boy
To go and overlook his merchandise
Beyond the seas; where he grew wondrous rich,
And left estates and monies to the poor,
And, at his birth-place, built a chapel floored
With marble, which he sent from foreign lands.
These thoughts, and may others of like sort,
Passed quickly through the mind of Isabel,
And her face brightened. The old Man was glad,
And thus resumed: — "Well, Isabel! this scheme
These two days has been meat and drink to me.
Far more than we have lost is left us yet.
   We have enough — I wish indeed that I
Were younger; — but this hope is a good hope.
Make ready Luke's best garments, of the best
Buy for him more, and let us send him forth
To-morrow, or the next day, or to-night:
   If he *could* go, the Boy should go tonight."

   Here Michael ceased, and to the fields went forth
With a light heart. The Housewife for five days
Was restless morn and night, and all day long
Wrought on with her best fingers to prepare
Things needful for the journey of her son.
But Isabel was glad when Sunday came
To stop her in her work: for, when she lay
By Michael's side, she through the last two nights
Heard him, how he was troubled in his sleep:
And when they rose at morning she could see
That all his hopes were gone. That day at noon
She said to Luke, while they two by themselves
Were sitting at the door, "Thou must not go:
We have no other Child but thee to lose,
None to remember — do not go away,
For if thou leave thy Father he will die."

The Youth made answer with a jocund voice;
And Isabel, when she had told her fears,
Recovered heart. That evening her best fare
Did she bring forth, and all together sat
Like happy people round a Christmas fire.

With daylight Isabel resumed her work;
And all the ensuing week the house appeared
As cheerful as a grove in Spring: at length
The expected letter from their kinsman came,
With kind assurances that he would do
His utmost for the welfare of the Boy;
To which, requests were added, that forthwith
He might be sent to him. Ten times or more
The letter was read over; Isabel
Went forth to show it to the neighbours round;
Nor was there at that time on English land
A prouder heart than Luke's. When Isabel
Had to her house returned, the old Man said,
"He shall depart to-morrow." To this word
The Housewife answered, talking much of things
Which, if at such short notice he should go,
Would surely be forgotten. But at length
She gave consent, and Michael was at ease.

Near the tumultuous brook of Green-head Ghyll,
In that deep valley, Michael had designed
To build a Sheep-fold; and, before he heard
The tidings of his melancholy loss,
For this same purpose he had gathered up
A heap of stones, which by the streamlet's edge
Lay thrown together, ready for the work.
With Luke that evening thitherward he walked;
And soon as they had reached the place he stopped,
And thus the old Man spake to him: — "My son,

Tomorrow thou wilt leave me: with full heart
I look upon thee, for thou art the same
That wert a promise to me ere thy birth,
And all thy life hast been my daily joy.
I will relate to thee some little part
Of our two histories; 'twill do thee good
When thou art from me, even if I should touch
On things thou canst not know of. — After thou
First cam'st into the world — as oft befalls
To new-born infants — thou didst sleep away
Two days, and blessings from thy Father's tongue
Then fell upon thee. Day by day passed on,
And still I loved thee with increasing love.
Never to living ear came sweeter sounds
Than when I heard thee by our own fireside
First uttering, without words, a natural tune;
While thou, a feeding babe, didst in thy joy
Sing at thy Mother's breast. Month followed month,
And in the open fields my life was passed
And on the mountains; else I think that thou
Hadst been brought up upon thy Father's knees.
But we were playmates, Luke: among these hills,
As well thou knowest, in us the old and young
Have played together, nor with me didst thou
Lack any pleasure which a boy can know."
Luke had a manly heart; but at these words
He sobbed aloud. The old Man grasped his hand,
And said, "Nay, do not take it so — I see
That these are things of which I need not speak.
— Even to the utmost I have been to thee
A kind and a good Father: and herein
I but repay a gift which I myself
Received at others' hands; for, though now old
Beyond the common life of man, I still
Remember them who loved me in my youth.

Both of them sleep together: here they lived,
As all their Forefathers had done; and, when
At length their time was come, they were not loth
To give their bodies to the family mould.
I wished that thou shouldst live the life they lived,
But 'tis a long time to look back, my Son,
And see so little gain from threescore years.
These fields were burthened when they came to me;
Till I was forty years of age, not more
Than half of my inheritance was mine.
I toiled and toiled; God blessed me in my work,
And till these three weeks past the land was free.
— It looks as if it never could endure
Another Master. Heaven forgive me, Luke,
If I judge ill for thee, but it seems good
That thou shouldst go."
                    At this the old Man paused;
Then, pointing to the stones near which they stood,
Thus, after a short silence, he resumed:
"This was a work for us; and now, my Son,
It is a work for me. But, lay one stone —
Here, lay it for me, Luke, with thine own hands.
Nay, Boy, be of good hope; — we both may live
To see a better day. At eighty-four
I still am strong and hale; — do thou thy part;
I will do mine. — I will begin again
With many tasks that were resigned to thee:
Up to the heights, and in among the storms,
Will I without thee go again, and do
All works which I was wont to do alone,
Before I knew thy face. — Heaven bless thee, Boy!
Thy heart these two weeks has been beating fast
With many hopes; it should be so — yes — yes —
I knew that thou couldst never have a wish
To leave me, Luke: thou hast been bound to me

Only by links of love: when thou art gone,
What will be left to us! — But I forget
My purposes. Lay now the corner-stone,
As I requested; and hereafter, Luke,
When thou art gone away, should evil men
Be thy companions, think of me, my Son,
And of this moment; hither turn thy thoughts,
And God will strengthen thee: amid all fear
And all temptation, Luke, I pray that thou
May'st bear in mind the life thy Fathers lived,
Who, being innocent, did for that cause
Bestir them in good deeds. Now, fare thee well —
When thou return'st, thou in this place wilt see
A work which is not here: a covenant
'Twill be between us; but, whatever fate
Befall thee, I shall love thee to the last,
And bear thy memory with me to the grave."

The Shepherd ended here; and Luke stooped down,
And, as his Father had requested, laid
The first stone of the Sheep-fold. At the sight
The old Man's grief broke from him; to his heart
He pressed his Son, he kissèd him and wept;
And to the house together they returned.
— Hushed was that House in peace, or seeming peace
Ere the night fell: — with morrow's dawn the Boy
Began his journey, and, when he had reached
The public way, he put on a bold face;
And all the neighbours, as he passed their doors,
Came forth with wishes and with farewell prayers,
That followed him till he was out of sight.

A good report did from their Kinsman come,
Of Luke and his well-doing: and the Boy

Wrote loving letters, full of wondrous news,
Which, as the Housewife phrased it, were throughout
"The prettiest letters that were ever seen."
Both parents read them with rejoicing hearts.
So, many months passed on: and once again
The Shepherd went about his daily work
With confident and cheerful thoughts; and now
Sometimes when he could find a leisure hour
He to that valley took his way, and there
Wrought at the Sheep-fold.   Meantime Luke began
To slacken in his duty; and, at length,
He in the dissolute city gave himself
To evil courses: ignominy and shame
Fell on him, so that he was driven at last
To seek a hiding-place beyond the seas.

   There is a comfort in the strength of love;
'Twill make a thing endurable, which else
Would overset the brain, or break the heart:
I have conversed with more than one who well
Remember the old Man, and what he was
Years after he had heard this heavy news.
His bodily frame had been from youth to age
Of an unusual strength.   Among the rocks
He went, and still looked up to sun and cloud,
And listened to the wind; and, as before,
Performed all kinds of labour for his sheep,
And for the land, his small inheritance.
And to that hollow dell from time to time
Did he repair, to build the Fold of which
His flock had need.   'Tis not forgotten yet
The pity which was then in every heart
For the old Man — and 'tis believed by all
That many and many a day he thither went,
And never lifted up a single stone.

There, by the Sheep-fold, sometimes was he seen
Sitting alone, or with his faithful Dog,
Then old, beside him, lying at his feet.
The length of full seven years, from time to time,
He at the building of this Sheep-fold wrought,
And left the work unfinished when he died.
Three years, or little more, did Isabel
Survive her Husband: at her death the estate
Was sold, and went into a stranger's hand.
The Cottage which was named the EVENING STAR.
Is gone — the ploughshare has been through the ground
On which it stood; great changes have been wrought
In all the neighbourhood: — yet the oak is left
That grew beside their door; and the remains
Of the unfinished Sheep-fold may be seen
Beside the boisterous brook of Green-head Ghyll.

Oct. 11–Dec. 9, 1800   *1800*

TO THE CUCKOO

O BLITHE New-comer! I have heard,
I hear thee and rejoice.
O Cuckoo! shall I call thee Bird,
Or but a wandering Voice?

While I am lying on the grass
Thy twofold shout I hear;
From hill to hill it seems to pass
At once far off, and near.

Though babbling only to the Vale,
Of sunshine and of flowers,
Thou bringest unto me a tale
Of visionary hours.

Thrice welcome, darling of the Spring!
Even yet thou art to me
No bird, but an invisible thing,
A voice, a mystery;

The same whom in my schoolboy days
I listened to; that Cry
Which made me look a thousand ways
In bush, and tree, and sky.

To seek thee did I often rove
Through woods and on the green;
And thou wert still a hope, a love;
Still longed for, never seen.

And I can listen to thee yet;
Can lie upon the plain
And listen, till I do beget
That golden time again.

O blessèd Bird! the earth we pace
Again appears to be
An unsubstantial, faery place;
That is fit home for Thee!

March 23–26, 1802   *1807*

RESOLUTION AND INDEPENDENCE

I

THERE was a roaring in the wind all night;
The rain came heavily and fell in floods;
But now the sun is rising calm and bright;

The birds are singing in the distant woods;
Over his own sweet voice the Stock-dove broods;
The Jay makes answer as the Magpie chatters;
And all the air is filled with pleasant noise of waters.

II

All things that love the sun are out of doors;
The sky rejoices in the morning's birth;
The grass is bright with rain-drops; — on the moors
The hare is running races in her mirth;
And with her feet she from the plashy earth
Raises a mist; that, glittering in the sun,
Runs with her all the way, wherever she doth run.

III

I was a Traveller then upon the moor;
I saw the hare that raced about with joy;
I heard the woods and distant waters roar;
Or heard them not, as happy as a boy:
The pleasant season did my heart employ:
My old remembrances went from me wholly;
And all the ways of men, so vain and melancholy.

IV

But, as it sometimes chanceth, from the might
Of joy in minds that can no further go,
As high as we have mounted in delight
In our dejection do we sink as low;
To me that morning did it happen so;
And fears and fancies thick upon me came;
Dim sadness — and blind thoughts, I knew not, nor
    could name.

V

I heard the sky-lark warbling in the sky;
And I bethought me of the playful hare:
Even such a happy Child of earth am I;
Even as these blissful creatures do I fare;
Far from the world I walk, and from all care;
But there may come another day to me —
Solitude, pain of heart, distress, and poverty.

VI

My whole life I have lived in pleasant thought,
As if life's business were a summer mood;
As if all needful things would come unsought
To genial faith, still rich in genial good;
But how can He expect that others should
Build for him, sow for him, and at his call
Love him, who for himself will take no heed at all?

VII

I thought of Chatterton, the marvellous Boy,
The sleepless Soul that perished in his pride;
Of Him who walked in glory and in joy
Following his plough, along the mountain-side:
By our own spirits are we deified:
We Poets in our youth begin in gladness;
But thereof come in the end despondency and madness.

VIII

Now, whether it were by peculiar grace,
A leading from above, a something given,
Yet it befell that, in this lonely place,
When I with these untoward thoughts had striven,
Beside a pool bare to the eye of heaven
I saw a Man before me unawares:
The oldest man he seemed that ever wore grey hairs.

IX

As a huge stone is sometimes seen to lie
Couched on the bald top of an eminence;
Wonder to all who do the same espy,
By what means it could thither come, and whence;
So that it seems a thing endued with sense:
Like a sea-beast crawled forth, that on a shelf
Of rock or sand reposeth, there to sun itself;

X

Such seemed this Man, not all alive nor dead,
Nor all asleep — in his extreme old age:
His body was bent double, feet and head
Coming together in life's pilgrimage;
As if some dire constraint of pain, or rage
Of sickness felt by him in times long past,
A more than human weight upon his frame had cast.

XI

Himself he propped, limbs, body, and pale face,
Upon a long grey staff of shaven wood:
And, still as I drew near with gentle pace,
Upon the margin of that moorish flood
Motionless as a cloud the old Man stood,
That heareth not the loud winds when they call;
And moveth all together, if it move at all.

XII

At length, himself unsettling, he the pond
Stirred with his staff, and fixedly did look
Upon the muddy water, which he conned,
As if he had been reading in a book:
And now a stranger's privilege I took;
And, drawing to his side, to him did say,
"This morning gives us promise of a glorious day."

XIII

A gentle answer did the old Man make,
In courteous speech which forth he slowly drew:
And him with further words I thus bespake,
"What occupation do you there pursue?
This is a lonesome place for one like you."
Ere he replied, a flash of mild surprise
Broke from the sable orbs of his yet-vivid eyes.

XIV

His words came feebly, from a feeble chest,
But each in solemn order followed each,
With something of a lofty utterance drest —
Choice word and measured phrase, above the reach
Of ordinary men; a stately speech;
Such as grave Livers do in Scotland use,
Religious men, who give to God and man their dues.

XV

He told, that to these waters he had come
To gather leeches, being old and poor:
Employment hazardous and wearisome!
And he had many hardships to endure:
From pond to pond he roamed, from moor to moor;
Housing, with God's good help, by choice or chance;
And in this way he gained an honest maintenance.

XVI

The old Man still stood talking by my side;
But now his voice to me was like a stream
Scarce heard; nor word from word could I divide;
And the whole body of the Man did seem
Like one whom I had met with in a dream;
Or like a man from some far region sent,
To give me human strength, by apt admonishment.

XVII

My former thoughts returned: the fear that kills;
And hope that is unwilling to be fed;
Cold, pain, and labour, and all fleshly ills;
And mighty Poets in their misery dead.
— Perplexed, and longing to be comforted,
My question eagerly did I renew,
"How is it that you live, and what is it you do?"

XVIII

He with a smile did then his words repeat;
And said that, gathering leeches, far and wide
He travelled; stirring thus about his feet
The waters of the pools where they abide.
"Once I could meet with them on every side;
But they have dwindled long by slow decay;
Yet still I persevere, and find them where I may."

XIX

While he was talking thus, the lonely place,
The old Man's shape, and speech — all troubled me:
In my mind's eye I seemed to see him pace
About the weary moors continually,
Wandering about alone and silently.
While I these thoughts within myself pursued,
He, having made a pause, the same discourse renewed.

XX

And soon with this he other matter blended,
Cheerfully uttered, with demeanour kind,
But stately in the main; and, when he ended,
I could have laughed myself to scorn to find
In that decrepit Man so firm a mind.
"God," said I, "be my help and stay secure;
I'll think of the Leech-gatherer on the lonely moor!"

May 3–July 4, 1802   *1807*

"SHE WAS A PHANTOM OF DELIGHT..."

She was a Phantom of delight
When first she gleamed upon my sight;
A lovely Apparition, sent
To be a moment's ornament;
Her eyes as stars of Twilight fair;
Like Twilight's, too, her dusky hair;
But all things else about her drawn
From May-time and the cheerful Dawn;
A dancing Shape, an Image gay,
To haunt, to startle, and way-lay.

I saw her upon nearer view,
A Spirit, yet a Woman too!
Her household motions light and free,
And steps of virgin-liberty;
A countenance in which did meet
Sweet records, promises as sweet;
A Creature not too bright or good
For human nature's daily food;
For transient sorrows, simple wiles,
Praise, blame, love, kisses, tears, and smiles.

And now I see with eye serene
The very pulse of the machine;
A Being breathing thoughtful breath,
A Traveller between life and death;
The reason firm, the temperate will,
Endurance, foresight, strength, and skill;
A perfect Woman, nobly planned,
To warn, to comfort, and command;
And yet a Spirit still, and bright
With something of angelic light.

1804   *1807*

"I WANDERED LONELY AS A CLOUD..."

I WANDERED lonely as a cloud
That floats on high o'er vales and hills,
When all at once I saw a crowd,
A host, of golden daffodils;
Beside the lake, beneath the trees,
Fluttering and dancing in the breeze.

Continuous as the stars that shine
And twinkle on the milky way,
They stretched in never-ending line
Along the margin of a bay:
Ten thousand saw I at a glance,
Tossing their heads in sprightly dance.

The waves beside them danced; but they
Out-did the sparkling waves in glee:
A poet could not but be gay,
In such a jocund company:
I gazed — and gazed — but little thought
What wealth the show to me had brought

For oft, when on my couch I lie
In vacant or in pensive mood,
They flash upon that inward eye
Which is the bliss of solitude;
And then my heart with pleasure fills,
And dances with the daffodils.

1804   *1807*

ODE TO DUTY

"Jam non consilio bonus, sed more eò perductus, ut non
tantum rectè facere possim, sed nisi rectè facere non
possim."

Stern Daughter of the Voice of God!
O Duty! if that name thou love
Who are a light to guide, a rod
To check the erring, and reprove;
Thou, who art victory and law
When empty terrors overawe;
From vain temptations dost set free;
And calm'st the weary strife of frail humanity!

There are who ask not if thine eye
Be on them; who, in love and truth,
Where no misgiving is, rely
Upon the genial sense of youth:
Glad Hearts! without reproach or blot;
Who do thy work, and know it not:
Oh! if through confidence misplaced
They fail, thy saving arms, dread Power! around them
         cast.

Serene will be our days and bright,
And happy will our nature be,
When love is an unerring light,
And joy its own security.
And they a blissful course may hold
Even now, who, not unwisely bold,
Live in the spirit of this creed;
Yet seek thy firm support, according to their need.

I, loving freedom, and untried;
No sport of every random gust,

Yet being to myself a guide,
Too blindly have reposed my trust:
And oft, when in my heart was heard
Thy timely mandate, I deferred
The task, in smoother walks to stray;
But thee I now would serve more strictly, if I may.

Through no disturbance of my soul,
Or strong compunction in me wrought,
I supplicate for thy control;
But in the quietness of thought:
Me this unchartered freedom tires;
I feel the weight of chance-desires:
My hopes no more must change their name,
I long for a repose that ever is the same.

Stern Lawgiver! yet thou dost wear
The Godhead's most benignant grace;
Nor know we anything so fair
As is the smile upon thy face:
Flowers laugh before thee on their beds
And fragrance in thy footing treads;
Thou dost preserve the stars from wrong;
And the most ancient heavens, through Thee, are fresh
and strong.

To humbler functions, awful Power!
I call thee: I myself commend
Unto thy guidance from this hour;
Oh, let my weakness have an end!
Give unto me, made lowly wise,
The spirit of self-sacrifice;
The confidence of reason give;
And in the light of truth thy Bondman let me live!

1804   *1807*

ELEGIAC STANZAS

Suggested by a picture of Peele Castle, in a storm, painted by Sir George Beaumont

I was thy neighbour once, thou rugged Pile!
Four summer weeks I dwelt in sight of thee:
I saw thee every day; and all the while
Thy Form was sleeping on a glassy sea.

So pure the sky, so quiet was the air!
So like, so very like, was day to day!
Whene'er I looked, thy Image still was there;
It trembled, but it never passed away.

How perfect was the calm! it seemed no sleep;
No mood, which season takes away, or brings:
I could have fancied that the mighty Deep
Was even the gentlest of all gentle Things.

Ah! then, if mine had been the Painter's hand,
To express what then I saw; and add the gleam,
The light that never was, on sea or land,
The consecration, and the Poet's dream;

I would have planted thee, thou hoary Pile
Amid a world how different from this!
Beside a sea that could not cease to smile;
On tranquil land, beneath a sky of bliss.

Thou shouldst have seemed a treasure-house divine
Of peaceful years; a chronicle of heaven; —
Of all the sunbeams that did ever shine
The very sweetest had to thee been given.

A Picture had it been of lasting ease,
Elysian quiet, without toil or strife;
No motion but the moving tide, a breeze,
Or merely silent Nature's breathing life.

Such, in the fond illusion of my heart,
Such Picture would I at that time have made:
And seen the soul of truth in every part,
A steadfast peace that might not be betrayed.

So once it would have been, — 'tis so no more;
I have submitted to a new control:
A power is gone, which nothing can restore;
A deep distress hath humanised my Soul.

Not for a moment could I now behold
A smiling sea, and be what I have been:
The feeling of my loss will ne'er be old;
This, which I know, I speak with mind serene.

Then, Beaumont, Friend! who would have been the
        Friend,
If he had lived, of Him whom I deplore,
This work of thine I blame not, but commend;
This sea in anger, and that dismal shore.

O 'tis a passionate Work! — yet wise and well,
Well chosen is the spirit that is here;
That Hulk which labours in the deadly swell,
This rueful sky, this pageantry of fear!

And this huge Castle, standing here sublime,
I love to see the look with which it braves,
Cased in the unfeeling armour of old time,
The lightning, the fierce wind, and trampling waves.

Farewell, farewell the heart that lives alone,
Housed in a dream, at distance from the Kind!
Such happiness, wherever it be known,
Is to be pitied; for 'tis surely blind.

But welcome fortitude, and patient cheer,
And frequent sights of what is to be borne!
Such sights, or worse, as are before me here. —
Not without hope we suffer and we mourn.

1805   *1807*

THE SOLITARY REAPER

BEHOLD her, single in the field,
Yon solitary Highland Lass!
Reaping and singing by herself;
Stop here, or gently pass!
Alone she cuts and binds the grain,
And sings a melancholy strain;
O listen! for the Vale profound
Is overflowing with the sound.

No Nightingale did ever chaunt
More welcome notes to weary bands
Of travellers in some shady haunt,
Among Arabian sands:
A voice so thrilling ne'er was heard
In spring-time from the Cuckoo-bird,
Breaking the silence of the seas
Among the farthest Hebrides.

Will no one tell me what she sings? —
Perhaps the plaintive numbers flow
For old, unhappy, far-off things,
And battles long ago:

Or is it some more humble lay,
Familiar matter of to-day?
Some natural sorrow, loss, or pain,
That has been, and may be again?

Whate'er the theme, the Maiden sang
As if her song could have no ending;
I saw her singing at her work,
And o'er the sickle bending: —
I listened, motionless and still;
And, as I mounted up the hill,
The music in my heart I bore,
Long after it was heard no more.

Nov., 1805   *1807*

CHARACTER OF THE HAPPY WARRIOR

Who is the happy Warrior? Who is he
That every man in arms should wish to be?
— It is the generous Spirit, who, when brought
Among the tasks of real life, hath wrought
Upon the plan that pleased his boyish thought:
Whose high endeavours are an inward light
That makes the path before him always bright:
Who, with a natural instinct to discern
What knowledge can perform, is diligent to learn;
Abides by this resolve, and stops not there,
But makes his moral being his prime care;
Who, doomed to go in company with Pain,
And Fear, and Bloodshed, miserable train!
Turns his necessity to glorious gain;
In face of these doth exercise a power
Which is our human nature's highest dower;

Controls them and subdues, transmutes, bereaves
Of their bad influence, and their good receives:
By objects, which might force the soul to abate
Her feeling, rendered more compassionate;
Is placable — because occasions rise
So often that demand such sacrifice;
More skilful in self-knowledge, even more pure,
As tempted more; more able to endure,
As more exposed to suffering and distress;
Thence, also, more alive to tenderness.
— 'Tis he whose law is reason; who depends
Upon that law as on the best of friends;
Whence, in a state where men are tempted still
To evil for a guard against worse ill,
And what in quality or act is best
Doth seldom on a right foundation rest,
He labours good on good to fix, and owes
To virtue every triumph that he knows:
— Who, if he rise to station of command,
Rises by open means; and there will stand
On honourable terms, or else retire,
And in himself possess his own desire;
Who comprehends his trust, and to the same
Keeps faithful with a singleness of aim;
And therefore does not stoop, nor lie in wait
For wealth, or honours, or for worldly state;
Whom they must follow; on whose head must fall,
Like showers of manna, if they come at all:
Whose powers shed round him in the common strife,
Or mild concerns of ordinary life,
A constant influence, a peculiar grace;
But who, if he be called upon to face
Some awful moment to which Heaven has joined
Great issues, good or bad for human kind,
Is happy as a Lover; and attired

With sudden brightness, like a Man inspired;
And, through the heat of conflict, keeps the law
In calmness made, and sees what he foresaw;
Or if an unexpected call succeed,
Come when it will, is equal to the need:
— He who, though thus endued as with a sense
And faculty for storm and turbulence,
Is yet a Soul whose master-bias leans
To homefelt pleasures and to gentle scenes;
Sweet images! which, wheresoe'er he be,
Are at his heart; and such fidelity
It is his darling passion to approve;
More brave for this, that he hath much to love: —
'Tis, finally, the Man, who, lifted high,
Conspicuous object in a Nation's eye,
Or left unthought-of in obscurity, —
Who, with a toward or untoward lot,
Prosperous or adverse, to his wish or not —
Plays, in the many games of life, that one
Where what he most doth value must be won:
Whom neither shape of danger can dismay,
Nor thought of tender happiness betray;
Who, not content that former worth stand fast,
Looks forward, persevering to the last,
From well to better, daily self-surpast:
Who, whether praise of him must walk the earth
For ever, and to noble deeds give birth,
Or he must fall, to sleep without his fame,
And leave a dead unprofitable name —
Finds comfort in himself and in his cause;
And, while the mortal mist is gathering, draws
His breath in confidence of Heaven's applause:
This is the happy Warrior; this is He
That every Man in arms should wish to be.

Dec., 1805, or Jan., 1806   *1807*

ODE

INTIMATIONS OF IMMORTALITY FROM RECOLLECTIONS
OF EARLY CHILDHOOD

The Child is father of the Man;
And I could wish my days to be
Bound each to each by natural piety.

I

THERE was a time when meadow, grove, and stream,
The earth, and every common sight,
    To me did seem
    Apparelled in celestial light,
The glory and the freshness of a dream.
It is not now as it hath been of yore; —
    Turn whereso'er I may,
    By night or day,
The things which I have seen I now can see no more.

II

    The Rainbow comes and goes,
    And lovely is the Rose,
    The Moon doth with delight
Look round her when the heavens are bare,
    Waters on a starry night
    Are beautiful and fair;
   The sunshine is a glorious birth;
   But yet I know, where'er I go,
That there hath past away a glory from the earth.

III

Now, while the birds thus sing a joyous song,
   And while the young lambs bound
    As to the tabor's sound,

To me alone there came a thought of grief:
A timely utterance gave that thought relief,
     And I again am strong:
The cataracts blow their trumpets from the steep;
No more shall grief of mine the season wrong;
I hear the Echoes through the mountains throng,
The Winds come to me from the fields of sleep,
      And all the earth is gay;
        Land and sea
    Give themselves up to jollity,
     And with the heart of May
    Doth every Beast keep holiday; —
      Thou Child of Joy,
Shout round me, let me hear thy shouts, thou happy
      Shepherd-boy!

IV

Ye blessèd Creatures, I have heard the call
   Ye to each other make; I see
The heavens laugh with you in your jubilee;
   My heart is at your festival,
    My head hath its coronal,
The fulness of your bliss, I feel — I feel it all.
     Oh evil day! if I were sullen
     While Earth herself is adorning,
      This sweet May-morning,
    And the Children are culling
      On every side,
    In a thousand valleys far and wide,
    Fresh flowers; while the sun shines warm,
And the Babe leaps up on his Mother's arm: —
    I hear, I hear, with joy I hear!
    — But there's a Tree, of many, one,
A single Field which I have looked upon,
Both of them speak of something that is gone:

The Pansy at my feet
Doth the same tale repeat:
Whither is fled the visionary gleam?
Where is it now, the glory and the dream?

V

Our birth is but a sleep and a forgetting:
The Soul that rises with us, our life's Star,
　　　Hath had elsewhere its setting,
　　　And cometh from afar:
　　　Not in entire forgetfulness,
　　　And not in utter nakedness,
But trailing clouds of glory do we come
　　　From God, who is our home:
Heaven lies about us in our infancy!
Shades of the prison-house begin to close
　　　Upon the growing Boy,
But He beholds the light, and whence it flows,
　　　He sees it in his joy;
The Youth, who daily farther from the east
　　　Must travel, still is Nature's Priest,
　　　And by the vision splendid
　　　Is on his way attended;
At length the Man perceives it die away,
And fade into the light of common day.

VI

Earth fills her lap with pleasures of her own;
Yearnings she hath in her own natural kind,
And, even with something of a Mother's mind,
　　　And no unworthy aim,
　　　The homely Nurse doth all she can
To make her Foster-child, her Inmate Man,
　　　Forget the glories he hath known,
And that imperial palace whence he came.

VII

Behold the Child among his new-born blisses,
A six years' Darling of a pigmy size!
See, where 'mid work of his own hand he lies,
Fretted by sallies of his mother's kisses,
With light upon him from his father's eyes!
See, at his feet, some little plan or chart,
Some fragment from his dream of human life,
Shaped by himself with newly-learned art;
   A wedding or a festival,
   A mourning or a funeral;
    And this hath now his heart,
    And unto this he frames his song.
    Then will he fit his tongue
To dialogues of business, love, or strife;
   But it will not be long
   Ere this be thrown aside,
   And with new joy and pride
The little Actor cons another part;
Filling from time to time his "humorous stage"
With all the Persons, down to palsied Age,
That Life brings with her in her equipage;
   As if his whole vocation
   Were endless imitation.

VIII

Thou, whose exterior semblance doth belie
   Thy Soul's immensity;
Thou best Philosopher, who yet dost keep
Thy heritage, thou Eye among the blind,
That, deaf and silent, read'st the eternal deep,
Haunted for ever by the eternal mind, —
   Mighty Prophet! Seer blest!
   On whom those truths do rest,

Which we are toiling all our lives to find,
In darkness lost, the darkness of the grave,
Thou, over whom thy Immortality
Broods like the Day, a Master o'er a Slave,
A Presence which is not to be put by;
Thou little Child, yet glorious in the might
Of heaven-born freedom on thy being's height,
Why with such earnest pains dost thou provoke
The years to bring the inevitable yoke,
Thus blindly with thy blessedness at strife?
Full soon thy Soul shall have her earthly freight,
And custom lie upon thee with a weight,
Heavy as frost, and deep almost as life!

CHILD HUSNOULD M

IX

O joy! that in our embers
Is something that doth live,
That nature yet remembers
What was so fugitive!
The thought of our past years in me doth breed
Perpetual benediction: not indeed
For that which is most worthy to be blest;
Delight and liberty, the simple creed
Of Childhood, whether busy or at rest,
With new-fledged hope still fluttering in his breast: —
Not for these I raise
The song of thanks and praise;
But for those obstinate questionings
Of sense and outward things,
Fallings from us, vanishings;
Blank misgivings of a Creature
Moving about in worlds not realised,
High instincts before which our mortal Nature
Did tremble like a guilty Thing surprised:

But for those first affections,
Those shadowy recollections,
Which, be they what they may,
Are yet the fountain-light of all our day,
Are yet a master-light of all our seeing;
Uphold us, cherish, and have power to make
Our noisy years seem moments in the being
Of the eternal Silence: truths that wake,
To perish never:
Which neither listlessness, nor mad endeavour,
Nor Man nor Boy,
Nor all that is at enmity with joy,
Can utterly abolish or destroy!
Hence in a season of calm weather
Though inland far we be,
Our Souls have sight of that immortal sea
Which brought us hither,
Can in a moment travel thither,
And see the Children sport upon the shore,
And hear the mighty waters rolling evermore.

X

Then sing, ye Birds, sing, sing a joyous song!
And let the young Lambs bound
As to the tabor's sound!
We in thought will join your throng,
Ye that pipe and ye that play,
Ye that through your hearts today
Feel the gladness of the May!
What though the radiance which was once so bright
Be now for ever taken from my sight,
Though nothing can bring back the hour
Of splendour in the grass, of glory in the flower;
We will grieve not, rather find
Strength in what remains behind;

In the primal sympathy
Which having been must ever be;
In the soothing thoughts that spring
Out of human suffering;
In the faith that looks through death,
In years that bring the philosophic mind.

XI

And O, ye Fountains, Meadows, Hills, and Groves,
Forebode not any severing of our loves!
Yet in my heart of hearts I feel your might;
I only have relinquished one delight
To live beneath your more habitual sway.
I love the Brooks which down their channels fret,
Even more than when I tripped lightly as they;
The innocent brightness of a new-born Day
  Is lovely yet;
The Clouds that gather round the setting sun
Do take a sober colouring from an eye
That hath kept watch o'er man's mortality;
Another race hath been, and other palms are won.
Thanks to the human heart by which we live,
Thanks to its tenderness, its joys, and fears,
To me the meanest flower that blows can give
Thoughts that do often lie too deep for tears.
1802–1804   *1807*

LAODAMIA

"WITH sacrifice before the rising morn
Vows have I made by fruitless hope inspired;
And from the infernal Gods, 'mid shades forlorn
Of night, my slaughtered Lord have I required:
Celestial pity I again implore; —
Restore him to my sight — great Jove, restore!"

So speaking, and by fervent love endowed
With faith, the Suppliant heavenward lifts her hands;
While, like the sun emerging from a cloud,
Her countenance brightens — and her eye expands;
Her bosom heaves and spreads, her stature grows;
And she expects the issue in repose.

O terror! what hath she perceived? — O joy!
What doth she look on? — whom doth she behold?
Her Hero slain upon the beach of Troy?
His vital presence? his corporeal mould?
It is — if sense deceive her not — 'tis He!
And a God leads him, wingèd Mercury!

Mild Hermes spake — and touched her with his wand
That calms all fear; "Such grace hath crowned thy
        prayer,
Laodamía! that at Jove's command
Thy Husband walks the paths of upper air:
He comes to tarry with thee three hours' space;
Accept the gift, behold him face to face!"

Forth sprang the impassioned Queen her Lord to clasp;
Again that consummation she essayed;
But unsubstantial Form eludes her grasp
As often as that eager grasp was made.
The Phantom parts — but parts to re-unite,
And re-assume his place before her sight.

"Protesiláus, lo! thy guide is gone!
Confirm, I pray, the vision with thy voice:
This is our palace, — yonder is thy throne;
Speak, and the floor thou tread'st on will rejoice.
Not to appal me have the gods bestowed
This precious boon; and blest a sad abode."

"Great Jove, Laodamía! doth not leave
His gifts imperfect: — Spectre though I be,
I am not sent to scare thee or deceive;
But in reward of thy fidelity.
And something also did my worth obtain;
For fearless virtue bringeth boundless gain.

"Thou knowest, the Delphic oracle foretold
That the first Greek who touched the Trojan strand
Should die; but me the threat could not withhold:
A generous cause a victim did demand;
And forth I leapt upon the sandy plain;
A self-devoted chief — by Hector slain."

"Supreme of Heroes — bravest, noblest, best!
Thy matchless courage I bewail no more,
Which then, when tens of thousands were deprest
By doubt, propelled thee to the fatal shore;
Thou found'st — and I forgive thee — here thou art —
A nobler counsellor than my poor heart.

"But thou, though capable of sternest deed,
Wert kind as resolute, and good as brave;
And he, whose power restores thee, hath decreed
Thou shouldst elude the malice of the grave:
Redundant are thy locks, thy lips as fair
As when their breath enriched Thessalian air.

"No Spectre greets me, — no vain Shadow this;
Come, blooming Hero, place thee by my side!
Give, on this well-known couch, one nuptial kiss
To me, this day, a second time thy bride!"
Jove frowned in heaven: the conscious Parcae threw
Upon those roseate lips a Stygian hue.

"This visage tells thee that my doom is past;
Nor should the change be mourned, even if the joys
Of sense were able to return as fast
And surely as they vanish. Earth destroys
Those raptures duly — Erebus disdains:
Calm pleasures there abide — majestic pains.

"Be taught, O faithful Consort, to control
Rebellious passion: for the Gods approve
The depth, and not the tumult, of the soul;
A fervent, not ungovernable, love
Thy transports moderate; and meekly mourn
When I depart, for brief is my sojourn —"

"Ah wherefore? — Did not Hercules by force
Wrest from the guardian Monster of the tomb
Alcestis, a reanimated corse,
Given back to dwell on earth in vernal bloom?
Medea's spells dispersed the weight of years,
And Æson stood a youth 'mid youthful peers.

"The Gods to us are merciful — and they
Yet further may relent: for mightier far
Than strength of nerve and sinew, or the sway
Of magic potent over sun and star,
Is love, though oft to agony distrest,
And though his favourite seat be feeble woman's breast.

"But if thou goest, I follow —" "Peace!" he said, —
She looked upon him and was calmed and cheered;
The ghastly colour from his lips had fled;
In his deportment, shape, and mien, appeared
Elysian beauty, melancholy grace,
Brought from a pensive though a happy place.

He spake of love, such love as Spirits feel
In worlds whose course is equable and pure;
No fears to beat away — no strife to heal —
The past unsighed for, and the future sure;
Spake of heroic arts in graver mood
Revived, with finer harmony pursued;

Of all that is most beauteous — imaged there
In happier beauty; more pellucid streams,
An ampler ether, a diviner air,
And fields invested with purpureal gleams;
Climes which the sun, who sheds the brightest day
Earth knows, is all unworthy to survey.

Yet there the Soul shall enter which hath earned
That privilege by virtue. — "Ill," said he,
"The end of man's existence I discerned,
Who from ignoble games and revelry
Could draw, when we had parted, vain delight,
While tears were thy best pastime, day and night;

"And while my youthful peers before my eyes
(Each hero following his peculiar bent)
Prepared themselves for glorious enterprise
By martial sports, — or, seated in the tent,
Chieftains and kings in council were detained;
What time the fleet at Aulis lay enchained.

"The wished-for wind was given: — I then revolved
The oracle, upon the silent sea;
And, if no worthier led the way, resolved
That, of a thousand vessels, mine should be
The foremost prow in pressing to the strand, —
Mine the first blood that tinged the Trojan sand.

"Yet bitter, oft-times bitter, was the pang
When of thy loss I thought, belovèd Wife!
On thee too fondly did my memory hang,
And on the joys we shared in mortal life, —
The paths which we had trod—these fountains, flowers;
My new-planned cities, and unfinished towers.

"But should suspense permit the Foe to cry,
'Behold they tremble! — haughty their array,
Yet of their number no one dares to die?'
In soul I swept the indignity away:
Old frailties then recurred: — but lofty thought,
In act embodied, my deliverance wrought.

"And Thou, though strong in love, art all too weak
In reason, in self-government too slow;
I counsel thee by fortitude to seek
Our blest re-union in the shades below.
The invisible world with thee hath sympathised;
Be thy affections raised and solemnised.

"Learn, by a mortal yearning, to ascend —
Seeking a higher object. Love was given,
Encouraged, sanctioned, chiefly for that end;
For this the passion to excess was driven —
That self might be annulled: her bondage prove
The fetters of a dream opposed to love." —

Aloud she shrieked! for Hermes reappears!
Round the dear Shade she would have clung — 'tis vain;
The hours are past — too brief had they been years;
And him no mortal effort can detain:
Swift, toward the realms that know not earthly day,
He through the portal takes his silent way,
And on the palace-floor a lifeless corse She lay.

Thus, all in vain exhorted and reproved,
She perished; and, as for a wilful crime,
By the just Gods whom no weak pity moved,
Was doomed to wear out her appointed time,
Apart from happy Ghosts, that gather flowers
Of blissful quiet 'mid unfading bowers.

— Yet tears to human suffering are due;
And mortal hopes defeated and o'erthrown
Are mourned by man, and not by man alone,
As fondly he believes. — Upon the side
Of Hellespont (such faith was entertained)
A knot of spiry trees for ages grew
From out the tomb of him for whom she died;
And ever, when such stature they had gained
That Ilium's walls were subject to their view,
The trees' tall summits withered at the sight;
A constant interchange of growth and blight!

1814   *1815*

TO A SKYLARK

ETHEREAL minstrel! pilgrim of the sky!
Dost thou despise the earth where cares abound?
Or, while the wings aspire, are heart and eye
Both with thy nest upon the dewy ground?
Thy nest which thou canst drop into at will,
Those quivering wings composed, that music still!

Leave to the nightingale her shady wood;
A privacy of glorious light is thine;
Whence thou dost pour upon the world a flood

Of harmony, with instinct more divine;
Type of the wise who soar, but never roam;
True to the kindred points of Heaven and Home!

1825   *1827*

SEPTEMBER, 1819

THE sylvan slopes with corn-clad fields
Are hung, as if with golden shields,
Bright trophies of the sun!
Like a fair sister of the sky,
Unruffled doth the blue lake lie,
The mountains looking on.

And, sooth to say, yon vocal grove,
Albeit uninspired by love,
By love untaught to ring,
May well afford to mortal ear
An impulse more profoundly dear
Than music of the Spring.

For *that* from turbulence and heat
Proceeds, from some uneasy seat
In nature's struggling frame,
Some region of impatient life:
And jealousy, and quivering strife,
Therein a portion claim.

This, this is holy; — while I hear
These vespers of another year,
This hymn of thanks and praise,
My spirit seems to mount above
The anxieties of human love,
And earth's precarious days.

But list! — though winter storms be nigh,
Unchecked is that soft harmony:
There lives Who can provide
For all His creatures; and in Him,
Even like the radiant Seraphim,
These choristers confide.

1819   *1820*

AT THE GRAVE OF BURNS
1803

SEVEN YEARS AFTER HIS DEATH

I SHIVER, Spirit fierce and bold,
At thought of what I now behold:
As vapours breathed from dungeons cold
   Strike pleasure dead,
So sadness comes from out the mould
   Where Burns is laid.

And have I then thy bones so near,
And thou forbidden to appear?
As if it were thyself that's here
   I shrink with pain;
And both my wishes and my fear
   Alike are vain.

Off weight — nor press on weight! — away
Dark thoughts! — they came, but not to stay;
With chastened feelings would I pay
   The tribute due
To him, and aught that hides his clay
   From mortal view.

Fresh as the flower, whose modest worth
He sang, his genius "glinted" forth,
Rose like a star that touching earth,
      For so it seems,
Doth glorify its humble birth
      With matchless beams.

The piercing eye, the thoughtful brow,
The struggling heart, where be they now? —
Full soon the Aspirant of the plough,
      The prompt, the brave,
Slept, with the obscurest, in the low
      And silent grave.

I mourned with thousands, but as one
More deeply grieved, for He was gone
Whose light I hailed when first it shone,
      And showed my youth
How Verse may build a princely throne
      On humble truth.

Alas! where'er the current tends,
Regret pursues and with it blends, —
Huge Criffel's hoary top ascends
      By Skiddaw seen, —
Neighbours we were, and loving friends
      We might have been;

True friends though diversely inclined;
But heart with heart and mind with mind,
Where the main fibres are entwined,
      Through Nature's skill,
May even by contraries be joined
      More closely still.

The tear will start, and let it flow;
Thou "poor Inhabitant below,"
At this dread moment — even so —
      Might we together
Have sate and talked where gowans blow,
      Or on wild heather.

What treasures would have then been placed
Within my reach; of knowledge graced
By fancy what a rich repast!
      But why go on? —
Oh! spare to sweep, thou mournful blast,
      His grave grass-grown.

There, too, a Son, his joy and pride,
(Not three weeks past the Stripling died,)
Lies gathered to his Father's side,
      Soul-moving sight!
Yet one to which is not denied
      Some sad delight.

For *he* is safe, a quiet bed
Hath early found among the dead,
Harboured where none can be misled,
      Wronged, or distrest;
And surely here it may be said
      That such are blest.

And oh for Thee, by pitying grace
Checked oft-times in a devious race,
May He, who halloweth the place
      Where Man is laid,
Receive thy Spirit in the embrace
      For which it prayed!

Sighing I turned away; but ere
Night fell I heard, or seemed to hear,
Music that sorrow comes not near,
    A ritual hymn,
Chanted in love that casts out fear
    By Seraphim.

Before 1807 (in part)   *1842*

THOUGHTS

SUGGESTED THE DAY FOLLOWING, ON THE BANKS OF NITH, NEAR THE POET'S RESIDENCE

Too frail to keep the lofty vow
That must have followed when his brow
Was wreathed — "The Vision" tells us how —
    With holly spray,
He faltered, drifted to and fro,
    And passed away.

Well might such thoughts, dear Sister, throng
Our minds when, lingering all too long,
Over the grave of Burns we hung
    In social grief —
Indulged as if it were a wrong
    To seek relief.

But, leaving each unquiet theme
Where gentlest judgments may misdeem,
And prompt to welcome every gleam
    Of good and fair,
Let us beside the limpid Stream
    Breathe hopeful air.

Enough of sorrow, wreck, and blight;
Think rather of those moments bright
When to the consciousness of right
    His course was true,
When Wisdom prospered in his sight
    And virtue grew.

Yes, freely let our hearts expand,
Freely as in youth's season bland,
When side by side, his Book in hand,
    We wont to stray,
Our pleasure varying at command
    Of each sweet Lay.

How oft inspired must he have trod
These pathways, yon far-stretching road!
There lurks his home; in that Abode,
    With mirth elate,
Or in his nobly-pensive mood,
    The Rustic sate.

Proud thoughts that Image overawes,
Before it humbly let us pause,
And ask of Nature from what cause
    And by what rules
She trained her Burns to win applause
    That shames the Schools.

Through busiest street and loneliest glen
Are felt the flashes of his pen;
He rules 'mid winter snows, and when
    Bees fill their hives;
Deep in the general heart of men
    His power survives.

What need of fields in some far clime
Where Heroes, Sages, Bards sublime,
And all that fetched the flowing rhyme
    From genuine springs,
Shall dwell together till old Time
    Folds up his wings?

Sweet Mercy! to the gates of Heaven
This Minstrel lead, his sins forgiven;
The rueful conflict, the heart riven
    With vain endeavour,
And memory of Earth's bitter leaven,
    Effaced for ever.

But why to Him confine the prayer,
When kindred thoughts and yearnings bear
On the frail heart the purest share
    With all that live? —
The best of what we do and are,
    Just God, forgive!

Finished, 1839   *1842*

WRITTEN AFTER THE DEATH OF CHARLES LAMB

To a good Man of most dear memory
This Stone is sacred. Here he lies apart
From the great city where he first drew breath,
Was reared and taught; and humbly earned his bread,
To the strict labours of the merchant's desk
By duty chained. Not seldom did those tasks

Tease, and the thought of time so spent depress,
His spirit, but the recompense was high;
Firm Independence, Bounty's rightful sire;
Affections, warm as sunshine, free as air;
And when the precious hours of leisure came,
Knowledge and wisdom, gained from converse sweet
With books, or while he ranged the crowded streets
With a keen eye, and overflowing heart:
So genius triumphed over seeming wrong,
And poured out truth in works by thoughtful love
Inspired — works potent over smiles and tears.
And as round mountain-tops the lightning plays,
Thus innocently sported, breaking forth
As from a cloud of some grave sympathy,
Humour and wild instinctive wit, and all
The vivid flashes of his spoken words.
From the most gentle creature nursed in fields
Had been derived the name he bore — a name,
Wherever Christian altars have been raised,
Hallowed to meekness and to innocence;
And if in him meekness at times gave way,
Provoked out of herself by troubles strange,
Many and strange, that hung about his life;
Still, at the centre of his being, lodged
A soul by resignation sanctified:
And if too often, self-reproached, he felt
That innocence belongs not to our kind,
A power that never ceased to abide in him,
Charity, 'mid the multitude of sins
That she can cover, left not his exposed
To an unforgiving judgment from just Heaven.
O, he was good, if e'er a good Man lived!

. . . .

From a reflecting mind and sorrowing heart
Those simple lines flowed with an earnest wish,
Though but a doubting hope, that they might serve
Fitly to guard the precious dust of him
Whose virtues called them forth. That aim is missed;
For much that truth most urgently required
Had from a faltering pen been asked in vain:
Yet, haply, on the printed page received,
The imperfect record, there, may stand unblamed
As long as verse of mine shall breathe the air
Of memory, or see the light of love.

    Thou wert a scorner of the fields, my Friend,
But more in show than truth; and from the fields,
And from the mountains, to thy rural grave
Transported, my soothed spirit hovers o'er
Its green untrodden turf, and blowing flowers;
And taking up a voice shall speak (tho' still
Awed by the theme's peculiar sanctity
Which words less free presumed not even to touch)
Of that fraternal love, whose heaven-lit lamp
From infancy, through manhood, to the last
Of threescore years, and to thy latest hour,
Burnt on with ever-strengthening light, enshrined
Within thy bosom.
          "Wonderful" hath been
The love established between man and man,
"Passing the love of women;" and between
Man and his help-mate in fast wedlock joined
Through God, is raised a spirit and soul of love
Without whose blissful influence Paradise
Had been no Paradise; and earth were now
A waste where creatures bearing human form,

Direst of savage beasts, would roam in fear,
Joyless and comfortless. Our days glide on;
And let him grieve who cannot choose but grieve
That he hath been an Elm without his Vine,
And her bright dower of clustering charities,
That, round his trunk and branches, might have clung
Enriching and adorning. Unto thee,
Not so enriched, not so adorned, to thee
Was given (say rather thou of later birth
Wert given to her) a Sister — 'tis a word
Timidly uttered, for she *lives*, the meek,
The self-restraining, and the ever-kind;
In whom thy reason and intelligent heart
Found — for all interests, hopes, and tender cares,
All softening, humanising, hallowing powers,
Whether withheld, or for her sake unsought —
More than sufficient recompense!
                      Her love
(What weakness prompts the voice to tell it here?)
Was as the love of mothers; and when years,
Lifting the boy to man's estate, had called
The long-protected to assume the part
Of a protector, the first filial tie
Was undissolved; and, in or out of sight,
Remained imperishably interwoven
With life itself. Thus, 'mid a shifting world
Did they together testify of time
And season's difference — a double tree
With two collateral stems sprung from one root;
Such were they — such thro' life they *might* have been
In union, in partition only such;
Otherwise wrought the will of the Most High;
Yet, thro' all visitations and all trials,

Still they were faithful; like two vessels launched
From the same beach one ocean to explore
With mutual help, and sailing — to their league
True, as inexorable winds, or bars
Floating or fixed of polar ice, allow

But turn we rather, let my spirit turn
With thine, O silent and invisible Friend!
To those dear intervals, nor rare nor brief,
When reunited, and by choice withdrawn
From miscellaneous converse, ye were taught
That the remembrance of foregone distress,
And the worse fear of future ill (which oft
Doth hang around it, as a sickly child
Upon its mother) may be both alike
Disarmed of power to unsettle present good
So prized, and things inward and outward held
In such an even balance, that the heart
Acknowledges God's grace, his mercy feels,
And in its depth of gratitude is still.

O gift divine of quiet sequestration!
The hermit, exercised in prayer and praise,
And feeding daily on the hope of heaven,
Is happy in his vow, and fondly cleaves
To life-long singleness; but happier far
Was to your souls, and, to the thoughts of others,
A thousand times more beautiful appeared,
Your *dual* loneliness. The sacred tie
Is broken; yet why grieve? for Time but holds
His moiety in trust, till Joy shall lead
To the blest world where parting is unknown.

November, 1835   *1837*

EVENING VOLUNTARIES

I

CALM is the fragrant air, and loth to lose
Day's grateful warmth, tho' moist with falling dews.
Look for the stars, you'll say that there are none;
Look up a second time, and, one by one,
You mark them twinkling out with silvery light,
And wonder how they could elude the sight!
The birds, of late so noisy in their bowers,
Warbled a while with faint and fainter powers,
But now are silent as the dim-seen flowers:
Nor does the village Church-clock's iron tone
The time's and season's influence disown;
Nine beats distinctly to each other bound
In drowsy sequence — how unlike the sound
That, in rough winter, oft inflicts a fear
On fireside listeners, doubting what they hear!
The shepherd, bent on rising with the sun,
Had closed his door before the day was done,
And now with thankful heart to bed doth creep,
And joins his little children in their sleep.
The bat, lured forth where trees the lane o'ershade,
Flits and reflits along the close arcade;
The busy dor-hawk chases the white moth
With burring note, which Industry and Sloth
Might both be pleased with, for it suits them both.
A stream is heard — I see it not, but know
By its soft music whence the waters flow:
Wheels and the tread of hoofs are heard no more;
One boat there was, but it will touch the shore
With the next dipping of its slackened oar;

Faint sound, that, for the gayest of the gay,
Might give to serious thought a moment's sway,
As a last token of man's toilsome day!

1832   *1835*

II

ON A HIGH PART OF THE COAST OF CUMBERLAND

Easter Sunday, April 7

THE AUTHOR'S SIXTY-THIRD BIRTHDAY

THE Sun, that seemed so mildly to retire,
Flung back from distant climes a streaming fire,
Whose blaze is now subdued to tender gleams,
Prelude of night's approach with soothing dreams.
Look round; — of all the clouds not one is moving;
'Tis the still hour of thinking, feeling, loving.
Silent, and steadfast as the vaulted sky,
The boundless plain of waters seems to lie: —
Comes that low sound from breezes rustling o'er
The grass-crowned headland that conceals the shore?
No; 'tis the earth-voice of the mighty sea,
Whispering how meek and gentle he *can* be!
   Thou Power supreme! who, arming to rebuke
Offenders, dost put off the gracious look,
And clothe thyself with terrors like the flood
Of Ocean roused into his fiercest mood,
Whatever discipline thy Will ordain
For the brief course that must for me remain;
Teach me with quick-eared spirit to rejoice
In admonitions of thy softest voice!
Whate'er the path these mortal feet may trace,
Breathe through my soul the blessing of thy grace,
Glad, through a perfect love, a faith sincere

Drawn from the wisdom that begins with fear,
Glad to expand; and, for a season, free
From finite cares, to rest absorbed in Thee!

April 7, 1833   *1835*

VI

Soft as a cloud is yon blue Ridge — the Mere
Seems firm as solid crystal, breathless, clear,
And motionless; and, to the gazer's eye,
Deeper than ocean, in the immensity
Of its vague mountains and unreal sky!
But, from the process in that still retreat,
Turn to minuter changes at our feet;
Observe how dewy Twilight has withdrawn
The crowd of daisies from the shaven lawn,
And has restored to view its tender green,
That, while the sun rode high, was lost beneath their
        dazzling sheen.
— An emblem this of what the sober Hour
Can do for minds disposed to feel its power!
Thus oft, when we in vain have wished away
The petty pleasures of the garish day,
Meek eve shuts up the whole usurping host
(Unbashful dwarfs each glittering at his post)
And leaves the disencumbered spirit free
To reassume a staid simplicity.

'Tis well — but what are helps of time and place,
When wisdom stands in need of nature's grace;
Why do good thoughts, invoked or not, descend,
Like Angels from their bowers, our virtues to befriend;
If yet To-morrow, unbelied, may say,
"I come to open out, for fresh display,
The elastic vanities of yesterday?"

1834   *1835*

Part Three

THIRTY–FIVE SONNETS

I

Nuns fret not at their convent's narrow room;
And hermits are contented with their cells;
And students with their pensive citadels;
Maids at the wheel, the weaver at his loom,
Sit blithe and happy; bees that soar for bloom,
High as the highest Peak of Furness-fells,
Will murmur by the hour in foxglove bells:
In truth the prison, unto which we doom
Ourselves, no prison is: and hence for me,
In sundry moods, 'twas pastime to be bound
Within the Sonnet's scanty plot of ground;
Pleased if some Souls (for such there needs must be)
Who have felt the weight of too much liberty,
Should find brief solace there, as I have found.

May, 1802–March, 1804   *1807*

II

Scorn not the Sonnet; Critic, you have frowned,
Mindless of its just honours; with this key
Shakspeare unlocked his heart; the melody

Of this small lute gave ease to Petrarch's wound;
A thousand times this pipe did Tasso sound;
With it Camöens soothed an exile's grief;
The Sonnet glittered a gay myrtle leaf
Amid the cypress with which Dante crowned
His visionary brow: a glow-worm lamp,
It cheered mild Spenser, called from Faery-land
To struggle through dark ways; and when a damp
Fell round the path of Milton, in his hand
The Thing became a trumpet; whence he blew
Soul-animating strains — alas, too few!

?   *1827*

III

1801

I GRIEVED for Buonaparté, with a vain
And an unthinking grief! The tenderest mood
Of that Man's mind — what can it be? what food
Fed his first hopes? what knowledge could *he* gain?
'Tis not in battles that from youth we train
The Governor who must be wise and good,
And temper with the sternness of the brain
Thoughts motherly, and meek as womanhood.
Wisdom doth live with children round her knees:
Books, leisure, perfect freedom, and the talk
Man holds with week-day man in the hourly walk
Of the mind's business: these are the degrees
By which true Sway doth mount; this is the stalk
True Power doth grow on; and her rights are these.

May 21, 1802   *1807*

IV

COMPOSED UPON WESTMINSTER BRIDGE, SEPTEMBER 3, 1802

EARTH has not anything to show more fair:
Dull would he be of soul who could pass by
A sight so touching in its majesty:
This City now doth, like a garment, wear
The beauty of the morning; silent, bare,
Ships, towers, domes, theatres, and temples lie
Open unto the fields, and to the sky;
All bright and glittering in the smokeless air.
Never did sun more beautifully steep
In his first splendour, valley, rock, or hill;
Ne'er saw I, never felt, a calm so deep!
The river glideth at his own sweet will:
Dear God! the very houses seem asleep;
And all that mighty heart is lying still!

1802   *1807*

V

IT is a beauteous evening, calm and free,
The holy time is quiet as a Nun
Breathless with adoration; the broad sun
Is sinking down in its tranquillity;
The gentleness of heaven broods o'er the Sea:
Listen! the mighty Being is awake,
And doth with his eternal motion make
A sound like thunder — everlastingly.
Dear Child! dear Girl! that walkest with me here,
If thou appear untouched by solemn thought,
Thy nature is not therefore less divine:
Thou liest in Abraham's bosom all the year;
And worshipp'st at the Temple's inner shrine,
God being with thee when we know it not.

Aug., 1802   *1807*

VI

TO TOUSSAINT L'OUVERTURE

TOUSSAINT, the most unhappy man of men!
Whether the whistling Rustic tend his plough
Within thy hearing, or thy head be now
Pillowed in some deep dungeon's earless den;—
O miserable Chieftain! where and when
Wilt thou find patience! Yet die not; do thou
Wear rather in thy bonds a cheerful brow:
Though fallen thyself, never to rise again,
Live, and take comfort. Thou hast left behind
Powers that will work for thee; air, earth, and skies;
There's not a breathing of the common wind
That will forget thee; thou hast great allies;
Thy friends are exultations, agonies,
And love, and man's unconquerable mind.

1802   *1807*

VII

ON THE EXTINCTION OF THE VENETIAN REPUBLIC

ONCE did She hold the gorgeous east in fee;
And was the safeguard of the west: the worth
Of Venice did not fall below her birth,
Venice, the eldest Child of Liberty.
She was a maiden City, bright and free;
No guile seduced, no force could violate;
And, when she took unto herself a Mate,
She must espouse the everlasting Sea.
And what if she had seen those glories fade,
Those titles vanish, and that strength decay;
Yet shall some tribute of regret be paid
When her long life hath reached its final day:
Men are we, and must grieve when even the Shade
Of that which once was great is passed away.

1802   *1807*

VIII

LONDON, 1802

MILTON! thou shouldst be living at this hour:
England hath need of thee: she is a fen
Of stagnant waters: altar, sword, and pen,
Fireside, the heroic wealth of hall and bower,
Have forefeited their ancient English dower
Of inward happiness. We are selfish men;
Oh! raise us up, return to us again;
And give us manners, virtue, freedom, power.
Thy soul was like a Star, and dwelt apart;
Thou hadst a voice whose sound was like the sea:
Pure as the naked heavens, majestic, free,
So didst thou travel on life's common way,
In cheerful godliness; and yet thy heart
The lowliest duties on herself did lay.

Sept., 1802   *1807*

IX

SEPTEMBER, 1802. NEAR DOVER

INLAND, within a hollow vale, I stood;
And saw, while sea was calm and air was clear,
The coast of France — the coast of France how near!
Drawn almost into frightful neighbourhood.
I shrunk; for verily the barrier flood
Was like a lake, or river bright and fair,
A span of waters; yet what power is there!
What mightiness for evil and for good!
Even so doth God protect us if we be
Virtuous and wise. Winds blow, and waters roll,
Strength to the brave, and Power, and Deity;
Yet in themselves are nothing! One decree
Spake laws to *them*, and said that by the soul
Only, the Nations shall be great and free.

Sept., 1802   *1807*

X

IT is not to be thought of that the Flood
Of British freedom, which, to the open sea
Of the world's praise, from dark antiquity
Hath flowed, "with pomp of waters unwithstood,"
Roused though it be full often to a mood
Which spurns the check of salutary bands,
That this most famous Stream in bogs and sands
Should perish; and to evil and to good
Be lost for ever.   In our halls is hung
Armoury of the invincible Knights of old:
We must be free or die, who speak the tongue
That Shakspeare spake; the faith and morals hold
Which Milton held. — In every thing we are sprung
Of Earth's first blood, have titles manifold.

1802 or 1803   *1807*

XI

"WITH how sad steps, O Moon, thou climb'st the sky,
How silently, and with how wan a face!"
Where art thou?   Thou so often seen on high
Running among the clouds a Wood-nymph's race!
Unhappy Nuns, whose common breath's a sigh
Which they would stifle, move at such a pace!
The northern Wind, to call thee to the chase,
Must blow to-night his bugle horn.   Had I
The power of Merlin, Goddess! this should be:
And all the stars, fast as the clouds were riven,
Should sally forth, to keep thee company,
Hurrying and sparkling through the clear blue heaven;
But, Cynthia! should to thee the palm be given,
Queen both for beauty and for majesty.

Before March, 1804   *1807*

XII

TO SLEEP

A FLOCK of sheep that leisurely pass by,
One after one; the sound of rain, and bees
Murmuring; the fall of rivers, winds and seas,
Smooth fields, white sheets of water, and pure sky;
I have thought of all by turns, and yet do lie
Sleepless! and soon the small birds' melodies
Must hear, first uttered from my orchard trees;
And the first cuckoo's melancholy cry.
Even thus last night, and two nights more, I lay
And could not win thee, Sleep! by any stealth:
So do not let me wear to-night away:
Without Thee what is all the morning's wealth?
Come, blessed barrier between day and day,
Dear mother of fresh thoughts and joyous health!
Before March, 1804   *1807*

XIII

TO THE MEN OF KENT. OCTOBER, 1803

VANGUARD of Liberty, ye men of Kent,
Ye children of a Soil that doth advance
Her haughty brow against the coast of France,
Now is the time to prove your hardiment!
To France be words of invitation sent!
They from their fields can see the countenance
Of your fierce war, may ken the glittering lance,
And hear you shouting forth your brave intent.
Left single, in bold parley, ye, of yore,
Did from the Norman win a gallant wreath;
Confirmed the charters that were yours before; —
No parleying now. In Britain is one breath;
We all are with you now from shore to shore; —
Ye men of Kent, 'tis victory or death!
Oct., 1803   *1807*

XIV

THE world is too much with us; late and soon,
Getting and spending, we lay waste our powers:
Little we see in Nature that is ours;
We have given our hearts away, a sordid boon!
This Sea that bares her bosom to the moon;
The winds that will be howling at all hours,
And are up-gathered now like sleeping flowers;
For this, for everything, we are out of tune;
It moves us not. — Great God! I'd rather be
A Pagan suckled in a creed outworn;
So might I, standing on this pleasant lea,
Have glimpses that would make me less forlorn;
Have sight of Proteus rising from the sea;
Or hear old Triton blow his wreathèd horn.

? *1807*

XV

COMPOSED BY THE SIDE OF GRASMERE LAKE

CLOUDS, lingering yet, extend in solid bars
Through the grey west; and lo! these waters, steeled
By breezeless air to smoothest polish, yield
A vivid repetition of the stars;
Jove, Venus, and the ruddy crest of Mars
Amid his fellows beauteously revealed
At happy distance from earth's groaning field,
Where ruthless mortals wage incessant wars.
Is it a mirror? — or the nether Sphere
Opening to view the abyss in which she feeds
Her own calm fires? — But list! a voice is near;
Great Pan himself low-whispering through the reeds,
"Be thankful, thou; for, if unholy deeds
Ravage the world, tranquillity is here!"

1807   *1819*

XVI

UPON THE SIGHT OF A BEAUTIFUL PICTURE
Painted by Sir G. H. Beaumont, Bart.

PRAISED be the Art whose subtle power could stay
Yon cloud, and fix it in that glorious shape;
Nor would permit the thin smoke to escape,
Nor those bright sunbeams to forsake the day;
Which stopped that band of travellers on their way,
Ere they were lost within the shady wood;
And showed the Bark upon the glassy flood
For ever anchored in her sheltering bay.
Soul-soothing Art! whom Morning, Noontide, Even,
Do serve with all their changeful pageantry;
Thou, with ambition modest yet sublime,
Here, for the sight of mortal man, hast given
To one brief moment caught from fleeting time
The appropriate calm of blest eternity.

Aug., 1811   *1815*

XVII

THE FRENCH AND THE SPANISH GUERILLAS

HUNGER, and sultry heat, and nipping blast
From bleak hill-top, and length of march by night
Through heavy swamp, or over snow-clad height —
These hardships ill-sustained, these dangers past,
The roving Spanish Bands are reached at last,
Charged, and dispersed like foam: but as a flight
Of scattered quails by signs do reunite,
So these, — and, heard of once again, are chased
With combinations of long-practised art
And newly-kindled hope; but they are fled —
Gone are they, viewless as the buried dead:
Where now? — Their sword is at the Foeman's heart!
And thus from year to year his walk they thwart,
And hang like dreams around his guilty bed.

1810 or 1811   *1815*

XVIII

SURPRISED by joy — impatient as the Wind
I turned to share the transport — Oh! with whom
But Thee, deep buried in the silent tomb,
That spot which no vicissitude can find?
Love, faithful love, recalled thee to my mind —
But how could I forget thee? Through what power,
Even for the least division of an hour,
Have I been so beguiled as to be blind
To my most grievous loss! — That thought's return
Was the worst pang that sorrow ever bore,
Save one, one only, when I stood forlorn,
Knowing my heart's best treasure was no more;
That neither present time, nor years unborn
Could to my sight that heavenly face restore.
After June, 1812   *1815*

XIX

SEPTEMBER, 1815

WHILE not a leaf seems faded; while the fields,
With ripening harvest prodigally fair,
In brightest sunshine bask; this nipping air,
Sent from some distant clime where Winter wields
His icy scimitar, a foretaste yields
Of bitter change, and bids the flowers beware;
And whispers to the silent birds, "Prepare
Against the threatening foe your trustiest shields."
For me, who under kindlier laws belong
To Nature's tuneful quire, this rustling dry
Through leaves yet green, and yon crystalline sky,
Announce a season potent to renew,
'Mid frost and snow, the instinctive joys of song,
And nobler cares than listless summer knew.
Dec., 1815   *1816*

XX

I watch, and long have watched, with calm regret
Yon slowly-sinking star — immortal Sire
(So might he seem) of all the glittering quire!
Blue ether still surrounds him — yet — and yet;
But now the horizon's rocky parapet
Is reached, where, forfeiting his bright attire,
He burns — transmuted to a dusky fire —
Then pays submissively the appointed debt
To the flying moments, and is seen no more.
Angels and gods! We struggle with our fate,
While health, power, glory, from their height decline,
Depressed; and then extinguished: and our state,
In this, how different, lost Star, from thine,
That no to-morrow shall our beams restore!
?   *1819*

XXI

WRITTEN UPON A BLANK LEAF IN "THE COMPLEAT ANGLER"

While flowing rivers yield a blameless sport,
Shall live the name of Walton: Sage benign!
Whose pen, the mysteries of the rod and line
Unfolding, did not fruitlessly exhort
To reverend watching of each still report
That Nature utters from her rural shrine.
Meek, nobly versed in simple discipline —
He found the longest summer day too short,
To his loved pastime given by sedgy Lee,
Or down the tempting maze of Shawford brook —
Fairer than life itself, in this sweet Book,
The cowslip-bank and shady willow-tree;
And the fresh meads — where flowed, from every nook
Of his full bosom, gladsome Piety!
?   *1819*

XXII

THE PLAIN OF DONNERDALE

THE old inventive Poets, had they seen,
Or rather felt, the entrancement that detains
Thy waters, Duddon! 'mid these flowery plains;
The still repose, the liquid lapse serene,
Transferred to bowers imperishably green,
Had beautified Elysium! But these chains
Will soon be broken; — a rough course remains,
Rough as the past; where Thou, of placid mien,
Innocuous as a firstling of the flock,
And countenanced like a soft cerulean sky,
Shalt change thy temper; and, with many a shock
Given and received in mutual jeopardy,
Dance, like a Bacchanal, from rock to rock,
Tossing her frantic thyrsus wide and high!

Between 1806–1820   1820

XXIII

NOT hurled precipitous from steep to steep;
Lingering no more 'mid flower-enamelled lands
And blooming thickets; nor by rocky bands
Held; but in radiant progress toward the Deep
Where mightiest rivers into powerless sleep
Sink, and forget their nature — *now* expands
Majestic Duddon, over smooth flat sands
Gliding in silence with unfettered sweep!
Beneath an ampler sky a region wide
Is opened round him: — hamlets, towers, and towns,
And blue-topped hills, behold him from afar;
In stately mien to sovereign Thames allied
Spreading his bosom under Kentish downs,
With commerce freighted, or triumphant war.

Between 1806–1820   1820

XXIV

AFTER-THOUGHT

I THOUGHT of Thee, my partner and my guide,
As being past away. — Vain sympathies!
For, backward, Duddon! as I cast my eyes,
I see what was, and is, and will abide;
Still glides the Stream, and shall for ever glide;
The Form remains, the Function never dies;
While we, the brave, the mighty, and the wise,
We Men, who in our morn of youth defied
The elements, must vanish; — be it so!
Enough, if something from our hands have power
To live, and act, and serve the future hour;
And if, as toward the silent tomb we go,
Through love, through hope, and faith's transcendent
    dower,
We feel that we are greater than we know.

Probably 1820   *1820*

XXV

MUTABILITY

FROM low to high doth dissolution climb,
And sink from high to low, along a scale
Of awful notes, whose concord shall not fail;
A musical but melancholy chime,
Which they can hear who meddle not with crime,
Nor avarice, nor over-anxious care.
Truth fails not; but her outward forms that bear
The longest date do melt like frosty rime,
That in the morning whitened hill and plain
And is no more; drop like the tower sublime
Of yesterday, which royally did wear
His crown of weeds, but could not even sustain
Some casual shout that broke the silent air,
Or the unimaginable touch of Time.

1821   *1822*

XXVI

RECOLLECTION OF THE PORTRAIT OF KING HENRY THE
EIGHTH, TRINITY LODGE, CAMBRIDGE

THE imperial Stature, the colossal stride,
Are yet before me; yet do I behold
The broad full visage, chest of amplest mould,
The vestments 'broidered with barbaric pride:
And lo! a poniard, at the Monarch's side,
Hangs ready to be grasped in sympathy
With the keen threatenings of that fulgent eye,
Below the white-rimmed bonnet, far descried,
Who trembles now at thy capricious mood?
'Mid those surrounding Worthies, haughty King,
We rather think, with grateful mind sedate,
How Providence educeth, from the spring
Of lawless will, unlooked-for streams of good,
Which neither force shall check nor time abate!

?   *1827*

XXVII

MARY QUEEN OF SCOTS

DEAR to the Loves, and to the Graces vowed,
The Queen drew back the wimple that she wore;
And to the throng, that on the Cumbrian shore
Her landing hailed, how touchingly she bowed!
And like a Star (that, from a heavy cloud
Of pine-tree foliage poised in air, forth darts,
When a soft summer gale at evening parts
The gloom that did its loveliness enshroud)
She smiled; but Time, the old Saturnian seer,
Sighed on the wing as her foot pressed the strand,
With step prelusive to a long array
Of woes and degradations hand in hand —
Weeping captivity, and shuddering fear
Stilled by the ensanguined block of Fotheringay!

1833   *1835*

XXVIII

TO THE CUCKOO

Not the whole warbling grove in concert heard
When sunshine follows shower, the breast can thrill
Like the first summons, Cuckoo! of thy bill,
With its twin notes inseparably paired.
The captive 'mid damp vaults unsunned, unaired,
Measuring the periods of his lonely doom,
That cry can reach; and to the sick man's room
Sends gladness, by no languid smile declared.
The lordly eagle-race through hostile search
May perish; time may come when never more
The wilderness shall hear the lion roar;
But, long as cock shall crow from household perch
To rouse the dawn, soft gales shall speed thy wing,
And thy erratic voice be faithful to the Spring!

? *1827*

XXIX

TO THE PLANET VENUS, AN EVENING STAR
Composed at Loch Lomond

Though joy attend Thee orient at the birth
Of dawn, it cheers the lofty spirit most
To watch thy course when Daylight, fled from earth,
In the grey sky hath left his lingering Ghost,
Perplexed as if between a splendour lost
And splendour slowly mustering. Since the Sun,
The absolute, the world-absorbing One,
Relinquished half his empire to the host
Emboldened by thy guidance, holy Star,
Holy as princely, who that looks on thee
Touching, as now, in thy humility
The mountain-borders of this seat of care,
Can question that thy countenance is bright,
Celestial Power, as much with love as light?

1831 *1835*

XXX

Desire we past illusions to recall?
To reinstate wild Fancy, would we hide
Truths whose thick veil Science has drawn aside?
No, — let this Age, high as she may, instal
In her esteem the thirst that wrought man's fall,
The universe is infinitely wide;
And conquering Reason, if self-glorified,
Can nowhere move uncrossed by some new wall
Or gulf of mystery, which thou alone,
Imaginative Faith! canst overleap,
In progress toward the fount of Love, — the throne
Of Power whose ministers the records keep
Of periods fixed, and laws established, less
Flesh to exalt than prove its nothingness.

1833   *1835*

XXXI

PLEA FOR THE HISTORIAN

Forbear to deem the Chronicler unwise,
Ungentle, or untouched by seemly ruth,
Who, gathering up all that Time's envious tooth
Has spared of sound and grave realities,
Firmly rejects those dazzling flatteries,
Dear as they are to unsuspecting Youth,
That might have drawn down Clio from the skies
To vindicate the majesty of truth.
Such was her office while she walked with men,
A Muse, who, not unmindful of her Sire
All-ruling Jove, whate'er the theme might be
Revered her Mother, sage Mnemosyne,
And taught her faithful servants how the lyre
Should animate, but not mislead, the pen.

?   *1842*

XXXII

THE LAST SUPPER, BY LEONARDO DA VINCI, IN THE REFEC-
TORY OF THE CONVENT OF MARIA DELLA GRAZIA — MILAN

THO' searching damps and many an envious flaw
Have marred this Work; the calm ethereal grace,
The love deep-seated in the Saviour's face,
The mercy, goodness, have not failed to awe
The Elements; as they do melt and thaw
The heart of the Beholder — and erase
(At least for one rapt moment) every trace
Of disobedience to the primal law.
The annunciation of the dreadful truth
Made to the Twelve, survives: lip, forehead, cheek,
And hand reposing on the board in ruth
Of what it utters, while the unguilty seek
Unquestionable meanings — still bespeak
A labour worthy of eternal youth!

1821   *1822*

XXXIII

A PLACE OF BURIAL IN THE SOUTH OF SCOTLAND

PART fenced by man, part by a rugged steep
That curbs a foaming brook, a Graveyard lies;
The hare's best couching-place for fearless sleep;
Which moonlit elves, far seen by credulous eyes,
Enter in dance. Of church, or sabbath ties,
No vestige now remains; yet thither creep
Bereft Ones, and in lowly anguish weep
Their prayers out to the wind and naked skies.
Proud tomb is none; but rudely-sculptured knights,
By humble choice of plain old times, are seen
Level with earth, among the hillocks green:
Union not sad, when sunny daybreak smites
The spangled turf, and neighbouring thickets ring
With *jubilate* from the choirs of spring!

1831   *1835*

XXXIV

Why art thou silent! Is thy love a plant
Of such weak fibre that the treacherous air
Of absence withers what was once so fair?
Is there no debt to pay, no boon to grant?
Yet have my thoughts for thee been vigilant —
Bound to thy service with unceasing care,
The mind's least generous wish a mendicant
For nought but what thy happiness could spare.
Speak — though this soft warm heart, once free to hold
A thousand tender pleasures, thine and mine,
Be left more desolate, more dreary cold
Than a forsaken bird's-nest filled with snow
'Mid its own bush of leafless eglantine —
Speak, that my torturing doubts their end may know!

Jan. 18, 1830   *1835*

XXXV

A poet! — He hath put his heart to school,
Nor dares to move unpropped upon the staff
Which Art hath lodged within his hand — must laugh
By precept only, and shed tears by rule.
Thy Art be Nature; the live current quaff,
And let the groveller sip his stagnant pool,
In fear that else, when Critics grave and cool
Have killed him, Scorn should write his epitaph.
How does the Meadow-flower its bloom unfold?
Because the lovely little flower is free
Down to its root, and, in that freedom, bold;
And so the grandeur of the Forest-tree
Comes not by casting in a formal mould,
But from its *own* divine vitality.

?   *1842*

WORDSWORTH ON THE RELATIONSHIP
OF *The Recluse, The Prelude,* AND *The Excursion*

I*

It may be proper to state whence the poem, of which "The Excursion" is a part, derives its Title of THE RECLUSE. — Several years ago, when the Author retired to his native mountains, with the hope of being enabled to construct a literary Work that might live, it was a reasonable thing that he should take a review of his own mind, and examine how far Nature and Education had qualified him for such employment. As subsidiary to this preparation, he undertook to record, in verse, the origin and progress of his own powers, as far as he was acquainted with them. That Work,† addressed to a dear Friend, most distinguished for his knowledge and genius, and to whom the Author's Intellect is deeply indebted, has been long finished; and the result of the investigation which gave rise to it was a determination to compose a philosophical poem, containing views of Man, Nature, and Society; and to be entitled, "The Recluse;" as having for its principal subject the sensations and opinions of a poet living in retirement. — The preparatory poem is biographical, and

* From the Preface to *The Excursion,* July 29, 1814.
† *The Prelude* [Ed].

conducts the history of the Author's mind to the point
when he was emboldened to hope that his faculties were
sufficiently matured for entering upon the arduous
labour which he had proposed to himself; and the two
Works have the same kind of relation to each other, if
he may so express himself, as the ante-chapel has to the
body of a gothic church. Continuing this allusion, he
may be permitted to add, that his minor Pieces, which
have been long before the Public, when they shall be
properly arranged, will be found by the attentive Reader
to have such connection with the main Work as may
give them claim to be likened to the little cells, ora-
tories, and sepulchral recesses, ordinarily included in
those edifices.

The Author would not have deemed himself justified
in saying, upon this occasion, so much of performances
either unfinished, or unpublished, if he had not thought
that the labour bestowed by him upon what he has here-
tofore and now laid before the Public, entitled him to
candid attention for such a statement as he thinks neces-
sary to throw light upon his endeavours to please and,
he would hope, to benefit his countrymen. — Nothing
further need be added, than that the first and third
parts of "The Recluse" will consist chiefly of medita-
tions in the Author's own person; and that in the inter-
mediate part ("The Excursion") the intervention of
characters speaking is employed, and something of a
dramatic form adopted.

II*

Such was the Author's language in the year 1814. It
will thence be seen, that the present Poem [*The Prelude*]

* From the Advertisement to *The Prelude*, dated July 13, 1850.

was intended to be introductory to the "Recluse," and that the "Recluse," if completed, would have consisted of Three Parts. Of these, the Second Part alone: viz. the "Excursion," was finished, and given to the world by the Author.

The First Book of the First Part of the "Recluse" still remains in manuscript*; but the Third Part was only planned. The materials of which it would have been formed have, however, been incorporated, for the most part, in the Author's other Publications, written subsequently to the "Excursion."

From THE RECLUSE

PART I—BOOK I

HOME IN GRASMERE

(Lines 754–860)

"On Man, on Nature, and on Human Life,
Musing in solitude, I oft perceive
Fair trains of imagery before me rise,
Accompanied by feelings of delight
Pure, or with no unpleasing sadness mixed;
And I am conscious of affecting thoughts
And dear remembrances, whose presence soothes
Or elevates the Mind, intent to weigh
The good and evil of our mortal state.
— To these emotions, whencesoe'er they come,
Whether from breath of outward circumstance,

---

* Part I, Book I, "Home in Grasmere," was posthumously published in 1888 [Ed.].

Or from the Soul — an impulse to herself —
I would give utterance in numerous verse.
Of Truth, of Grandeur, Beauty, Love, and Hope,
And melancholy Fear subdued by Faith;
Of blessèd consolations in distress;
Of moral strength, and intellectual Power;
Of joy in widest commonalty spread;
Of the individual Mind that keeps her own
Inviolate retirement, subject there
To Conscience only, and the law supreme
Of that Intelligence which governs all —
I sing: — 'fit audience let me find though few!'

"So prayed, more gaining than he asked, the Bard —
In holiest mood. Urania, I shall need
Thy guidance, or a greater Muse, if such
Descend to earth or dwell in highest heaven!
For I must tread on shadowy ground, must sink
Deep — and, aloft ascending, breathe in worlds
To which the heaven of heavens is but a veil.
All strength — all terror, single or in bands,
That ever was put forth in personal form —
Jehovah — with his thunder, and the choir
Of shouting Angels, and the empyreal thrones —
I pass them unalarmed. Not Chaos, not
The darkest pit of lowest Erebus,
Nor aught of blinder vacancy, scooped out
By help of dreams — can breed such fear and awe
As fall upon us often when we look
Into our Minds, into the Mind of Man —
My haunt, and the main region of my song.
— Beauty — a living Presence of the earth,
Surpassing the most fair ideal Forms
Which craft of delicate Spirits hath composed
From earth's materials — waits upon my steps;

Pitches her tents before me as I move,
An hourly neighbour. Paradise, and groves
Elysian, Fortunate Fields — like those of old
Sought in the Atlantic Main — why should they be
A history only of departed things,
Or a mere fiction of what never was?
For the discerning intellect of Man,
When wedded to this goodly universe
In love and holy passion, shall find these
A simple produce of the common day.
— I, long before the blissful hour arrives,
Would chant, in lonely peace, the spousal verse
Of this great consummation: — and, by words
Which speak of nothing more than what we are,
Would I arouse the sensual from their sleep
Of Death, and win the vacant and the vain
To noble raptures; while my voice proclaims
How exquisitely the individual Mind
(And the progressive powers perhaps no less
Of the whole species) to the external World
Is fitted: — and how exquisitely, too —
Theme this but little heard of among men —
The external World is fitted to the Mind;
And the creation (by no lower name
Can it be called) which they with blended might
Accomplish: — this is our high argument.
— Such grateful haunts foregoing, if I oft
Must turn elsewhere — to travel near the tribes
And fellowships of men, and see ill sights
Of madding passions mutually inflamed;
Must hear Humanity in fields and groves
Pipe solitary anguish; or must hang
Brooding above the fierce confederate storm
Of sorrow, barricadoed evermore
Within the walls of cities — may these sounds

Have their authentic comment; that even these
Hearing, I be not downcast or forlorn! —
Descend, prophetic Spirit! that inspir'st
The human Soul of universal earth,
Dreaming on things to come; and dost possess
A metropolitan temple in the hearts
Of mighty Poets: upon me bestow
A gift of genuine insight; that my Song
With star-like virtue in its place may shine,
Shedding benignant influence, and secure,
Itself, from all malevolent effect
Of those mutations that extend their sway
Throughout the nether sphere! — And if with this
I mix more lowly matter; with the thing
Contemplated, describe the Mind and Man
Contemplating; and who, and what he was —
The transitory Being that beheld
The Vision; when and where, and how he lived; —
Be not this labour useless. If such theme
May sort with highest objects, then — dread Power!
Whose gracious favour is the primal source
Of all illumination, — may my Life
Express the image of a better time,
More wise desires, and simpler manners; — nurse
My Heart in genuine freedom: all pure thoughts
Be with me; — so shall thy unfailing love
Guide, and support, and cheer me to the end!"

Between 1800–1814   *1888*

THE PRELUDE
OR
GROWTH OF A POET'S MIND

An Autobiographical Poem

BOOK FIRST

INTRODUCTION — CHILDHOOD AND SCHOOL-TIME

OH THERE is blessing in this gentle breeze,
A visitant that while it fans my cheek
Doth seem half-conscious of the joy it brings
From the green fields, and from yon azure sky.
Whate'er its mission, the soft breeze can come
To none more grateful than to me; escaped
From the vast city, where I long had pined
A discontented sojourner: now free,
Free as a bird to settle where I will.
What dwelling shall receive me? in what vale   10
Shall be my harbour? underneath what grove
Shall I take up my home? and what clear stream
Shall with its murmur lull me into rest?
The earth is all before me. With a heart
Joyous, nor scared at its own liberty,
I look about; and should the chosen guide
Be nothing better than a wandering cloud,
I cannot miss my way. I breathe again!
Trances of thought and mountings of the mind

Come fast upon me: it is shaken off,   20
That burthen of my own unnatural self,
The heavy weight of many a weary day
Not mine, and such as were not made for me.
Long months of peace (if such bold word accord
With any promises of human life),
Long months of ease and undisturbed delight
Are mine in prospect; whither shall I turn,
By road or pathway, or through trackless field,
Up hill or down, or shall some floating thing
Upon the river point me out my course?   30

Dear Liberty! Yet what would it avail
But for a gift that consecrates the joy?
For I, methought, while the sweet breath of heaven
Was blowing on my body, felt within
A correspondent breeze, that gently moved
With quickening virtue, but is now become
A tempest, a redundant energy,
Vexing its own creation. Thanks to both,
And their congenial powers, that, while they join
In breaking up a long-continued frost,   40
Bring with them vernal promises, the hope
Of active days urged on by flying hours, —
Days of sweet leisure, taxed with patient thought
Abstruse, nor wanting punctual service high,
Matins and vespers of harmonious verse!

Thus far, O Friend! did I, not used to make
A present joy the matter of a song,
Pour forth that day my soul in measured strains
That would not be forgotten, and are here
Recorded: to the open fields I told   50
A prophecy: poetic numbers came
Spontaneously to clothe in priestly robe

A renovated spirit singled out,
Such hope was mine, for holy services.
My own voice cheered me, and, far more, the mind's
Internal echo of the imperfect sound;
To both I listened, drawing from them both
A cheerful confidence in things to come.

    Content and not unwilling now to give
A respite to this passion, I paced on   60
With brisk and eager steps; and came, at length,
To a green shady place, where down I sate
Beneath a tree, slackening my thoughts by choice
And settling into gentler happiness.
T'was autumn, and a clear and placid day,
With warmth, as much as needed, from a sun
Two hours declined towards the west; a day
With silver clouds, and sunshine on the grass,
And in the sheltered and the sheltering grove
A perfect stillness.   Many were the thoughts   70
Encouraged and dismissed, till choice was made
Of a known Vale, whither my feet should turn,
Nor rest till they had reached the very door
Of the one cottage which methought I saw.
No picture of mere memory ever looked
So fair; and while upon the fancied scene
I gazed with growing love, a higher power
Than Fancy gave assurance of some work
Of glory there forthwith to be begun,
Perhaps too there performed.   Thus long I mused,   80
Nor e'er lost sight of what I mused upon,
Save when, amid the stately grove of oaks,
Now here, now there, an acorn, from its cup
Dislodged, through sere leaves rustled, or at once
To the bare earth dropped with a startling sound.
From that soft couch I rose not, till the sun

Had almost touched the horizon; casting then
A backward glance upon the curling cloud
Of city smoke, by distance ruralised;
Keen as a Truant or a Fugitive,   90
But as a Pilgrim resolute, I took,
Even with the chance equipment of that hour,
The road that pointed toward the chosen Vale.

It was a splendid evening, and my soul
Once more made trial of her strength, nor lacked
Æolian visitations; but the harp
Was soon defrauded, and the banded host
Of harmony dispersed in straggling sounds,
And lastly utter silence! "Be it so;
Why think of anything but present good?"   100
So, like a home-bound labourer, I pursued
My way beneath the mellowing sun, that shed
Mild influence; nor left in me one wish
Again to bend the Sabbath of that time
To a servile yoke. What need of many words?
A pleasant loitering journey, through three days
Continued, brought me to my hermitage.
I spare to tell of what ensued, the life
In common things — the endless store of things,
Rare, or at least so seeming, every day   110
Found all about me in one neighbourhood —
The self-congratulation, and, from morn
To night, unbroken cheerfulness serene.
But speedily an earnest longing rose
To brace myself to some determined aim,
Reading or thinking; either to lay up
New stores, or rescue from decay the old
By timely interference: and therewith
Came hopes still higher, that with outward life
I might endue some airy phantasies   120

That had been floating loose about for years,
And to such beings temperately deal forth
The many feelings that oppressed my heart.
That hope hath been discouraged; welcome light
Dawns from the east, but dawns to disappear
And mock me with a sky that ripens not
Into a steady morning: if my mind,
Remembering the bold promise of the past,
Would gladly grapple with some noble theme,
Vain is her wish; where'er she turns she finds   130
Impediments from day to day renewed.

   And now it would content me to yield up
Those lofty hopes awhile, for present gifts
Of humbler industry. But, oh, dear Friend!
The Poet, gentle creature as he is,
Hath, like the Lover, his unruly times;
His fits when he is neither sick nor well,
Though no distress be near him but his own
Unmanageable thoughts: his mind, best pleased
While she as duteous as the mother dove   140
Sits brooding, lives not always to that end,
But like the innocent bird, hath goadings on
That drive her as in trouble through the groves;
With me is now such passion, to be blamed
No otherwise than as it lasts too long.

   When, as becomes a man who would prepare
For such an arduous work, I through myself
Make rigorous inquisition, the report
Is often cheering; for I neither seem
To lack that first great gift, the vital soul,   150
Nor general Truths, which are themselves a sort
Of Elements and Agents, Under-powers,
Subordinate helpers of the living mind:

Nor am I naked of external things,
Forms, images, nor numerous other aids
Of less regard, though won perhaps with toil
And needful to build up a Poet's praise.
Time, place, and manners do I seek, and these
Are found in plenteous store, but nowhere such
As may be singled out with steady choice;   160
No little band of yet remembered names
Whom I, in perfect confidence, might hope
To summon back from lonesome banishment,
And make them dwellers in the hearts of men
Now living, or to live in future years.
Sometimes the ambitious Power of choice, mistaking
Proud spring-tide swellings for a regular sea,
Will settle on some British theme, some old
Romantic tale by Milton left unsung;
More often turning to some gentle place   170
Within the groves of Chivalry, I pipe
To shepherd swains, or seated harp in hand,
Amid reposing knights by a river side
Or fountain, listen to the grave reports
Of dire enchantments faced and overcome
By the strong mind, and tales of warlike feats,
Where spear encountered spear, and sword with sword
Fought, as if conscious of the blazonry
That the shield bore, so glorious was the strife;
Whence inspiration for a song that winds   180
Through ever-changing scenes of votive quest
Wrongs to redress, harmonious tribute paid
To patient courage and unblemished truth,
To firm devotion, zeal unquenchable,
And Christian meekness hallowing faithful loves.
Sometimes, more sternly moved, I would relate
How vanquished Mithridates northward passed,
And, hidden in the cloud of years, became

Odin, the Father of a race by whom
Perished the Roman Empire: how the friends   190
And followers of Sertorius, out of Spain
Flying, found shelter in the Fortunate Isles,
And left their usages, their arts and laws,
To disappear by a slow gradual death,
To dwindle and to perish one by one,
Starved in those narrow bounds: but not the soul
Of Liberty, which fifteen hundred years
Survived, and, when the European came
With skill and power that might not be withstood,
Did, like a pestilence, maintain its hold   200
And wasted down by glorious death that race
Of natural heroes: or I would record
How, in tyrannic times, some high-souled man,
Unnamed among the chronicles of kings,
Suffered in silence for Truth's sake: or tell,
How that one Frenchman, through continued force
Of meditation on the inhuman deeds
Of those who conquered first the Indian Isles,
Went single in his ministry across
The Ocean; not to comfort the oppressed,   210
But, like a thirsty wind, to roam about
Withering the Oppressor: how Gustavus sought
Help at his need in Dalecarlia's mines:
How Wallace fought for Scotland; left the name
Of Wallace to be found, like a wild flower,
All over his dear Country; left the deeds
Of Wallace, like a family of Ghosts,
To people the steep rocks and river banks,
Her natural sanctuaries, with a local soul
Of independence and stern liberty.   220
Sometimes it suits me better to invent
A tale from my own heart, more near akin
To my own passions and habitual thoughts;

Some variegated story, in the main
Lofty, but the unsubstantial structure melts
Before the very sun that brightens it,
Mist into air dissolving! Then a wish,
My last and favourite aspiration, mounts
With yearning toward some philosophic song
Of Truth that cherishes our daily life;   230
With meditations passionate from deep
Recesses in man's heart, immortal verse
Thoughtfully fitted to the Orphean lyre;
But from this awful burthen I full soon
Take refuge and beguile myself with trust
That mellower years will bring a riper mind
And clearer insight. Thus my days are past
In contradiction; with no skill to part
Vague longing, haply bred by want of power,
From paramount impulse not to be withstood,   240
A timorous capacity, from prudence,
From circumspection, infinite delay.
Humility and modest awe, themselves
Betray me, serving often for a cloak
To a more subtle selfishness; that now
Locks every function up in blank reserve,
Now dupes me, trusting to an anxious eye
That with intrusive restlessness beats off
Simplicity and self-presented truth.
Ah! better far than this, to stray about   250
Voluptuously through fields and rural walks,
And ask no record of the hours, resigned
To vacant musing, unreproved neglect
Of all things, and deliberate holiday.
Far better never to have heard the name
Of zeal and just ambition, than to live
Baffled and plagued by a mind that every hour
Turns recreant to her task; takes heart again,

Then feels immediately some hollow thought
Hang like an interdict upon her hopes.   260
This is my lot; for either still I find
Some imperfection in the chosen theme,
Or see of absolute accomplishment
Much wanting, so much wanting, in myself,
That I recoil and droop, and seek repose
In listlessness from vain perplexity,
Unprofitably travelling toward the grave,
Like a false steward who hath much received
And renders nothing back.
                        Was it for this
That one, the fairest of all rivers, loved   270
To blend his murmurs with my nurse's song,
And, from his alder shades and rocky falls,
And from his fords and shallows, sent a voice
That flowed along my dreams? For this, didst thou,
O Derwent! winding among grassy holms
Where I was looking on, a babe in arms,
Make ceaseless music that composed my thoughts
To more than infant softness, giving me
Amid the fretful dwellings of mankind
A foretaste, a dim earnest, of the calm   280
That Nature breathes among the hills and groves.

   When he had left the mountains and received
On his smooth breast the shadow of those towers
That yet survive, a shattered monument
Of feudal sway, the bright blue river passed
Along the margin of our terrace walk;
A tempting playmate whom we dearly loved.
Oh, many a time have I, a five years' child,
In a small mill-race severed from his stream,
Made one long bathing of a summer's day;   290
Basked in the sun, and plunged and basked again

Alternate, all a summer's day, or scoured
The sandy fields, leaping through flowery groves
Of yellow ragwort; or, when rock and hill,
The woods, and distant Skiddaw's lofty height,
Were bronzed with deepest radiance, stood alone
Beneath the sky, as if I had been born
On Indian plains, and from my mother's hut
Had run abroad in wantonness, to sport
A naked savage, in the thunder shower.   300

Fair seed-time had my soul, and I grew up
Fostered alike by beauty and by fear:
Much favoured in my birth-place, and no less
In that belovèd Vale to which erelong
We were transplanted; there were we let loose
For sports of wider range. Ere I had told
Ten birth-days, when among the mountain slopes
Frost, and the breath of frosty wind, had snapped
The last autumnal crocus, 't was my joy
With store of springes o'er my shoulder hung   310
To range the open heights where woodcocks run
Along the smooth green turf. Through half the night,
Scudding away from snare to snare, I plied
That anxious visitation; — moon and stars
Were shining o'er my head. I was alone,
And seemed to be a trouble to the peace
That dwelt among them. Sometimes it befell
In these night wanderings, that a strong desire
O'erpowered my better reason, and the bird
Which was the captive of another's toil   320
Became my prey; and when the deed was done
I heard among the solitary hills
Low breathings coming after me, and sounds
Of undistinguishable motion, steps
Almost as silent as the turf they trod.

Nor less, when spring had warmed the cultured Vale,
Moved we as plunderers where the mother-bird
Had in high places built her lodge; though mean
Our object and inglorious, yet the end
Was not ignoble. Oh! when I have hung   330
Above the raven's nest, by knots of grass
And half-inch fissures in the slippery rock
But ill sustained, and almost (so it seemed)
Suspended by the blast that blew amain,
Shouldering the naked crag, oh, at that time
While on the perilous ridge I hung alone,
With what strange utterance did the loud dry wind
Blow through my ear! the sky seemed not a sky
Of earth — and with what motion moved the clouds!

Dust as we are, the immortal spirit grows   340
Like harmony in music; there is a dark
Inscrutable workmanship that reconciles
Discordant elements, makes them cling together
In one society. How strange, that all
The terrors, pains, and early miseries,
Regrets, vexations, lassitudes interfused
Within my mind, should e'er have borne a part,
And that a needful part, in making up
The calm existence that is mine when I
Am worthy of myself! Praise to the end!   350
Thanks to the means which Nature deigned to employ;
Whether her fearless visitings, or those
That came with soft alarm, like hurtless light
Opening the peaceful clouds; or she would use
Severer interventions, ministry
More palpable, as best might suit her aim.

One summer evening (led by her) I found
A little boat tied to a willow tree

Within a rocky cove, its usual home.
Straight I unloosed her chain, and stepping in   360
Pushed from the shore. It was an act of stealth
And troubled pleasure, nor without the voice
Of mountain-echoes did my boat move on;
Leaving behind her still, on either side,
Small circles glittering idly in the moon,
Until they melted all into one track
Of sparkling light. But now, like one who rows,
Proud of his skill, to reach a chosen point
With an unswerving line, I fixed my view
Upon the summit of a craggy ridge,   370
The horizon's utmost boundary; far above
Was nothing but the stars and the grey sky.
She was an elfin pinnace; lustily
I dipped my oars into the silent lake,
And, as I rose upon the stroke, my boat
Went heaving through the water like a swan;
When, from behind that craggy steep till then
The horizon's bound, a huge peak, black and huge,
As if with voluntary power instinct,
Upreared its head. I struck and struck again,   380
And growing still in stature the grim shape
Towered up between me and the stars, and still,
For so it seemed, with purpose of its own
And measured motion like a living thing,
Strode after me. With trembling oars I turned,
And through the silent water stole my way
Back to the covert of the willow tree;
There in her mooring-place I left my bark, —
And through the meadows homeward went, in grave
And serious mood; but after I had seen   390
That spectacle, for many days, my brain
Worked with a dim and undetermined sense
Of unknown modes of being; o'er my thoughts

There hung a darkness, call it solitude
Or blank desertion. No familiar shapes
Remained, no pleasant images of trees,
Of sea or sky, no colours of green fields;
But huge and mighty forms, that do not live
Like living men, moved slowly through the mind
By day, and were a trouble to my dreams.   400

    Wisdom and Spirit of the universe!
Thou Soul that art the eternity of thought
That givest to forms and images a breath
And everlasting motion, not in vain
By day or star-light thus from my first dawn
Of childhood didst thou intertwine for me
The passions that build up our human soul;
Not with the mean and vulgar works of man,
But with high objects, with enduring things —
With life and nature — purifying thus   410
The elements of feeling and of thought,
And sanctifying, by such discipline,
Both pain and fear, until we recognise
A grandeur in the beatings of the heart.
Nor was this fellowship vouchsafed to me
With stinted kindness. In November days,
When vapours rolling down the valley made
A lonely scene more lonesome, among woods,
At noon and 'mid the calm of summer nights,
When, by the margin of the trembling lake,   420
Beneath the gloomy hills homeward I went
In solitude, such intercourse was mine;
Mine was it in the fields both day and night,
And by the waters, all the summer long.

    And in the frosty season, when the sun
Was set, and visible for many a mile

The cottage windows blazed through twilight gloom,
I heeded not their summons: happy time
It was indeed for all of us — for me
It was a time of rapture!   Clear and loud   430
The village clock tolled six, — I wheeled about,
Proud and exulting like an untired horse
That cares not for his home.   All shod with steel,
We hissed along the polished ice in games
Confederate, imitative of the chase
And woodland pleasures, — the resounding horn,
The pack loud chiming, and the hunted hare.
So through the darkness and the cold we flew,
And not a voice was idle; with the din
Smitten, the precipices rang aloud;   440
The leafless trees and every icy crag
Tinkled like iron; while far distant hills
Into the tumult sent an alien sound
Of melancholy not unnoticed, while the stars
Eastward were sparkling clear, and in the west
The orange sky of evening died away.
Not seldom from the uproar I retired
Into a silent bay, or sportively
Glanced sideway, leaving the tumultuous throng,
To cut across the reflex of a star   450
That fled, and, flying still before me, gleamed
Upon the glassy plain; and oftentimes,
When we had given our bodies to the wind,
And all the shadowy banks on either side
Came sweeping through the darkness, spinning
          still
The rapid line of motion, then at once
Have I, reclining back upon my heels,
Stopped short; yet still the solitary cliffs
Wheeled by me — even as if the earth had rolled
With visible motion her diurnal round!   460

Behind me did they stretch in solemn train,
Feebler and feebler, and I stood and watched
Till all was tranquil as a dreamless sleep.

  Ye Presences of Nature in the sky
And on the earth! Ye Visions of the hills!
And Souls of lonely places! can I think
A vulgar hope was yours when ye employed
Such ministry, when ye, through many a year
Haunting me thus among my boyish sports,
On caves and trees, upon the woods and hills,   470
Impressed, upon all forms, the characters
Of danger or desire; and thus did make
The surface of the universal earth,
With triumph and delight, with hope and fear,
Work like a sea?
                    Not uselessly employed,
Might I pursue this theme through every change
Of exercise and play, to which the year
Did summon us in his delightful round.

  We were a noisy crew; the sun in heaven
Beheld not vales more beautiful than ours;   480
Nor saw a band in happiness and joy
Richer, or worthier of the ground they trod.
I could record with no reluctant voice
The woods of autumn, and their hazel bowers
With milk-white clusters hung; the rod and line,
True symbol of hope's foolishness, whose strong
And unreproved enchantment led us on
By rocks and pools shut out from every star,
All the green summer, to forlorn cascades
Among the windings hid of mountain brooks.   490
— Unfading recollections! at this hour
The heart is almost mine with which I felt,

From some hill-top on sunny afternoons,
The paper kite high among fleecy clouds
Pull at her rein like an impetuous courser;
Or, from the meadows sent on gusty days,
Beheld her breast the wind, then suddenly
Dashed headlong, and rejected by the storm.

    Ye lowly cottages wherein we dwelt,
A ministration of your own was yours;   500
Can I forget you, being as you were
So beautiful among the pleasant fields
In which ye stood? or can I here forget
The plain and seemly countenance with which
Ye dealt out your plain comforts?   Yet had ye
Delights and exultations of your own.
Eager and never weary we pursued
Our home-amusements by the warm peat-fire
At evening, when with pencil, and smooth slate
In square divisions parcelled out and all   510
With crosses and with cyphers scribbled o'er,
We schemed and puzzled, head opposed to head
In strife too humble to be named in verse:
Or round the naked table, snow-white deal,
Cherry or maple, sate in close array,
And to the combat, Loo or Whist, led on
A thick-ribbed army; not, as in the world,
Neglected and ungratefully thrown by
Even for the very service they had wrought,
But husbanded through many a long campaign.   520
Uncouth assemblage was it, where no few
Had changed their functions: some, plebeian cards
Which Fate, beyond the promise of their birth
Had dignified, and called to represent
The persons of departed potentates.
Oh, with what echoes on the board they fell!

Ironic diamonds, — clubs, hearts, diamonds, spades,
A congregation piteously akin!
Cheap matter offered they to boyish wit,
Those sooty knaves, precipitated down   530
With scoffs and taunts, like Vulcan out of heaven:
The paramount ace, a moon in her eclipse,
Queens gleaming through their splendour's last decay,
And monarchs surly at the wrongs sustained
By royal visages.   Meanwhile abroad
Incessant rain was falling, or the frost
Raged bitterly, with keen and silent tooth;
And, interrupting oft that eager game,
From under Esthwaite's splitting fields of ice
The pent-up air, struggling to free itself,   540
Gave out to meadow grounds and hills a loud
Protracted yelling, like the noise of wolves
Howling in troops along the Bothnic Main.

   Nor, sedulous as I have been to trace
How Nature by extrinsic passion first
Peopled the mind with forms sublime or fair,
And made me love them, may I here omit
How other pleasures have been mine, and joys
Of subtler origin; how I have felt,
Not seldom even in that tempestuous time,   550
Those hallowed and pure motions of the sense
Which seem, in their simplicity, to own
An intellectual charm; that calm delight
Which, if I err not, surely must belong
To those first-born affinities that fit
Our new existence to existing things,
And, in our dawn of being, constitute
The bond of union between life and joy.

   Yes, I remember when the changeful earth,

And twice five summers on my mind had stamped   560
The faces of the moving year, even then
I held unconscious intercourse with beauty
Old as creation, drinking in a pure
Organic pleasure from the silver wreaths
Of curling mist, or from the level plain
Of waters coloured by impending clouds.

The sands of Westmoreland, the creeks and bays
Of Cumbria's rocky limits, they can tell
How, when the Sea threw off his evening shade,
And to the shepherd's hut on distant hills   570
Sent welcome notice of the rising moon,
How I have stood, to fancies such as these
A stranger, linking with the spectacle
No conscious memory of a kindred sight,
And bringing with me no peculiar sense
Of quietness or peace; yet have I stood,
Even while mine eye hath moved o'er many a league
Of shining water, gathering as it seemed,
Through every hair-breadth in that field of light,
New pleasure like a bee among the flowers.   580

Thus oft amid those fits of vulgar joy
Which, through all seasons, on a child's pursuits
Are prompt attendants, 'mid that giddy bliss
Which, like a tempest, works along the blood
And is forgotten; even then I felt
Gleams like the flashing of a shield; — the earth
And common face of Nature spake to me
Rememberable things; sometimes, 'tis true,
By chance collisions and quaint accidents
(Like those ill-sorted unions, work supposed   590
Of evil-minded fairies), yet not vain
Nor profitless, if haply they impressed

Collateral objects and appearances,
Albeit lifeless then, and doomed to sleep
Until maturer seasons called them forth
To impregnate and to elevate the mind.
— And if the vulgar joy by its own weight
Wearied itself out of the memory,
The scenes which were a witness of that joy
Remained in their substantial lineaments   600
Depicted on the brain, and to the eye
Were visible, a daily sight; and thus
By the impressive discipline of fear,
By pleasure and repeated happiness,
So frequently repeated, and by force
Of obscure feelings representative
Of things forgotten, these same scenes so bright,
So beautiful, so majestic in themselves,
Though yet the day was distant, did become
Habitually dear, and all their forms   610
And changeful colours by invisible links
Were fastened to the affections.
                              I began
My story early — not misled, I trust,
By an infirmity of love for days
Disowned by memory — ere the breath of spring
Planting my snowdrops among winter snows:
Nor will it seem to thee, O Friend ! so prompt
In sympathy, that I have lengthened out
With fond and feeble tongue a tedious tale.
Meanwhile, my hope has been, that I might fetch   620
Invigorating thoughts from former years;
Might fix the wavering balance of my mind,
And haply meet reproaches too, whose power
May spur me on, in manhood now mature
To honourable toil.   Yet should these hopes
Prove vain and thus should neither I be taught

To understand myself, nor thou to know
With better knowledge how the heart was framed
Of him thou lovest; need I dread from thee
Harsh judgments, if the song be loth to quit   630
Those recollected hours that have the charm
Of visionary things, those lovely forms
And sweet sensations that throw back our life,
And almost make remotest infancy
A visible scene, on which the sun is shining?

One end at least hath been attained; my mind
Hath been revived, and if this genial mood
Desert me not, forthwith shall be brought down
Through later years the story of my life.
The road lies plain before me; — 'tis a theme   640
Single and of determined bounds; and hence
I choose it rather at this time, than work
Of ampler or more varied argument,
Where I might be discomfited and lost:
And certain hopes are with me, that to thee
This labour will be welcome, honoured Friend!

BOOK SECOND

SCHOOL-TIME (*continued*)

THUS far, O Friend! have we, though leaving much
Unvisited, endeavoured to retrace
The simple ways in which my childhood walked;
Those chiefly that first led me to the love
Of rivers, woods, and fields. The passion yet
Was in its birth, sustained as might befall
By nourishment that came unsought; for still
From week to week, from month to month, we lived
A round of tumult. Duly were our games

Prolonged in summer till the daylight failed; 10
No chair remained before the doors; the bench
And threshold steps were empty; fast asleep
The labourer, and the old man who had sate
A later lingerer; yet the revelry
Continued and the loud uproar: at last,
When all the ground was dark, and twinkling stars
Edged the black clouds, home and to bed we went,
Feverish with weary joints and beating minds.
Ah! is there one who ever has been young,
Nor needs a warning voice to tame the pride 20
Of intellect and virtue's self-esteem?
One is there, though the wisest and the best
Of all mankind, who covets not at times
Union that cannot be; — who would not give
If so he might, to duty and to truth
The eagerness of infantine desire?
A tranquillising spirit presses now
On my corporeal frame, so wide appears
The vacancy between me and those days
Which yet have such self-presence in my mind, 30
That, musing on them, often do I seem
Two consciousnesses, conscious of myself
And of some other Being. A rude mass
Of native rock, left midway in the square
Of our small market village, was the goal
Or centre of these sports; and when, returned
After long absence, thither I repaired,
Gone was the old grey stone, and in its place
A smart Assembly-room usurped the ground
That had been ours. There let the fiddle scream, 40
And be ye happy! Yet, my Friends! I know
That more than one of you will think with me
Of those soft starry nights, and that old Dame
From whom the stone was named, who there had sate,

And watched her table with its huckster's wares
Assiduous, through the length of sixty years.

    We ran a boisterous course; the year span round
With giddy motion. But the time approached
That brought with it a regular desire
For calmer pleasures, when the winning forms   50
Of Nature were collaterally attached
To every scheme of holiday delight
And every boyish sport, less grateful else
And languidly pursued.
                      When summer came,
Our pastime was, on bright half-holidays,
To sweep along the plain of Windermere
With rival oars; and the selected bourne
Was now an Island musical with birds
That sang and ceased not; now a Sister Isle
Beneath the oaks' umbrageous covert, sown   60
With lilies of the valley like a field;
And now a third small Island, where survived
In solitude the ruins of a shrine
Once to Our Lady dedicate, and served
Daily with chaunted rites. In such a race
So ended, disappointment could be none,
Uneasiness, or pain, or jealousy:
We rested in the shade, all pleased alike,
Conquered and conqueror. Thus the pride of strength,
And the vain-glory of superior skill,   70
Were tempered; thus was gradually produced
A quiet independence of the heart:
And to my Friend who knows me I may add,
Fearless of blame, that hence for future days
Ensued a diffidence and modesty,
And I was taught to feel, perhaps too much,
The self-sufficing power of Solitude.

Our daily meals were frugal, Sabine fare!
More than we wished we knew the blessing then
Of vigorous hunger — hence corporeal strength   80
Unsapped by delicate viands; for, exclude
A little weekly stipend, and we lived
Through three divisions of the quartered year
In penniless poverty. But now to school
From the half-yearly holidays returned,
We came with weightier purses, that sufficed
To furnish treats more costly than the Dame
Of the old grey stone, from her scant board, supplied.
Hence rustic dinners on the cool green ground,
Or in the woods, or by a river side   90
Or shady fountains, while among the leaves
Soft airs were stirring, and the mid-day sun
Unfelt shone brightly round us in our joy.
Nor is my aim neglected if I tell
How sometimes, in the length of those half-years,
We from our funds drew largely; — proud to curb,
And eager to spur on, the galloping steed;
And with the courteous inn-keeper, whose stud
Supplied our want, we haply might employ
Sly subterfuge, if the adventure's bound   100
Were distant: some famed temple where of yore
The Druids worshipped, or the antique walls
Of that large abbey, where within the Vale
Of Nightshade, to St. Mary's honour built,
Stands yet a mouldering pile with fractured arch,
Belfry, and images, and living trees;
A holy scene! — Along the smooth green turf
Our horses grazed. To more than inland peace,
Left by the west wind sweeping overhead
From a tumultuous ocean, trees and towers   110
In that sequestered valley may be seen,
Both silent and both motionless alike;

Such the deep shelter that is there, and such
The safeguard for repose and quietness.

   Our steeds remounted and the summons given,
With whip and spur we through the chauntry flew
In uncouth race, and left the cross-legged knight,
And the stone-abbot, and that single wren
Which one day sang so sweetly in the nave
Of the old church, that — though from recent showers
The earth was comfortless, and, touched by faint   121
Internal breezes, sobbings of the place
And respirations, from the roofless walls
The shuddering ivy dripped large drops — yet still
So sweetly 'mid the gloom the invisible bird
Sang to herself, that there I could have made
My dwelling-place, and lived for ever there
To hear such music. Through the walls we flew
And down the valley, and, a circuit made
In wantonness of heart, through rough and smooth 130
We scampered homewards. Oh, ye rocks and streams,
And that still spirit shed from evening air!
Even in this joyous time I sometimes felt
Your presence, when with slackened step we breathed
Along the sides of the steep hills, or when
Lighted by gleams of moonlight from the sea
We beat with thundering hoofs the level sand.

   Midway on long Winander's eastern shore,
Within the crescent of a pleasant bay,
A tavern stood; no homely-featured house,   140
Primeval like its neighbouring cottages,
But 't was a splendid place, the door beset
With chaises, grooms, and liveries, and within
Decanters, glasses, and the blood-red wine.
In ancient times, and ere the Hall was built

On the large island, had this dwelling been
More worthy of a poet's love, a hut,
Proud of its own bright fire and sycamore shade.
But — though the rhymes were gone that once inscribed
The threshold, and large golden characters, 150
Spread o'er the spangled sign-board, had dislodged
The old Lion and usurped his place, in slight
And mockery of the rustic painter's hand —
Yet, to this hour, the spot to me is dear
With all its foolish pomp. The garden lay
Upon a slope surmounted by a plain
Of a small bowling-green; beneath us stood
A grove, with gleams of water through the trees
And over the tree-tops; nor did we want
Refreshment, strawberries and mellow cream. 160
There, while through half an afternoon we played
On the smooth platform, whether skill prevailed
Or happy blunder triumphed, bursts of glee
Made all the mountains ring. But, ere night-fall
When in our pinnace we returned at leisure
Over the shadowy lake, and to the beach
Of some small island steered our course with one,
The Minstrel of the Troop, and left him there,
And rowed off gently, while he blew his flute
Alone upon the rock — oh, then, the calm 170
And dead still water lay upon my mind
Even with a weight of pleasure, and the sky,
Never before so beautiful, sank down
Into my heart, and held me like a dream!
Thus were my sympathies enlarged, and thus
Daily the common range of visible things
Grew dear to me: already I began
To love the sun; a boy I loved the sun,
Not as I since have loved him, as a pledge
And surety of our earthly life, a light 180

Which we behold and feel we are alive;
Nor for his bounty to so many worlds —
But for this cause, that I had seen him lay
His beauty on the morning hills, had seen
The western mountain touch his setting orb,
In many a thoughtless hour, when, from excess
Of happiness, my blood appeared to flow
For its own pleasure, and I breathed with joy.
And, from like feelings, humble though intense,
To patriotic and domestic love   190
Analogous, the moon to me was dear;
For I could dream away my purposes,
Standing to gaze upon her while she hung
Midway between the hills as if she knew
No other region, but belonged to thee,
Yea, appertained by a peculiar right
To thee and thy grey huts, thou one dear Vale!

Those incidental charms which first attached
My heart to rural objects, day by day
Grew weaker, and I hasten on to tell   200
How Nature, intervenient till this time
And secondary, now at length was sought
For her own sake. But who shall parcel out
His intellect by geometric rules,
Split like a province into round and square?
Who knows the individual hour in which
His habits were first sown, even as a seed?
Who that shall point as with a wand and say
"This portion of the river of my mind
Came from yon fountain?" Thou, my Friend! art one
More deeply read in thy own thoughts; to thee   211
Science appears but what in truth she is,
Not as our glory and our absolute boast,
But as a succedaneum, and a prop
To our infirmity. No officious slave

Art thou of that false secondary power
By which we multiply distinctions, then
Deem that our puny boundaries are things
That we perceive, and not that we have made.
To thee, unblinded by these formal arts,   220
The unity of all hath been revealed,
And thou wilt doubt, with me less aptly skilled
Than many are to range the faculties
In scale and order, class the cabinet
Of their sensations, and in voluble phrase
Run through the history and birth of each
As of a single independent thing.
Hard task, vain hope, to analyse the mind,
If each most obvious and particular thought,
Not in a mystical and idle sense,   230
But in the words of Reason deeply weighed,
Hath no beginning.
                    Blest the infant Babe,
(For with my best conjecture I would trace
Our Being's earthly progress,) blest the Babe,
Nursed in his Mother's arms, who sinks to sleep
Rocked on his Mother's breast; who with his soul
Drinks in the feelings of his Mother's eye!
For him, in one dear Presence, there exists
A virtue which irradiates and exalts
Objects through widest intercourse of sense;   240
No outcast he, bewildered and depressed:
Along his infant veins are interfused
The gravitation and the filial bond
Of nature that connect him with the world.
Is there a flower, to which he points with hand
Too weak to gather it, already love
Drawn from love's purest earthly fount for him
Hath beautified that flower; already shades
Of pity cast from inward tenderness

Do fall around him upon aught that bears   250
Unsightly marks of violence or harm.
Emphatically such a Being lives,
Frail creature as he is, helpless as frail,
An inmate of this active universe:
For, feeling has to him imparted power
That through the growing faculties of sense
Doth like an agent of the one great Mind
Create, creator and receiver both,
Working but in alliance with the works
Which it beholds. — Such, verily, is the first   260
Poetic spirit of our human life,
By uniform control of after years,
In most, abated or suppressed; in some,
Through every change of growth and of decay,
Pre-eminent till death.
                              From early days,
Beginning not long after that first time
In which, a Babe, by intercourse of touch
I held mute dialogues with my Mother's heart,
I have endeavoured to display the means
Whereby this infant sensibility,   270
Great birthright of our being, was in me
Augmented and sustained. Yet is a path
More difficult before me; and I fear
That in its broken windings we shall need
The chamois' sinews, and the eagle's wing:
For now a trouble came into my mind
From unknown causes. I was left alone
Seeking the visible world, nor knowing why.
The props of my affections were removed,
And yet the building stood, as if sustained   280
By its own spirit! All that I beheld
Was dear, and hence to finer influxes
The mind lay open to a more exact

And close communion. Many are our joys
In youth, but oh! what happiness to live
When every hour brings palpable access
Of knowledge, when all knowledge is delight,
And sorrow is not there! The seasons came,
And every season wheresoe'er I moved
Unfolded transitory qualities,   290
Which, but for this most watchful power of love,
Had been neglected; left a register
Of permanent relations, else unknown.
Hence life, and change, and beauty, solitude
More active ever than "best society" —
Society made sweet as solitude
By silent inobtrusive sympathies,
And gentle agitations of the mind
From manifold distinctions, difference
Perceived in things, where, to the unwatchful eye,   300
No difference is, and hence, from the same source,
Sublimer joy; for I would walk alone,
Under the quiet stars, and at that time
Have felt whate'er there is of power in sound
To breathe an elevated mood, by form
Or image unprofaned; and I would stand,
If the night blackened with a coming storm,
Beneath some rock, listening to notes that are
The ghostly language of the ancient earth,
Or make their dim abode in distant winds.   310
Thence did I drink the visionary power;
And deem not profitless those fleeting moods
Of shadowy exultation: not for this,
That they are kindred to our purer mind
And intellectual life; but that the soul,
Remembering how she felt, but what she felt
Remembering not, retains an obscure sense
Of possible sublimity, whereto

With growing faculties she doth aspire,
With faculties still growing, feeling still   320
That whatsoever point they gain, they yet
Have something to pursue.
                   And not alone,
'Mid gloom and tumult, but no less 'mid fair
And tranquil scenes, that universal power
And fitness in the latent qualities
And essences of things, by which the mind
Is moved with feelings of delight, to me
Came strengthened with a superadded soul,
A virtue not its own. My morning walks
Were early; — oft before the hours of school   330
I travelled round our little lake, five miles
Of pleasant wandering. Happy time! more dear
For this, that one was by my side, a Friend,
Then passionately loved; with heart how full
Would he peruse these lines! For many years
Have since flowed in between us, and, our minds
Both silent to each other, at this time
We live as if those hours had never been.
Nor seldom did I lift our cottage latch
Far earlier, ere one smoke-wreath had risen   340
From human dwelling, or the vernal thrush
Was audible; and sate among the woods
Alone upon some jutting eminence,
At the first gleam of dawn-light, when the Vale,
Yet slumbering, lay in utter solitude.
How shall I seek the origin? where find
Faith in the marvellous things which then I felt?
Oft in these moments such a holy calm
Would overspread my soul, that bodily eyes
Were utterly forgotten, and what I saw   350
Appeared like something in myself, a dream,
A prospect in the mind.

'T were long to tell
What spring and autumn, what the winter snows,
And what the summer shade, what day and night,
Evening and morning, sleep and waking, thought
From sources inexhaustible, poured forth
To feed the spirit of religious love
In which I walked with Nature. But let this
Be not forgotten, that I still retained
My first creative sensibility;   360
That by the regular action of the world
My soul was unsubdued. A plastic power
Abode with me; a forming hand, at times
Rebellious, acting in a devious mood;
A local spirit of his own, at war
With general tendency, but, for the most,
Subservient strictly to external things
With which it communed. An auxiliar light
Came from my mind, which on the setting sun
Bestowed new splendour; the melodious birds,   370
The fluttering breezes, fountains that run on
Murmuring so sweetly in themselves, obeyed
A like dominion, and the midnight storm
Grew darker in the presence of my eye:
Hence my obeisance, my devotion hence,
And hence my transport.
                    Nor should this, perchance,
Pass unrecorded, that I still had loved
The exercise and produce of a toil,
Than analytic industry to me
More pleasing, and whose character I deem   380
Is more poetic as resembling more
Creative agency.   The song would speak
Of that interminable building reared
By observation of affinities
In objects where no brotherhood exists

To passive minds.   My seventeenth year was come
And, whether from this habit rooted now
So deeply in my mind, or from excess
In the great social principle of life
Coercing all things into sympathy,   390
To unorganic natures were transferred
My own enjoyments; or the power of truth
Coming in revelation, did converse
With things that really are; I, at this time,
Saw blessings spread around me like a sea.
Thus while the days flew by, and years passed on,
From Nature and her overflowing soul,
I had received so much, that all my thoughts
Were steeped in feeling; I was only then
Contented, when with bliss ineffable   400
I felt the sentiment of Being spread
O'er all that moves and all that seemeth still;
O'er all that, lost beyond the reach of thought
And human knowledge, to the human eye
Invisible, yet liveth to the heart;
O'er all that leaps and runs, and shouts and sings,
Or beats the gladsome air; o'er all that glides
Beneath the wave, yea, in the wave itself,
And mighty depth of waters.   Wonder not
If high the transport, great the joy I felt,   410
Communing in this sort through earth and heaven
With every form of creature, as it looked
Towards the Uncreated with a countenance
Of adoration, with an eye of love.
One song they sang, and it was audible,
Most audible, then, when the fleshly ear,
O'ercome by humblest prelude of that strain,
Forgot her functions, and slept undisturbed.

    If this be error, and another faith
Find easier access to the pious mind,   420

Yet were I grossly destitute of all
Those human sentiments that make this earth
So dear, if I should fail with grateful voice
To speak of you, ye mountains, and ye lakes
And sounding cataracts, ye mists and winds
That dwell among the hills where I was born.
If in my youth I have been pure in heart,
If, mingling with the world, I am content
With my own modest pleasures, and have lived
With God and Nature communing, removed   430
From little enmities and low desires —
The gift is yours; if in these times of fear,
This melancholy waste of hopes o'erthrown,
If, 'mid indifference and apathy,
And wicked exultation when good men
On every side fall off, we know not how,
To selfishness, disguised in gentle names
Of peace and quiet and domestic love
Yet mingled not unwillingly with sneers
On visionary minds; if, in this time   440
Of dereliction and dismay, I yet
Despair not of our nature, but retain
A more than Roman confidence, a faith
That fails not, in all sorrow my support,
The blessing of my life — the gift is yours,
Ye winds and sounding cataracts! 't is yours,
Ye mountains! thine, O Nature! Thou hast fed
My lofty speculations; and in thee,
For this uneasy heart of ours, I find
A never-failing principle of joy   450
And purest passion.
                Thou, my Friend! wert reared
In the great city, 'mid far other scenes;
But we, by different roads, at length have gained
The selfsame bourne. And for this cause to thee
I speak, unapprehensive of contempt,

The insinuated scoff of coward tongues,
And all that silent language which so oft
In conversation between man and man
Blots from the human countenance all trace
Of beauty and of love. For thou hast sought   460
The truth in solitude, and, since the days
That gave thee liberty, full long desired,
To serve in Nature's temple, thou has been
The most assiduous of her ministers;
In many things my brother, chiefly here
In this our deep devotion.
                   Fare thee well!
Health and the quiet of a healthful mind
Attend thee! seeking oft the haunts of men,
And yet more often living with thyself,
And for thyself, so haply shall thy days   470
Be many, and a blessing to mankind.

BOOK THIRD

RESIDENCE AT CAMBRIDGE

IT WAS a dreary morning when the wheels
Rolled over a wide plain o'erhung with clouds,
And nothing cheered our way till first we saw
The long-roofed chapel of King's College lift
Turrets and pinnacles in answering files,
Extended high above a dusky grove.

Advancing, we espied upon the road
A student clothed in gown and tasselled cap,
Striding along as if o'ertasked by Time,
Or covetous of exercise and air;   10
He passed — nor was I master of my eyes

Till he was left an arrow's flight behind.
As near and nearer to the spot we drew,
It seemed to suck us in with an eddy's force.
Onward we drove beneath the Castle; caught,
While crossing Magdalene Bridge, a glimpse of Cam;
And at the *Hoop* alighted, famous Inn.

My spirit was up, my thoughts were full of hope;
Some friends I had, acquaintances who there
Seemed friends, poor simple schoolboys, now hung
     round   20
With honour and importance; in a world
Of welcome faces up and down I roved;
Questions, directions, warnings and advice,
Flowed in upon me, from all sides; fresh day
Of pride and pleasure! to myself I seemed
A man of business and expense, and went
From shop to shop about my own affairs,
To Tutor or to Tailor, as befell,
From street to street with loose and careless mind.

I was the Dreamer, they the Dream; I roamed   30
Delighted through the motley spectacle;
Gowns grave, or gaudy, doctors, students, streets,
Courts, cloisters, flocks of churches, gateways, towers:
Migration strange for a stripling of the hills,
A northern villager.
               As if the change
Had waited on some Fairy's wand, at once
Behold me rich in monies, and attired
In splendid garb, with hose of silk, and hair
Powdered like rimy trees, when frost is keen.
My lordly dressing-gown, I pass it by,   40
With other signs of manhood that supplied
The lack of beard. — The weeks went roundly on,

With invitations, suppers, wine and fruit,
Smooth housekeeping within, and all without
Liberal, and suiting gentleman's array.

　The Evangelist St. John my patron was:
Three Gothic courts are his, and in the first
Was my abiding-place, a nook obscure;
Right underneath, the College kitchens made
A humming sound, less tuneable than bees,　　50
But hardly less industrious; with shrill notes
Of sharp command and scolding intermixed.
Near me hung Trinity loquacious clock,
Who never let the quarters, night or day,
Slip by him unproclaimed, and told the hours
Twice over with a male and female voice.
Her pealing organ was my neighbour too;
And from my pillow, looking forth by light
Of moon or favouring stars, I could behold
The antechapel where the statue stood　　60
Of Newton with his prism and silent face,
The marble index of a mind for ever
Voyaging through strange seas of Thought, alone.

　Of College labours, of the Lecturer's room
All studded round, as thick as chairs could stand,
With loyal students, faithful to their books,
Half-and-half idlers, hardy recusants,
And honest dunces — of important days,
Examinations, when the man was weighed
As in a balance! of excessive hopes,　　70
Trembling withal and commendable fears,
Small jealousies, and triumphs good or bad —
Let others that know more speak as they know.
Such glory was but little sought by me,
And little won. Yet from the first crude days

Of settling time in this untried abode,
I was disturbed at times by prudent thoughts,
Wishing to hope without a hope, some fears
About my future worldly maintenance,
And, more than all, a strangeness in the mind,   80
A feeling that I was not for that hour,
Nor for that place. But wherefore be cast down?
For (not to speak of Reason and her pure
Reflective acts to fix the moral law
Deep in the conscience, nor of Christian Hope,
Bowing her head before her sister Faith
As one far mightier), hither I had come,
Bear witness Truth, endowed with holy powers
And faculties, whether to work or feel.
Oft when the dazzling show no longer new   90
Had ceased to dazzle, ofttimes did I quit
My comrades, leave the crowd, buildings and groves,
And as I paced alone the level fields
Far from those lovely sights and sounds sublime
With which I had been conversant, the mind
Drooped not; but there into herself returning,
With prompt rebound seemed fresh as heretofore.
At least I more distinctly recognised
Her native instincts: let me dare to speak
A higher language, say that now I felt   100
What independent solaces were mine,
To mitigate the injurious sway of place
Or circumstance, how far soever changed
In youth, or *to* be changed in manhood's prime;
Or for the few who shall be called to look
On the long shadows in our evening years,
Ordained percursors to the night of death.
As if awakened, summoned, roused, constrained,
I looked for universal things; perused
The common countenance of earth and sky: 110
Earth, nowhere unembellished by some trace

Of that first Paradise whence man was driven;
And sky, whose beauty and bounty are expressed
By the proud name she bears — the name of Heaven.
I called on both to teach me what they might;
Or, turning the mind in upon herself,
Pored, watched, expected, listened, spread my thoughts
And spread them with a wider creeping; felt
Incumbencies more awful, visitings
Of the Upholder of the tranquil soul,   120
That tolerates the indignities of Time,
And, from the centre of Eternity
All finite motions overruling, lives
In glory immutable. But peace! enough
Here to record that I was mounting now
To such community with highest truth —
A track pursuing, not untrod before,
From strict analogies by thought supplied
Or consciousnesses not to be subdued.
To every natural form, rock, fruits, or flower,   130
Even the loose stones that cover the highway,
I gave a moral life: I saw them feel,
Or linked them to some feeling: the great mass
Lay imbedded in a quickening soul, and all
That I beheld respired with inward meaning.
Add that whate'er of Terror or of Love
Or Beauty, Nature's daily face put on
From transitory passion, unto this
I was as sensitive as waters are
To the sky's influence in a kindred mood   140
Of passion; was obedient as a lute
That waits upon the touches of the wind.
Unknown, unthought of, yet I was most rich —
I had a world about me — 't was my own;
I made it, for it only lived to me,
And to the God who sees into the heart.

Such sympathies, though rarely, were betrayed
By outward gestures and by visible looks:
Some called it madness — so indeed it was,
If child-like fruitfulness in passing joy, 150
If steady moods of thoughtfulness matured
To inspiration, sort with such a name;
If prophecy be madness; if things viewed
By poets in old time, and higher up
By the first men, earth's first inhabitants,
May in these tutored days no more be seen
With undisordered sight. But leaving this,
It was no madness, for the bodily eye
Amid my strongest workings evermore
Was searching out the lines of difference 160
As they lie hid in all external forms,
Near or remote, minute or vast; an eye
Which, from a tree, a stone, a withered leaf,
To the broad ocean and the azure heavens
Spangled with kindred multitudes of stars,
Could find no surface where its power might sleep;
Which spake perpetual logic to my soul,
And by an unrelenting agency
Did bind my feelings even as in a chain.

    And here, O Friend! have I retraced my life 170
Up to an eminence, and told a tale
Of matters which not falsely may be called
The glory of my youth. Of genius, power,
Creation and divinity itself
I have been speaking, for my theme has been
What has passed within me. Not of outward things
Done visibly for other minds, words, signs,
Symbols or actions, but of my own heart
Have I been speaking, and my youthful mind.
O Heavens! how awful is the might of souls, 180

And what they do within themselves while yet
The yoke of earth is new to them, the world
Nothing but a wild field where they were sown.
This is, in truth, heroic argument,
This genuine prowess, which I wished to touch
With hand however weak, but in the main
It lies far hidden from the reach of words.
Points have we all of us within our souls
Where all stand single; this I feel, and make
Breathings for incommunicable powers;   **190**
But is not each a memory to himself,
And, therefore, now that we must quit this theme,
I am not heartless, for there's not a man
That lives who hath not known his god-like hours,
And feels not what an empire we inherit
As natural beings in the strength of Nature.

  No more: for now into a populous plain
We must descend. A Traveller I am,
Whose tale is only of himself; even so,
So be it, if the pure of heart be prompt   **200**
To follow, and if thou, my honoured Friend!
Who in these thoughts art ever at my side,
Support, as heretofore, my fainting steps.

  It hath been told, that when the first delight
That flashed upon me from this novel show
Had failed, the mind returned into herself;
Yet true it is, that I had made a change
In climate, and my nature's outward coat
Changed also slowly and insensibly.
Full oft the quiet and exalted thoughts   **210**
Of loneliness gave way to empty noise
And superficial pastimes; now and then
Forced labour, and more frequently forced hopes;

And, worst of all, a treasonable growth
Of indecisive judgments, that impaired
And shook the mind's simplicity. — And yet
This was a gladsome time. Could I behold —
Who, less insensible than sodden clay
In a sea-river's bed at ebb of tide,
Could have beheld — with undelighted heart,   220
So many happy youths, so wide and fair
A congregation in its budding-time
Of health, and hope, and beauty, all at once
So many divers samples from the growth
Of life's sweet season — could have seen unmoved
That miscellaneous garland of wild flowers
Decking the matron temples of a place
So famous through the world? To me, at least,
It was a goodly prospect: for, in sooth,
Though I had learnt betimes to stand unpropped,   230
And independent musings pleased me so
That spells seemed on me when I was alone,
Yet could I only cleave to solitude
In lonely places; if a throng was near
That way I leaned by nature; for my heart
Was social, and loved idleness and joy.

Not seeking those who might participate
My deeper pleasures (nay, I had not once,
Though not unused to mutter lonesome songs,
Even with myself divided such delight,   240
Or looked that way for aught that might be clothed
In human language), easily I passed
From the remembrances of better things,
And slipped into the ordinary works
Of careless youth, unburthened, unalarmed.
Caverns there were within my mind which sun
Could never penetrate, yet did there not

Want store of leafy *arbours* where the light
Might enter in at will. Companionships,
Friendships, acquaintances, were welcome all.   250
We sauntered, played, or rioted; we talked
Unprofitable talk at morning hours;
Drifted about along the streets and walks,
Read lazily in trivial books, went forth
To gallop through the country in blind zeal
Of senseless horsemanship, or on the breast
Of Cam sailed boisterously, and let the stars
Come forth, perhaps without one quiet thought.

  Such was the tenor of the second act
In this new life. Imagination slept,   260
And yet not utterly. I could not print
Ground where the grass had yielded to the steps
Of generations of illustrious men,
Unmoved. I could not always lightly pass
Through the same gateways, sleep where they had slept,
Wake where they waked, range that inclosure old,
That garden of great intellects, undisturbed.
Place also by the side of this dark sense
Of noble feeling, that those spiritual men,
Even the great Newton's own ethereal self,   270
Seemed humbled in these precincts, thence to be
The more endeared. Their several memories here
(Even like their persons in their portraits clothed
With the accustomed garb of daily life)
Put on a lowly and a touching grace
Of more distinct humanity, that left
All genuine admiration unimpaired.

  Beside the pleasant Mill of Trompington
I laughed with Chaucer in the hawthorn shade;
Heard him, while birds were warbling, tell his tales   280

Of amorous passion. And that gentle Bard,
Chosen by the Muses for their Page of State —
Sweet Spenser, moving through his clouded heaven
With the moon's beauty and the moon's soft pace,
I called him Brother, Englishman, and Friend!
Yea, our blind Poet, who in his later day,
Stood almost single; uttering odious truth —
Darkness before, and danger's voice behind,
Soul awful — if the earth has ever lodged
An awful soul — I seemed to see him here   290
Familiarly, and in his scholar's dress
Bounding before me, yet a stripling youth —
A boy, no better, with his rosy cheeks
Angelical, keen eye, courageous look,
And conscious step of purity and pride.
Among the band of my compeers was one
Whom chance had stationed in the very room
Honoured by Milton's name. O temperate Bard!
Be it confest that, for the first time, seated
Within thy innocent lodge and oratory,   300
One of a festive circle, I poured out
Libations, to thy memory drank, till pride
And gratitude grew dizzy in a brain
Never excited by the fumes of wine
Before that hour, or since. Then, forth I ran
From the assembly; through a length of streets,
Ran, ostrich-like, to reach our chapel door
In not a desperate or opprobious time,
Albeit long after the importunate bell
Had stopped, with wearisome Cassandra voice   310
No longer haunting the dark winter night.
Call back, O Friend! a moment to thy mind,
The place itself and fashion of the rites.
With careless ostentation shouldering up
My surplice, through the inferior throng I clove

Of the plain Burghers, who in audience stood
On the last skirts of their permitted ground,
Under the pealing organ. Empty thoughts!
I am ashamed of them: and that great Bard,
And thou, O Friend! who in thy ample mind   320
Hast placed me high above my best deserts,
Ye will forgive the weakness of that hour,
In some of its unworthy vanities,
Brother to many more.

            In this mixed sort
The months passed on, remissly, not given up
To wilful alienation from the right,
Or walks of open scandal, but in vague
And loose indifference, easy likings, aims
Of a low pitch — duty and zeal dismissed,
Yet Nature, or a happy course of things   330
Not doing in their stead the needful work.
The memory languidly revolved, the heart
Reposed in noontide rest, the inner pulse
Of contemplation almost failed to beat.
Such life might not inaptly be compared
To a floating island, an amphibious spot
Unsound, of spongy texture, yet withal
Not wanting a fair face of water weeds
And pleasant flowers. The thirst of living praise,
Fit reverence for the glorious Dead, the sight   340
Of those long vistas, sacred catacombs,
Where mighty *minds* lie visibly entombed,
Have often stirred the heart of youth, and bred
A fervent love of rigorous discipline. —
Alas! such high emotion touched not me.
Look was there none within these walls to shame
My easy spirits, and discountenance
Their light composure, far less to instil
A calm resolve of mind, firmly addressed

To puissant efforts. Nor was this the blame 350
Of others but my own; I should, in truth,
As far as doth concern my single self,
Misdeem most widely, lodging it elsewhere:
For I, bred up 'mid Nature's luxuries,
Was a spoiled child, and, rambling like the wind,
As I had done in daily intercourse
With those crystalline rivers, solemn heights,
And mountains, ranging like a fowl of the air,
I was ill-tutored for captivity;
To quit my pleasure, and, from month to month, 360
Take up a station calmly on the perch
Of sedentary peace. Those lovely forms
Had also left less space within my mind,
Which, wrought upon instinctively, had found
A freshness in those objects of her love,
A winning power, beyond all other power.
Not that I slighted books, — that were to lack
All sense, — but other passions in me ruled,
Passions more fervent, making me less prompt
To in-door study than was wise or well, 370
Or suited to those years. Yet I, though used
In magisterial liberty to rove,
Culling such flowers of learning as might tempt
A random choice, could shadow forth a place
(If now I yield not to a flattering dream)
Whose studious aspect should have bent me down
To instantaneous service; should at once
Have made me pay to science and to arts
And written lore, acknowledged my liege lord,
A homage frankly offered up, like that 380
Which I had paid to Nature. Toil and pains
In this recess, by thoughtful Fancy built,
Should spread from heart to heart; and stately groves,
Majestic edifices, should not want

A corresponding dignity within.
The congregating temper that pervades
Our unripe years, not wasted, should be taught
To minister to works of high attempt —
Works which the enthusiast would perform with love.
Youth should be awed, religiously possessed   390
With a conviction of the power that waits
On knowledge, when sincerely sought and prized
For its own sake, on glory and on praise
If but by labour won, and fit to endure
The passing day; should learn to put aside
Her trappings here, should strip them off abashed
Before antiquity and stedfast truth
And strong book-mindedness; and over all
A healthy sound simplicity should reign,
A seemly plainness, name it what you will,   400
Republican or pious.
                                    If these thoughts
Are a gratuitous emblazonry
That mocks the recreant age *we* live in, then
Be Folly and False-seeming free to affect
Whatever formal gait of discipline
Shall raise them highest in their own esteem —
Let them parade among the Schools at will,
But spare the House of God. Was ever known
The witless shepherd who persists to drive
A flock that thirsts not to a pool disliked?   410
A weight must surely hang on days begun
And ended with such mockery. Be wise,
Ye Presidents and Deans, and, till the spirit
Of ancient times revive, and youth be trained
At home in pious service, to your bells
Give seasonable rest, for 't is a sound
Hollow as ever vexed the tranquil air;
And your officious doings bring disgrace

On the plain steeples of our English Church,
Whose worship, 'mid remotest village trees,   420
Suffers for this. Even Science, too, at hand
In daily sight of this irreverence,
Is smitten thence with an unnatural taint,
Loses her just authority, falls beneath
Collateral suspicion, else unknown.
This truth escaped me not, and I confess,
That having 'mid my native hills given loose
To a schoolboy's vision, I had raised a pile
Upon the basis of the coming time,
That fell in ruins round me. Oh, what joy   430
To see a sanctuary for our country's youth
Informed with such a spirit as might be
Its own protection; a primeval grove,
Where, though the shades with cheerfulness were filled,
Nor indigent of songs warbled from crowds
In under-coverts, yet the countenance
Of the whole place should bear a stamp of awe;
A habitation sober and demure
For ruminating creatures; a domain
For quiet things to wander in; a haunt   440
In which the heron should delight to feed
By the shy rivers, and the pelican
Upon the cypress spire in lonely thought
Might sit and sun himself. — Alas! Alas!
In vain for such solemnity I looked;
Mine eyes were crossed by butterflies, ears vexed
By chattering popinjays; the inner heart
Seemed trivial, and the impresses without
Of a too gaudy region.
                    Different sight
Those venerable Doctors saw of old,   450
When all who dwelt within these famous walls
Led in abstemiousness a studious life;

When, in forlorn and naked chambers cooped
And crowded, o'er the ponderous books they hung
Like caterpillars eating out their way
In silence, or with keen devouring noise
Not to be tracked or fathered. Princes then
At matins froze, and couched at curfew-time,
Trained up through piety and zeal to prize
Spare diet, patient labour, and plain weeds.   460
O seat of Arts! renowned throughout the world!
Far different service in those homely days
The Muses' modest nurslings underwent
From their first childhood: in that glorious time
When Learning, like a stranger come from far,
Sounding through Christian lands her trumpets, roused
Peasant and king; when boys and youths, the growth
Of raggèd villages and crazy huts,
Forsook their homes, and, errant in the quest
Of Patron, famous school or friendly nook,   470
Where, pensioned, they in shelter might sit down,
From town to town and through wide scattered realms
Journeyed with ponderous folios in their hands;
And often, starting from some covert place,
Saluted the chance comer on the road,
Crying, "An obolus, a penny give
To a poor scholar!" — when illustrious men,
Lovers of truth, by penury constrained,
Bucer, Erasmus, or Melancthon, read
Before the doors or windows of their cells   480
By moonshine through mere lack of taper light.

    But peace to vain regrets! We see but darkly
Even when we look behind us, and best things
Are not so pure by nature that they needs
Must keep to all, as fondly all believe,
Their highest promise. If the mariner,

When at reluctant distance he hath passed
Some tempting island, could but know the ills
That must have fallen upon him had he brought
His bark to land upon the wished-for shore,   490
Good cause would oft be his to thank the surf
Whose white belt scared him thence, or wind that blew
Inexorably adverse: for myself
I grieve not; happy is the gownèd youth,
Who only misses what I missed, who falls
No lower than I fell.
                                        I did not love,
Judging not ill perhaps, the timid course
Of our scholastic studies; could have wished
To see the river flow with ampler range
And freer pace; but more, far more, I grieved   500
To see displayed among an eager few,
Who in the field of contest persevered,
Passions unworthy of youth's generous heart
And mounting spirit, pitiably repaid,
When so disturbed, whatever palms are won.
From these I turned to travel with the shoal
Of more unthinking natures, easy minds
And pillowy; yet not wanting love that makes
The day pass lightly on, when foresight sleeps,
And wisdom and the pledges interchanged   510
With our own inner being are forgot.

   Yet was this deep vacation not given up
To utter waste. Hitherto I had stood
In my own mind remote from social life,
(At least from what we commonly so name,)
Like a lone shepherd on a promontory,
Who lacking occupation looks far forth
Into the boundless sea, and rather makes
Than finds what he beholds. And sure it is,

That this first transit from the smooth delights   520
And wild outlandish walks of simple youth
To something that resembles an approach
Towards human business, to a privileged world
Within a world, a midway residence
With all its intervenient imagery,
Did better suit my visionary mind,
Far better, than to have been bolted forth,
Thrust out abruptly into Fortune's way
Among the conflicts of substantial life;
By a more just gradation did lead on   530
To higher things; more naturally matured,
For permanent possession, better fruits,
Whether of truth or virtue, to ensue.
In serious mood, but oftener, I confess,
With playful zest of fancy, did we note
(How could we less?) the manners and the ways
Of those who lived distinguished by the badge
Of good or ill report; or those with whom
By frame of Academic discipline
We were perforce connected, men whose sway   540
And known authority of office served
To set our minds on edge, and did no more.
Nor wanted we rich pastime of this kind,
Found everywhere, but chiefly in the ring
Of the grave Elders, men unscoured, grotesque
In character, tricked out like aged trees
Which through the lapse of their infirmity
Give ready place to any random seed
·That chooses to be reared upon their trunks.

  Here on my view, confronting vividly   550
Those shepherd swains whom I had lately left
Appeared a different aspect of old age;
How different! yet both distinctly marked,

Objects embossed to catch the general eye,
Or portraitures for special use designed,
As some might seem, so aptly do they serve
To illustrate Nature's book of rudiments —
That book upheld as with maternal care
When she would enter on her tender scheme
Of teaching comprehension with delight,   560
And mingling playful with pathetic thoughts.

   The surfaces of artificial life
And manners finely wrought, the delicate race
Of colours, lurking, gleaming up and down
Through that state arras woven with silk and gold;
This wily interchange of snaky hues,
Willingly or unwillingly revealed,
I neither knew nor cared for; and as such
Were wanting here, I took what might be found
Of less elaborate fabric. At this day   570
I smile, in many a mountain solitude
Conjuring up scenes as obsolete in freaks
Of character, in points of wit as broad,
As aught by wooden images performed
For entertainment of the gaping crowd
At wake or fair. And oftentimes do flit
Remembrances before me of old men —
Old humourists, who have been long in their graves,
And having almost in my mind put off
Their human names, have into phantoms passed   580
Of texture midway between life and books.

   I play the loiterer: 't is enough to note
That here in dwarf proportions were expressed
The limbs of the great world; its eager strifes
Collaterally pourtrayed, as in mock fight,

A tournament of blows, some hardly dealt
Though short of mortal combat; and whate'er
Might in this pageant be supposed to hit
An artless rustic's notice, this way less,
More that way, was not wasted upon me —   590
And yet the spectacle may well demand
A more substantial name, no mimic show,
Itself a living part of a live whole,
A creek in the vast sea; for, all degrees
And shapes of spurious fame and short-lived praise
Here sate in state, and fed with daily alms
Retainers won away from solid good;
And here was Labour, his own bond-slave; Hope,
That never set the pains against the prize;
Idleness halting with his weary clog,   600
And poor misguided Shame, and witless Fear,
And simple Pleasure foraging for Death;
Honour misplaced, and Dignity astray;
Feuds, factions, flatteries, enmity, and guile,
Murmuring submission, and bald government,
(The idol weak as the idolater),
And Decency and Custom starving Truth,
And blind Authority beating with his staff
The child that might have led him; Emptiness
Followed as of good omen, and meek Worth   610
Left to herself unheard of and unknown.

Of these and other kindred notices
I cannot say what portion is in truth
The naked recollection of that time,
And what may rather have been called to life
By after-meditation. But delight
That, in an easy temper lulled asleep,
Is still with Innocence its own reward,
This was not wanting. Carelessly I roamed

As through a wide museum from whose stores　620
A casual rarity is singled out
And has its brief perusal, then gives way
To others, all supplanted in their turn;
Till 'mid this crowded neighbourhood of things
That are by nature most unneighbourly,
The head turns round and cannot right itself;
And though an aching and a barren sense
Of gay confusion still be uppermost,
With few wise longings and but little love,
Yet to the memory something cleaves at last,　630
Whence profit may be drawn in times to come.

　Thus in submissive idleness, my Friend!
The labouring time of autumn, winter, spring,
Eight months! rolled pleasingly away; the ninth
Came and returned me to my native hills.

BOOK FOURTH

SUMMER VACATION

Bright was the summer's noon when quickening steps
Followed each other till a dreary moor
Was crossed, a bare ridge clomb, upon whose top
Standing alone, as from a rampart's edge,
I overlooked the bed of Windermere,
Like a vast river, stretching in the sun.
With exultation, at my feet I saw
Lake, islands, promontories, gleaming bays,
A universe of Nature's fairest forms
Proudly revealed with instantaneous burst,　10
Magnificent, and beautiful, and gay.
I bounded down the hill shouting amain

For the old Ferryman; to the shout the rocks
Replied, and when the Charon of the flood
Had staid his oars, and touched the jutting pier,
I did not step into the well-known boat
Without a cordial greeting. Thence with speed
Up the familiar hill I took my way
Towards that sweet Valley where I had been reared;
'T was but a short hour's walk, ere veering round   20
I saw the snow-white church upon her hill
Sit like a thronèd Lady, sending out
A gracious look all over her domain.
Yon azure smoke betrays the lurking town;
With eager footsteps I advance and reach
The cottage threshold where my journey closed.
Glad welcome had I, with some tears, perhaps,
From my old Dame, so kind and motherly,
While she perused me with a parent's pride.
The thoughts of gratitude shall fall like dew   30
Upon thy grave, good creature! While my heart
Can beat never will I forget thy name.
Heaven's blessing be upon thee where thou liest
After thy innocent and busy stir
In narrow cares, thy little daily growth
Of calm enjoyments, after eighty years,
And more than eighty, of untroubled life;
Childless, yet by the strangers to thy blood
Honoured with little less than filial love.
What joy was mine to see thee once again,   40
Thee and thy dwelling, and a crowd of things
About its narrow precincts all beloved,
And many of them seeming yet my own!
Why should I speak of what a thousand hearts
Have felt, and every man alive can guess?
The rooms, the court, the garden were not left
Long unsaluted, nor the sunny seat

Round the stone table under the dark pine,
Friendly to studious or to festive hours;
Nor that unruly child of mountain birth,   56
The famous brook, who, soon as he was boxed
Within our garden, found himself at once,
As if by trick insidious and unkind,
Stripped of his voice and left to dimple down
(Without an effort and without a will)
A channel paved by man's officious care.
I looked at him and smiled, and smiled again,
And in the press of twenty thousand thoughts,
"Ha," quoth I, "pretty prisoner, are you there?"
Well might sarcastic Fancy then have whispered,   60
"An emblem here behold of thy own life;
In its late course of even days with all
Their smooth enthralment;" but the heart was full,
Too full for that reproach. My aged Dame
Walked proudly at my side: she guided me;
I willing, nay — nay, wishing to be led.
— The face of every neighbour whom I met
Was like a volume to me; some were hailed
Upon the road, some busy at their work,
Unceremonious greetings interchanged   70
With half the length of a long field between.
Among my schoolfellows I scattered round
Like recognitions, but with some constraint
Attended, doubtless, with a little pride,
But with more shame, for my habiliments,
The transformation wrought by gay attire.
Not less delighted did I take my place
At our domestic table: and, dear Friend!
In this endeavour simply to relate
A Poet's history, may I leave untold   80
The thankfulness with which I laid me down
In my accustomed bed, more welcome now

Perhaps than if it had been more desired
Or been more often thought of with regret;
That lowly bed whence I had heard the wind
Roar, and the rain beat hard; where I so oft
Had lain awake on summer nights to watch
The moon in splendour couched among the leaves
Of a tall ash, that near our cottage stood;
Had watched her with fixed eyes while to and fro   90
In the dark summit of the waving tree
She rocked with every impulse of the breeze.

    Among the favourites whom it pleased me well
To see again, was one by ancient right
Our inmate, a rough terrier of the hills;
By birth and call of nature pre-ordained
To hunt the badger and unearth the fox
Among the impervious crags, but having been
From youth our own adopted, he had passed
Into a gentler service. And when first   100
The boyish spirit flagged, and day by day
Along my veins I kindled with the stir,
The fermentation, and the vernal heat
Of poesy, affecting private shades
Like a sick Lover, then this dog was used
To watch me, an attendant and a friend,
Obsequious to my steps early and late,
Though often of such dilatory walk
Tired, and uneasy at the halts I made.
A hundred times when, roving high and low,   110
I have been harassed with the toil of verse,
Much pains and little progress, and at once
Some lovely Image in the song rose up
Full-formed, like Venus rising from the sea;
Then have I darted forwards to let loose
My hand upon his back with stormy joy,

Caressing him again and yet again.
And when at evening on the public way
I sauntered, like a river murmuring
And talking to itself when all things else   120
Are still, the creature trotted on before;
Such was his custom; but whene'er he met
A passenger approaching, he would turn
To give me timely notice, and straightway,
Grateful for that admonishment, I hushed
My voice, composed my gait, and, with the air
And mien of one whose thoughts are free, advanced
To give and take a greeting that might save
My name from piteous rumours, such as wait
On men suspected to be crazed in brain.   130

Those walks well worthy to be prized and loved —
Regretted! — that word, too, was on my tongue,
But they were richly laden with all good,
And cannot be remembered but with thanks
And gratitude, and perfect joy of heart —
Those walks in all their freshness now came back
Like a returning Spring.   When first I made
Once more the circuit of our little lake,
If ever happiness hath lodged with man,
That day consummate happiness was mine,   140
Wide-spreading, steady, calm, contemplative.
The sun was set, or setting, when I left
Our cottage door, and evening soon brought on
A sober hour, not winning or serene,
For cold and raw the air was, and untuned:
But as a face we love is sweetest then
When sorrow damps it, or, whatever look
It chance to wear, is sweetest if the heart
Have fulness in herself; even so with me
It fared that evening.   Gently did my soul   150

Put off her veil, and, self-transmuted, stood
Naked, as in the presence of her God.
While on I walked, a comfort seemed to touch
A heart that had not been disconsolate:
Strength came where weakness was not known to be,
At least not felt; and restoration came
Like an intruder knocking at the door
Of unacknowledged weariness. I took
The balance, and with firm hand weighed myself.
— Of that external scene which round me lay,   160
Little, in this abstraction, did I see;
Remembered less; but I had inward hopes
And swellings of the spirit, was rapt and soothed,
Conversed with promises, had glimmering views
How life pervades the undecaying mind;
How the immortal soul with God-like power
Informs, creates, and thaws the deepest sleep
That time can lay upon her; how on earth,
Man, if he do but live within the light
Of high endeavours, daily spreads abroad   170
His being armed with strength that cannot fail.
Nor was there want of milder thoughts, of love,
Of innocence, and holiday repose;
And more than pastoral quiet, 'mid the stir
Of boldest projects, and a peaceful end
At last, or glorious, by endurance won.
Thus musing, in a wood I sate me down
Alone, continuing there to muse: the slopes
And heights meanwhile were slowly overspread
With darkness, and before a rippling breeze   180
The long lake lengthened out its hoary line,
And in the sheltered coppice where I sate,
Around me from among the hazel leaves,
Now here, now there, moved by the straggling wind,
Came ever and anon a breath-like sound,

Quick as the pantings of the faithful dog,
The off and on companion of my walk;
And such, at times, believing them to be,
I turned my head to look if he were there;
Then into solemn thought I passed once more.   190

   A freshness also found I at this time
In human Life, the daily life of those
Whose occupations really I loved;
The peaceful scene oft filled me with surprise
Changed like a garden in the heat of spring
After an eight-days' absence. For (to omit
The things which were the same and yet appeared
Far otherwise) amid this rural solitude,
A narrow Vale where each was known to all,
'T was not indifferent to a youthful mind   200
To mark some sheltering bower or sunny nook
Where an old man had used to sit alone,
Now vacant; pale-faced babes whom I had left
In arms, now rosy prattlers at the feet
Of a pleased grandame tottering up and down;
And growing girls whose beauty, filched away
With all its pleasant promises, was gone
To deck some slighted playmate's homely cheek.

   Yes, I had something of a subtler sense,
And often looking round was moved to smiles   210
Such as a delicate work of humour breeds;
I read, without design, the opinions, thoughts,
Of those plain-living people now observed
With clearer knowledge; with another eye
I saw the quiet woodman in the woods,
The shepherd roam the hills. With new delight,
This chiefly, did I note my grey-haired Dame;
Saw her go forth to church or other work

Of state equipped in monumental trim;
Short velvet cloak, (her bonnet of the like),   220
A mantle such as Spanish Cavaliers
Wore in old times. Her smooth domestic life,
Affectionate without disquietude,
Her talk, her business, pleased me; and no less
Her clear though shallow stream of piety
That ran on Sabbath days a fresher course;
With thoughts unfelt till now I saw her read
Her Bible on hot Sunday afternoons,
And loved the book, when she had dropped asleep
And made of it a pillow for her head.   230

   Nor less do I remember to have felt,
Distinctly manifested at this time,
A human-heartedness about my love
For objects hitherto the absolute wealth
Of my own private being and no more;
Which I had loved, even as a blessed spirit
Or Angel, if he were to dwell on earth,
Might love in individual happiness.
But now there opened on me other thoughts
Of change, congratulation or regret,   240
A pensive feeling! It spread far and wide;
The trees, the mountains shared it, and the brooks,
The stars of Heaven, now seen in their old haunts —
White Sirius glittering o'er the southern crags,
Orion with his belt, and those fair Seven,
Acquaintances of every little child,
And Jupiter, my own belovèd star!
Whatever shadings of mortality,
Whatever imports from the world of death
Had come among these objects heretofore,   250
Were, in the main, of mood less tender: strong,
Deep, gloomy were they, and severe; the scatterings

Of awe or tremulous dread, that had given way
In later youth to yearnings of a love
Enthusiastic, to delight and hope.

    As one who hangs down-bending from the side
Of a slow-moving boat, upon the breast
Of a still water, solacing himself
With such discoveries as his eye can make
Beneath him in the bottom of the deep,   260
Sees many beauteous sights — weeds, fishes, flowers,
Grots, pebbles, roots of trees, and fancies more,
Yet often is perplexed, and cannot part
The shadow from the substance, rocks and sky,
Mountains and clouds, reflected in the depth
Of the clear flood, from things which there abide
In their true dwelling; now is crossed by gleam
Of his own image, by a sunbeam now,
And wavering motions sent he knows not whence,
Impediments that make his task more sweet;   270
Such pleasant office have we long pursued
Incumbent o'er the surface of past time
With like success, nor often have appeared
Shapes fairer or less doubtfully discerned
Than these to which the Tale, indulgent Friend!
Would now direct thy notice. Yet in spite
Of pleasure won, and knowledge not withheld,
There was an inner falling off — I loved,
Loved deeply all that had been loved before,
More deeply even than ever: but a swarm   280
Of heady schemes jostling each other, gawds,
And feast and dance, and public revelry,
And sports and games (too grateful in themselves,
Yet in themselves less grateful, I believe,
Than as they were a badge glossy and fresh
Of manliness and freedom) all conspired

To lure my mind from firm habitual quest
Of feeding pleasures, to depress the zeal
And damp those yearnings which had once been mine —
A wild, unworldly-minded youth, given up   290
To his own eager thoughts. It would demand
Some skill, and longer time than may be spared
To paint these vanities, and how they wrought
In haunts where they, till now, had been unknown.
It seemed the very garments that I wore
Preyed on my strength, and stopped the quiet stream
Of self-forgetfulness.

                Yes, that heartless chase
Of trivial pleasures was a poor exchange
For books and nature at that early age.
'T is true, some casual knowledge might be gained   300
Of character or life; but at that time,
Of manners put to school I took small note,
And all my deeper passions lay elsewhere.
Far better had it been to exalt the mind
By solitary study, to uphold
Intense desire through meditative peace;
And yet, for chastisement of these regrets,
The memory of one particular hour
Doth here rise up against me. 'Mid a throng
Of maids and youths, old men, and matrons staid,   310
A medley of all tempers, I had passed
The night in dancing, gaiety, and mirth,
With din of instruments and shuffling feet,
And glancing forms, and tapers glittering,
And unaimed prattle flying up and down;
Spirits upon the stretch, and here and there
Slight shocks of young love-liking interspersed,
Whose transient pleasure mounted to the head,
And tingled through the veins. Ere we retired,
The cock had crowed, and now the eastern sky   320

Was kindling, not unseen, from humble copse
And open field, through which the pathway wound,
And homeward led my steps.   Magnificent
The morning rose, in memorable pomp,
Glorious as e'er I had beheld — in front,
The sea lay laughing at a distance; near,
The solid mountains shone, bright as the clouds,
Grain-tinctured, drenched in empyrean light;
And in the meadows and the lower grounds
Was all the sweetness of a common dawn —   330
Dews, vapours, and the melody of birds,
And labourers going forth to till the fields.
Ah! need I say, dear Friend! that to the brim
My heart was full; I made no vows, but vows
Were then made for me; bond unknown to me
Was given, that I should be, else sinning greatly,
A dedicated Spirit.   On I walked
In thankful blessedness, which yet survives.

    Strange rendezvous!   My mind was at that time
A parti-coloured show of grave and gay,   340
Solid and light, short-sighted and profound;
Of inconsiderate habits and sedate,
Consorting in one mansion unreproved.
The worth I knew of powers that I possessed,
Though slighted and too oft misused.   Besides,
That summer, swarming as it did with thoughts
Transient and idle, lacked not intervals
When Folly from the frown of fleeting Time
Shrunk, and the mind experienced in herself
Conformity as just as that of old   350
To the end and written spirit of God's works,
Whether held forth in Nature or in Man,
Through pregnant vision, separate or conjoined.

When from our better selves we have too long
Been parted by the hurrying world, and droop,
Sick of its business, of its pleasures tired,
How gracious, how benign, is Solitude;
How potent a mere image of her sway;
Most potent when impressed upon the mind
With an appropriate human centre — hermit,   360
Deep in the bosom of the wilderness;
Votary (in vast cathedral, where no foot
Is treading, where no other face is seen)
Kneeling at prayers; or watchman on the top
Of lighthouse, beaten by Atlantic waves;
Or as the soul of that great Power is met
Sometimes embodied on a public road,
When, for the night deserted, it assumes
A character of quiet more profound
Than pathless wastes.
              Once, when those summer months
Were flown, and autumn brought its annual show
Of oars with oars contending, sails with sails,
Upon Winander's spacious breast, it chanced
That — after I had left a flower-decked room
(Whose in-door pastime, lighted up, survived
To a late hour), and spirits overwrought
Were making night do penance for a day
Spent in a round of strenuous idleness —
My homeward course led up a long ascent,
Where the road's watery surface, to the top   380
Of that sharp rising, glittered to the moon
And bore the semblance of another stream
Stealing with silent lapse to join the brook
That murmured in the vale. All else was still;
No living thing appeared in earth or air,
And, save the flowing water's peaceful voice,
Sound there was none — but, lo! an uncouth shape,

Shown by a sudden turning of the road,
So near that, slipping back into the shade
Of a thick hawthorn, I could mark him well, 390
Myself unseen. He was of stature tall,
A span above man's common measure, tall,
Stiff, lank, and upright; a more meagre man
Was never seen before by night or day.
Long were his arms, pallid his hands; his mouth
Looked ghastly in the moonlight: from behind,
A mile-stone propped him; I could also ken
That he was clothed in military garb,
Though faded, yet entire. Companionless,
No dog attending, by no staff sustained, 400
He stood, and in his very dress appeared
A desolation, a simplicity,
To which the trappings of a gaudy world
Make a strange back-ground. From his lips, ere long,
Issued low muttered sounds, as if of pain
Or some uneasy thought; yet still his form
Kept the same awful steadiness — at his feet
His shadow lay, and moved not. From self-blame
Not wholly free, I watched him thus; at length
Subduing my heart's specious cowardice, 410
I left the shady nook where I had stood
And hailed him. Slowly from his resting-place
He rose, and with a lean and wasted arm
In measured gesture lifted to his head
Returned my salutation; then resumed
His station as before; and when I asked
His history, the veteran, in reply,
Was neither slow nor eager; but, unmoved,
And with a quiet uncomplaining voice,
A stately air of mild indifference, 420
He told in few plain words a soldier's tale —
That in the Tropic Islands he had served,

Whence he had landed scarcely three weeks past;
That on his landing he had been dismissed,
And now was travelling towards his native home.
This heard, I said, in pity, "Come with me."
He stooped, and straightway from the ground took up
An oaken staff by me yet unobserved —
A staff which must have dropped from his slack hand
And lay till now neglected in the grass.   430
Though weak his step and cautious, he appeared
To travel without pain, and I beheld,
With an astonishment but ill suppressed,
His ghostly figure moving at my side;
Nor could I, while we journeyed thus, forbear
To turn from present hardships to the past,
And speak of war, battle, and pestilence,
Sprinkling this talk with questions, better spared,
On what he might himself have seen or felt.
He all the while was in demeanour calm,   440
Concise in answer; solemn and sublime
He might have seemed, but that in all he said
There was a strange half-absence, as of one
Knowing too well the importance of his theme,
But feeling it no longer.   Our discourse
Soon ended, and together on we passed
In silence through a wood gloomy and still.
Up-turning, then, along an open field,
We reached a cottage.   At the door I knocked,
And earnestly to charitable care   450
Commended him as a poor friendless man,
Belated and by sickness overcome.
Assured that now the traveller would repose
In comfort, I entreated that henceforth
He would not linger in the public ways,
But ask for timely furtherance and help
Such as his state required.   At this reproof,

With the same ghastly mildness in his look,
He said, "My trust is in the God of Heaven,
And in the eye of him who passes me!"   460

   The cottage door was speedily unbarred,
And now the soldier touched his hat once more
With his lean hand, and in a faltering voice,
Whose tone bespake reviving interests
Till then unfelt, he thanked me; I returned
The farewell blessing of the patient man,
And so we parted. Back I cast a look,
And lingered near the door a little space,
Then sought with quiet heart my distant home.

BOOK FIFTH

BOOKS

When Contemplation, like the night-calm felt
Through earth and sky, spreads widely, and sends deep
Into the soul its tranquillising power,
Even then I sometimes grieve for thee, O Man,
Earth's paramount Creature! not so much for woes
That thou endurest; heavy though that weight be,
Cloud-like it mounts, or touched with light divine
Doth melt away; but for those palms achieved
Through length of time, by patient exercise
Of study and hard thought; there, there, it is   10
That sadness finds its fuel.   Hitherto,
In progress through this Verse, my mind hath looked
Upon the speaking face of earth and heaven
As her prime teacher, intercourse with man
Established by the sovereign Intellect,
Who through that bodily image hath diffused,
As might appear to the eye of fleeting time,

A deathless spirit.　Thou also, man! hast wrought,
For commerce of thy nature with herself,
Things that aspire to unconquerable life;　　　　20
And yet we feel — we cannot choose but feel —
That they must perish.　Tremblings of the heart
It gives, to think that our immortal being
No more shall need such garments; and yet man,
As long as he shall be the child of earth,
Might almost "weep to have" what he may lose,
Nor be himself extinguished, but survive,
Abject, depressed, forlorn, disconsolate.
A thought is with me sometimes, and I say, —
Should the whole frame of earth by inward throes　30
Be wrenched, or fire come down from far to scorch
Her pleasant habitations, and dry up
Old Ocean, in his bed left singed and bare,
Yet would the living Presence still subsist
Victorious, and composure would ensue,
And kindlings like the morning — presage sure
Of day returning and of life revived.
But all the meditations of mankind,
Yea, all the adamantine holds of truth
By reason built, or passion, which itself　　　　40
Is highest reason in a soul sublime;
The consecrated works of Bard and Sage,
Sensuous or intellectual, wrought by men,
Twin labourers and heirs of the same hopes;
Where would they be?　Oh! why hath not the Mind
Some element to stamp her image on
In nature somewhat nearer to her own?
Why, gifted with such powers to send abroad
Her spirit, must it lodge in shrines so frail?

　　One day, when from my lips a like complaint　　50
Had fallen in presence of a studious friend,

He with a smile made answer, that in truth
'T was going far to seek disquietude;
But on the front of his reproof confessed
That he himself had oftentimes given way
To kindred hauntings.   Whereupon I told,
That once in the stillness of a summer's noon,
While I was seated in a rocky cave
By the sea-side, perusing, so it chanced,
The famous history of the errant knight   60
Recorded by Cervantes, these same thoughts
Beset me, and to height unusual rose,
While listlessly I sate, and, having closed
The book, had turned my eyes toward the wide sea.
On poetry and geometric truth,
And their high privilege of lasting life,
From all internal injury exempt,
I mused; upon these chiefly: and at length,
My senses yielding to the sultry air,
Sleep seized me, and I passed into a dream.   70
I saw before me stretched a boundless plain
Of sandy wilderness, all black and void,
And as I looked around, distress and fear
Came creeping over me, when at my side,
Close at my side, an uncouth shape appeared
Upon a dromedary, mounted high.
He seemed an Arab of the Bedouin tribes:
A lance he bore, and underneath one arm
A stone, and in the opposite hand a shell
Of a surpassing brightness.   At the sight   80
Much I rejoiced, not doubting but a guide
Was present, one who with unerring skill
Would through the desert lead me; and while yet
I looked and looked, self-questioned what this freight
Which the new-comer carried through the waste
Could mean, the Arab told me that the stone

(To give it in the language of the dream)
Was "Euclid's Elements," and "This," said he,
"Is something of more worth;" and at the word
Stretched forth the shell, so beautiful in shape,   90
In colour so resplendent, with command
That I should hold it to my ear.   I did so,
And heard that instant in an unknown tongue,
Which yet I understood, articulate sounds,
A loud prophetic blast of harmony;
An Ode, in passion uttered, which foretold
Destruction to the children of the earth
By deluge, now at hand.   No sooner ceased
The song, than the Arab with calm look declared
That all would come to pass of which the voice   100
Had given forewarning, and that he himself
Was going then to bury those two books:
The one that held acquaintance with the stars,
And wedded soul to soul in purest bond
Of reason, undisturbed by space or time;
The other that was a god, yea many gods,
Had voices more than all the winds, with power
To exhilarate the spirit, and to soothe,
Through every clime, the heart of human kind.
While this was uttering, strange as it may seem,   110
I wondered not, although I plainly saw
The one to be a stone, the other a shell;
Nor doubted once but that they both were books,
Having a perfect faith in all that passed.
Far stronger, now, grew the desire I felt
To cleave unto this man; but when I prayed
To share his enterprise, he hurried on
Reckless of me: I followed, not unseen,
For oftentimes he cast a backward look,
Grasping his twofold treasure. — Lance in rest,   120
He rode, I keeping pace with him; and now

He, to my fancy, had become the knight
Whose tale Cervantes tells; yet not the knight,
But was an Arab of the desert too;
Of these was neither, and was both at once.
His countenance, meanwhile, grew more disturbed;
And, looking backwards when he looked, mine eyes
Saw, over half the wilderness diffused,
A bed of glittering light: I asked the cause:
"It is," said he, "the waters of the deep   130
Gathering upon us;" quickening then the pace
Of the unwieldy creature he bestrode,
He left me: I called after him aloud;
He heeded not; but, with his twofold charge
Still in his grasp, before me, full in view,
Went hurrying o'er the illimitable waste,
With the fleet waters of a drowning world
In chase of him; whereat I waked in terror,
And saw the sea before me, and the book,
In which I had been reading, at my side.   140

    Full often, taking from the world of sleep
This Arab phantom, which I thus beheld,
This semi-Quixote, I to him have given
A substance, fancied him a living man,
A gentle dweller in the desert, crazed
By love and feeling, and internal thought
Protracted among endless solitudes;
Have shaped him wandering upon this quest!
Nor have I pitied him; but rather felt
Reverence was due to a being thus employed;   150
And thought that, in the blind and awful lair
Of such a madness, reason did lie couched.
Enow there are on earth to take in charge
Their wives, their children, and their virgin loves,
Or whatsoever else the heart holds dear;

Enow to stir for these; yea, will I say,
Contemplating in soberness the approach
Of an event so dire, by signs in earth
Or heaven made manifest, that I could share
That maniac's fond anxiety, and go   160
Upon like errand.   Oftentimes at least
Me hath such strong entrancement overcome,
When I have held a volume in my hand,
Poor earthly casket of immortal verse,
Shakespeare, or Milton, labourers divine!

   Great and benign, indeed, must be the power
Of living nature, which could thus so long
Detain me from the best of other guides
And dearest helpers, left unthanked, unpraised,
Even in the time of lisping infancy;   170
And later down, in prattling childhood even,
While I was travelling back among those days,
How could I ever play an ingrate's part?
Once more should I have made those bowers resound,
By intermingling strains of thankfulness
With their own thoughtless melodies; at least
It might have well beseemed me to repeat
Some simply fashioned tale, to tell again,
In slender accents of sweet verse, some tale
That did bewitch me then, and soothes me now.   180
O Friend! O Poet! brother of my soul,
Think not that I could pass along untouched
By these remembrances.   Yet wherefore speak?
Why call upon a few weak words to say
What is already written in the hearts
Of all that breathe? — what in the path of all
Drops daily from the tongue of every child,
Wherever man is found?   The trickling tear
Upon the cheek of listening Infancy

Proclaims it, and the insuperable look   190
That drinks as if it never could be full.

   That portion of my story I shall leave
There registered: whatever else of power
Or pleasure sown, or fostered thus, may be
Peculiar to myself, let that remain
Where still it works, though hidden from all search
Among the depths of time.   Yet is it just
That here, in memory of all books which lay
Their sure foundations in the heart of man,
Whether by native prose, or numerous verse,   200
That in the name of all inspired souls —
From Homer the great Thunderer, from the voice
That roars along the bed of Jewish song,
And that more varied and elaborate,
Those trumpet-tones of harmony that shake
Our shores in England, — from those loftiest notes
Down to the low and wren-like warblings, made
For cottagers and spinners at the wheel,
And sun-burnt travellers resting their tired limbs,
Stretched under wayside hedge-rows, ballad tunes,   210
Food for the hungry ears of little ones,
And of old men who have survived their joys —
'T is just that in behalf of these, the works,
And of the men that framed them, whether known
Or sleeping nameless in their scattered graves,
That I should here assert their rights, attest
Their honours, and should, once for all, pronounce
Their benediction; speak of them as Powers
For ever to be hallowed; only less,
For what we are and what we may become,   220
Than Nature's self, which is the breath of God,
Or His pure Word by miracle revealed.

Rarely and with reluctance would I stoop
To transitory themes; yet I rejoice,
And, by these thoughts admonished, will pour out
Thanks with uplifted heart, that I was reared
Safe from an evil which these days have laid
Upon the children of the land, a pest
That might have dried me up, body and soul.
This verse is dedicate to Nature's self,   230
And things that teach as Nature teaches: then,
Oh! where had been the Man, the Poet where,
Where had we been, we two, belovèd Friend!
If in the season of unperilous choice,
In lieu of wandering, as we did, through vales
Rich with indigenous produce, open ground
Of Fancy, happy pastures ranged at will,
We had been followed, hourly watched, and noosed,
Each in his several melancholy walk
Stringed like a poor man's heifer at its feed,   240
Led through the lanes in forlorn servitude;
Or rather like a stallèd ox debarred
From touch of growing grass, that may not taste
A flower till it have yielded up its sweets
A prelibation to the mower's scythe.

Behold the parent hen amid her brood,
Though fledged and feathered, and well pleased to part
And straggle from her presence, still a brood,
And she herself from the maternal bond
Still undischarged; yet doth she little more   250
Than move with them in tenderness and love,
A centre to the circle which they make;
And now and then, alike from need of theirs
And call of her own natural appetites,
She scratches, ransacks up the earth for food,
Which they partake at pleasure.   Early died

My honoured Mother, she who was the heart
And hinge of all our learnings and our loves:
She left us destitute, and, as we might,
Trooping together.   Little suits it me   260
To break upon the sabbath of her rest
With any thought that looks at others' blame;
Nor would I praise her but in perfect love.
Hence am I checked: but let me boldly say,
In gratitude, and for the sake of truth,
Unheard by her, that she, not falsely taught,
Fetching her goodness rather from times past,
Than shaping novelties for times to come,
Had no presumption, no such jealousy,
Nor did by habit of her thoughts mistrust   270
Our nature, but had virtual faith that He
Who fills the mother's breast with innocent milk,
Doth also for our nobler part provide,
Under His great correction and control,
As innocent instincts, and as innocent food;
Or draws, for minds that are left free to trust
In the simplicities of opening life,
Sweet honey out of spurned or dreaded weeds.
This was her creed, and therefore she was pure
From anxious fear of error or mishap,   280
And evil, overweeningly so called;
Was not puffed up by false unnatural hopes,
Nor selfish with unnecessary cares,
Nor with impatience from the season asked
More than its timely produce; rather loved
The hours for what they are, than from regard
Glanced on their promises in restless pride.
Such was she — not from faculties more strong
Than others have, but from the times, perhaps,
And spot in which she lived, and through a grace   290
Of modest meekness, simple-mindedness,

A heart that found benignity and hope,
Being itself benign.
                    My drift I fear
Is scarcely obvious; but, that common sense
May try this modern system by its fruits,
Leave let me take to place before her sight
A specimen pourtrayed with faithful hand.
Full early trained to worship seemliness,
This model of a child is never known
To mix in quarrels; that were far beneath   300
Its dignity; with gifts he bubbles o'er
As generous as a fountain; selfishness
May not come near him, nor the little throng
Of flitting pleasures tempt him from his path;
The wandering beggars propagate his name,
Dumb creatures find him tender as a nun,
And natural or supernatural fear,
Unless it leap upon him in a dream,
Touches him not.   To enhance the wonder, see
How arch his notices, how nice his sense   310
Of the ridiculous; not blind is he
To the broad follies of the licensed world,
Yet innocent himself withal, though shrewd,
And can read lectures upon innocence;
A miracle of scientific lore,
Ships he can guide across the pathless sea,
And tell you all their cunning; he can read
The inside of the earth, and spell the stars;
He knows the policies of foreign lands;
Can string you names of districts, cities, towns, 320
The whole world over, tight as beads of dew
Upon a gossamer thread; he sifts, he weighs;
All things are put to question; he must live
Knowing that he grows wiser every day
Or else not live at all, and seeing too

Each little drop of wisdom as it falls
Into the dimpling cistern of his heart:
For this unnatural growth the trainer blame,
Pity the tree. — Poor human vanity,
Wert thou extinguished, little would be left   330
Which he could truly love; but how escape?
For, ever as a thought of purer birth
Rises to lead him toward a better clime,
Some intermeddler still is on the watch
To drive him back, and pound him, like a stray,
Within the pinfold of his own conceit.
Meanwhile old grandame earth is grieved to find
The playthings, which her love designed for him,
Unthought of: in their woodland beds the flowers
Weep, and the river sides are all forlorn.   340
Oh! give us once again the wishing-cap
Of Fortunatus, and the invisible coat
Of Jack the Giant-killer, Robin Hood,
And Sabra in the forest with St. George!
The child, whose love is here, at least, doth reap
One precious gain, that he forgets himself.

These mighty workmen of our later age,
Who, with a broad highway, have overbridged
The froward chaos of futurity,
Tamed to their bidding; they who have the skill   350
To manage books, and things, and make them act
On infant minds as surely as the sun
Deals with a flower; the keepers of our time,
The guides and wardens of our faculties,
Sages who in their prescience would control
All accidents, and to the very road
Which they have fashioned would confine us down,
Like engines; when will their presumption learn,
That in the unreasoning progress of the world

A wiser spirit is at work for us,   360
A better eye than theirs, most prodigal
Of blessings, and most studious of our good,
Even in what seem our most unfruitful hours?

There was a Boy: ye knew him well, ye cliffs
And islands of Winander! — many a time
At evening, when the earliest stars began
To move along the edges of the hills,
Rising or setting, would he stand alone
Beneath the trees or by the glimmering lake,
And there, with fingers interwoven, both hands   370
Pressed closely palm to palm, and to his mouth
Uplifted, he, as through an instrument,
Blew mimic hootings to the silent owls,
That they might answer him; and they would shout
Across the watery vale, and shout again,
Responsive to his call, with quivering peals,
And long halloos and screams, and echoes loud,
Redoubled and redoubled, concourse wild
Of jocund din; and, when a lengthened pause
Of silence came and baffled his best skill,   380
Then sometimes, in that silence while he hung
Listening, a gentle shock of mild surprise
Has carried far into his heart the voice
Of mountain torrents; or the visible scene
Would enter unawares into his mind,
With all its solemn imagery, its rocks,
Its woods, and that uncertain heaven, received
Into the bosom of the steady lake.

This Boy was taken from his mates, and died
In childhood, ere he was full twelve years old.   390
Fair is the spot, most beautiful the vale
Where he was born; the grassy churchyard hangs

Upon a slope above the village school,
And through that churchyard when my way has led
On summer evenings, I believe that there
A long half hour together I have stood
Mute, looking at the grave in which he lies!
Even now appears before the mind's clear eye
That self-same village church; I see her sit
(The thronèd Lady whom erewhile we hailed)   400
On her green hill, forgetful of this Boy
Who slumbers at her feet, — forgetful, too,
Of all her silent neighbourhood of graves,
And listening only to the gladsome sounds
That, from the rural school ascending, play
Beneath her and about her.   May she long
Behold a race of young ones like to those
With whom I herded! — (easily, indeed,
We might have fed upon a fatter soil
Of arts and letters — but be that forgiven) —   410
A race of real children; not too wise,
Too learned, or too good; but wanton, fresh,
And bandied up and down by love and hate;
Not unresentful where self-justified;
Fierce, moody, patient, venturous, modest, shy;
Mad at their sports like withered leaves in winds;
Though doing wrong and suffering, and full oft
Bending beneath our life's mysterious weight
Of pain, and doubt, and fear, yet yielding not
In happiness to the happiest upon earth.   420
Simplicity in habit, truth in speech,
Be these the daily strengtheners of their minds;
May books and Nature be their early joy!
And knowledge, rightly honoured with that name —
Knowledge not purchased by the loss of power!

   Well do I call to mind the very week

When I was first intrusted to the care
Of that sweet Valley; when its paths, its shores,
And brooks were like a dream of novelty
To my half-infant thoughts; that very week, 430
While I was roving up and down alone,
Seeking I knew not what, I chanced to cross
One of those open fields, which, shaped like ears,
Make green peninsulas on Esthwaite's Lake:
Twilight was coming on, yet through the gloom
Appeared distinctly on the opposite shore
A heap of garments, as if left by one
Who might have there been bathing. Long I watched,
But no one owned them; meanwhile the calm lake
Grew dark with all the shadows on its breast, 440
And, now and then, a fish up-leaping snapped
The breathless stillness. The succeeding day,
Those unclaimed garments telling a plain tale
Drew to the spot an anxious crowd; some looked
In passive expectation from the shore,
While from a boat others hung o'er the deep,
Sounding with grappling irons and long poles.
At last, the dead man, 'mid that beauteous scene
Of trees and hills and water, bolt upright
Rose, with his ghastly face, a spectre shape 450
Of terror; yet no soul-debasing fear,
Young as I was, a child not nine years old,
Possessed me, for my inner eye had seen
Such sights before, among the shining streams
Of faery land, the forest of romance.
Their spirit hallowed the sad spectacle
With decoration of ideal grace;
A dignity, a smoothness, like the works
Of Grecian art, and purest poesy.

A precious treasure had I long possessed, 460

A little yellow, canvas-covered book,
A slender abstract of the Arabian tales;
And, from companions in a new abode,
When first I learnt, that this dear prize of mine
Was but a block hewn from a mighty quarry —
That there were four large volumes, laden all
With kindred matter, 't was to me, in truth,
A promise scarcely earthly. Instantly,
With one not richer than myself, I made
A covenant that each should lay aside   470
The moneys he possessed, and hoard up more
Till our joint savings had amassed enough
To make this book our own. Through several months,
In spite of all temptation, we preserved
Religiously that vow; but firmness failed,
Nor were we ever masters of our wish.

And when thereafter to my father's house
The holidays returned me, there to find
That golden store of books which I had left,
What joy was mine! How often in the course   480
Of those glad respites, though a soft west wind
Ruffled the waters to the angler's wish,
For a whole day together, have I lain
Down by thy side, O Derwent! murmuring stream,
On the hot stones, and in the glaring sun,
And there have read, devouring as I read,
Defrauding the day's glory, desperate!
Till with a sudden bound of smart reproach,
Such as an idler deals with in his shame,
I to the sport betook myself again.   490

A gracious spirit o'er this earth presides,
And o'er the heart of man; invisibly
It comes, to works of unreproved delight,

And tendency benign, directing those
Who care not, know not, think not, what they do.
The tales that charm away the wakeful night
In Araby; romances; legends penned
For solace by dim light of monkish lamps;
Fictions, for ladies of their love, devised
By youthful squires; adventures endless, spun   500
By the dismantled warrior in old age,
Out of the bowels of those very schemes
In which his youth did first extravagate;
These spread like day, and something in the shape
Of these will live till man shall be no more.
Dumb yearnings, hidden appetites, are ours,
And *they must* have their food. Our childhood sits,
Our simple childhood, sits upon a throne
That hath more power than all the elements.
I guess not what this tells of Being past,   510
Nor what it augurs of the life to come;
But so it is; and, in that dubious hour —
That twilight — when we first begin to see
This dawning earth, to recognise, expect,
And, in the long probation that ensues,
The time of trial, ere we learn to live
In reconcilement with our stinted powers;
To endure this state of meagre vassalage,
Unwilling to forego, confess, submit,
Uneasy and unsettled, yoke-fellows   520
To custom, mettlesome, and not yet tamed
And humbled down — oh! then we feel, we feel,
We know where we have friends.   Ye dreamers, then,
Forgers of daring tales! we bless you then,
Impostors, drivellers, dotards, as the ape
Philosophy will call you: *then* we feel
With what, and how great might ye are in league,
Who make our wish, our power, our thought a deed,

An empire, a possession, — ye whom time
And seasons serve; all Faculties to whom   530
Earth crouches, the elements are potter's clay,
Space like a heaven filled up with northern lights,
Here, nowhere, there, and everywhere at once.

   Relinquishing this lofty eminence
For ground, though humbler, not the less a tract
Of the same isthmus, which our spirits cross
In progress from their native continent
To earth and human life, the Song might dwell
On that delightful time of growing youth,
When craving for the marvellous gives way   540
To strengthening love for things that we have seen;
When sober truth and steady sympathies,
Offered to notice by less daring pens,
Take firmer hold of us, and words themselves
Move us with conscious pleasure.
                                        I am sad
At thought of rapture now for ever flown;
Almost to tears I sometimes could be sad
To think of, to read over, many a page,
Poems withal of name, which at that time
Did never fail to entrance me, and are now   550
Dead in my eyes, dead as a theatre
Fresh emptied of spectators.   Twice five years
Or less I might have seen, when first my mind
With conscious pleasure opened to the charm
Of words in tuneful order, found them sweet
For their own *sakes*, a passion, and a power;
And phrases pleased me chosen for delight,
For pomp, or love.   Oft, in the public roads
Yet unfrequented, while the morning light
Was yellowing the hill tops, I went abroad   560
With a dear friend, and for the better part

Of two delightful hours we strolled along
By the still borders of the misty lake,
Repeating favourite verses with one voice,
Or conning more, as happy as the birds
That round us chaunted. Well might we be glad,
Lifted above the ground by airy fancies,
More bright than madness or the dreams of wine;
And, though full oft the objects of our love
Were false, and in their splendour overwrought,   570
Yet was there surely then no vulgar power
Working within us, — nothing less, in truth,
Than that most noble attribute of man,
Though yet untutored and inordinate,
That wish for something loftier, more adorned,
Than is the common aspect, daily garb,
Of human life. What wonder, then, if sounds
Of exultation echoed through the groves!
For, images, and sentiments, and words,
And everything encountered or pursued   580
In that delicious world of poesy,
Kept holiday, a never-ending show,
With music, incense, festival, and flowers!

    Here must we pause: this only let me add,
From heart-experience, and in humblest sense
Of modesty, that he, who in his youth
A daily wanderer among woods and fields
With living Nature hath been intimate,
Not only in that raw unpractised time
Is stirred to ecstasy, as others are,   590
By glittering verse; but further, doth receive,
In measure only dealt out to himself,
Knowledge and increase of enduring joy
From the great Nature that exists in works
Of mighty Poets. Visionary power

Attends the motions of the viewless winds,
Embodied in the mystery of words:
There, darkness makes abode, and all the host
Of shadowy things work endless changes, — there,
As in a mansion like their proper home,   600
Even forms and substances are circumfused
By that transparent veil with light divine,
And, through the turnings intricate of verse,
Present themselves as objects recognised,
In flashes, and with glory not their own.

BOOK SIXTH

CAMBRIDGE AND THE ALPS

THE leaves were fading when to Esthwaite's banks
And the simplicities of cottage life
I bade farewell; and, one among the youth
Who, summoned by that season, reunite
As scattered birds troop to the fowler's lure,
Went back to Granta's cloisters, not so prompt
Or eager, though as gay and undepressed
In mind, as when I thence had taken flight
A few short months before. I turned my face
Without repining from the coves and heights   10
Clothed in the sunshine of the withering fern;
Quitted, not loth, the mild magnificence
Of calmer lakes and louder streams; and you,
Frank-hearted maids of rocky Cumberland,
You and your not unwelcome days of mirth,
Relinquished, and your nights of revelry,
And in my own unlovely cell sate down
In lightsome mood — such privilege has youth
That cannot take long leave of pleasant thoughts.

The bonds of indolent society   20
Relaxing in their hold, henceforth I lived
More to myself.   Two winters may be passed
Without a separate notice: many books
Were skimmed, devoured, or studiously perused,
But with no settled plan.   I was detached
Internally from academic cares;
Yet independent study seemed a course
Of hardy disobedience toward friends
And kindred, proud rebellion and unkind.
This spurious virtue, rather let it bear   30
A name it now deserves, this cowardice,
Gave treacherous sanction to that over-love
Of freedom which encouraged me to turn
From regulations even of my own
As from restraints and bonds.   Yet who can tell —
Who knows what thus may have been gained, both then
And at a later season, or preserved;
What love of nature, what original strength
Of contemplation, what intuitive truths
The deepest and the best, what keen research,   40
Unbiassed, unbewildered, and unawed?

   The Poet's soul was with me at that time;
Sweet meditations, the still overflow
Of present happiness, while future years
Lacked not anticipations, tender dreams,
No few of which have since been realised;
And some remain, hopes for my future life.
Four years and thirty, told this very week,
Have I been now a sojourner on earth,
By sorrow not unsmitten; yet for me   50
Life's morning radiance hath not left the hills,
Her dew is on the flowers.   Those were the days
Which also first emboldened me to trust

With firmness, hitherto but slightly touched
By such a daring thought, that I might leave
Some monument behind me which pure hearts
Should reverence.   The instinctive humbleness,
Maintained even by the very name and thought
Of printed books and authorship, began
To melt away; and further, the dread awe   60
Of mighty names was softened down and seemed
Approachable, admitting fellowship
Of modest sympathy.   Such aspect now,
Though not familiarly, my mind put on,
Content to observe, to achieve, and to enjoy.

  All winter long, whenever free to choose,
Did I by night frequent the College grove
And tributary walks; the last, and oft
The only one, who had been lingering there
Through hours of silence, till the porter's bell,   70
A punctual follower on the stroke of nine,
Rang with its blunt unceremonious voice;
Inexorable summons!   Lofty elms,
Inviting shades of opportune recess,
Bestowed composure on a neighbourhood
Unpeaceful in itself.   A single tree
With sinuous trunk, boughs exquisitely wreathed,
Grew there; an ash which Winter for himself
Decked out with pride, and with outlandish grace:
Up from the ground, and almost to the top,   80
The trunk and every master branch were green
With clustering ivy, and the lightsome twigs
And outer spray profusely tipped with seeds
That hung in yellow tassels, while the air
Stirred them, not voiceless.   Often have I stood
Foot-bound uplooking at this lovely tree
Beneath a frosty moon.   The hemisphere

Of magic fiction, verse of mine perchance
May never tread; but scarcely Spenser's self
Could have more tranquil visions in his youth,   90
Or could more bright appearances create
Of human forms with superhuman powers,
Than I beheld, loitering on calm clear nights
Alone, beneath this fairy work of earth.

On the vague reading of a truant youth
'T were idle to descant.   My inner judgment
Not seldom differed from my taste in books,
As if it appertained to another mind,
And yet the books which then I valued most
Are dearest to me *now;* for, having scanned,   100
Not heedlessly, the laws, and watched the forms
Of Nature, in that knowledge I possessed
A standard, often usefully applied,
Even when unconsciously, to things removed
From a familiar sympathy. — In fine,
I was a better judge of thoughts than words,
Misled in estimating words, not only
By common inexperience of youth,
But by the trade in classic niceties,
The dangerous craft, of culling term and phrase   110
From languages that want the living voice
To carry meaning to the natural heart;
To tell us what is passion, what is truth,
What reason, what simplicity and sense.

Yet may we not entirely overlook
The pleasure gathered from the rudiments
Of geometric science.   Though advanced
In these enquiries, with regret I speak,
No farther than the threshold, there I found
Both elevation and composed delight: 120

With Indian awe and wonder, ignorance pleased
With its own struggles, did I meditate
On the relation those abstractions bear
To Nature's laws, and by what process led,
Those immaterial agents bowed their heads
Duly to serve the mind of earth-born man;
From star to star, from kindred sphere to sphere,
From system on to system without end.

More frequently from the same source I drew
A pleasure quiet and profound, a sense   130
Of permanent and universal sway,
And paramount belief; there, recognised
A type, for finite natures, of the one
Supreme Existence, the surpassing life
Which — to the boundaries of space and time,
Of melancholy space and doleful time,
Superior and incapable of change,
Nor touched by welterings of passion — is,
And hath the name of, God.   Transcendent peace
And silence did await upon these thoughts   140
That were a frequent comfort to my youth.

'T is told by one whom stormy waters threw,
With fellow-sufferers by the shipwreck spared,
Upon a desert coast, that having brought
To land a single volume, saved by chance,
A treatise of Geometry, he wont,
Although of food and clothing destitute,
And beyond common wretchedness depressed,
To part from company and take this book
(Then first a self-taught pupil in its truths)   150
To spots remote, and draw his diagrams
With a long staff upon the sand, and thus
Did oft beguile his sorrow, and almost

Forget his feeling: so (if like effect
From the same cause produced, 'mid outward things
So different, may rightly be compared),
So was it then with me, and so will be
With Poets ever. Mighty is the charm
Of those abstractions to a mind beset
With images and haunted by herself,   160
And specially delightful unto me
Was that clear synthesis built up aloft
So gracefully; even then when it appeared
Not more than a mere plaything, or a toy
To sense embodied: not the thing it is
In verity, an independent world,
Created out of pure intelligence.

 Such dispositions then were mine unearned
By aught, I fear, of genuine desert —
Mine, through heaven's grace and inborn aptitudes. 170
And not to leave the story of that time
Imperfect, with these habits must be joined,
Moods melancholy, fits of spleen, that loved
A pensive sky, sad days, and piping winds,
The twilight more than dawn, autumn than spring;
A treasured and luxurious gloom of choice
And inclination mainly, and the mere
Redundancy of youth's contentedness.
— To time thus spent, add multitudes of hours
Pilfered away, by what the Bard who sang 180
Of the Enchanter Indolence hath called
"Good-natured lounging," and behold a map
Of my collegiate life — far less intense
Than duty called for, or, without regard
To duty, *might* have sprung up of itself
By change of accidents, or even, to speak
Without unkindness, in another place.

Yet why take refuge in that plea? — the fault,
This I repeat, was mine; mine be the blame.

In summer, making quest for works of art,   190
Or scenes renowned for beauty, I explored
That streamlet whose blue current works its way
Between romantic Dovedale's spiry rocks;
Pried into Yorkshire dales, or hidden tracts
Of my own native region, and was blest
Between these sundry wanderings with a joy
Above all joys, that seemed another morn
Risen on mid noon; blest with the presence, Friend,
Of that sole Sister, her who hath been long
Dear to thee also, thy true friend and mine,   200
Now, after separation desolate,
Restored to me — such absence that she seemed
A gift then first bestowed. The varied banks
Of Emont, hitherto unnamed in song,
And that monastic castle, 'mid tall trees,
Low standing by the margin of the stream,
A mansion visited (as fame reports)
By Sidney, where, in sight of our Helvellyn,
Or stormy Cross-fell, snatches he might pen
Of his Arcadia, by fraternal love   210
Inspired; — that river and those mouldering towers
Have seen us side by side, when, having clomb
The darksome windings of a broken stair,
And crept along a ridge of fractured wall,
Not without trembling, we in safety looked
Forth, through some Gothic window's open space,
And gathered with one mind a rich reward
From the far-stretching landscape, by the light
Of morning beautified, or purple eve;
Or, not less pleased, lay on some turret's head.   220
Catching from tufts of grass and hare-bell flowers

Their faintest whisper to the passing breeze,
Given out while mid-day heat oppressed the plains.

Another maid there was, who also shed
A gladness o'er that season, then to me,
By her exulting outside look of youth
And placid under-countenance, first endeared;
That other spirit, Coleridge! who is now
So near to us, that meek confiding heart,
So reverenced by us both.   O'er paths and fields   230
In all that neighbourhood, through narrow lanes
Of eglantine, and through the shady woods,
And o'er the Border Beacon, and the waste
Of naked pools, and common crags that lay
Exposed on the bare fell, were scattered love,
The spirit of pleasure, and youth's golden gleam.
O Friend! we had not seen thee at that time,
And yet a power is on me, and a strong
Confusion, and I seem to plant thee there.
Far art thou wandered now in search of health   240
And milder breezes, — melancholy lot!
But thou art with us, with us in the past,
The present, with us in the times to come.
There is no grief, no sorrow, no despair,
No languor, no dejection, no dismay,
No absence scarcely can there be, for those
Who love as we do.   Speed thee well! divide
With us thy pleasure; thy returning strength,
Receive it daily as a joy of ours;
Share with us thy fresh spirits, whether gift   250
Of gales Etesian or of tender thoughts.

I, too, have been a wanderer; but, alas!
How different the fate of different men.
Though mutually unknown, yea nursed and reared

As if in several elements, we were framed
To bend at last to the same discipline,
Predestined, if two beings ever were,
To seek the same delights, and have one health,
One happiness.   Throughout this narrative,
Else sooner ended, I have borne in mind   260
For whom it registers the birth, and marks the growth,
Of gentleness, simplicity, and truth,
And joyous loves, that hallow innocent days
Of peace and self-command.   Of rivers, fields,
And groves I speak to thee, my Friend! to thee,
Who, yet a liveried schoolboy, in the depths
Of the huge city, on the leaded roof
Of that wide edifice, thy school and home,
Wert used to lie and gaze upon the clouds
Moving in heaven; or, of that pleasure tired,   270
To shut thine eyes, and by internal light
See trees, and meadows, and thy native stream,
Far distant, thus beheld from year to year
Of a long exile.   Nor could I forget,
In this late portion of my argument,
That scarcely, as my term of pupilage
Ceased, had I left those academic bowers
When thou wert thither guided.   From the heart
Of London, and from cloisters there, thou camest,
And didst sit down in temperance and peace,   280
A rigorous student.   What a stormy course
Then followed.   Oh! it is a pang that calls
For utterance, to think what easy change
Of circumstances might to thee have spared
A world of pain, ripened a thousand hopes,
For ever withered.   Through this retrospect
Of my collegiate life I still have had
Thy after-sojourn in the self-same place
Present before my eyes, have played with times

And accidents as children do with cards,   290
Or as a man, who, when his house is built,
A frame locked up in wood and stone, doth still,
As impotent fancy prompts, by his fireside,
Rebuild it to his liking. I have thought
Of thee, thy learning, gorgeous eloquence,
And all the strength and plumage of thy youth,
Thy subtle speculations, toils abstruse
Among the schoolmen, and Platonic forms
Of wild ideal pageantry, shaped out
From things well-matched or ill, and words for things,
The self-created sustenance of a mind   301
Debarred from Nature's living images,
Compelled to be a life unto herself,
And unrelentingly possessed by thirst
Of greatness, love, and beauty. Not alone,
Ah! surely not in singleness of heart
Should I have seen the light of evening fade
From smooth Cam's silent waters: had we met,
Even at that early time, needs must I trust
In the belief, that my maturer age,   310
My calmer habits, and more steady voice,
Would with an influence benign have soothed,
Or chased away, the airy wretchedness
That battened on thy youth. But thou hast trod
A march of glory, which doth put to shame
These vain regrets; health suffers in thee, else
Such grief for thee would be the weakest thought
That ever harboured in the breast of man.

A passing word erewhile did lightly touch
On wanderings of my own, that now embraced   326
With livelier hope a region wider far.

When the third summer freed us from restraint,

A youthful friend, he too a mountaineer,
Not slow to share my wishes, took his staff,
And sallying forth, we journeyed side by side,
Bound to the distant Alps.   A hardy slight,
Did this unprecedented course imply,
Of college studies and their set rewards;
Nor had, in truth, the scheme been formed by me
Without uneasy forethought of the pain,   330
The censures, and ill-omening, of those
To whom my worldly interests were dear.
But Nature then was sovereign in my mind,
And mighty forms, seizing a youthful fancy,
Had given a charter to irregular hopes.
In any age of uneventful calm
Among the nations, surely would my heart
Have been possessed by similar desire;
But Europe at that time was thrilled with joy,
France standing on the top of golden hours,   340
And human nature seeming born again.

   Lightly equipped, and but a few brief looks
Cast on the white cliffs of our native shore
From the receding vessel's deck, we chanced
To land at Calais on the very eve
Of that great federal day; and there we saw,
In a mean city, and among a few,
How bright a face is worn when joy of one
Is joy for tens of millions.   Southward thence
We held our way, direct through hamlets, towns,   350
Gaudy with reliques of that festival,
Flowers left to wither on triumphal arcs,
And window-garlands.   On the public roads,
And, once, three days successively, through paths
By which our toilsome journey was abridged,
Among sequestered villages we walked

And found benevolence and blessedness
Spread like a fragrance everywhere, when spring
Hath left no corner of the land untouched;
Where elms for many and many a league in files   360
With their thin umbrage, on the stately roads
Of that great kingdom, rustled o'er our heads,
For ever near us as we paced along:
How sweet at such a time, with such delight
On every side, in prime of youthful strength,
To feed a Poet's tender melancholy
And fond conceit of sadness, with the sound
Of undulations varying as might please
The wind that swayed them; once, and more than once,
Unhoused beneath the evening star we saw   370
Dances of liberty, and, in late hours
Of darkness, dances in the open air
Deftly prolonged, though grey-haired lookers on
Might waste their breath in chiding.
                                        Under hills —
The vine-clad hills and slopes of Burgundy,
Upon the bosom of the gentle Saone
We glided forward with the flowing stream.
Swift Rhone! thou wert the *wings* on which we cut
A winding passage with majestic ease
Between thy lofty rocks.   Enchanting show   380
Those woods and farms and orchards did present,
And single cottages and lurking towns,
Reach after reach, succession without end
Of deep and stately vales!   A lonely pair
Of strangers, till day closed, we sailed along
Clustered together with a merry crowd
Of those emancipated, a blithe host
Of travellers, chiefly delegates, returning
From the great spousals newly solemnised
At their chief city, in the sight of Heaven.   390

Like bees they swarmed, gaudy and gay as bees;
Some vapoured in the unruliness of joy,
And with their swords flourished as if to fight
The saucy air.   In this proud company
We landed — took with them our evening meal,
Guests welcome almost as the angels were
To Abraham of old.   The supper done,
With flowing cups elate and happy thoughts
We rose at signal given, and formed a ring
And, hand in hand, danced round and round the board;
All hearts were open, every tongue was loud   401
With amity and glee; we bore a name
Honoured in France, the name of Englishmen,
And hospitably did they give us hail,
As their forerunners in a glorious course;
And round and round the board we danced again.
With these blithe friends our voyage we renewed
At early dawn.   The monastery bells
Made a sweet jingling in our youthful ears;
The rapid river flowing without noise,   410
And each uprising or receding spire
Spake with a sense of peace, at intervals
Touching the heart amid the boisterous crew
By whom we were encompassed.   Taking leave
Of this glad throng, foot-travellers side by side,
Measuring our steps in quiet, we pursued
Our journey, and ere twice the sun had set
Beheld the Convent of Chartreuse, and there
Rested within an awful *solitude:*
Yes; for even then no other than a place   420
Of soul-affecting *solitude* appeared
That far-famed region, though our eyes had seen,
As toward the sacred mansion we advanced,
Arms flashing, and a military glare
Of riotous men commissioned to expel

The blameless inmates, and belike subvert
That frame of social being, which so long
Had bodied forth the ghostliness of things
In silence visible and perpetual calm.
— "Stay, stay your sacrilegious hands!" — The voice
Was Nature's, uttered from her Alpine throne;   431
I heard it then and seem to hear it now —
"Your impious work forbear, perish what may,
Let this one temple last, be this one spot
Of earth devoted to eternity!"
She ceased to speak, but while St. Bruno's pines
Waved their dark tops, not silent as they waved,
And while below, along their several beds,
Murmured the sister streams of Life and Death,
Thus by conflicting passions pressed, my heart   440
Responded; "Honour to the patriot's zeal!
Glory and hope to new-born Liberty!
Hail to the mighty projects of the time!
Discerning sword that Justice wields, do thou
Go forth and prosper; and, ye purging fires,
Up to the loftiest towers of Pride ascend,
Fanned by the breath of angry Providence.
But oh! if Past and Future be the wings
On whose support harmoniously conjoined
Moves the great spirit of human knowledge, spare   450
These courts of mystery, where a step advanced
Between the portals of the shadowy rocks
Leaves far behind life's treacherous vanities,
For penitential tears and trembling hopes
Exchanged — to equalise in God's pure sight
Monarch and peasant: be the house redeemed
With its unworldly votaries, for the sake
Of conquest over sense, hourly achieved
Through faith and meditative reason, resting
Upon the word of heaven-imparted truth,   460

Calmly triumphant   and for humbler claim
Of that imaginative impulse sent
From these majestic floods, yon shining cliffs,
The untransmuted shapes of many worlds,
Cerulean ether's pure inhabitants,
These forests unapproachable by death,
That shall endure as long as man endures,
To think, to hope, to worship, and to feel,
To struggle, to be lost within himself
In trepidation, from the blank abyss   470
To look with bodily eyes, and be consoled."
Not seldom since that moment have I wished
That thou, O Friend! the trouble or the calm
Hadst shared, when, from profane regards apart,
In sympathetic reverence we trod
The floors of those dim cloisters, till that hour,
From their foundation, strangers to the presence
Of unrestricted and unthinking man.
Abroad, how cheeringly the sunshine lay
Upon the open lawns! Vallombre's groves   480
Entering, we fed the soul with darkness; thence
Issued, and with uplifted eyes beheld,
In different quarters of the bending sky,
The cross of Jesus stand erect, as if
Hands of angelic powers had fixed it there,
Memorial reverenced by a thousand storms;
Yet then, from the undiscriminating sweep
And rage of one State-whirlwind, insecure.

   'T is not my present purpose to retrace
That variegated journey step by step.   490
A march it was of military speed,
And Earth did change her images and forms
Before us, fast as clouds are changed in heaven.
Day after day, up early and down late,

From hill to vale we dropped, from vale to hill
Mounted — from province on to province swept,
Keen hunters in a chase of fourteen weeks,
Eager as birds of prey, or as a ship
Upon the stretch, when winds are blowing fair:
Sweet coverts did we cross of pastoral life,   500
Enticing valleys, greeted them and left
Too soon, while yet the very flash and gleam
Of salutation were not passed away.
Oh! sorrow for the youth who could have seen,
Unchastened, unsubdued, unawed, unraised
To patriarchal dignity of mind,
And pure simplicity of wish and will,
Those sanctified abodes of peaceful man,
Pleased (though to hardship born, and compassed round
With danger, varying as the seasons change),   510
Pleased with his daily task, or, if not pleased,
Contented, from the moment that the dawn
(Ah! surely not without attendant gleams
Of soul-illumination) calls him forth
To industry, by glistenings flung on rocks,
Whose evening shadows lead him to repose.

   Well might a stranger look with bounding heart
Down on a green recess, the first I saw
Of those deep haunts, an aboriginal vale,
Quiet and lorded over and possessed   520
By naked huts, wood-built, and sown like tents
Or Indian cabins over the fresh lawns
And by the river side.
                    That very day,
From a bare ridge we also first beheld
Unveiled the summit of Mont Blanc, and grieved
To have a soulless image on the eye
That had usurped upon a living thought

That never more could be.   The wondrous Vale
Of Chamouny stretched far below, and soon
With its dumb cataracts and streams of ice,   530
A motionless array of mighty waves,
Five rivers broad and vast, made rich amends,
And reconciled us to realities;
There small birds warble from the leafy trees,
The eagle soars high in the element,
There doth the reaper bind the yellow sheaf,
The maiden spread the haycock in the sun,
While Winter like a well-tamed lion walks,
Descending from the mountain to make sport
Among the cottages by beds of flowers.   540

Whate'er in this wide circuit we beheld,
Or heard, was fitted to our unripe state
Of intellect and heart.   With such a book
Before our eyes, we could not choose but read
Lessons of genuine brotherhood, the plain
And universal reason of mankind,
The truths of young and old.   Nor, side by side
Pacing, two social pilgrims, or alone
Each with his humour, could we fail to abound
In dreams and fictions, pensively composed: 550
Dejection taken up for pleasure's sake,
And gilded sympathies, the willow wreath,
And sober posies of funereal flowers,
Gathered among those solitudes sublime
From formal gardens of the lady Sorrow,
Did sweeten many a meditative hour.

Yet still in me with those soft luxuries
Mixed something of stern mood, an underthirst
Of vigour seldom utterly allayed:
And from that source how different a sadness   560

Would issue, let one incident make known.
When from the Vallais we had turned, and clomb
Along the Simplon's steep and rugged road,
Following a band of muleteers, we reached
A halting-place, where all together took
Their noon-tide meal.   Hastily rose our guide,
Leaving us at the board; awhile we lingered,
Then paced the beaten downward way that led
Right to a rough stream's edge, and there broke off;
The only track now visible was one   570
That from the torrent's further brink held forth
Conspicuous invitation to ascend
A lofty mountain.   After brief delay
Crossing the unbridged stream, that road we took,
And clomb with eagerness, till anxious fears
Intruded, for we failed to overtake
Our comrades gone before.   By fortunate chance,
While every moment added doubt to doubt,
A peasant met us, from whose mouth we learned
That to the spot which had perplexed us first   580
We must descend, and there should find the road,
Which in the stony channel of the stream
Lay a few steps, and then along its banks;
And, that our future course, all plain to sight,
Was downwards, with the current of that stream.
Loth to believe what we so grieved to hear,
For still we had hopes that pointed to the clouds,
We questioned him again, and yet again;
But every word that from the peasant's lips
Came in reply, translated by our feelings,   590
Ended in this, — *that we had crossed the Alps*.

    Imagination — here the Power so called
Through sad incompetence of human speech,
That awful Power rose from the mind's abyss

Like an unfathered vapour that enwraps,
At once, some lonely traveller.   I was lost;
Halted without an effort to break through;
But to my conscious soul I now can say —
"I recognise thy glory:" in such strength
Of usurpation, when the light of sense   600
Goes out, but with a flash that has revealed
The invisible world, doth greatness make abode,
There harbours; whether we be young or old,
Our destiny, our being's heart and home,
Is with infinitude, and only there;
With hope it is, hope that can never die,
Effort, and expectation, and desire,
And something evermore about to be.
Under such banners militant, the soul
Seeks for no trophies, struggles for no spoils   610
That may attest her prowess, blest in thoughts
That are their own perfection and reward,
Strong in herself and in beatitude
That hides her, like the mighty flood of Nile
Poured from his fount of Abyssinian clouds
To fertilise the whole Egyptian plain.

    The melancholy slackening that ensued
Upon those tidings by the peasant given
Was soon dislodged.   Downwards we hurried fast,
And, with the half-shaped road which we had missed,
Entered a narrow chasm.   The brook and road   621
Were fellow-travellers in this gloomy strait,
And with them did we journey several hours
At a slow pace.   The immeasurable height
Of woods decaying, never to be decayed,
The stationary blasts of waterfalls,
And in the narrow rent at every turn
Winds thwarting winds, bewildered and forlorn,

The torrents shooting from the clear blue sky,
The rocks that muttered close upon our ears,   630
Black drizzling crags that spake by the way-side
As if a voice were in them, the sick sight
And giddy prospect of the raving stream,
The unfettered clouds and region of the Heavens,
Tumult and peace, the darkness and the light —
Were all like workings of one mind, the features
Of the same face, blossoms upon one tree;
Characters of the great Apocalypse,
The types and symbols of Eternity,
Of first, and last, and midst, and without end.   640

That night our lodging was a house that stood
Alone within the valley, at a point
Where, tumbling from aloft, a torrent swelled
The rapid stream whose margin we had trod;
A dreary mansion, large beyond all need,
With high and spacious rooms, deafened and stunned
By noise of waters, making innocent sleep
Lie melancholy among weary bones.

Uprisen betimes, our journey we renewed,
Led by the stream, ere noon-day magnified   650
Into a lordly river, broad and deep,
Dimpling along in silent majesty,
With mountains for its neighbours, and in view
Of distant mountains and their snowy tops,
And thus proceeding to Locarno's Lake,
Fit resting-place for such a visitant.
Locarno! spreading out in width like Heaven,
How dost thou cleave to the poetic heart,
Back in the sunshine of the memory;
And Como! thou, a treasure whom the earth   660
Keeps to herself, confined as in a depth

Of Abyssinian privacy. I spake
Of thee, thy chestnut woods, and garden plots
Of Indian corn tended by dark-eyed maids;
Thy lofty steeps, and pathways roofed with vines,
Winding from house to house, from town to town
Sole link that binds them to each other; walks,
League after league, and cloistral avenues,
Where silence dwells if music be not there:
While yet a youth undisciplined in verse,   670
Through fond ambition of that hour I strove
To chant your praise; nor can approach you now
Ungreeted by a more melodious Song,
Where tones of Nature smoothed by learned Art
May flow in lasting current. Like a breeze
Or sunbeam over your domain I passed
In motion without pause; but ye have left
Your beauty with me, a serene accord
Of forms and colours, passive, yet endowed
In their submissiveness with power as sweet   680
And gracious, almost, might I dare to say,
As virtue is, or goodness; sweet as love,
Or the remembrance of a generous deed,
Or mildest visitations of pure thought,
When God, the giver of all joy, is thanked
Religiously, in silent blessedness;
Sweet as this last herself, for such it is.

With those delightful pathways we advanced,
For two days' space in presence of the Lake,
That, stretching far among the Alps, assumed   690
A character more stern. The second night,
From sleep awakened, and misled by sound
Of the church clock telling the hours with strokes
Whose import then we had not learned, we rose
By moonlight, doubting not that day was nigh,

And that meanwhile, by no uncertain path,
Along the winding margin of the lake,
Led, as before, we should behold the scene
Hushed in profound repose. We left the town
Of Gravedona with this hope; but soon   700
Were lost, bewildered among woods immense,
And on a rock sate down, to wait for day.
An open place it was, and overlooked,
From high, the sullen water far beneath,
On which a dull red image of the moon
Lay bedded, changing oftentimes its form
Like an uneasy snake.   From hour to hour
We sate and sate, wondering, as if the night
Had been ensnared by witchcraft.   On the rock
At last we stretched our weary limbs for sleep,   710
But *could not* sleep, tormented by the stings
Of insects, which, with noise like that of noon,
Filled all the woods: the cry of unknown birds;
The mountains more by blackness visible
And their own size, than any outward light;
The breathless wilderness of clouds; the clock
That told, with unintelligible voice,
The widely parted hours; the noise of streams,
And sometimes rustling motions nigh at hand,
That did not leave us free from personal fear;   720
And, lastly, the withdrawing moon, that set
Before us, while she still was high in heaven; —
These were our food; and such a summer's night
Followed that pair of golden days that shed
On Como's Lake, and all that round it lay,
Their fairest, softest, happiest influence.

But here I must break off, and bid farewell
To days, each offering some new sight, or fraught
With some untried adventure, in a course

Prolonged till sprinklings of autumnal snow   730
Checked our unwearied steps. Let this alone
Be mentioned as a parting word, that not
In hollow exultation, dealing out
Hyperboles of praise comparative;
Not rich one moment to be poor for ever;
Not prostrate, overborne, as if the mind
Herself were nothing, a mere pensioner
On outward forms — did we in presence stand
Of that magnificent region. On the front
Of this whole Song is written that my heart   740
Must, in such Temple, needs have offered up
A different worship. Finally, whate'er
I saw, or heard, or felt, was but a stream
That flowed into a kindred stream; a gale,
Confederate with the current of the soul,
To speed my voyage; every sound or sight,
In its degree of power, administered
To grandeur or to tenderness, — to the one
Directly, but to tender thoughts by means
Less often instantaneous in effect;   750
Led me to these by paths that, in the main,
Were more circuitous, but not less sure
Duly to reach the point marked out by Heaven.

Oh, most belovèd Friend! a glorious time,
A happy time that was; triumphant looks
Were then the common language of all eyes;
As if awaked from sleep, the Nations hailed
Their great expectancy: the fife of war
Was then a spirit-stirring sound indeed,
A blackbird's whistle in a budding grove.   760
We left the Swiss exulting in the fate
Of their near neighbours; and, when shortening fast
Our pilgrimage, nor distant far from home,

We crossed the Brabant armies on the fret
For battle in the cause of Liberty.
A stripling, scarcely of the household then
Of social life, I looked upon these things
As from a distance; heard, and saw, and felt,
Was touched, but with no intimate concern;
I seemed to move along them, as a bird   770
Moves through the air, or as a fish pursues
Its sport, or feeds in its proper element;
I wanted not that joy, I did not need
Such help; the ever-living universe,
Turn where I might, was opening out its glories,
And the independent spirit of pure youth
Called forth, at every season, new delights,
Spread round my steps like sunshine o'er green fields.

BOOK SEVENTH

RESIDENCE IN LONDON

Six changeful years have vanished since I first
Poured out (saluted by that quickening breeze
Which met me issuing from the City's walls)
A glad preamble to this Verse: I sang
Aloud, with fervour irresistible
Of short-lived transport, like a torrent bursting,
From a black thunder-cloud, down Scafell's side
To rush and disappear. But soon broke forth
(So willed the Muse) a less impetuous stream,
That flowed awhile with unabating strength,   10
Then stopped for years; not audible again
Before last primrose-time. Belovèd Friend!
The assurance which then cheered some heavy thoughts
On thy departure to a foreign land

Has failed; too slowly moves the promised work.
Through the whole summer have I been at rest,
Partly from voluntary holiday,
And part through outward hindrance. But I heard,
After the hour of sunset yester-even,
Sitting within doors between light and dark, 20
A choir of redbreasts gathered somewhere near
My threshold, — minstrels from the distant woods
Sent in on Winter's service, to announce,
With preparation artful and benign,
That the rough lord had left the surly North
On his accustomed journey. The delight,
Due to this timely notice, unawares
Smote me, and, listening, I in whispers said,
"Ye heartsome Choristers, ye and I will be
Associates, and, unscared by blustering winds, 30
Will chant together." Thereafter, as the shades
Of twilight deepened, going forth, I spied
A glow-worm underneath a dusky plume
Or canopy of yet unwithered fern,
Clear-shining, like a hermit's taper seen
Through a thick forest. Silence touched me here
No less than sound had done before; the child
Of Summer, lingering, shining, by herself,
The voiceless worm on the unfrequented hills,
Seemed sent on the same errand with the choir 40
Of Winter that had warbled at my door,
And the whole year breathed tenderness and love.

 The last night's genial feeling overflowed
Upon this morning, and my favourite grove,
Tossing in sunshine its dark boughs aloft,
As if to make the strong wind visible,
Wakes in me agitations like its own,
A spirit friendly to the Poet's task,

Which we will now resume with lively hope,
Nor checked by aught of tamer argument   50
That lies before us, needful to be told.

   Returned from that excursion, soon I bade
Farewell for ever to the sheltered seats
Of gownèd students, quitted hall and bower,
And every comfort of that privileged ground,
Well pleased to pitch a vagrant tent among
The unfenced regions of society.

   Yet, undetermined to what course of life
I should adhere, and seeming to possess
A little space of intermediate time   60
At full command, to London first I turned,
In no disturbance of excessive hope,
By personal ambition unenslaved,
Frugal as there was need, and, though self-willed,
From dangerous passions free.   Three years had flown
Since I had felt in heart and soul the shock
Of the huge town's first presence, and had paced
Her endless streets, a transient visitant:
Now, fixed amid that concourse of mankind
Where Pleasure whirls about incessantly,   70
And life and labour seem but one, I filled
An idler's place; an idler well content
To have a house (what matter for a home?)
That owned him; living cheerfully abroad
With unchecked fancy ever on the stir,
And all my young affections out of doors.

There was a time when whatsoe'er is feigned
Of airy palaces, and gardens built
By Genii of romance; or hath in grave

Authentic history been set forth of Rome,   80
Alcairo, Babylon, or Persepolis;
Or given upon report by pilgrim friars,
Of golden cities ten months' journey deep
Among Tartarian wilds — fell short, far short,
Of what my fond simplicity believed
And thought of London — held me by a chain
Less strong of wonder and obscure delight.
Whether the bolt of childhood's Fancy shot
For me beyond its ordinary mark,
'Twere vain to ask; but in our flock of boys   90
Was One, a cripple from his birth, whom chance
Summoned from school to London; fortunate
And envied traveller! When the Boy returned,
After short absence, curiously I scanned
His mien and person, nor was free, in sooth,
From disappointment, not to find some change
In look and air, from that new region brought,
As if from Fairy-land. Much I questioned him;
And every word he uttered, on my ears
Fell flatter than a cagèd parrot's note,   100
That answers unexpectedly awry,
And mocks the prompter's listening. Marvellous things
Had vanity (quick Spirit that appears
Almost as deeply seated and as strong
In a Child's heart as fear itself) conceived
For my enjoyment. Would that I could now
Recall what then I pictured to myself,
Of mitred Prelates, Lords in ermine clad,
The King, and the King's Palace, and, not last,
Nor least, Heaven bless him! the renowned Lord Mayor.
Dreams not unlike to those which once begat   111
A change of purpose in young Whittington,
When he, a friendless and a drooping boy,
Sate on a stone, and heard the bells speak out

Articulate music.   Above all, one thought
Baffled my understanding: how men lived
Even next-door neighbours, as we say, yet still
Strangers, not knowing each the other's name.

Oh, wondrous power of words, by simple faith
Licensed to take the meaning that we love!   120
Vauxhall and Ranelagh!   I then had heard
Of your green groves, and wilderness of lamps
Dimming the stars, and fireworks magical,
And gorgeous ladies, under splendid domes,
Floating in dance, or warbling high in air
The songs of spirits!   Nor had Fancy fed
With less delight upon that other class
Of marvels, broad-day wonders permanent:
The River proudly bridged; the dizzy top
And Whispering Gallery of St. Paul's; the tombs   130
Of Westminster; the Giants of Guildhall;
Bedlam, and those carved maniacs at the gates,
Perpetually recumbent; Statues — man,
And the horse under him — in gilded pomp
Adorning flowery gardens, 'mid vast squares;
The Monument, and that Chamber of the Tower
Where England's sovereigns sit in long array,
Their steeds bestriding, — every mimic shape
Cased in the gleaming mail the monarch wore,
Whether for gorgeous tournament addressed,   140
Or life or death upon the battle-field.
Those bold imaginations in due time
Had vanished, leaving others in their stead:
And now I looked upon the living scene;
Familiarly perused it; oftentimes,
In spite of strongest disappointment, pleased
Through courteous self-submission, as a tax
Paid to the object by prescriptive right.

  Rise up, thou monstrous ant-hill on the plain
Of a too busy world!   Before me flow,   150
Thou endless stream of men and moving things!
Thy every-day appearance, as it strikes —
With wonder heightened, or sublimed by awe —
On strangers, of all ages; the quick dance
Of colours, lights, and forms; the deafening din;
The comers and the goers face to face,
Face after face; the string of dazzling wares,
Shop after shop, with symbols, blazoned names,
And all the tradesman's honours overhead:
Here, fronts of houses, like a title-page,   160
With letters huge inscribed from top to toe,
Stationed above the door, like guardian saints;
There, allegoric shapes, female or male,
Or physiognomies of real men,
Land-warriors, kings, or admirals of the sea,
Boyle, Shakspeare, Newton, or the attractive head
Of some quack-doctor, famous in his day.

  Meanwhile the roar continues, till at length,
Escaped as from an enemy, we turn
Abruptly into some sequestered nook,   170
Still as a sheltered place when winds blow loud!
At leisure, thence, through tracts of thin resort,
And sights and sounds that come at intervals,
We take our way.   A raree-show is here,
With children gathered round; another street
Presents a company of dancing dogs,
Or dromedary, with an antic pair
Of monkeys on his back; a minstrel band
Of Savoyards; or, single and alone,
An English ballad-singer.   Private courts,   180
Gloomy as coffins, and unsightly lanes
Thrilled by some female vendor's scream, belike

The very shrillest of all London cries,
May then entangle our impatient steps;
Conducted through those labyrinths, unawares,
To privileged regions and inviolate,
Where from their airy lodges studious lawyers
Look out on waters, walks, and gardens green.

 Thence back into the throng, until we reach,
Following the tide that slackens by degrees,   190
Some half-frequented scenes, where wider streets
Bring straggling breezes of suburban air.
Here files of ballads dangle from dead walls;
Advertisements, of giant-size, from high
Press forward, in all colours, on the sight;
These, bold in conscious merit, lower down;
That, fronted with a most imposing word,
Is, peradventure, one in masquerade.
As on the broadening causeway we advance,
Behold, turned upwards, a face hard and strong 200
In lineaments, and red with over-toil.
'T is one encountered here and everywhere;
A travelling cripple, by the trunk cut short,
And stumping on his arms. In sailor's garb
Another lies at length, beside a range
Of well-formed characters, with chalk inscribed
Upon the smooth flat stones: the Nurse is here,
The Bachelor, that loves to sun himself,
The military Idler, and the Dame,
That field-ward takes her walk with decent steps. 210

 Now homeward through the thickening hubbub, where
See, among less distinguishable shapes,
The begging scavenger, with hat in hand;
The Italian, as he thrids his way with care,
Steadying, far-seen, a frame of images

Upon his head; with basket at his breast
The Jew; the stately and slow-moving Turk,
With freight of slippers piled beneath his arm!

Enough; — the mighty concourse I surveyed
With no unthinking mind, well pleased to note   220
Among the crowd all specimens of man,
Through all the colours which the sun bestows,
And every character of form and face:
The Swede, the Russian; from the genial south,
The Frenchman and the Spaniard; from remote
America, the Hunter-Indian; Moors,
Malays, Lascars, the Tartar, the Chinese,
And Negro Ladies in white muslin gowns.

At leisure, then, I viewed, from day to day,
The spectacles within doors, — birds and beasts   230
Of every nature, and strange plants convened
From every clime; and, next, those sights that ape
The absolute presence of reality,
Expressing, as in mirror, sea and land,
And what earth is, and what she has to show.
I do not here allude to subtlest craft,
By means refined attaining purest ends,
But imitations, fondly made in plain
Confession of man's weakness and his loves.
Whether the Painter, whose ambitious skill   240
Submits to nothing less than taking in
A whole horizon's circuit, do with power,
Like that of angels or commissioned spirits,
Fix us upon some lofty pinnacle,
Or in a ship on waters, with a world
Of life, and life-like mockery beneath,
Above, behind, far stretching and before;
Or more mechanic artist represent

By scale exact, in model, wood or clay,
From blended colours also borrowing help,   250
Some miniature of famous spots or things, —
St. Peter's Church; or, more aspiring aim,
In microscopic vision, Rome herself;
Or, haply, some choice rural haunt, — the Falls
Of Tivoli; and, high upon that steep,
The Sibyl's mouldering Temple! every tree,
Villa, or cottage, lurking among rocks
Throughout the landscape; tuft, stone, scratch minute —
All that the traveller sees when he is there.

Add to these exhibitions, mute and still,   260
Others of wider scope, where living men,
Music, and shifting pantomimic scenes,
Diversified the allurement.   Need I fear
To mention by its name, as in degree,
Lowest of these and humblest in attempt,
Yet richly graced with honours of her own,
Half-rural Sadler's Wells?   Though at that time
Intolerant, as is the way of youth
Unless itself be pleased, here more than once
Taking my seat, I saw (nor blush to add,   270
With ample recompense) giants and dwarfs,
Clowns, conjurors, posture-masters, harlequins,
Amid the uproar of the rabblement,
Perform their feats.   Nor was it mean delight
To watch crude Nature work in untaught minds;
To note the laws and progress of belief;
Though obstinate on this way, yet on that
How willingly we travel, and how far!
To have, for instance, brought upon the scene
The champion, Jack the Giant-killer: Lo!   280
He dons his coat of darkness; on the stage
Walks, and achieves his wonders, from the eye

Of living Mortal covert, "as the moon
Hid in her vacant interlunar cave."
Delusion bold! and how can it be wrought?
The garb he wears is black as death, the word
"*Invisible*" flames forth upon his chest.

Here, too, were "forms and pressures of the time,"
Rough, bold, as Grecian comedy displayed
When Art was young; dramas of living men,   290
And recent things yet warm with life; a sea-fight,
Shipwreck, or some domestic incident
Divulged by Truth and magnified by Fame;
Such as the daring brotherhood of late
Set forth, too serious theme for that light place —
I mean, O distant Friend! a story drawn
From our own ground, — the Maid of Buttermere, —
And how, unfaithful to a virtuous wife
Deserted and deceived, the Spoiler came
And wooed the artless daughter of the hills,   300
And wedded her, in cruel mockery
Of love and marriage bonds.   These words to thee
Must needs bring back the moment when we first,
Ere the broad world rang with the maiden's name,
Beheld her serving at the cottage inn;
Both stricken, as she entered or withdrew,
With admiration of her modest mien
And carriage, marked by unexampled grace.
We since that time not unfamiliarly
Have seen her, — her discretion have observed,   310
Her just opinions, delicate reserve,
Her patience, and humility of mind
Unspoiled by commendation and the excess
Of public notice — an offensive light
To a meek spirit suffering inwardly.

From this memorial tribute to my theme
I was returning, when, with sundry forms
Commingled — shapes which met me in the way
That we must tread — thy image rose again,
Maiden of Buttermere!   She lives in peace   320
Upon the spot where she was born and reared;
Without contamination doth she live
In quietness, without anxiety:
Beside the mountain chapel, sleeps in earth
Her new-born infant, fearless as a lamb
That, thither driven from some unsheltered place,
Rests underneath the little rock-like pile
When storms are raging.   Happy are they both —
Mother and child! — These feelings, in themselves
Trite, do yet scarcely seem so when I think   330
On those ingenuous moments of our youth
Ere we have learnt by use to slight the crimes
And sorrows of the world.   Those simple days
Are now my theme; and, foremost of the scenes,
Which yet survive in memory, appears
One, at whose centre sate a lovely Boy,
A sportive infant, who, for six months' space,
Not more, had been of age to deal about
Articulate prattle — Child as beautiful
As ever clung around a mother's neck,   340
Or father fondly gazed upon with pride.
There, too, conspicuous for stature tall
And large dark eyes, beside her infant stood
The mother; but, upon her cheeks diffused,
False tints too well accorded with the glare
From play-house lustres thrown without reserve
On every object near.   The Boy had been
The pride and pleasure of all lookers-on
In whatsoever place, but seemed in this
A sort of alien scattered from the clouds.   350

Of lusty vigour, more than infantine
He was in limb, in cheek a summer rose
Just three parts blown — a cottage-child — if e'er,
By cottage-door on breezy mountain-side,
Or in some sheltering vale, was seen a babe
By Nature's gifts so favoured.   Upon a board
Decked with refreshments had this child been placed,
His little stage in the vast theatre,
And there he sate, surrounded with a throng
Of chance spectators, chiefly dissolute men   360
And shameless women, treated and caressed;
Ate, drank, and with the fruit and glasses played,
While oaths and laughter and indecent speech
Were rife about him as the songs of birds
Contending after showers.   The mother now
Is fading out of memory, but I see
The lovely Boy as I beheld him then
Among the wretched and the falsely gay,
Like one of those who walked with hair unsinged
Amid the fiery furnace.   Charms and spells   370
Muttered on black and spiteful instigation
Have stopped, as some believe, the kindliest growths.
Ah, with how different spirit might a prayer
Have been preferred, that this fair creature, checked
By special privilege of Nature's love,
Should in his childhood be detained for ever!
But with its universal freight the tide
Hath rolled along, and this bright innocent,
Mary! may now have lived till he could look
With envy on thy nameless babe that sleeps,   380
Beside the mountain chapel, undisturbed.

Four rapid years had scarcely then been told
Since, travelling southward from our pastoral hills,
I heard, and for the first time in my life,

The voice of woman utter blasphemy —
Saw woman as she is, to open shame
Abandoned, and the pride of public vice;
I shuddered, for a barrier seemed at once
Thrown in that from humanity divorced
Humanity, splitting the race of man   390
In twain, yet leaving the same outward form.
Distress of mind ensued upon the sight,
And ardent meditation.   Later years
Brought to such spectacle a milder sadness,
Feelings of pure commiseration, grief
For the individual and the overthrow
Of her soul's beauty; farther I was then
But seldom led, or wished to go; in truth
The sorrow of the passion stopped me there.

But let me now, less moved, in order take   400
Our argument.   Enough is said to show
How casual incidents of real life,
Observed where pastime only had been sought,
Outweighed, or put to flight, the set events
And measured passions of the stage, albeit
By Siddons trod in the fulness of her power.
Yet was the theatre my dear delight;
The very gilding, lamps and painted scrolls,
And all the mean upholstery of the place,
Wanted not animation, when the tide   410
Of pleasure ebbed but to return as fast
With the ever-shifting figures of the scene,
Solemn or gay: whether some beauteous dame
Advanced in radiance through a deep recess
Of thick entangled forest, like the moon
Opening the clouds; or sovereign king, announced
With flourishing trumpet, came in full-blown state
Of the world's greatness, winding round with train

Of courtiers, banners, and a length of guards,
Or captive led in abject weeds, and jingling   420
His slender manacles; or romping girl
Bounced, leapt, and pawed the air; or mumbling sire,
A scare-crow pattern of old age dressed up
In all the tatters of infirmity
All loosely put together, hobbled in,
Stumping upon a cane with which he smites,
From time to time, the solid boards, and makes them
Prate somewhat loudly of the whereabout
Of one so overloaded with his years.
But what of this! the laugh, the grin, grimace,   430
The antics striving to outstrip each other,
Were all received, the least of them not lost,
With an unmeasured welcome.   Through the night,
Between the show, and many-headed mass
Of the spectators, and each several nook
Filled with its fray or brawl, how eagerly
And with what flashes, as it were, the mind
Turned this way — that way! sportive and alert
And watchful, as a kitten when at play,
While winds are eddying round her, among straws   440
And rustling leaves.   Enchanting age and sweet!
Romantic almost, looked at through a space,
How small, of intervening years!   For then,
Though surely no mean progress had been made
In meditations holy and sublime,
Yet something of a girlish child-like gloss
Of novelty survived for scenes like these;
Enjoyment haply handed down from times
When at a country-playhouse, some rude barn
Tricked out for that proud use, if I perchance   450
Caught, on a summer evening through a chink
In the old wall, an unexpected glimpse
Of daylight, the bare thought of where I was

Gladdened me more than if I had been led
Into a dazzling cavern of romance,
Crowded with Genii busy among works
Not to be looked at by the common sun.

    The matter that detains us now may seem,
To many, neither dignified enough
Nor arduous, yet will not be scorned by them,   460
Who, looking inward, have observed the ties
That bind the perishable hours of life
Each to the other, and the curious props
By which the world of memory and thought
Exists and is sustained.   More lofty themes,
Such as at least do wear a prouder face,
Solicit our regard; but when I think
Of these, I feel the imaginative power
Languish within me; even then it slept,
When, pressed by tragic sufferings, the heart   470
Was more than full; amid my sobs and tears
It slept, even in the pregnant season of youth.
For though I was most passionately moved
And yielded to all changes of the scene
With an obsequious promptness, yet the storm
Passed not beyond the suburbs of the mind;
Save when realities of act and mien,
The incarnation of the spirits that move
In harmony amid the Poet's world,
Rose to ideal grandeur, or, called forth   480
By power of contrast, made me recognise,
As at a glance, the things which I had shaped,
And yet not shaped, had seen and scarcely seen,
When, having closed the mighty Shakspeare's page,
I mused, and thought, and felt, in solitude.

    Pass we from entertainments, that are such

Professedly, to others titled higher,
Yet, in the estimate of youth at least,
More near akin to those than names imply, —
I mean the brawls of lawyers in their courts   490
Before the ermined judge, or that great stage
Where senators, tongue-favoured men, perform,
Admired and envied.   Oh! the beating heart,
When one among the prime of these rose up, —
One, of whose name from childhood we had heard
Familiarly, a household term, like those,
The Bedfords, Glosters, Salsburys, of old,
Whom the fifth Harry talks of.   Silence! hush!
This is no trifler, no short-flighted wit,
No stammerer of a minute, painfully   500
Delivered.   No! the Orator hath yoked
The Hours, like young Aurora, to his car:
Thrice welcome Presence! how can patience e'er
Grow weary of attending on a track
That kindles with such glory!   All are charmed,
Astonished; like a hero in romance,
He winds away his never-ending horn;
Words follow words, sense seems to follow sense:
What memory and what logic! till the strain
Transcendent, superhuman as it seemed,   510
Grows tedious even in a young man's ear.

     Genius of Burke! forgive the pen seduced
By specious wonders, and too slow to tell
Of what the ingenuous, what bewildered men,
Beginning to mistrust their boastful guides,
And wise men, willing to grow wiser, caught,
Rapt auditors! from thy most eloquent tongue —
Now mute, for ever mute in the cold grave.
I see him, — old, but vigorous in age, —
Stand like an oak whose stag-horn branches start   520

Out of its leafy brow, the more to awe
The younger brethren of the grove. But some —
While he forewarns, denounces, launches forth,
Against all systems built on abstract rights,
Keen ridicule; the majesty proclaims
Of Institutes and Laws, hallowed by time;
Declares the vital power of social ties
Endeared by Custom; and with high disdain,
Exploding upstart Theory, insists
Upon the allegiance to which men are born —   530
Some — say at once a froward multitude —
Murmur (for truth is hated, where not loved)
As the winds fret within the Æolian cave,
Galled by their monarch's chain. The times were big
With ominous change, which, night by night, provoked
Keen struggles, and black clouds of passion raised;
But memorable moments intervened,
When Wisdom, like the Goddess from Jove's brain,
Broke forth in armour of resplendent words,
Startling the Synod. Could a youth, and one   540
In ancient story versed, whose breast had heaved
Under the weight of classic eloquence,
Sit, see, and hear, unthankful, uninspired?

Nor did the Pulpit's oratory fail
To achieve its higher triumph. Not unfelt
Were its admonishments, nor lightly heard
The awful truths delivered thence by tongues
Endowed with various power to search the soul;
Yet ostentation, domineering, oft
Poured forth harangues, how sadly out of place! —   550
There have I seen a comely bachelor,
Fresh from a toilette of two hours, ascend
His rostrum, with seraphic glance look up,
And, in a tone elaborately low

Beginning, lead his voice through many a maze
A minuet course; and, winding up his mouth,
From time to time, into an orifice
Most delicate, a lurking eyelet, small,
And only not invisible, again
Open it out, diffusing thence a smile   560
Of rapt irradiation, exquisite.
Meanwhile the Evangelists, Isaiah, Job,
Moses, and he who penned, the other day,
The Death of Abel, Shakspeare, and the Bard
Whose genius spangled o'er a gloomy theme
With fancies thick as his inspiring stars,
And Ossian (doubt not — 't is the naked truth)
Summoned from streamy Morven — each and all
Would, in their turns, lend ornaments and flowers
To entwine the crook of eloquence that helped   570
This pretty Shepherd, pride of all the plains,
To rule and guide his captivated flock.

I glance but at a few conspicuous marks,
Leaving a thousand others, that, in hall,
Court, theatre, conventicle, or shop,
In public room or private, park or street,
Each fondly reared on his own pedestal,
Looked out for admiration. Folly, vice,
Extravagance in gesture, mien, and dress,
And all the strife of singularity,   580
Lies to the ear, and lies to every sense —
Of these, and of the living shapes they wear,
There is no end. Such candidates for regard,
Although well pleased to be where they were found,
I did not hunt after, nor greatly prize,
Nor made unto myself a secret boast
Of reading them with quick and curious eye;
But, as a common produce, things that are

To-day, to-morrow will be, took of them
Such willing note, as, on some errand bound   590
That asks not speed, a traveller might bestow
On sea-shells that bestrew the sandy beach,
Or daisies swarming through the fields of June.

But foolishness and madness in parade,
Though most at home in this their dear domain,
Are scattered everywhere, no rarities,
Even to the rudest novice of the Schools.
Me, rather, it employed, to note, and keep
In memory, those individual sights
Of courage, or integrity, or truth,   600
Or tenderness, which there, set off by foil,
Appeared more touching.   One will I select —
A Father — for he bore that sacred name ; —
Him saw I, sitting in an open square,
Upon a corner-stone of that low wall,
Wherein were fixed the iron pales that fenced
A spacious grass-plot ; there, in silence, sate
This One Man, with a sickly babe outstretched
Upon his knee, whom he had thither brought
For sunshine, and to breathe the fresher air.   610
Of those who passed, and me who looked at him,
He took no heed ; but in his brawny arms
(The Artificer was to the elbow bare,
And from his work this moment had been stolen)
He held the child, and, bending over it,
As if he were afraid both of the sun
And of the air, which he had come to seek,
Eyed the poor babe with love unutterable.

As the black storm upon the mountain top
Sets off the sunbeam in the valley, so   620
That huge fermenting mass of human-kind

Serves as a solemn back-ground, or relief,
To single forms and objects, whence they draw,
For feeling and contemplative regard,
More than inherent liveliness and power.
How oft, amid those overflowing streets,
Have I gone forward with the crowd, and said
Unto myself, "The face of every one
That passes by me is a mystery!"
Thus have I looked, nor ceased to look, oppressed   630
By thoughts of what and whither, when and how,
Until the shapes before my eyes became
A second-sight procession, such as glides
Over still mountains, or appears in dreams;
And once, far-travelled in such mood, beyond
The reach of common indication, lost
Amid the moving pageant, I was smitten
Abruptly, with the view (a sight not rare)
Of a blind Beggar, who, with upright face,
Stood, propped against a wall, upon his chest   640
Wearing a written paper, to explain
His story, whence he came, and who he was.
Caught by the spectacle my mind turned round
As with the might of waters; and apt type
This label seemed of the utmost we can know,
Both of ourselves and of the universe;
And, on the shape of that unmoving man,
His steadfast face and sightless eyes, I gazed,
As if admonished from another world.

    Though reared upon the base of outward things,   650
Structures like these the excited spirit mainly
Builds for herself; scenes different there are,
Full-formed, that take, with small internal help,
Possession of the faculties, — the peace
That comes with night; the deep solemnity

Of nature's intermediate hours of rest,
When the great tide of human life stands still:
The business of the day to come, unborn,
Of that gone by, locked up, as in the grave;
The blended calmness of the heavens and earth,　660
Moonlight and stars, and empty streets, and sounds
Unfrequent as in deserts; at late hours
Of winter evenings, when unwholesome rains
Are falling hard, with people yet astir,
The feeble salutation from the voice
Of some unhappy woman, now and then
Heard as we pass, when no one looks about,
Nothing is listened to. But these, I fear,
Are falsely catalogued; things that are, are not,
As the mind answers to them, or the heart　670
Is prompt, or slow, to feel. What say you, then,
To times, when half the city shall break out
Full of one passion, vengeance, rage, or fear?
To executions, to a street on fire,
Mobs, riots, or rejoicings? From these sights
Take one, — that ancient festival, the Fair,
Holden where martyrs suffered in past time,
And named of St. Bartholomew; there, see
A work completed to our hands, that lays,
If any spectacle on earth can do,　680
The whole creative powers of man asleep! —
For once, the Muse's help will we implore,
And she shall lodge us, wafted on her wings,
Above the press and danger of the crowd,
Upon some showman's platform. What a shock
For eyes and ears! what anarchy and din,
Barbarian and infernal, — a phantasma,
Monstrous in colour, motion, shape, sight, sound!
Below, the open space, through every nook
Of the wide area, twinkles, is alive　690

With heads; the midway region, and above,
Is thronged with staring pictures and huge scrolls,
Dumb proclamations of the Prodigies;
With chattering monkeys dangling from their poles,
And children whirling in their roundabouts;
With those that stretch the neck and strain the eyes,
And crack the voice in rivalship, the crowd
Inviting; with buffoons against buffoons
Grimacing, writhing, screaming, — him who grinds
The hurdy-gurdy, at the fiddle weaves,   700
Rattles the salt-box, thumps the kettle-drum,
And him who at the trumpet puffs his cheeks,
The silver-collared Negro with his timbrel,
Equestrians, tumblers, women, girls, and boys,
Blue-breeched, pink-vested, with high-towering
        plumes. —
All moveables of wonder, from all parts,
Are here — Albinos, painted Indians, Dwarfs,
The Horse of knowledge, and the learned Pig,
The Stone-eater, the man that swallows fire,
Giants, Ventriloquists, the Invisible Girl,   710
The Bust that speaks and moves its goggling eyes,
The Wax-work, Clock-work, all the marvellous craft
Of modern Merlins, Wild Beasts, Puppet-shows,
All out-o'-the-way, far-fetched, perverted things,
All freaks of nature, all Promethean thoughts
Of man, his dulness, madness, and their feats
All jumbled up together, to compose
A Parliament of Monsters. Tents and Booths
Meanwhile, as if the whole were one vast mill,
Are vomiting, receiving on all sides,   720
Men, Women, three-years' Children, Babes in arms.

    Oh, blank confusion! true epitome
Of what the mighty City is herself,

To thousands upon thousands of her sons,
Living amid the same perpetual whirl
Of trivial objects, melted and reduced
To one identity, by differences
That have no law, no meaning, and no end —
Oppression, under which even highest minds
Must labour, whence the strongest are not free.   730
But though the picture weary out the eye,
By nature an unmanageable sight,
It is not wholly so to him who looks
In steadiness, who hath among least things
An under-sense of greatest; sees the parts
As parts, but with a feeling of the whole.
This, of all acquisitions, first awaits
On sundry and most widely different modes
Of education, nor with least delight
On that through which I passed. Attention springs,   740
And comprehensiveness and memory flow,
From early converse with the works of God
Among all regions; chiefly where appear
Most obviously simplicity and power.
Think, how the everlasting streams and woods,
Stretched and still stretching far and wide, exalt
The roving Indian, on his desert sands:
What grandeur not unfelt, what pregnant show
Of beauty, meets the sun-burnt Arab's eye:
And, as the sea propels, from zone to zone,   750
Its currents; magnifies its shoals of life
Beyond all compass; spreads, and sends aloft
Armies of clouds, — even so, its powers and aspects
Shape for mankind, by principles as fixed,
The views and aspirations of the soul
To majesty. Like virtue have the forms
Perennial of the ancient hills; nor less
The changeful language of their countenances

Quickens the slumbering mind, and aids the thoughts,
However multitudinous, to move   760
With order and relation. This, if still,
As hitherto, in freedom I may speak,
Not violating any just restraint,
As may be hoped, of real modesty, —
This did I feel, in London's vast domain.
The Spirit of Nature was upon me there;
The soul of Beauty and enduring Life
Vouchsafed her inspiration, and diffused,
Through meagre lines and colours, and the press
Of self-destroying, transitory things,   770
Composure, and ennobling Harmony.

BOOK EIGHTH

RETROSPECT — LOVE OF NATURE LEADING TO LOVE OF MAN

WHAT sounds are those, Helvellyn, that are heard
Up to thy summit, through the depth of air
Ascending, as if distance had the power
To make the sounds more audible? What crowd
Covers, or sprinkles o'er, yon village green?
Crowd seems it, solitary hill! to thee,
Though but a little family of men,
Shepherds and tillers of the ground — betimes
Assembled with their children and their wives,
And here and there a stranger interspersed.   10
They hold a rustic fair — a festival,
Such as, on this side now, and now on that,
Repeated through his tributary vales,
Helvellyn, in the silence of his rest,
Sees annually, if clouds towards either ocean

Blown from their favourite resting-place, or mists
Dissolved, have left him an unshrouded head.
Delightful day it is for all who dwell
In this secluded glen, and eagerly
They give it welcome. Long ere heat of noon,   20
From byre or field the kine were brought; the sheep
Are penned in cotes; the chaffering is begun.
The heifer lows, uneasy at the voice
Of a new master; bleat the flocks aloud.
Booths are there none; a stall or two is here;
A lame man or a blind, the one to beg,
The other to make music; hither, too,
From far, with basket, slung upon her arm,
Of hawker's wares — books, pictures, combs, and pins —
Some aged woman finds her way again,   30
Year after year, a punctual visitant!
There also stands a speech-maker by rote,
Pulling the strings of his boxed raree-show;
And in the lapse of many years may come
Prouder itinerant, mountebank, or he
Whose wonders in a covered wain lie hid.
But one there is, the loveliest of them all,
Some sweet lass of the valley, looking out
For gains, and who that sees her would not buy?
Fruits of her father's orchard are her wares,   40
And with the ruddy produce she walks round
Among the crowd, half pleased with, half ashamed
Of, her new office, blushing restlessly.
The children now are rich, for the old to-day
Are generous as the young; and, if content
With looking on, some ancient wedded pair
Sit in the shade together; while they gaze,
"A cheerful smile unbends the wrinkled brow,
The days departed start again to life,
And all the scenes of childhood reappear,   50

Faint, but more tranquil, like the changing sun
To him who slept at noon and wakes at eve."
Thus gaiety and cheerfulness prevail,
Spreading from young to old, from old to young,
And no one seems to want his share. — Immense
Is the recess, the circumambient world
Magnificent, by which they are embraced:
They move about upon the soft green turf:
How little they, they and their doings, seem,
And all that they can further or obstruct!   60
Through utter weakness pitiably dear,
As tender infants are: and yet how great!
For all things serve them: them the morning light
Loves, as it glistens on the silent rocks;
And them the silent rocks, which now from high
Look down upon them; the reposing clouds;
The wild brooks prattling from invisible haunts;
And old Helvellyn, conscious of the stir
Which animates this day their calm abode.

With deep devotion, Nature, did I feel,   70
In that enormous City's turbulent world
Of men and things, what benefit I owed
To thee, and those domains of rural peace,
Where to the sense of beauty first my heart
Was opened; tract more exquisitely fair
Than that famed paradise of ten thousand trees,
Or Gehol's matchless gardens, for delight
Of the Tartarian dynasty composed
(Beyond that mighty wall, not fabulous,
China's stupendous mound) by patient toil   80
Of myriads and boon nature's lavish help;
There, in a clime from widest empire chosen,
Fulfilling (could enchantment have done more?)
A sumptuous dream of flowery lawns, with domes

Of pleasure sprinkled over, shady dells
For eastern monasteries, sunny mounts
With temples crested, bridges, gondolas,
Rocks, dens, and groves of foliage taught to melt
Into each other their obsequious hues,
Vanished and vanishing in subtle chase,   90
Too fine to be pursued; or standing forth
In no discordant opposition, strong
And gorgeous as the colours side by side
Bedded among rich plumes of tropic birds;
And mountains over all, embracing all;
And all the landscape, endlessly enriched
With waters running, falling, or asleep.

But lovelier far than this, the paradise
Where I was reared; in Nature's primitive gifts
Favoured no less, and more to every sense   100
Delicious, seeing that the sun and sky,
The elements, and seasons as they change,
Do find a worthy fellow-labourer there —
Man free, man working for himself, with choice
Of time, and place, and object; by his wants,
His comforts, native occupations, cares,
Cheerfully led to individual ends
Or social, and still followed by a train
Unwooed, unthought-of even — simplicity,
And beauty, and inevitable grace.   110

Yea, when a glimpse of those imperial bowers
Would to a child be transport over-great,
When but a half-hour's roam through such a place
Would leave behind a dance of images,
That shall break in upon his sleep for weeks;
Even then the common haunts of the green earth,
And ordinary interests of man,

Which they embosom, all without regard
As both may seem, are fastening on the heart
Insensibly, each with the other's help.　　120
For me, when my affections first were led
From kindred, friends, and playmates, to partake
Love for the human creature's absolute self,
That noticeable kindliness of heart
Sprang out of fountains, there abounding most,
Where sovereign Nature dictated the tasks
And occupations which her beauty adorned,
And Shepherds were the men that pleased me first;
Not such as Saturn ruled 'mid Latian wilds,
With arts and laws so tempered, that their lives　　130
Left, even to us toiling in this late day,
A bright tradition of the golden age;
Not such as, 'mid Arcadian fastnesses
Sequestered, handed down among themselves
Felicity, in Grecian song renowned;
Nor such as — when an adverse fate had driven,
From house and home, the courtly band whose fortunes
Entered, with Shakspeare's genius, the wild woods
Of Arden — amid sunshine or in shade
Culled the best fruits of Time's uncounted hours,　　140
Ere Phœbe sighed for the false Ganymede;
Or there where Perdita and Florizel
Together danced, Queen of the feast, and King;
Nor such as Spenser fabled.　True it is,
That I had heard (what he perhaps had seen)
Of maids at sunrise bringing in from far
Their May-bush, and along the streets in flocks
Parading with a song of taunting rhymes,
Aimed at the laggards slumbering within doors;
Had also heard, from those who yet remembered,　　150
Tales of the May-pole dance, and wreaths that decked
Porch, door-way, or kirk-pillar; and of youths,

Each with his maid, before the sun was up,
By annual custom, issuing forth in troops,
To drink the waters of some sainted well,
And hang it round with garlands. Love survives;
But, for such purpose, flowers no longer grow:
The times, too sage, perhaps too proud, have dropped
These lighter graces; and the rural ways
And manners which my childhood looked upon   160
Were the unluxuriant produce of a life
Intent on little but substantial needs,
Yet rich in beauty, beauty that was felt.
But images of danger and distress,
Man suffering among awful Powers and Forms;
Of this I heard, and saw enough to make
Imagination restless; nor was free
Myself from frequent perils; nor were tales
Wanting, — the tragedies of former times,
Hazards and strange escapes, of which the rocks   170
Immutable, and everflowing streams,
Where'er I roamed, were speaking monuments.

Smooth life had flock and shepherd in old time,
Long springs and tepid winters, on the banks
Of delicate Galesus; and no less
Those scattered along Adria's myrtle shores:
Smooth life had herdsman, and his snow-white **herd**
To triumphs and to sacrificial rites
Devoted, on the inviolable stream
Of rich Clitumnus; and the goat-herd lived   180
As calmly, underneath the pleasant brows
Of cool Lucretilis, where the pipe was heard
Of Pan, Invisible God, thrilling the rocks
With tutelary music, from all harm
The fold protecting. I myself, mature
In manhood then, have seen a pastoral tract

Like one of these, where Fancy might run wild,
Though under skies less generous, less serene:
There, for her own delight had Nature framed
A pleasure-ground, diffused a fair expanse 190
Of level pasture, islanded with groves
And banked with woody risings; but the Plain
Endless, here opening widely out, and there
Shut up in lesser lakes or beds of lawn
And intricate recesses, creek or bay
Sheltered within a shelter, where at large
The shepherd strays, a rolling hut his home.
Thither he comes with spring-time, there abides
All summer, and at sunrise ye may hear
His flageolet to liquid notes of love 200
Attuned, or sprightly fife resounding far.
Nook is there none, nor tract of that vast space
Where passage opens, but the same shall have
In turn its visitant, telling there his hours
In unlaborious pleasure, with no task
More toilsome than to carve a beechen bowl
For spring or fountain, which the traveller finds,
When through the region he pursues at will
His devious course. A glimpse of such sweet life
I saw when, from the melancholy walls 210
Of Goslar, once imperial, I renewed
My daily walk along that wide champaign,
That, reaching to her gates, spreads east and west,
And northwards, from beneath the mountainous verge
Of the Hercynian forest. Yet, hail to you
Moors, mountains, headlands, and ye hollow vales,
Ye long deep channels for the Atlantic's voice,
Powers of my native region! Ye that seize
The heart with firmer grasp! Your snows and streams
Ungovernable, and your terrifying winds, 220
That howl so dismally for him who treads

Companionless your awful solitudes!
There, 't is the shepherd's task the winter long
To wait upon the storms: of their approach
Sagacious, into sheltering coves he drives
His flock, and thither from the homestead bears
A toilsome burden up the craggy ways,
And deals it out, their regular nourishment
Strewn on the frozen snow. And when the spring
Looks out, and all the pastures dance with lambs,   230
And when the flock, with warmer weather, climbs
Higher and higher, him his office leads
To watch their goings, whatsoever track
The wanderers choose. For this he quits his home
At day-spring, and no sooner doth the sun
Begin to strike him with a fire-like heat,
Than he lies down upon some shining rock,
And breakfasts with his dog. When they have stolen,
As is their wont, a pittance from strict time,
For rest not needed or exchange of love,   240
Then from his couch he starts; and now his feet
Crush out a livelier fragrance from the flowers
Of lowly thyme, by Nature's skill enwrought
In the wild turf: the lingering dews of morn
Smoke round him, as from hill to hill he hies,
His staff protending like a hunter's spear,
Or by its aid leaping from crag to crag,
And o'er the brawling beds of unbridged streams.
Philosophy, methinks, at Fancy's call,
Might deign to follow him through what he does   250
Or sees in his day's march; himself he feels,
In those vast regions where his service lies,
A freeman, wedded to his life of hope
And hazard, and hard labour interchanged
With that majestic indolence so dear
To native man. A rambling schoolboy, thus,

I felt his presence in his own domain,
As of a lord and master, or a power,
Or genius, under Nature, under God,
Presiding; and severest solitude   260
Had more commanding looks when he was there.
When up the lonely brooks on rainy days
Angling I went, or trod the trackless hills
By mists bewildered, suddenly mine eyes
Have glanced upon him distant a few steps,
In size a giant, stalking through thick fog,
His sheep like Greenland bears; or, as he stepped
Beyond the boundary line of some hill-shadow,
His form hath flashed upon me, glorified
By the deep radiance of the setting sun: 270
Or him have I descried in distant sky,
A solitary object and sublime,
Above all height! like an aerial cross
Stationed alone upon a spiry rock
Of the Chartreuse, for worship. Thus was man
Ennobled outwardly before my sight,
And thus my heart was early introduced
To an unconscious love and reverence
Of human nature; hence the human form
To me became an index of delight,   280
Of grace and honour, power and worthiness.
Meanwhile this creature — spiritual almost
As those of books, but more exalted far;
Far more of an imaginative form
Than the gay Corin of the groves, who lives
For his own fancies, or to dance by the hour,
In coronal, with Phyllis in the midst —
Was, for the purposes of kind, a man
With the most common; husband, father; learned,
Could teach, admonish; suffered with the rest   290
From vice and folly, wretchedness and fear;

Of this I little saw, cared less for it,
But something must have felt.
                 Call ye these appearances —
Which I beheld of shepherds in my youth,
This sanctity of Nature given to man —
A shadow, a delusion, ye who pore
On the dead letter, miss the spirit of things;
Whose truth is not a motion or a shape
Instinct with vital functions, but a block
Or waxen image which yourselves have made,   300
And ye adore! But blessèd be the God
Of Nature and of Man that this was so;
That men before my inexperienced eyes
Did first present themselves thus purified,
Removed, and to a distance that was fit:
And so we all of us in some degree
Are led to knowledge, wheresoever led,
And howsoever; were it otherwise,
And we found evil fast as we find good
In our first years, or think that it is found,   310
How could the innocent heart bear up and live!
But doubly fortunate my lot; not here
Alone, that something of a better life
Perhaps was round me than it is the privilege
Of most to move in, but that first I looked
At Man through objects that were great or fair;
First communed with him by their help. And thus
Was founded a sure safeguard and defence
Against the weight of meanness, selfish cares,
Coarse manners, vulgar passions, that beat in   320
On all sides from the ordinary world
In which we traffic. Starting from this point
I had my face turned toward the truth, began
With an advantage furnished by that kind
Of prepossession, without which the soul

Receives no knowledge that can bring forth good,
No genuine insight ever comes to her.
From the restraint of over-watchful eyes
Preserved, I moved about, year after year,
Happy, and now most thankful that my walk   330
Was guarded from too early intercourse
With the deformities of crowded life,
And those ensuing laughters and contempts,
Self-pleasing, which, if we would wish to think
With a due reverence on earth's rightful lord,
Here placed to be the inheritor of heaven,
Will not permit us; but pursue the mind,
That to devotion willingly would rise,
Into the temple and the temple's heart.

    Yet deem not, Friend! that human kind with me   340
Thus early took a place pre-eminent;
Nature herself was, at this unripe time,
But secondary to my own pursuits
And animal activities, and all
Their trivial pleasures; and when these had drooped
And gradually expired, and Nature, prized
For her own sake, became my joy, even then —
And upwards through late youth, until not less
Than two-and-twenty summers had been told —
Was Man in my affections and regards   350
Subordinate to her, her visible forms
And viewless agencies: a passion, she,
A rapture often, and immediate love
Ever at hand; he, only a delight
Occasional, an accidental grace,
His hour being not yet come.   Far less had then
The inferior creatures, beast or bird, attuned
My spirit to that gentleness of love,

(Though they had long been carefully observed),
Won from me those minute obeisances   360
Of tenderness, which I may number now
With my first blessings.   Nevertheless, on these
The light of beauty did not fall in vain,
Or grandeur circumfuse them to no end.

  But when that first poetic faculty
Of plain Imagination and severe,
No longer a mute influence of the soul,
Ventured, at some rash Muse's earnest call,
To try her strength among harmonious words;
And to book-notions and the rules of art   370
Did knowingly conform itself; there came
Among the simple shapes of human life
A wilfulness of fancy and conceit;
And Nature and her objects beautified
These fictions, as in some sort, in their turn,
They burnished her.   From touch of this new power
Nothing was safe: the elder-tree that grew
Beside the well-known charnel-house had then
A dismal look: the yew-tree had its ghost,
That took his station there for ornament: 380
The dignities of plain occurrence then
Were tasteless, and truth's golden mean, a point
Where no sufficient pleasure could be found.
Then, if a widow, staggering with the blow
Of her distress, was known to have turned her steps
To the cold grave in which her husband slept,
One night, or haply more than one, through pain
Or half-insensate impotence of mind,
The fact was caught at greedily, and there
She must be visitant the whole year through,   390
Wetting the turf with never-ending tears.

   Through quaint obliquities I might pursue
These cravings; when the foxglove, one by one,
Upwards through every stage of the tall stem,
Had shed beside the public way its bells,
And stood of all dismantled, save the last
Left at the tapering ladder's top, that seemed
To bend as doth a slender blade of grass
Tipped with a rain-drop, Fancy loved to seat,
Beneath the plant despoiled, but crested still   400
With this last relic, soon itself to fall,
Some vagrant mother, whose arch little ones,
All unconcerned by her dejected plight,
Laughed as with rival eagerness their hands
Gathered the purple cups that round them lay,
Strewing the turf's green slope.
                                        A diamond light
(Whene'er the summer sun, declining, smote
A smooth rock wet with constant springs) was seen
Sparkling from out a copse-clad bank that rose
Fronting our cottage.   Oft beside the hearth   410
Seated, with open door, often and long
Upon this restless lustre have I gazed,
That made my fancy restless as itself.
'T was now for me a burnished silver shield
Suspended over a knight's tomb, who lay
Inglorious, buried in the dusky wood:
An entrance now into some magic cave
Or palace built by fairies of the rock;
Nor could I have been bribed to disenchant
The spectacle, by visiting the spot.   420
Thus wilful Fancy, in no hurtful mood,
Engrafted far-fetched shapes on feelings bred
By pure Imagination: busy Power
She was, and with her ready pupil turned
Instinctively to human passions, then

Least understood.   Yet, 'mid the fervent swarm
Of these vagaries, with an eye so rich
As mine was through the bounty of a grand
And lovely region, I had forms distinct
To steady me: each airy thought revolved   430
Round a substantial centre, which at once
Incited it to motion, and controlled.
I did not pine like one in cities bred,
As was thy melancholy lot, dear Friend!
Great Spirit as thou art, in endless dreams
Of sickliness, disjoining, joining, things
Without the light of knowledge.   Where the harm,
If, when the woodman languished with disease
Induced by sleeping nightly on the ground
Within his sod-built cabin, Indian-wise,   440
I called the pangs of disappointed love,
And all the sad etcetera of the wrong,
To help him to his grave?   Meanwhile the man,
If not already from the woods retired
To die at home, was haply, as I knew,
Withering by slow degrees, 'mid gentle airs,
Birds, running streams, and hills so beautiful
On golden evenings, while the charcoal pile
Breathed up its smoke, an image of his ghost
Or spirit that full soon must take her flight.   450
Nor shall we not be tending towards that point
Of sound humanity to which our Tale
Leads, though by sinuous ways, if here I show
How Fancy, in a season when she wove
Those slender cords, to guide the unconscious Boy
For the Man's sake, could feed at Nature's call
Some pensive musings which might well beseem
Maturer years.
            A grove there is whose boughs
Stretch from the western marge of Thurstonmere,

With length of shade so thick, that whoso glides   460
Along the line of low-roofed water, moves
As in a cloister. Once — while, in that shade
Loitering, I watched the golden beams of light
Flung from the setting sun, as they reposed
In silent beauty on the naked ridge
Of a high eastern hill — thus flowed my thoughts
In a pure stream of words fresh from the heart:
Dear native Regions, wheresoe'er shall close
My mortal course, there will I think on you;
Dying, will cast on you a backward look;   470
Even as this setting sun (albeit the Vale
Is no where touched by one memorial gleam)
Doth with the fond remains of his last power
Still linger, and a farewell lustre sheds,
On the dear mountain-tops where first he rose.

   Enough of humble arguments; recall,
My Song! those high emotions which thy voice
Has heretofore made known; that bursting forth
Of sympathy, inspiring and inspired,
When everywhere a vital pulse was felt,   480
And all the several frames of things, like stars,
Through every magnitude distinguishable,
Shone mutually indebted, or half lost
Each in the other's blaze, a galaxy
Of life and glory. In the midst stood Man,
Outwardly, inwardly contemplated,
As, of all visible natures, crown, though born
Of dust, and kindred to the worm; a Being,
Both in perception and discernment, first
In every capability of rapture,   490
Through the divine effect of power and love;
As, more than anything we know, instinct

With godhead, and, by reason and by will,
Acknowledging dependency sublime.

Ere long, the lonely mountains left, I moved,
Begirt, from day to day, with temporal shapes
Of vice and folly thrust upon my view,
Objects of sport, and ridicule, and scorn,
Manners and characters discriminate,
And little bustling passions that eclipse,   500
As well they might, the impersonated thought,
The idea, or abstraction of the kind.

An idler among academic bowers,
Such was my new condition, as at large
Has been set forth; yet here the vulgar light
Of present, actual, superficial life,
Gleaming through colouring of other times,
Old usages and local privilege,
Was welcomed, softened, if not solemnised.
This notwithstanding, being brought more near   510
To vice and guilt, forerunning wretchedness,
I trembled, — thought, at times, of human life
With an indefinite terror and dismay,
Such as the storms and angry elements
Had bred in me; but gloomier far, a dim
Analogy to uproar and misrule,
Disquiet, danger, and obscurity.

It might be told (but wherefore speak of things
Common to all?) that, seeing, I was led
Gravely to ponder — judging between good   520
And evil, not as for the mind's delight
But for her guidance — one who was to *act*,
As sometimes to the best of feeble means
I did, by human sympathy impelled:

And, through dislike and most offensive pain,
Was to the truth conducted; of this faith
Never forsaken, that, by acting well,
And understanding, I should learn to love
The end of life, and everything we know.

　　Grave Teacher, stern Preceptress! for at times　　530
Thou canst put on an aspect most severe;
London, to thee I willingly return.
Erewhile my verse played idly with the flowers
Enwrought upon thy mantle; satisfied
With that amusement, and a simple look
Of child-like inquisition now and then
Cast upwards on thy countenance, to detect
Some inner meanings which might harbour there.
But how could I in mood so light indulge,
Keeping such fresh remembrance of the day,　　540
When, having thridded the long labyrinth
Of the suburban villages, I first
Entered thy vast dominion?　On the roof
Of an itinerant vehicle I sate,
With vulgar men about me, trivial forms
Of houses, pavement, streets, of men and things, — ·
Mean shapes on every side: but, at the instant,
When to myself it fairly might be said,
The threshold now is overpast, (how strange
That aught external to the living mind　　550
Should have such mighty sway! yet so it was),
A weight of ages did at once descend
Upon my heart; no thought embodied, no
Distinct remembrances, but weight and power, —
Power growing under weight: alas! I feel
That I am trifling: 't was a moment's pause, —
All that took place within me came and went

As in a moment; yet with Time it dwells,
And grateful memory, as a thing divine.

The curious traveller, who, from open day,   560
Hath passed with torches into some huge cave,
The Grotto of Antiparos, or the Den
In old time haunted by that Danish Witch,
Yordas; he looks around and sees the vault
Widening on all sides; sees, or thinks he sees,
Erelong, the massy roof above his head,
That instantly unsettles and recedes, —
Substance and shadow, light and darkness, all
Commingled, making up a canopy
Of shapes and forms and tendencies to shape   570
That shift and vanish, change and interchange
Like spectres, — ferment silent and sublime!
That after a short space works less and less,
Till, every effort, every motion gone,
The scene before him stands in perfect view
Exposed, and lifeless as a written book! —
But let him pause awhile, and look again,
And a new quickening shall succeed, at first
Beginning timidly, then creeping fast,
Till the whole cave, so late a senseless mass,   580
Busies the eye with images and forms
Boldly assembled, — here is shadowed forth
From the projections, wrinkles, cavities,
A variegated landscape, — there the shape
Of some gigantic warrior clad in mail,
The ghostly semblance of a hooded monk,
Veiled nun, or pilgrim resting on his staff:
Strange congregation! yet not slow to meet
Eyes that perceive through minds that can inspire.

Even in such sort had I at first been moved,   590

Nor otherwise continued to be moved,
As I explored the vast metropolis,
Fount of my country's destiny and the world's;
That great emporium, chronicle at once
And burial-place of passions, and their home
Imperial, their chief living residence.

With strong sensations teeming as it did
Of past and present, such a place must needs
Have pleased me, seeking knowledge at that time
Far less than craving power; yet knowledge came,   600
Sought or unsought, and influxes of power
Came, of themselves, or at her call derived
In fits of kindliest apprehensiveness,
From all sides, when whate'er was in itself
Capacious found, or seemed to find, in me
A correspondent amplitude of mind;
Such is the strength and glory of our youth!
The human nature unto which I felt
That I belonged, and reverenced with love,
Was not a punctual presence, but a spirit   610
Diffused through time and space, with aid derived
Of evidence from monuments, erect,
Prostrate, or leaning towards their common rest
In earth, the widely scattered wreck sublime
Of vanished nations, or more clearly drawn
From books and what they picture and record.

'T is true, the history of our native land —
With those of Greece compared and popular Rome,
And in our high-wrought modern narratives
Stript of their harmonising soul, the life   620
Of manners and familiar incidents —

Had never much delighted me.   And less
Than other intellects had mine been used
To lean upon extrinsic circumstance
Of record or tradition; but a sense
Of what in the Great City had been done
And suffered, and was doing, suffering, still,
Weighed with me, could support the test of thought;
And, in despite of all that had gone by,
Or was departing never to return,   630
There I conversed with majesty and power
Like independent natures.   Hence the place
Was thronged with impregnations like the Wilds
In which my early feelings had been nursed —
Bare hills and valleys, full of caverns, rocks,
And audible seclusions, dashing lakes,
Echoes and waterfalls, and pointed crags
That into music touch the passing wind.
Here then my young imagination found
No uncongenial element;   could here   640
Among new objects serve or give command,
Even as the heart's occasions might require,
To forward reason's else too-scrupulous march.
The effect was, still more elevated views
Of human nature.   Neither vice nor guilt,
Debasement undergone by body or mind,
Nor all the misery forced upon my sight,
Misery not lightly passed, but sometimes scanned
Most feelingly, could overthrow my trust
In what we *may* become; induce belief   650
That I was ignorant, had been falsely taught,
A solitary, who with vain conceits
Had been inspired, and walked about in dreams.
From those sad scenes when meditation turned,
Lo! everything that was indeed divine
Retained its purity inviolate,

Nay brighter shone, by this portentous gloom
Set off; such opposition as aroused
The mind of Adam, yet in Paradise
Though fallen from bliss, when in the East he saw   660
Darkness ere day's mid course, and morning light
More orient in the western cloud, that drew
O'er the blue firmament a radiant white,
Descending slow with something heavenly fraught.

  Add also, that among the multitudes
Of that huge city, oftentimes was seen
Affectingly set forth, more than elsewhere
Is possible, the unity of man,
One spirit over ignorance and vice
Predominant, in good and evil hearts;   670
One sense for moral judgments, as one eye
For the sun's light.   The soul when smitten thus
By a sublime *idea*, whencesoe'er
Vouchsafed for union or communion, feeds
On the pure bliss, and takes her rest with God.

  Thus from a very early age, O Friend!
My thoughts by slow gradations had been drawn
To human-kind, and to the good and ill
Of human life: Nature had led me on;
And oft amid the "busy hum" I seemed   680
To travel independent of her help,
As if I had forgotten her; but no,
The world of human-kind outweighed not hers
In my habitual thoughts; the scale of love,
Though filling daily, still was light, compared
With that in which *her* mighty objects lay.

BOOK NINTH

RESIDENCE IN FRANCE

EVEN as a river, — partly (it might seem)
Yielding to old remembrances, and swayed
In part by fear to shape a way direct,
That would engulph him soon in the ravenous sea —
Turns, and will measure back his course, far back,
Seeking the very regions which he crossed
In his first outset; so have we, my Friend!
Turned and returned with intricate delay.
Or as a traveller, who has gained the brow
Of some aerial Down, while there he halts   10
For breathing-time, is tempted to review
The region left behind him; and, if aught
Deserving notice have escaped regard,
Or been regarded with too careless eye,
Strives, from that height, with one and yet one more
Last look, to make the best amends he may:
So have we lingered. Now we start afresh
With courage, and new hope risen on our toil.
Fair greetings to this shapeless eagerness,
Whene'er it comes! needful in work so long,   20
Thrice needful to the argument which now
Awaits us! Oh, how much unlike the past!

  Free as a colt at pasture on the hill,
I ranged at large, through London's wide domain,
Month after month. Obscurely did I live,
Not seeking frequent intercourse with men,
By literature, or elegance, or rank,
Distinguished. Scarcely was a year thus spent
Ere I forsook the crowded solitude,

With less regret for its luxurious pomp, 30
And all the nicely-guarded shows of art,
Than for the humble book-stalls in the streets,
Exposed to eye and hand where'er I turned.

France lured me forth; the realm that I had crossed
So lately, journeying toward the snow-clad Alps.
But now, relinquishing the scrip and staff,
And all enjoyment which the summer sun
Sheds round the steps of those who meet the day
With motion constant as his own, I went
Prepared to sojourn in a pleasant town, 40
Washed by the current of the stately Loire.

Through Paris lay my readiest course, and there
Sojourning a few days, I visited
In haste, each spot of old or recent fame,
The latter chiefly; from the field of Mars
Down to the suburbs of St. Antony,
And from Mont Martre southward to the Dome
Of Geneviève. In both her clamorous Halls,
The National Synod and the Jacobins,
I saw the Revolutionary Power 50
Toss like a ship at anchor, rocked by storms;
The Arcades I traversed, in the Palace huge
Of Orleans; coasted round and round the line
Of Tavern, Brothel, Gaming-house, and Shop,
Great rendezvous of worst and best, the walk
Of all who had a purpose, or had not;
I stared and listened, with a stranger's ears,
To Hawkers and Haranguers, hubbub wild!
And hissing Factionists with ardent eyes,
In knots, or pairs, or single. Not a look 60
Hope takes, or Doubt or Fear is forced to wear,
But seemed there present; and I scanned them all,

Watched every gesture uncontrollable,
Of anger, and vexation, and despite,
All side by side, and struggling face to face,
With gaiety and dissolute idleness.

Where silent zephyrs sported with the dust
Of the Bastille, I sate in the open sun,
And from the rubbish gathered up a stone,
And pocketed the relic, in the guise   70
Of an enthusiast: yet, in honest truth,
I looked for something that I could not find,
Affecting more emotion than I felt;
For 't is most certain, that these various sights,
However potent their first shock, with me
Appeared to recompense the traveller's pains
Less than the painted Magdalene of Le Brun,
A beauty exquisitely wrought, with hair
Dishevelled, gleaming eyes, and rueful cheek
Pale and bedropped with overflowing tears.   80

But hence to my more permanent abode
I hasten; there, by novelties in speech,
Domestic manners, customs, gestures, looks,
And all the attire of ordinary life,
Attention was engrossed; and, thus amused,
I stood 'mid those concussions, unconcerned,
Tranquil almost, and careless as a flower
Glassed in a green-house, or a parlour shrub
That spreads its leaves in unmolested peace,
While every bush and tree, the country through,   90
Is shaking to the roots: indifference this
Which may seem strange: but I was unprepared
With needful knowledge, had abruptly passed
Into a theatre, whose stage was filled
And busy with an action far advanced.

Like others, I had skimmed, and sometimes read
With care, the master pamphlets of the day;
Nor wanted such half-insight as grew wild
Upon that meagre soil, helped out by talk
And public news; but having never seen   100
A chronicle that might suffice to show
Whence the main organs of the public power
Had sprung, their transmigrations, when and how
Accomplished, giving thus unto events
A form and body; all things were to me
Loose and disjointed, and the affections left
Without a vital interest. At that time,
Moreover, the first storm was overblown,
And the strong hand of outward violence
Locked up in quiet. For myself, I fear   110
Now, in connection with so great a theme,
To speak (as I must be compelled to do)
Of one so unimportant; night by night
Did I frequent the formal haunts of men,
Whom, in the city, privilege of birth
Sequestered from the rest, societies
Polished in arts, and in punctilio versed;
Whence, and from deeper causes, all discourse
Of good and evil of the time was shunned
With scrupulous care; but these restrictions soon   120
Proved tedious, and I gradually withdrew
Into a noisier world, and thus ere long
Became a patriot; and my heart was all
Given to the people, and my love was theirs.

    A band of military Officers,
Then stationed in the city, were the chief
Of my associates: some of these wore swords
That had been seasoned in the wars, and all
Were men well-born; the chivalry of France.

In age and temper differing, they had yet   130
One spirit ruling in each heart; alike
(Save only one, hereafter to be named)
Were bent upon undoing what was done:
This was their rest and only hope; therewith
No fear had they of bad becoming worse,
For worst to them was come; nor would have stirred,
Or deemed it worth a moment's thought to stir,
In anything, save only as the act
Looked thitherward.   One, reckoning by years,
Was in the prime of manhood, and erewhile   140
He had sate lord in many tender hearts;
Though heedless of such honours now, and changed:
His temper was quite mastered by the times,
And they had blighted him, had eaten away
The beauty of his person, doing wrong
Alike to body and to mind: his port,
Which once had been erect and open, now
Was stooping and contracted, and a face,
Endowed by Nature with her fairest gifts
Of symmetry and light and bloom, expressed,   150
As much as any that was ever seen,
A ravage out of season, made by thoughts
Unhealthy and vexatious.   With the hour,
That from the press of Paris duly brought
Its freight of public news, the fever came,
A punctual visitant, to shake this man,
Disarmed his voice and fanned his yellow cheek
Into a thousand colours; while he read,
Or mused, his sword was haunted by his touch
Continually, like an uneasy place   160
In his own body.   'T was in truth an hour
Of universal ferment; mildest men
Were agitated; and commotions, strife
Of passion and opinion, filled the walls

Of peaceful houses with unquiet sounds.
The soil of common life was, at that time,
Too hot to tread upon. Oft said I then,
And not then only, "What a mockery this
Of history, the past and that to come!
Now do I feel how all men are deceived,   170
Reading of nations and their works, in faith,
Faith given to vanity and emptiness;
Oh! laughter for the page that would reflect
To future times the face of what now is!"
The land all swarmed with passion, like a plain
Devoured by locusts, — Carra, Gorsas, — add
A hundred other names, forgotten now,
Nor to be heard of more; yet they were powers,
Like earthquakes, shocks repeated day by day,
And felt through every nook of town and field.   180

   Such was the state of things. Meanwhile the chief
Of my associates stood prepared for flight
To augment the band of emigrants in arms
Upon the borders of the Rhine, and leagued
With foreign foes mustered for instant war.
This was their undisguised intent, and they
Were waiting with the whole of their desires
The moment to depart.
                        An Englishman,
Born in a land whose very name appeared
To license some unruliness of mind;   190
A stranger, with youth's further privilege,
And the indulgence that a half-learnt speech
Wins from the courteous; I, who had been else
Shunned and not tolerated, freely lived
With these defenders of the Crown, and talked,
And heard their notions; nor did they disdain
The wish to bring me over to their cause.

But though untaught by thinking or by books
To reason well of polity or law,
And nice distinctions, then on every tongue,   200
Of natural rights and civil; and to acts
Of nations and their passing interests
(If with unworldly ends and aims compared)
Almost indifferent, even the historian's tale
Prizing but little otherwise than I prized
Tales of the poets, as it made the heart
Beat high, and filled the fancy with fair forms,
Old heroes and their sufferings and their deeds;
Yet in the regal sceptre, and the pomp
Of orders and degrees, I nothing found   210
Then, or had ever, even in crudest youth,
That dazzled me, but rather what I mourned
And ill could brook, beholding that the best
Ruled not, and feeling that they ought to rule.

For, born in a poor district, and which yet
Retaineth more of ancient homeliness,
Than any other nook of English ground,
It was my fortune scarcely to have seen,
Through the whole tenor of my school-day time,
The face of one, who, whether boy or man,   220
Was vested with attention or respect
Through claims of wealth or blood; nor was it least
Of many benefits, in later years
Derived from academic institutes
And rules, that they held something up to view
Of a Republic, where all stood thus far
Upon equal ground; that we were brothers all
In honour, as in one community,
Scholars and gentlemen; where, furthermore,
Distinction open lay to all that came,   230
And wealth and titles were in less esteem

Than talents, worth, and prosperous industry.
Add unto this, subservience from the first
To presences of God's mysterious power
Made manifest in Nature's sovereignty,
And fellowship with venerable books,
To sanction the proud workings of the soul,
And mountain liberty.   It could not be
But that one tutored thus should look with awe
Upon the faculties of man, receive   240
Gladly the highest promises, and hail,
As best, the government of equal rights
And individual worth.   And hence, O Friend!
If at the first great outbreak I rejoiced
Less than might well befit my youth, the cause
In part lay here, that unto me the events
Seemed nothing out of nature's certain course,
A gift that was come rather late than soon.
No wonder, then, if advocates like these,
Inflamed by passion, blind with prejudice,   250
And stung with injury, at this riper day,
Were impotent to make my hopes put on
The shape of theirs, my understanding bend
In honour to their honour: zeal, which yet
Had slumbered, now in opposition burst
Forth like a Polar summer: every word
They uttered was a dart, by counter-winds
Blown back upon themselves; their reason seemed
Confusion-stricken by a higher power
Than human understanding, their discourse   260
Maimed, spiritless; and, in their weakness strong,
I triumphed.
              Meantime, day by day, the roads
Were crowded with the bravest youth of France,
And all the promptest of her spirits, linked
In gallant soldiership, and posting on

To meet the war upon her frontier bounds.
Yet at this very moment do tears start
Into mine eyes: I do not say I weep —
I wept not then, — but tears have dimmed my sight,
In memory of the farewells of that time,   270
Domestic severings, female fortitude
At dearest separation, patriot love
And self-devotion, and terrestrial hope,
Encouraged with a martyr's confidence;
Even files of strangers merely seen but once,
And for a moment, men from far with sound
Of music, martial tunes, and banners spread,
Entering the city, here and there a face,
Or person, singled out among the rest,
Yet still a stranger and beloved as such;   280
Even by these passing spectacles my heart
Was oftentimes uplifted, and they seemed
Arguments sent from Heaven to prove the cause
Good, pure, which no one could stand up against,
Who was not lost, abandoned, selfish, proud,
Mean, miserable, wilfully depraved,
Hater perverse of equity and truth.

    Among that band of Officers was one,
Already hinted at, of other mould —
A patriot, thence rejected by the rest,   290
And with an oriental loathing spurned,
As of a different caste.   A meeker man
Than this lived never, nor a more benign,
Meek though enthusiastic.   Injuries
Made *him* more gracious, and his nature then
Did breathe its sweetness out most sensibly,
As aromatic flowers on Alpine turf,
When foot hath crushed them.   He through the events
Of that great change wandered in perfect faith,

As through a book, an old romance, or tale   300
Of Fairy, or some dream of actions wrought
Behind the summer clouds.   By birth he ranked
With the most noble, but unto the poor
Among mankind he was in service bound,
As by some tie invisible, oaths professed
To a religious order.   Man he loved
As man; and, to the mean and the obscure,
And all the homely in their homely works,
Transferred a courtesy which had no air
Of condescension; but did rather seem   310
A passion and a gallantry, like that
Which he, a soldier, in his idler day
Had paid to woman: somewhat vain he was,
Or seemed so, yet it was not vanity,
But fondness, and a kind of radiant joy
Diffused around him, while he was intent
On works of love or freedom, or revolved
Complacently the progress of a cause,
Whereof he was a part: yet this was meek
And placid, and took nothing from the man   320
That was delightful.   Oft in solitude
With him did I discourse about the end
Of civil government, and its wisest forms;
Of ancient loyalty, and chartered rights,
Custom and habit, novelty and change;
Of self-respect, and virtue in the few
For patrimonial honour set apart,
And ignorance in the labouring multitude.
For he, to all intolerance indisposed,
Balanced these contemplations in his mind;   330
And I, who at that time was scarcely dipped
Into the turmoil, bore a sounder judgment
Than later days allowed; carried about me,
With less alloy to its integrity,

The experience of past ages, as, through help
Of books and common life, it makes sure way
To youthful minds, by objects over near
Not pressed upon, nor dazzled or misled
By struggling with the crowd for present ends.

But though not deaf, nor obstinate to find   340
Error without excuse upon the side
Of them who strove against us, more delight
We took, and let this freely be confessed,
In painting to ourselves the miseries
Of royal courts, and that voluptuous life
Unfeeling, where the man who is of soul
The meanest thrives the most; where dignity,
True personal dignity, abideth not;
A light, a cruel, and vain world cut off
From the natural inlets of just sentiment,   350
From lowly sympathy and chastening truth;
Where good and evil interchange their names,
And thirst for bloody spoils abroad is paired
With vice at home.   We added dearest themes —
Man and his noble nature, as it is
The gift which God has placed within his power,
His blind desires and steady faculties
Capable of clear truth, the one to break
Bondage, the other to build liberty
On firm foundations, making social life,   360
Through knowledge spreading and imperishable,
As just in regulation, and as pure
As individual in the wise and good.

We summoned up the honourable deeds
Of ancient Story, thought of each bright spot,
That would be found in all recorded time,
Of truth preserved and error passed away;

Of single spirits that catch the flame from Heaven,
And how the multitudes of men will feed
And fan each other; thought of sects, how keen   370
They are to put the appropriate nature on,
Triumphant over every obstacle
Of custom, language, country, love, or hate,
And what they do and suffer for their creed;
How far they travel, and how long endure;
How quickly mighty Nations have been formed,
From least beginnings; how, together locked
By new opinions, scattered tribes have made
One body, spreading wide as clouds in heaven.
To aspirations then of our own minds   380
Did we appeal; and, finally, beheld
A living confirmation of the whole
Before us, in a people from the depth
Of shameful imbecility uprisen,
Fresh as the morning star.   Elate we looked
Upon their virtues; saw, in rudest men,
Self-sacrifice the firmest; generous love,
And continence of mind, and sense of right,
Uppermost in the midst of fiercest strife.

   Oh, sweet it is, in academic groves,   390
Or such retirement, Friend! as we have known
In the green dales beside our Rotha's stream,
Greta, or Derwent, or some nameless rill,
To ruminate, with interchange of talk,
On rational liberty, and hope in man,
Justice and peace.   But far more sweet such toil —
Toil, say I, for it leads to thoughts abstruse —
If nature then be standing on the brink
Of some great trial, and we hear the voice
Of one devoted, — one whom circumstance   400
Hath called upon to embody his deep sense

In action, give it outwardly a shape,
And that of benediction, to the world.
Then doubt is not, and truth is more than truth, —
A hope it is, and a desire; a creed
Of zeal, by an authority Divine
Sanctioned, of danger, difficulty, or death.
Such conversation, under Attic shades,
Did Dion hold with Plato; ripened thus
For a Deliverer's glorious task, — and such   410
He, on that ministry already bound,
Held with Eudemus and Timonides,
Surrounded by adventurers in arms,
When those two vessels with their daring freight,
For the Sicilian Tyrant's overthrow,
Sailed from Zacynthus, — philosophic war,
Led by Philosophers.   With harder fate,
Though like ambition, such was he, O Friend!
Of whom I speak.   So Beaupuis (let the name
Stand near the worthiest of Antiquity)   420
Fashioned his life; and many a long discourse,
With like persuasion honoured, we maintained:
He, on his part, accoutred for the worst,
He perished fighting, in supreme command,
Upon the borders of the unhappy Loire,
For liberty, against deluded men,
His fellow-countrymen; and yet most blessed
In this, that he the fate of later times
Lived not to see, nor what we now behold,
Who have as ardent hearts as he had then.   430

   Along that very Loire, with festal mirth
Resounding at all hours, and innocent yet
Of civil slaughter, was our frequent walk;
Or in wide forests of continuous shade,
Lofty and over-arched, with open space

Beneath the trees, clear footing many a mile —
A solemn region.   Oft amid those haunts,
From earnest dialogues I slipped in thought,
And let remembrance steal to other times,
When, o'er those interwoven roots, moss-clad,   440
And smooth as marble or a waveless sea,
Some Hermit, from his cell forth-strayed, might pace
In sylvan meditation undisturbed;
As on the pavement of a Gothic church
Walks a lone Monk, when service hath expired,
In peace and silence.   But if e'er was heard, —
Heard, though unseen, — a devious traveller,
Retiring or approaching from afar
With speed and echoes loud of trampling hoofs
From the hard floor reverberated, then   450
It was Angelica thundering through the woods
Upon her palfrey, or that gentle maid
Erminia, fugitive as fair as she.
Sometimes methought I saw a pair of knights
Joust underneath the trees, that as in storm
Rocked high above their heads; anon, the din
Of boisterous merriment, and music's roar,
In sudden proclamation, burst from haunt
Of Satyrs in some viewless glade, with dance
Rejoicing o'er a female in the midst,   460
A mortal beauty, their unhappy thrall.
The width of those huge forests, unto me
A novel scene, did often in this way
Master my fancy while I wandered on
With that revered companion.   And sometimes —
When to a convent in a meadow green,
By a brook-side, we came, a roofless pile,
And not by reverential touch of Time
Dismantled, but by violence abrupt —
In spite of those heart-bracing colloquies,   470

In spite of real fervour, and of that
Less genuine and wrought up within myself —
I could not but bewail a wrong so harsh,
And for the Matin-bell to sound no more
Grieved, and the twilight taper, and the cross
High on the topmost pinnacle, a sign
(How welcome to the weary traveller's eyes!)
Of hospitality and peaceful rest.
And when the partner of those varied walks
Pointed upon occasion to the site   480
Of Romorentin, home of ancient kings,
To the imperial edifice of Blois,
Or to that rural castle, name now slipped
From my remembrance, where a lady lodged,
By the first Francis wooed, and bound to him
In chains of mutual passion, from the tower,
As a tradition of the country tells,
Practised to commune with her royal knight
By cressets and love-beacons, intercourse
'Twixt her high-seated residence and his   490
Far off at Chambord on the plain beneath;
Even here, though less than with the peaceful house
Religious, 'mid those frequent monuments
Of Kings, their vices and their better deeds,
Imagination, potent to inflame
At times with virtuous wrath and noble scorn,
Did also often mitigate the force
Of civic prejudice, the bigotry,
So call it, of a youthful patriot's mind;
And on these spots with many gleams I looked   500
Of chivalrous delight.   Yet not the less,
Hatred of absolute rule, where will of one
Is law for all, and of that barren pride
In them who, by immunities unjust,
Between the sovereign and the people stand,

His helper and not theirs, laid stronger hold
Daily upon mè, mixed with pity too
And love; for where hope is, there love will be
For the abject multitude.   And when we chanced
One day to meet a hunger-bitten girl,   510
Who crept along fitting her languid gait
Unto a heifer's motion, by a cord
Tied to her arm, and picking thus from the lane
Its sustenance, while the girl with pallid hands
Was busy knitting in a heartless mood
Of solitude, and at the sight my friend
In agitation said, "'T is against *that*
That we are fighting," I with him believed
That a benignant spirit was abroad
Which might not be withstood, that poverty   520
Abject as this would in a little time
Be found no more, that we should see the earth
Unthwarted in her wish to recompense
The meek, the lowly, patient child of toil,
All institutes for ever blotted out
That legalised exclusion, empty pomp
Abolished, sensual state and cruel power
Whether by edict of the one or few;
And finally, as sum and crown of all,
Should see the people having a strong hand   530
In framing their own laws; whence better days
To all mankind.   But, these things set apart,
Was not this single confidence enough
To animate the mind that ever turned
A thought to human welfare?   That henceforth
Captivity by mandate without law
Should cease; and open accusation lead
To sentence in the hearing of the world,
And open punishment, if not the air
Be free to breathe in, and the heart of man   540

Dread nothing. From this height I shall not stoop
To humbler matter that detained us oft
In thought or conversation, public acts,
And public persons, and emotions wrought
Within the breast, as ever-varying winds
Of record or report swept over us;
But I might here, instead, repeat a tale,
Told by my Patriot friend, of sad events,
That prove to what low depth had struck the roots,
How widely spread the boughs, of that old tree   550
Which, as a deadly mischief, and a foul
And black dishonour, France was weary of.

Oh, happy time of youthful lovers, (thus
The story might begin,) oh, balmy time,
In which a love-knot, on a lady's brow,
Is fairer than the fairest star in Heaven!
So might — and with that prelude *did* begin
The record; and, in faithful verse, was given
The doleful sequel.
                        But our little bark
On a strong river boldly hath been launched;   560
And from the driving current should we turn
To loiter wilfully within a creek,
Howe'er attractive, Fellow voyager!
Would'st thou not chide? Yet deem not my pains lost.
For Vaudracour and Julia (so were named
The ill-fated pair) in that plain tale will draw
Tears from the hearts of others, when their own
Shall beat no more. Thou, also, there may'st read,
At leisure, how the enamoured youth was driven,
By public power abased, to fatal crime,   570
Nature's rebellion against monstrous law;
How, between heart and heart, oppression thrust
Her mandates, severing whom true love had joined,

Harassing both; until he sank and pressed
The couch his fate had made for him; supine,
Save when the stings of viperous remorse,
Trying their strength, enforced him to start up,
Aghast and prayerless. Into a deep wood
He fled, to shun the haunts of human kind;
There dwelt, weakened in spirit more and more;   580
Nor could the voice of Freedom, which through France
Full speedily resounded, public hope,
Or personal memory of his own worst wrongs,
Rouse him; but, hidden in those gloomy shades,
His days he wasted, — an imbecile mind.

BOOK TENTH

RESIDENCE IN FRANCE (*continued*)

IT WAS a beautiful and silent day
That overspread the countenance of earth,
Then fading with unusual quietness, —
A day as beautiful as e'er was given
To soothe regret, though deepening what it soothed,
When by the gliding Loire I paused, and cast
Upon his rich domains, vineyard and tilth,
Green meadow-ground, and many-coloured woods,
Again, and yet again, a farewell look;
Then from the quiet of that scene passed on,   10
Bound to the fierce Metropolis.   From his throne
The King had fallen, and that invading host —
Presumptuous cloud, on whose black front was written
The tender mercies of the dismal wind
That bore it — on the plains of Liberty
Had burst innocuous.   Say in bolder words,
They — who had come elate as eastern hunters

Banded beneath the Great Mogul, when he
Erewhile went forth from Agra or Lahore,
Rajahs and Omrahs in his train, intent   20
To drive their prey enclosed within a ring
Wide as a province, but, the signal given,
Before the point of the life-threatening spear
Narrowing itself by moments — they, rash men,
Had seen the anticipated quarry turned
Into avengers, from whose wrath they fled
In terror.   Disappointment and dismay
Remained for all whose fancies had run wild
With evil expectations; confidence
And perfect triumph for the better cause.   30

   The State — as if to stamp the final seal
On her security, and to the world
Show what she was, a high and fearless soul,
Exulting in defiance, or heart-stung
By sharp resentment, or belike to taunt
With spiteful gratitude the baffled League,
That had stirred up her slackening faculties
To a new transition — when the King was crushed
Spared not the empty throne, and in proud haste
Assumed the body and venerable name   40
Of a Republic.   Lamentable crimes,
'T is true, had gone before this hour, dire work
Of massacre, in which the senseless sword
Was prayed to as a judge; but these were past,
Earth free from them for ever, as was thought, —
Ephemeral monsters, to be seen but once!
Things that could only show themselves and die.

   Cheered with this hope, to Paris I returned,
And ranged, with ardour heretofore unfelt,

The spacious city, and in progress passed 50
The prison where the unhappy Monarch lay,
Associate with his children and his wife
In bondage; and the palace, lately stormed
With roar of cannon by a furious host.
I crossed the square (an empty area then!)
Of the Carrousel, where so late had lain
The dead, upon the dying heaped, and gazed
On this and other spots, as doth a man
Upon a volume whose contents he knows
Are memorable, but from him locked up, 60
Being written in a tongue he cannot read,
So that he questions the mute leaves with pain,
And half upbraids their silence. But that night
I felt most deeply in what world I was,
What ground I trod on, and what air I breathed.
High was my room and lonely, near the roof
Of a large mansion or hotel, a lodge
That would have pleased me in more quiet times;
Nor was it wholly without pleasure then.
With unextinguished taper I kept watch, 70
Reading at intervals; the fear gone by
Pressed on me almost like a fear to come.
I thought of those September massacres,
Divided from me by one little month,
Saw them and touched: the rest was conjured up
From tragic fictions or true history,
Remembrances and dim admonishments.
The horse is taught his manage, and no star
Of wildest course but treads back his own steps;
For the spent hurricane the air provides 80
As fierce a successor; the tide retreats
But to return out of its hiding-place
In the great deep; all things have second birth;
The earthquake is not satisfied at once;

And in this way I wrought upon myself,
Until I seemed to hear a voice that cried,
To the whole city, "Sleep no more." The trance
Fled with the voice to which it had given birth;
But vainly comments of a calmer mind
Promised soft peace and sweet forgetfulness.   90
The place, all hushed and silent as it was,
Appeared unfit for the repose of night,
Defenceless as a wood where tigers roam.

  With early morning towards the Palace-walk
Of Orleans eagerly I turned: as yet
The streets were still; not so those long Arcades;
There, 'mid a peal of ill-matched sounds and cries,
That greeted me on entering, I could hear
Shrill voices from the hawkers in the throng,
Bawling, "Denunciation of the Crimes   100
Of Maximilian Robespierre;" the hand,
Prompt as the voice, held forth a printed speech,
The same that had been recently pronounced,
When Robespierre, not ignorant for what mark
Some words of indirect reproof had been
Intended, rose in hardihood, and dared
The man who had an ill surmise of him
To bring his charge in openness; whereat,
When a dead pause ensued, and no one stirred,
In silence of all present, from his seat   110
Louvet walked single through the avenue,
And took his station in the Tribune, saying,
"I, Robespierre, accuse thee!" Well is known
The inglorious issue of that charge, and how
He, who had launched the startling thunderbolt,
The one bold man, whose voice the attack had sounded,
Was left without a follower to discharge
His perilous duty, and retire lamenting

That Heaven's best aid is wasted upon men
Who to themselves are false.
                                    But these are things 120
Of which I speak, only as they were storm
Or sunshine to my individual mind,
No further.   Let me then relate that now —
In some sort seeing with my proper eyes
That Liberty, and Life, and Death, would soon
To the remotest corners of the land
Lie in the arbitrement of those who ruled
The capital City; what was struggled for,
And by what combatants victory must be won;
The indecision on their part whose aim   130
Seemed best, and the straightforward path of those
Who in attack or in defence were strong
Through their impiety — my inmost soul
Was agitated; yea, I could almost
Have prayed that throughout earth upon all men,
By patient exercise of reason made
Worthy of liberty, all spirits filled
With zeal expanding in Truth's holy light,
The gift of tongues might fall, and power arrive
From the four quarters of the winds to do   140
For France, what without help she could not do,
A work of honour; think not that to this
I added, work of safety: from all doubt
Or trepidation for the end of things
Far was I, far as angels are from guilt.

    Yet did I grieve, nor only grieved, but thought
Of opposition and of remedies:
An insignificant stranger and obscure,
And one, moreover, little graced with power
Of eloquence even in my native speech,   150
And all unfit for tumult or intrigue,

Yet would I at this time with willing heart
Have undertaken for a cause so great
Service however dangerous.   I revolved,
How much the destiny of Man had still
Hung upon single persons; that there was,
Transcendent to all local patrimony,
One nature, as there is one sun in heaven;
That objects, even as they are great, thereby
Do come within the reach of humblest eyes;   160
That Man is only weak through his mistrust
And want of hope where evidence divine
Proclaims to him that hope should be most sure;
Nor did the inexperience of my youth
Preclude conviction, that a spirit strong
In hope, and trained to noble aspirations,
A spirit thoroughly faithful to itself,
Is for Society's unreasoning herd
A domineering instinct, serves at once
For way and guide, a fluent receptacle   170
That gathers up each petty straggling rill
And vein of water, glad to be rolled on
In safe obedience; that a mind, whose rest
Is where it ought to be, in self-restraint,
In circumspection and simplicity,
Falls rarely in entire discomfiture
Below its aim, or meets with, from without,
A treachery that foils it or defeats;
And, lastly, if the means on human will,
Frail human will, dependent should betray   180
Him who too boldly trusted them, I felt
That 'mid the loud distractions of the world
A sovereign voice subsists within the soul,
Arbiter undisturbed of right and wrong,
Of life and death, in majesty severe
Enjoining, as may best promote the aims

Of truth and justice, either sacrifice,
From whatsoever region of our cares
Or our infirm affections Nature pleads,
Earnest and blind, against the stern decree.   190

  On the other side, I called to mind those truths
That are the commonplaces of the schools —
(A theme for boys, too hackneyed for their sires,)
Yet, with a revelation's liveliness,
In all their comprehensive bearings known
And visible to philosophers of old,
Men who, to business of the world untrained,
Lived in the shade; and to Harmodius known
And his compeer Aristogiton, known
To Brutus — that tyrannic power is weak,   200
Hath neither gratitude, nor faith, nor love,
Nor the support of good or evil men
To trust in; that the godhead which is ours
Can never utterly be charmed or stilled;
That nothing hath a natural right to last
But equity and reason; that all else
Meets foes irreconcilable, and at best
Lives only by variety of disease.

  Well might my wishes be intense, my thoughts
Strong and perturbed, not doubting at that time   210
But that the virtue of one paramount mind
Would have abashed those impious crests — have
    quelled
Outrage and bloody power, and — in despite
Of what the People long had been and were
Through ignorance and false teaching, sadder proof
Of immaturity, and — in the teeth
Of desperate opposition from without —
Have cleared a passage for just government,

And left a solid birthright to the State,
Redeemed, according to example given   320
By ancient lawgivers.
               In this frame of mind,
Dragged by a chain of harsh necessity,
So seemed it, — now I thankfully acknowledge,
Forced by the gracious providence of Heaven, —
To England I returned, else (though assured
That I both was and must be of small weight,
No better than a landsman on the deck
Of a ship struggling with a hideous storm)
Doubtless, I should have then made common cause
With some who perished; haply perished too,   330
A poor mistaken and bewildered offering, —
Should to the breast of Nature have gone back,
With all my resolutions, all my hopes,
A Poet only to myself, to men
Useless, and even, beloved Friend! a soul
To thee unknown!
               Twice had the trees let fall
Their leaves, as often Winter had put on
His hoary crown, since I had seen the surge
Beat against Albion's shore, since ear of mine
Had caught the accents of my native speech   340
Upon our native country's sacred ground.
A patriot of the world, how could I glide
Into communion with her sylvan shades,
Erewhile my tuneful haunt? It pleased me more
To abide in the great City, where I found
The general air still busy with the stir
Of that first memorable onset made
By a strong levy of humanity
Upon the traffickers in Negro blood;
Effort which, though defeated, had recalled   350
To notice old forgotten principles,

And through the nation spread a novel heat
Of virtuous feeling. For myself, I own
That this particular strife had wanted power
To rivet my affections; nor did now
Its unsuccessful issue much excite
My sorrow; for I brought with me the faith
That, if France prospered, good men would not long
Pay fruitless worship to humanity,
And this most rotten branch of human shame,   260
Object, so seemed it, of superfluous pains,
Would fall together with its parent tree.
What, then, were my emotions, when in arms
Britain put forth her free-born strength in league,
Oh, pity and shame! with those confederate Powers!
Not in my single self alone I found,
But in the minds of all ingenuous youth,
Change and subversion from that hour. No shock
Given to my moral nature had I known
Down to that very moment; neither lapse   270
Nor turn of sentiment that might be named
A revolution, save at this one time;
All else was progress on the self-same path
On which, with a diversity of pace,
I had been travelling: this a stride at once
Into another region. As a light
And pliant harebell, swinging in the breeze
On some grey rock — its birth-place — so had I
Wantoned, fast rooted on the ancient tower
Of my beloved country, wishing not   280
A happier fortune than to wither there:
Now was I from that pleasant station torn
And tossed about in whirlwind. I rejoiced,
Yea, afterwards — truth most painful to record! —
Exulted, in the triumph of my soul,
When Englishmen by thousands were o'erthrown,

Left without glory on the field, or driven,
Brave hearts! to shameful flight.   It was a grief, —
Grief call it not, 't was anything but that, —
A conflict of sensations without name,   290
Of which *he* only, who may love the sight
Of a village steeple, as I do, can judge,
When, in the congregation bending all
To their great Father, prayers were offered up,
Or praises for our country's victories;
And, 'mid the simple worshippers, perchance
I only, like an uninvited guest
Whom no one owned, sate silent, shall I add,
Fed on the day of vengeance yet to come.

   Oh! much have they to account for, who could tear,
By violence, at one decisive rent,   301
From the best youth in England their dear pride,
Their joy, in England; this, too, at a time
In which worst losses easily might wean
The best of names, when patriotic love
Did of itself in modesty give way,
Like the Precursor when the Deity
Is come Whose harbinger he was; a time
In which apostasy from ancient faith
Seemed but conversion to a higher creed;   310
Withal a season dangerous and wild,
A time when sage Experience would have snatched
Flowers out of any hedge-row to compose
A chaplet in contempt of his grey locks.

   When the proud fleet that bears the red-cross flag
In that unworthy service was prepared
To mingle, I beheld the vessels lie,
A brood of gallant creatures, on the deep;
I saw them in their rest, a sojourner

Through a whole month of calm and glassy days   320
In that delightful island which protects
Their place of convocation — there I heard,
Each evening, pacing by the still sea-shore,
A monitory sound that never failed, —
The sunset cannon.   While the orb went down
In the tranquillity of nature, came
That voice, ill requiem! seldom heard by me
Without a spirit overcast by dark
Imaginations, sense of woes to come,
Sorrow for human kind, and pain of heart.   330

In France, the men, who, for their desperate ends,
Had plucked up mercy by the roots, were glad
Of this new enemy.   Tyrants, strong before
In wicked pleas, were strong as demons now;
And thus, on every side beset with foes,
The goaded land waxed mad; the crimes of few
Spread into madness of the many; blasts
From hell came sanctified like airs from heaven.
The sternness of the just, the faith of those
Who doubted not that Providence had times   340
Of vengeful retribution, theirs who throned
The human Understanding paramount
And made of that their God, the hopes of men
Who were content to barter short-lived pangs
For a paradise of ages, the blind rage
Of insolent tempers, the light vanity
Of intermeddlers, steady purposes
Of the suspicious, slips of the indiscreet,
And all the accidents of life — were pressed
Into one service, busy with one work.   350
The Senate stood aghast, her prudence quenched,
Her wisdom stifled, and her justice scared,
Her frenzy only active to extol

Past outrages, and shape the way for new,
Which no one dared to oppose or mitigate.

Domestic carnage now filled the whole year
With feast-days; old men from the chimney-nook,
The maiden from the bosom of her love,
The mother from the cradle of her babe,
The warrior from the field — all perished, all —   360
Friends, enemies, of all parties, ages, ranks,
Head after head, and never heads enough
For those that bade them fall.   They found their joy,
They made it proudly, eager as a child,
(If like desires of innocent little ones
May with such heinous appetites be compared),
Pleased in some open field to exercise
A toy that mimics with revolving wings
The motion of a wind-mill; though the air
Do of itself blow fresh, and make the vanes   370
Spin in his eyesight, *that* contents him not,
But with the plaything at arm's length, he sets
His front against the blast, and runs amain,
That it may whirl the faster.
                                      Amid the depth
Of those enormities, even thinking minds
Forgot, at seasons, whence they had their being,
Forgot that such a sound was ever heard
As Liberty upon earth: yet all beneath
Her innocent authority was wrought,
Nor could have been, without her blessed name.   380
The illustrious wife of Roland, in the hour
Of her composure, felt that agony,
And gave it vent in her last words.   O Friend!
It was a lamentable time for man,
Whether a hope had e'er been his or not:
A woful time for them whose hopes survived

The shock; most woful for those few who still
Were flattered, and had trust in human kind:
They had the deepest feeling of the grief.
Meanwhile the Invaders fared as they deserved: 390
The Herculean Commonwealth had put forth her arms,
And throttled with an infant godhead's might
The snakes about her cradle; that was well,
And as it should be; yet no cure for them
Whose souls were sick with pain of what would be
Hereafter brought in charge against mankind.
Most melancholy at that time, O Friend!
Were my day-thoughts, — my nights were miserable;
Through months, through years, long after the last beat
Of those atrocities, the hour of sleep   400
To me came rarely charged with natural gifts,
Such ghastly visions had I of despair
And tyranny, and implements of death;
And innocent victims sinking under fear,
And momentary hope, and worn-out prayer,
Each in his separate cell, or penned in crowds
For sacrifice, and struggling with fond mirth
And levity in dungeons, where the dust
Was laid with tears. Then suddenly the scene
Changed, and the unbroken dream entangled me   410
In long orations, which I strove to plead
Before unjust tribunals, — with a voice
Labouring, a brain confounded, and a sense,
Death-like, of treacherous desertion, felt
In the last place of refuge — my own soul.

When I began in youth's delightful prime
To yield myself to Nature, when that strong
And holy passion overcame me first,
Nor day nor night, evening or morn, was free
From its oppression.   But, O Power Supreme!   420

Without Whose call this world would cease to breathe,
Who from the fountain of Thy grace dost fill
The veins that branch through every frame of life,
Making man what he is, creature divine,
In single or in social eminence,
Above the rest raised infinite ascents
When reason that enables him to be
Is not sequestered — what a change is here!
How different ritual for this after-worship,
What countenance to promote this second love!   430
The first was service paid to things which lie
Guarded within the bosom of Thy will.
Therefore to serve was high beatitude;
Tumult was therefore gladness, and the fear
Ennobling, venerable; sleep secure,
And waking thoughts more rich than happiest dreams.

But as the ancient Prophets, borne aloft
In vision, yet constrained by natural laws
With them to take a troubled human heart,
Wanted not consolations, nor a creed   440
Of reconcilement, then when they denounced,
On towns and cities, wallowing in the abyss
Of their offences, punishment to come;
Or saw, like other men, with bodily eyes,
Before them, in some desolated place,
The wrath consummate and the threat fulfilled;
So, with devout humility be it said,
So did a portion of that spirit fall
On me uplifted from the vantage-ground
Of pity and sorrow to a state of being   450
That through the time's exceeding fierceness saw
Glimpses of retribution, terrible,
And in the order of sublime behests:
But, even if that were not, amid the awe

Of unintelligible chastisement,
Not only acquiescences of faith
Survived, but daring sympathies with power,
Motions not treacherous or profane, else why
Within the folds of no ungentle breast
Their dread vibration to this hour prolonged? 460
Wild blasts of music thus could find their way
Into the midst of turbulent events;
So that worst tempests might be listened to.
Then was the truth received into my heart,
That, under heaviest sorrow earth can bring,
If from the affliction somewhere do not grow
Honour which could not else have been, a faith,
An elevation, and a sanctity,
If new strength be not given nor old restored,
The blame is ours, not Nature's.   When a taunt 470
Was taken up by scoffers in their pride,
Saying, "Behold the harvest that we reap
From popular government and equality,"
I clearly saw that neither these nor aught
Of wild belief engrafted on their names
By false philosophy had caused the woe,
But a terrific reservoir of guilt
And ignorance filled up from age to age,
That could no longer hold its loathsome charge,
But burst and spread in deluge through the land. 480

   And as the desert hath green spots, the sea
Small islands scattered amid stormy waves,
So *that* disastrous period did not want
Bright sprinklings of all human excellence,
To which the silver wands of saints in Heaven
Might point with rapturous joy.   Yet not the less,
For those examples, in no age surpassed,
Of fortitude and energy and love,

And human nature faithful to herself
Under worst trials, was I driven to think   490
Of the glad times when first I traversed France
A youthful pilgrim; above all reviewed
That eventide, when under windows bright
With happy faces and with garlands hung,
And through a rainbow-arch that spanned the street,
Triumphal pomp for liberty confirmed,
I paced, a dear companion at my side,
The town of Arras, whence with promise high
Issued, on delegation to sustain
Humanity and right, *that* Robespierre,   500
He who thereafter, and in how short time!
Wielded the sceptre of the Atheist crew.
When the calamity spread far and wide —
And this same city, that did then appear
To outrun the rest in exultation, groaned
Under the vengeance of her cruel son,
As Lear reproached the winds — I could almost
Have quarrelled with that blameless spectacle
For lingering yet an image in my mind
To mock me under such a strange reverse.   510

    O Friend! few happier moments have been mine
Than that which told the downfall of this Tribe
So dreaded, so abhorred.   The day deserves
A separate record.   Over the smooth sands
Of Leven's ample estuary lay
My journey, and beneath a genial sun,
With distant prospect among gleams of sky
And clouds and intermingling mountain tops,
In one inseparable glory clad,
Creatures of one ethereal substance met   520
In consistory, like a diadem
Or crown of burning seraphs as they sit

In the empyrean.   Underneath that pomp
Celestial, lay unseen the pastoral vales
Among whose happy fields I had grown up
From childhood.   On the fulgent spectacle,
That neither passed away nor changed, I gazed
Enrapt; but brightest things are wont to draw
Sad opposites out of the inner heart,
As even their pensive influence drew from mine.   530
How could it otherwise? for not in vain
That very morning had I turned aside
To seek the ground where, 'mid a throng of graves,
An honoured teacher of my youth was laid,
And on the stone were graven by his desire
Lines from the churchyard elegy of Gray.
This faithful guide, speaking from his death-bed,
Added no farewell to his parting counsel,
But said to me, "My head will soon lie low;"
And when I saw the turf that covered him,   540
After the lapse of full eight years, those words,
With sound of voice and countenance of the Man,
Came back upon me, so that some few tears
Fell from me in my own despite.   But now
I thought, still traversing that widespread plain,
With tender pleasure of the verses graven
Upon his tombstone, whispering to myself:
He loved the Poets, and, if now alive,
Would have loved me, as one not destitute
Of promise, nor belying the kind hope   550
That he had formed, when I, at his command,
Began to spin, with toil, my earliest songs.

      As I advanced, all that I saw or felt
Was gentleness and peace.   Upon a small
And rocky island near, a fragment stood,
(Itself like a sea rock) the low remains

(With shells encrusted, dark with briny weeds)
Of a dilapidated structure, once
A Romish chapel, where the vested priest
Said matins at the hour that suited those   560
Who crossed the sands with ebb of morning tide.
Not far from that still ruin all the plain
Lay spotted with a variegated crowd
Of vehicles and travellers, horse and foot,
Wading beneath the conduct of their guide
In loose procession through the shallow stream
Of inland waters; the great sea meanwhile
Heaved at safe distance, far retired.   I paused,
Longing for skill to paint a scene so bright
And cheerful, but the foremost of the band   570
As he approached, no salutation given
In the familiar language of the day,
Cried, "Robespierre is dead!" nor was a doubt,
After strict question, left within my mind
That he and his supporters all were fallen.

  Great was my transport, deep my gratitude
To everlasting Justice, by this fiat
Made manifest.   "Come now, ye golden times,"
Said I forth-pouring on those open sands
A hymn of triumph: "as the morning comes   580
From out the bosom of the night, come ye:
Thus far our trust is verified; behold!
They who with clumsy desperation brought
A river of Blood, and preached that nothing else
Could cleanse the Augean stable, by the might
Of their own helper have been swept away;
Their madness stands declared and visible;
Elsewhere will safety now be sought, and earth
March firmly towards righteousness and peace." —
Then schemes I framed more calmly, when and how 590

The madding factions might be tranquillised,
And how through hardships manifold and long
The glorious renovation would proceed.
Thus interrupted by uneasy bursts
Of exultation, I pursued my way
Along that very shore which I had skimmed
In former days, when — spurring from the Vale
Of Nightshade, and St. Mary's mouldering fane,
And the stone abbot, after circuit made
In wantonness of heart, a joyous band   600
Of schoolboys hastening to their distant home
Along the margin of the moonlight sea —
We beat with thundering hoofs the level sand.

BOOK ELEVENTH

FRANCE (*concluded*)

FROM that time forth, Authority in France
Put on a milder face; Terror had ceased,
Yet everything was wanting that might give
Courage to them who looked for good by light
Of rational Experience, for the shoots
And hopeful blossoms of a second spring:
Yet, in me, confidence was unimpaired;
The Senate's language, and the public acts
And measures of the Government, though both
Weak, and of heartless omen, had not power   10
To daunt me; in the People was my trust:
And, in the virtues which mine eyes had seen,
I knew that wound external could not take
Life from the young Republic; that new foes
Would only follow, in the path of shame,
Their brethren, and her triumphs be in the end
Great, universal, irresistible.

This intuition led me to confound
One victory with another, higher far, —
Triumphs of unambitious peace at home,   20
And noiseless fortitude.   Beholding still
Resistance strong as heretofore, I thought
That what was in degree the same was likewise
The same in quality, — that, as the worse
Of the two spirits then at strife remained
Untired, the better, surely, would preserve
The heart that first had roused him.   Youth maintains,
In all conditions of society,
Communion more direct and intimate
With Nature, — hence, ofttimes, with reason too —   30
Than age or manhood, even.   To Nature then,
Power had reverted: habit, custom, law,
Had left an interregnum's open space
For *her* to move about in, uncontrolled.
Hence could I see how Babel-like their task,
Who, by the recent deluge stupified,
With their whole souls went culling from the day
Its petty promises, to build a tower
For their own safety; laughed with my compeers
At gravest heads, by enmity to France   40
Distempered, till they found, in every blast
Forced from the street-disturbing newsman's horn,
For her great cause record or prophecy
Of utter ruin.   How might we believe
That wisdom could, in any shape, come near
Men clinging to delusions so insane?
And thus, experience proving that no few
Of our opinions had been just, we took
Like credit to ourselves where less was due,
And thought that other notions were as sound,   50
Yea, could not but be right, because we saw
That foolish men opposed them.

To a strain
More animated I might here give way,
And tell, since juvenile errors are my theme,
What in those days, through Britain, was performed
To turn *all* judgments out of their right course;
But this is passion over-near ourselves,
Reality too close and too intense,
And intermixed with something, in my mind,
Of scorn and condemnation personal,   60
That would profane the sanctity of verse.
Our Shepherds, they say merely, at that time
Acted, or seemed at least to act, like men
Thirsting to make the guardian crook of law
A tool of murder; they who ruled the State —
Though with such awful proof before their eyes
That he, who would sow death, reaps death, or worse,
And can reap nothing better — child-like longed
To imitate, not wise enough to avoid;
Or left (by mere timidity betrayed)   70
The plain straight road, for one no better chosen
Than if their wish had been to undermine
Justice, and make an end of Liberty.

But from these bitter truths I must return
To my own history.   It hath been told
That I was led to take an eager part
In arguments of civil polity,
Abruptly, and indeed before my time:
I had approached, like other youths, the shield
Of human nature from the golden side,   80
And would have fought, even to the death, to attest
The quality of the metal which I saw.
What there is best in individual man,
Of wise in passion, and sublime in power,
Benevolent in small societies,

And great in large ones, I had oft revolved,
Felt deeply, but not thoroughly understood
By reason: nay, far from it; they were yet,
As cause was given me afterwards to learn,
Not proof against the injuries of the day;   90
Lodged only at the sanctuary's door,
Not safe within its bosom.   Thus prepared,
And with such general insight into evil,
And of the bounds which sever it from good,
As books and common intercourse with life
Must needs have given — to the inexperienced mind,
When the world travels in a beaten road,
Guide faithful as is needed — I began
To meditate with ardour on the rule
And management of nations; what it is   100
And ought to be; and strove to learn how far
Their power or weakness, wealth or poverty,
Their happiness or misery, depends
Upon their laws, and fashion of the State.

   O pleasant exercise of hope and joy!
For mighty were the auxiliars which then stood
Upon our side, us who were strong in love!
Bliss was it in that dawn to be alive,
But to be young was very Heaven!   O times,
In which the meagre, stale, forbidding ways   110
Of custom, law, and statute, took at once
The attraction of a country in romance!
When Reason seemed the most to assert her rights,
When most intent on making of herself
A prime enchantress — to assist the work,
Which then was going forward in her name!
Not favoured spots alone, but the whole Earth,
The beauty wore of promise — that which sets
(As at some moments might not be unfelt

Among the bowers of Paradise itself)   120
The budding rose above the rose full blown.
What temper at the prospect did not wake
To happiness unthought of? The inert
Were roused, and lively natures rapt away!
They who had fed their childhood upon dreams,
The play-fellows of fancy, who had made
All powers of swiftness, subtilty, and strength
Their ministers, — who in lordly wise had stirred
Among the grandest objects of the sense,
And dealt with whatsoever they found there 130
As if they had within some lurking right
To wield it; — they, too, who of gentle mood
Had watched all gentle motions, and to these
Had fitted their own thoughts, schemers more mild,
And in the region of their peaceful selves; —
Now was it that *both* found, the meek and lofty
Did both find, helpers to their hearts' desire,
And stuff at hand, plastic as they could wish, —
Were called upon to exercise their skill,
Not in Utopia, — subterranean fields, —   140
Or some secreted island, Heaven knows where!
But in the very world, which is the world
Of all of us, — the place where, in the end,
We find our happiness, or not at all!

  Why should I not confess that Earth was then
To me, what an inheritance, new-fallen,
Seems, when the first time visited, to one
Who thither comes to find in it his home?
He walks about and looks upon the spot
With cordial transport, moulds it and remoulds, 150
And is half-pleased with things that are amiss,
'T will be such joy to see them disappear.

An active partisan, I thus convoked
From every object pleasant circumstances
To suit my ends; I moved among mankind
With genial feelings still predominant;
When erring, erring on the better part,
And in the kinder spirit; placable,
Indulgent, as not uninformed that men
See as they have been taught — Antiquity　　　160
Gives rights to error; and aware, no less
That throwing off oppression must be work
As well of License as of Liberty;
And above all — for this was more than all —
Not caring if the wind did now and then
Blow keen upon an eminence that gave
Prospect so large into futurity;
In brief, a child of Nature, as at first,
Diffusing only those affections wider
That from the cradle had grown up with me,　　　170
And losing, in no other way than light
Is lost in light, the weak in the more strong.

In the main outline, such it might be said
Was my condition, till with open war
Britain opposed the liberties of France.
This threw me first out of the pale of love;
Soured and corrupted, upwards to the source,
My sentiments; was not, as hitherto,
A swallowing up of lesser things in great,
But change of them into their contraries;　　　180
And thus a way was opened for mistakes
And false conclusions, in degree as gross,
In kind more dangerous. What had been a pride,
Was now a shame; my likings and my loves
Ran in new channels, leaving old ones dry;
And hence a blow that, in maturer age,

Would but have touched the judgment, struck more
    deep
Into sensations near the heart: meantime,
As from the first, wild theories were afloat,
To whose pretensions, sedulously urged,   190
I had but lent a careless ear, assured
That time was ready to set all things right,
And that the multitude, so long oppressed,
Would be oppressed no more.

                        But when events
Brought less encouragement, and unto these
The immediate proof of principles no more
Could be entrusted, while the events themselves,
Worn out in greatness, stripped of novelty,
Less occupied the mind, and sentiments
Could through my understanding's natural growth   200
No longer keep their ground, by faith maintained
Of inward consciousness, and hope that laid
Her hand upon her object — evidence
Safer, of universal application, such
As could not be impeached, was sought elsewhere.

    But now, become oppressors in their turn,
Frenchmen had changed a war of self-defence
For one of conquest, losing sight of all
Which they had struggled for: up mounted now,
Openly in the eye of earth and heaven,   210
The scale of liberty. I read her doom.
With anger vexed, with disappointment sore,
But not dismayed, nor taking to the shame
Of a false prophet. While resentment rose,
Striving to hide, what nought could heal, the wounds
Of mortified presumption, I adhered
More firmly to old tenets, and, to prove
Their temper, strained them more; and thus, in heat

Of contest, did opinions every day
Grow into consequence, till round my mind   220
They clung, as if they were its life, nay more,
The very being of the immortal soul.

   This was the time, when, all things tending fast
To depravation, speculative schemes —
That promised to abstract the hopes of Man
Out of his feelings, to be fixed thenceforth
For ever in a purer element —
Found ready welcome.   Tempting region *that*
For Zeal to enter and refresh herself,
Where passions had the privilege to work,   230
And never hear the sound of their own names.
But, speaking more in charity, the dream
Flattered the young, pleased with extremes, nor least
With that which makes our Reason's naked self
The object of its fervour.   What delight!
How glorious! in self-knowledge and self-rule,
To look through all the frailties of the world,
And, with a resolute mastery shaking off
Infirmities of nature, time, and place,
Build social upon personal Liberty,   240
Which, to the blind restraints of general laws,
Superior, magisterially adopts
One guide, the light of circumstances, flashed
Upon an independent intellect.
Thus expectation rose again; thus hope,
From her first ground expelled, grew proud once more.
Oft, as my thoughts were turned to human kind,
I scorned indifference; but, inflamed with thirst
Of a secure intelligence, and sick
Of other longing, I pursued what seemed   250
A more exalted nature; wished that Man
Should start out of his earthy, worm-like state,

And spread abroad the wings of Liberty,
Lord of himself, in undisturbed delight —
A noble aspiration! *yet* I feel
(Sustained by worthier as by wiser thoughts)
The aspiration, nor shall ever cease
To feel it; — but return we to our course.

   Enough, 't is true — could such a plea excuse
Those aberrations — had the clamorous friends   260
Of ancient Institutions said and done
To bring disgrace upon their very names;
Disgrace, of which, custom and written law,
And sundry moral sentiments as props
Or emanations of those institutes,
Too justly bore a part.   A veil had been
Uplifted; why deceive ourselves? in sooth,
'T was even so; and sorrow for the man
Who either had not eyes wherewith to see,
Or, seeing, had forgotten!   A strong shock   270
Was given to old opinions; all men's minds
Had felt its power, and mine was both let loose,
Let loose and goaded.   After what hath been
Already said of patriotic love,
Suffice it here to add, that, somewhat stern
In temperament, withal a happy man,
And therefore bold to look on painful things,
Free likewise of the world, and thence more bold,
I summoned my best skill, and toiled, intent
To anatomise the frame of social life;   280
Yea, the whole body of society
Searched to its heart. Share with me, Friend! the wish
That some dramatic tale, endued with shapes
Livelier, and flinging out less guarded words
Than suit the work we fashion, might set forth
What then I learned, or think I learned, of truth,

And the errors into which I fell, betrayed
By present objects, and by reasonings false
From their beginnings, inasmuch as drawn
Out of a heart that had been turned aside   290
From Nature's way by outward accidents,
And which was thus confounded, more and more
Misguided, and misguiding.   So I fared,
Dragging all precepts, judgments, maxims, creeds,
Like culprits to the bar; calling the mind,
Suspiciously, to establish in plain day
Her titles and her honours; now believing,
Now disbelieving; endlessly perplexed
With impulse, motive, right and wrong, the ground
Of obligation, what the rule and whence   300
The sanction; till, demanding formal *proof*,
And seeking it in every thing, I lost
All feeling of conviction, and, in fine,
Sick, wearied out with contrarieties,
Yielded up moral questions in despair.

   This was the crisis of that strong disease,
This the soul's last and lowest ebb; I drooped,
Deeming our blessèd reason of least use
Where wanted most: "The lordly attributes
Of will and choice," I bitterly exclaimed,   310
"What are they but a mockery of a Being
Who hath in no concerns of his a test
Of good and evil; knows not what to fear
Or hope for, what to covet or to shun;
And who, if those could be discerned, would yet
Be little profited, would see, and ask
Where is the obligation to enforce?
And, to acknowledged law rebellious, still,
As selfish passion urged, would act amiss;
The dupe of folly, or the slave of crime."   320

Depressed, bewildered thus, I did not walk
With scoffers, seeking light and gay revenge
From indiscriminate laughter, nor sate down
In reconcilement with an utter waste
Of intellect; such sloth I could not brook,
(Too well I loved, in that my spring of life,
Pains-taking thoughts, and truth, their dear reward)
But turned to abstract science, and there sought
Work for the reasoning faculty enthroned
Where the disturbances of space and time —   330
Whether in matters various, properties
Inherent, or from human will and power
Derived — find no admission.   Then it was —
Thanks to the bounteous Giver of all good! —
That the belovèd Sister in whose sight
Those days were passed, now speaking in a voice
Of sudden admonition — like a brook
That did but *cross* a lonely road, and now
Is seen, heard, felt, and caught at every turn,
Companion never lost through many a league —   340
Maintained for me a saving intercourse
With my true self; for, though bedimmed and changed
Much, as it seemed, I was no further changed
Than as a clouded and a waning moon:
She whispered still that brightness would return;
She, in the midst of all, preserved me still
A Poet, made me seek beneath that name,
And that alone, my office upon earth;
And, lastly, as hereafter will be shown,
If willing audience fail not, Nature's self,   350
By all varieties of human love
Assisted, led me back through opening day
To those sweet counsels between head and heart
Whence grew that genuine knowledge, fraught with
        peace,

Which, through the later sinkings of this cause,
Hath still upheld me, and upholds me now
In the catastrophe (for so they dream,
And nothing less), when, finally to close
And seal up all the gains of France, a Pope
Is summoned in, to crown an Emperor —   360
This last opprobrium, when we see a people
That once looked up in faith, as if to Heaven
For manna, take a lesson from the dog
Returning to his vomit; when the sun
That rose in splendour, was alive, and moved
In exultation with a living pomp
Of clouds — his glory's natural retinue —
Hath dropped all functions by the gods bestowed,
And, turned into a gewgaw, a machine,
Sets like an Opera phantom.
                              Thus, O Friend!   370
Through times of honour and through times of shame
Descending, have I faithfully retraced
The perturbations of a youthful mind
Under a long-lived storm of great events —
A story destined for thy ear, who now,
Among the fallen of nations, dost abide
Where Etna, over hill and valley, casts
His shadow stretching towards Syracuse,
The city of Timoleon! Righteous Heaven!
How are the mighty prostrated! They first,   380
They first of all that breathe should have awaked
When the great voice was heard from out the tombs
Of ancient heroes. If I suffered grief
For ill-requited France, by many deemed
A trifler only in her proudest day;
Have been distressed to think of what she once
Promised, now is; a far more sober cause
Thine eyes must see of sorrow in a land,

To the reanimating influence lost
Of memory, to virtue lost and hope,   390
Though with the wreck of loftier years bestrewn.

But indignation works where hope is not,
And thou, O Friend! wilt be refreshed.   There is
One great society alone on earth:
The noble Living and the noble Dead.

Thine be such converse strong and sanative,
A ladder for thy spirit to reascend
To health and joy and pure contentedness;
To me the grief confined, that thou art gone
From this last spot of earth, where Freedom now   400
Stands single in her only sanctuary;
A lonely wanderer, art gone, by pain
Compelled and sickness, at this latter day,
This sorrowful reverse for all mankind.
I feel for thee, must utter what I feel:
The sympathies erewhile in part discharged,
Gather afresh, and will have vent again:
My own delights do scarcely seem to me
My own delights; the lordly Alps themselves,
Those rosy peaks, from which the Morning looks   410
Abroad on many nations, are no more
For me that image of pure gladsomeness
Which they were wont to be.   Through kindred scenes,
For purpose, at a time, how different!
Thou tak'st thy way, carrying the heart and soul
That Nature gives to Poets, now by thought
Matured, and in the summer of their strength.
Oh! wrap him in your shades, ye giant woods,
On Etna's side; and thou, O flowery field
Of Enna! is there not some nook of thine,   420
From the first play-time of the infant world

Kept sacred to restorative delight,
When from afar invoked by anxious love?

   Child of the mountains, among shepherds reared,
Ere yet familiar with the classic page,
I learnt to dream of Sicily; and lo,
The gloom, that, but a moment past, was deepened
At thy command, at her command gives way;
A pleasant promise, wafted from her shores,
Comes o'er my heart: in fancy I behold   430
Her seas yet smiling, her once happy vales;
Nor can my tongue give utterance to a name
Of note belonging to that honoured isle,
Philosopher or Bard, Empedocles,
Or Archimedes, pure abstracted soul!
That doth not yield a solace to my grief:
And, O Theocritus, so far have some
Prevailed among the powers of heaven and earth,
By their endowments, good or great, that they
Have had, as thou reportest, miracles   440
Wrought for them in old time: yea, not unmoved,
When thinking on my own beloved friend,
I hear thee tell how bees with honey fed
Divine Comates, by his impious lord
Within a chest imprisoned; how they came
Laden from blooming grove or flowery field,
And fed him there, alive, month after month,
Because the goatherd, blessèd man! had lips
Wet with the Muses' nectar.
                           Thus I soothe
The pensive moments by this calm fire-side,   450
And find a thousand bounteous images
To cheer the thoughts of those I love, and mine.
Our prayers have been accepted; thou wilt stand
On Etna's summit, above earth and sea,

Triumphant, winning from the invaded heavens
Thoughts without bound, magnificent designs,
Worthy of poets who attuned their harps
In wood or echoing cave, for discipline
Of heroes; or, in reverence to the gods,
'Mid temples, served by sapient priests, and choirs 460
Of virgins crowned with roses.   Not in vain
Those temples, where they in their ruins yet
Survive for inspiration, shall attract
Thy solitary steps: and on the brink
Thou wilt recline of pastoral Arethuse;
Or, if that fountain be in truth no more,
Then, near some other spring — which, by the name
Thou gratulatest, willingly deceived —
I see thee longer a glad votary,
And not a captive pining for his home. 470

BOOK   TWELFTH

IMAGINATION AND TASTE, HOW IMPAIRED
AND RESTORED

Long time have human ignorance and guilt
Detained us, on what spectacles of woe
Compelled to look, and inwardly oppressed
With sorrow, disappointment, vexing thoughts,
Confusion of the judgment, zeal decayed,
And, lastly, utter loss of hope itself
And things to hope for!   Not with these began
Our song, and not with these our song must end.
Ye motions of delight, that haunt the sides
Of the green hills; ye breezes and soft airs, 10
Whose subtle intercourse with breathing flowers,
Feelingly watched, might teach Man's haughty race

How without injury to take, to give
Without offence; ye who, as if to show
The wondrous influence of power gently used,
Bend the complying heads of lordly pines,
And, with a touch, shift the stupendous clouds
Through the whole compass of the sky; ye brooks,
Muttering along the stones, a busy noise
By day, a quiet sound in silent night;   20
Ye waves, that out of the great deep steal forth
In a calm hour to kiss the pebbly shore,
Not mute, and then retire, fearing no storm;
And you, ye groves, whose ministry it is
To interpose the covert of your shades,
Even as a sleep, between the heart of man
And outward troubles, between man himself,
Not seldom, and his own uneasy heart:
Oh! that I had a music and a voice
Harmonious as your own, that I might tell   30
What ye have done for me.   The morning shines,
Nor heedeth Man's perverseness; Spring returns, —
I saw the Spring return, and could rejoice,
In common with the children of her love,
Piping on boughs, or sporting on fresh fields,
Or boldly seeking pleasure nearer heaven
On wings that navigate cerulean skies.
So neither were complacency, nor peace,
Nor tender yearnings, wanting for my good
Through these distracted times; in Nature still   40
Glorying, I found a counterpoise in her,
Which, when the spirit of evil reached its height,
Maintained for me a secret happiness.

This narrative, my Friend! hath chiefly told
Of intellectual power, fostering love,
Dispensing truth, and, over men and things

Where reason yet might hesitate, diffusing
Prophetic sympathies of genial faith:
So was I favoured — such my happy lot —
Until that natural graciousness of mind   50
Gave way to overpressure from the times
And their disastrous issues.   What availed,
When spells forbade the voyager to land,
That fragrant notice of a pleasant shore
Wafted, at intervals, from many a bower
Of blissful gratitude and fearless love?
Dare I avow that wish was mine to see,
And hope that future times *would* surely see,
The man to come, parted, as by a gulph,
From him who had been; that I could no more   60
Trust the elevation which had made me one
With the great family that still survives
To illuminate the abyss of ages past,
Sage, warrior, patriot, hero; for it seemed
That their best virtues were not free from taint
Of something false and weak, that could not stand
The open eye of Reason.   Then I said,
"Go to the Poets, they will speak to thee
More perfectly of purer creatures; — yet
If reason be nobility in man,   70
Can aught be more ignoble than the man
Whom they delight in, blinded as he is
By prejudice, the miserable slave
Of low ambition or distempered love?"

    In such strange passion, if I may once more
Review the past, I warred against myself —
A bigot to a new idolatry —
Like a cowled monk who hath forsworn the world,
Zealously laboured to cut off my heart
From all the sources of her former strength;   80

And as, by simple waving of a wand,
The wizard instantaneously dissolves
Palace or grove, even so could I unsoul
As readily by syllogistic words
Those mysteries of being which have made,
And shall continue evermore to make,
Of the whole human race one brotherhood.

    What wonder, then, if, to a mind so far
Perverted, even the visible Universe
Fell under the dominion of a taste   90
Less spiritual, with microscopic view
Was scanned, as I had scanned the moral world?

    O Soul of Nature! excellent and fair!
That didst rejoice with me, with whom I, too,
Rejoiced through early youth, before the winds
And roaring waters, and in lights and shades
That marched and countermarched about the hills
In glorious apparition, Powers on whom
I daily waited, now all eye and now
All ear; but never long without the heart   100
Employed, and man's unfolding intellect:
O Soul of Nature! that, by laws divine
Sustained and governed, still dost overflow
With an impassioned life, what feeble ones
Walk on this earth! how feeble have I been
When thou wert in thy strength! Nor this through
          stroke
Of human suffering, such as justifies
Remissness and inaptitude of mind,
But through presumption; even in pleasure pleased
Unworthily, disliking here, and there   110
Liking; by rules of mimic art transferred
To things above all art; but more, — for this,

Although a strong infection of the age,
Was never much my habit — giving way
To a comparison of scene with scene,
Bent overmuch on superficial things,
Pampering myself with meagre novelties
Of colour and proportion; to the moods
Of time and season, to the moral power,
The affections and the spirit of the place,   120
Insensible. Nor only did the love
Of sitting thus in judgment interrupt
My deeper feelings, but another cause,
More subtle and less easily explained,
That almost seems inherent in the creature,
A twofold frame of body and of mind.
I speak in recollection of a time
When the bodily eye, in every stage of life
The most despotic of our senses, gained
Such strength in *me* as often held my mind   130
In absolute dominion.   Gladly here,
Entering upon abstruser argument,
Could I endeavour to unfold the means
Which Nature studiously employs to thwart
This tyranny, summons all the senses each
To counteract the other, and themselves,
And makes them all, and the objects with which all
Are conversant, subservient in their turn
To the great ends of Liberty and Power.
But leave we this: enough that my delights   140
(Such as they were) were sought insatiably.
Vivid the transport, vivid though not profound;
I roamed from hill to hill, from rock to rock,
Still craving combinations of new forms,
New pleasure, wider empire for the sight,
Proud of her own endowments, and rejoiced
To lay the inner faculties asleep.

Amid the turns and counterturns, the strife
And various trials of our complex being,
As we grow up, such thraldom of that sense   150
Seems hard to shun.   And yet I knew a maid,
A young enthusiast, who escaped these bonds;
Her eye was not the mistress of her heart;
Far less did rules prescribed by passive taste,
Or barren intermeddling subtleties,
Perplex her mind; but, wise as women are
When genial circumstance hath favoured them,
She welcomed what was given, and craved no more;
Whate'er the scene presented to her view
That was the best, to that she was attuned   160
By her benign simplicity of life,
And through a perfect happiness of soul,
Whose variegated feelings were in this
Sisters, that they were each some new delight.
Birds in the bower, and lambs in the green field,
Could they have known her, would have loved;
            methought
Her very presence such a sweetness breathed,
That flowers, and trees, and even the silent hills,
And everything she looked on, should have had
An intimation how she bore herself   170
Towards them and to all creatures.   God delights
In such a being; for, her common thoughts
Are piety, her life is gratitude.

Even like this maid, before I was called forth
From the retirement of my native hills,
I loved whate'er I saw: nor lightly loved,
But most intensely; never dreamt of aught
More grand, more fair, more exquisitely framed
Than those few nooks to which my happy feet
Were limited.   I had not at that time   180

Lived long enough, nor in the least survived
The first diviner influence of this world,
As it appears to unaccustomed eyes.
Worshipping them among the depth of things,
As piety ordained, could I submit
To measured admiration, or to aught
That should preclude humility and love?
I felt, observed, and pondered; did not judge,
Yea, never thought of judging; with the gift
Of all this glory filled and satisfied.   190
And afterwards, when through the gorgeous Alps
Roaming, I carried with me the same heart:
In truth, the degradation — howsoe'er
Induced, effect, in whatsoe'er degree,
Of custom that prepares a partial scale
In which the little oft outweighs the great;
Or any other cause that hath been named;
Or lastly, aggravated by the times
And their impassioned sounds, which well might make
The milder minstrelsies of rural scenes   200
Inaudible — was transient; I had known
Too forcibly, too early in my life,
Visitings of imaginative power
For this to last: I shook the habit off
Entirely and for ever, and again
In Nature's presence stood, as now I stand,
A sensitive being, a *creative* soul.

   There are in our existence spots of time,
That with distinct pre-eminence retain
A renovating virtue, whence — depressed   210
By false opinion and contentious thought,
Or aught of heavier or more deadly weight,
In trivial occupations, and the round
Of ordinary intercourse — our minds

Are nourished and invisibly repaired;
A virtue, by which pleasure is enhanced,
That penetrates, enables us to mount,
When high, more high, and lifts us up when fallen.
This efficacious spirit chiefly lurks
Among those passages of life that give   220
Profoundest knowledge to what point, and how,
The mind is lord and master — outward sense
The obedient servant of her will.   Such moments
Are scattered everywhere, taking their date
From our first childhood.   I remember well,
That once, while yet my inexperienced hand
Could scarcely hold a bridle, with proud hopes
I mounted, and we journeyed towards the hills:
An ancient servant of my father's house
Was with me, my encourager and guide: 230
We had not travelled long, ere some mischance
Disjoined me from my comrade; and, through fear
Dismounting, down the rough and stony moor
I led my horse, and, stumbling on, at length
Came to a bottom, where in former times
A murderer had been hung in iron chains.
The gibbet-mast had mouldered down, the bones
And iron case were gone; but on the turf,
Hard by, soon after that fell deed was wrought,
Some unknown hand had carved the murderer's name.
The monumental letters were inscribed   241
In times long past; but still, from year to year
By superstition of the neighbourhood,
The grass is cleared away, and to this hour
The characters are fresh and visible:
A casual glance had shown them, and I fled,
Faltering and faint, and ignorant of the road:
Then, reascending the bare common, saw
A naked pool that lay beneath the hills,

The beacon on the summit, and, more near,   250
A girl, who bore a pitcher on her head,
And seemed with difficult steps to force her way
Against the blowing wind.   It was, in truth,
An ordinary sight; but I should need
Colours and words that are unknown to man,
To paint the visionary dreariness
Which, while I looked all round for my lost guide,
Invested moorland waste and naked pool,
The beacon crowning the lone eminence,
The female and her garments vexed and tossed   260
By the strong wind.   When, in the blessèd hours
Of early love, the loved one at my side,
I roamed, in daily presence of this scene,
Upon the naked pool and dreary crags,
And on the melancholy beacon, fell
A spirit of pleasure and youth's golden gleam;
And think ye not with radiance more sublime
For these remembrances, and for the power
They had left behind?   So feeling comes in aid
Of feeling, and diversity of strength   270
Attends us, if but once we have been strong.
Oh! mystery of man, from what a depth
Proceed thy honours.   I am lost, but see
In simple childhood something of the base
On which thy greatness stands; but this I feel,
That from thyself it comes, that thou must give,
Else never canst receive.   The days gone by
Return upon me almost from the dawn
Of life: the hiding-places of man's power
Open; I would approach them, but they close.   280
I see by glimpses now; when age comes on,
May scarcely see at all; and I would give,
While yet we may, as far as words can give,
Substance and life to what I feel, enshrining,

Such is my hope, the spirit of the Past
For future restoration. — Yet another
Of these memorials : —
                        One Christmas-time,
On the glad eve of its dear holidays,
Feverish, and tired, and restless, I went forth
Into the fields, impatient for the sight   290
Of those led palfreys that should bear us home;
My brothers and myself.   There rose a crag,
That, from the meeting-point of two highways
Ascending, overlooked them both, far stretched;
Thither, uncertain on which road to fix
My expectation, thither I repaired,
Scout-like, and gained the summit; 't was a day
Tempestuous, dark, and wild, and on the grass
I sate half-sheltered by a naked wall;
Upon my right hand couched a single sheep,   300
Upon my left a blasted hawthorn stood;
With those companions at my side, I watched,
Straining my eyes intensely, as the mist
Gave intermitting prospect of the copse
And plain beneath.   Ere we to school returned, —
That dreary time, — ere we had been ten days
Sojourners in my father's house, he died;
And I and my three brothers, orphans then,
Followed his body to the grave.   The event,
With all the sorrow that it brought, appeared   310
A chastisement; and when I called to mind
That day so lately past, when from the crag
I looked in such anxiety of hope;
With trite reflections of morality,
Yet in the deepest passion, I bowed low
To God, Who thus corrected my desires;
And afterwards, the wind and sleety rain,
And all the business of the elements,

The single sheep, and the one blasted tree,
And the bleak music from that old stone wall,   320
The noise of wood and water, and the mist
That on the line of each of those two roads
Advanced in such indisputable shapes;
All these were kindred spectacles and sounds
To which I oft repaired, and thence would drink,
As at a fountain; and on winter nights,
Down to this very time, when storm and rain
Beat on my roof, or, haply, at noon-day,
While in a grove I walk, whose lofty trees,
Laden with summer's thickest foliage, rock   330
In a strong wind, some working of the spirit,
Some inward agitations thence are brought,
Whate'er their office, whether to beguile
Thoughts over busy in the course they took,
Or animate an hour of vacant ease.

BOOK THIRTEENTH

IMAGINATION AND TASTE, HOW IMPAIRED AND RESTORED (*concluded*)

FROM Nature doth emotion come, and moods
Of calmness equally are Nature's gift:
This is her glory; these two attributes
Are sister horns that constitute her strength.
Hence Genius, born to thrive by interchange
Of peace and excitation, finds in her
His best and purest friend; from her receives
That energy by which he seeks the truth,
From her that happy stillness of the mind
Which fits him to receive it when unsought.   10

   Such benefit the humblest intellects
Partake of, each in their degree; 't is mine

To speak, what I myself have known and felt;
Smooth task! for words find easy way, inspired
By gratitude, and confidence in truth.
Long time in search of knowledge did I range
The field of human life, in heart and mind
Benighted; but, the dawn beginning now
To re-appear, 't was proved that not in vain
I had been taught to reverence a Power　　　　20
That is the visible quality and shape
And image of right reason; that matures
Her processes by steadfast laws; gives birth
To no impatient or fallacious hopes,
No heat of passion or excessive zeal,
No vain conceits; provokes to no quick turns
Of self-applauding intellect; but trains
To meekness, and exalts by humble faith;
Holds up before the mind intoxicate
With present objects, and the busy dance　　　　30
Of things that pass away, a temperate show
Of objects that endure; and by this course
Disposes her, when over-fondly set
On throwing off incumbrances, to seek
In man, and in the frame of social life,
Whate'er there is desirable and good
Of kindred permanence, unchanged in form
And function, or, through strict vicissitude,
Of life and death, revolving.　Above all
Were re-established now those watchful thoughts　　　40
Which, seeing little worthy or sublime
In what the Historian's pen so much delights
To blazon — power and energy detached
From moral purpose — early tutored me
To look with feelings of fraternal love
Upon the unassuming things that hold
A silent station in this beauteous world.

Thus moderated, thus composed, I found
Once more in Man an object of delight,
Of pure imagination, and of love;   50
And, as the horizon of my mind enlarged,
Again I took the intellectual eye
For my instructor, studious more to see
Great truths, than touch and handle little ones.
Knowledge was given accordingly; my trust
Became more firm in feelings that had stood
The test of such a trial; clearer far
My sense of excellence — of right and wrong:
The promise of the present time retired
Into its true proportion; sanguine schemes,   60
Ambitious projects, pleased me less; I sought
For present good in life's familiar face,
And built thereon my hopes of good to come.

With settling judgments now of what would last
And what would disappear; prepared to find
Presumption, folly, madness, in the men
Who thrust themselves upon the passive world
As Rulers of the world; to see in these,
Even when the public welfare is their aim,
Plans without thought, or built on theories   70
Vague and unsound; and having brought the books
Of modern statists to their proper test,
Life, human life, with all its sacred claims
Of sex and age, and heaven-descended rights,
Mortal, or those beyond the reach of death;
And having thus discerned how dire a thing
Is worshipped in that idol proudly named
"The Wealth of Nations," *where* alone that wealth
Is lodged, and how increased; and having gained
A more judicious knowledge of the worth   80
And dignity of individual man,

No composition of the brain, but man
Of whom we read, the man whom we behold
With our own eyes — I could not but enquire —
Not with less interest than heretofore,
But greater, though in spirit more subdued —
Why is this glorious creature to be found
One only in ten thousand?   What one is,
Why may not millions be?   What bars are thrown
By Nature in the way of such a hope?   90
Our animal appetites and daily wants,
Are these obstructions insurmountable?
If not, then others vanish into air.
"Inspect the basis of the social pile:
Enquire," said I, "how much of mental power
And genuine virtue they possess who live
By bodily toil, labour exceeding far
Their due proportion, under all the weight
Of that injustice which upon ourselves
Ourselves entail."   Such estimate to frame   100
I chiefly looked (what need to look beyond?)
Among the natural abodes of men,
Fields with their rural works; recalled to mind
My earliest notices; with these compared
The observations made in later youth,
And to that day continued. — For, the time
Had never been when throes of mighty Nations
And the world's tumult unto me could yield,
How far soe'er transported and possessed,
Full measure of content; but still I craved   110
An intermingling of distinct regards
And truths of individual sympathy
Nearer ourselves.   Such often might be gleaned
From the great City, else it must have proved
To me a heart-depressing wilderness;
But much was wanting: therefore did I turn

To you, ye pathways, and ye lonely roads;
Sought you enriched with everything I prized,
With human kindnesses and simple joys.

Oh! next to one dear state of bliss, vouchsafed,   120
Alas! to few in this untoward world,
The bliss of walking daily in life's prime
Through field or forest with the maid we love,
While yet our hearts are young, while yet we breathe
Nothing but happiness, in some lone nook,
Deep vale, or anywhere, the home of both,
From which it would be misery to stir:
Oh! next to such enjoyment of our youth,
In my esteem, next to such dear delight,
Was that of wandering on from day to day   130
Where I could meditate in peace, and cull
Knowledge that step by step might lead me on
To wisdom; or, as lightsome as a bird
Wafted upon the wind from distant lands,
Sing notes of greeting to strange fields or groves,
Which lacked not voice to welcome me in turn;
And, when that pleasant toil had ceased to please,
Converse with men, where if we meet a face
We almost meet a friend, on naked heaths
With long long ways before, by cottage bench,   140
Or well-spring where the weary traveller rests.

Who doth not love to follow with his eye
The windings of a public way? the sight,
Familiar object as it is, hath wrought
On my imagination since the morn
Of childhood, when a disappearing line,
One daily present to my eyes, that crossed
The naked summit of a far-off hill

Beyond the limits that my feet had trod,
Was like an invitation into space　　　　　150
Boundless, or guide into eternity.
Yes, something of the grandeur which invests
The mariner, who sails the roaring sea
Through storm and darkness, early in my mind
Surrounded, too, the wanderers of the earth;
Grandeur as much, and loveliness far more.
Awed have I been by strolling Bedlamites;
From many other uncouth vagrants (passed
In fear) have walked with quicker step; but why
Take note of this?　When I began to enquire,　　　　　160
To watch and question those I met, and speak
Without reserve to them, the lonely roads
Were open schools in which I daily read
With most delight the passions of mankind,
Whether by words, looks, sighs, or tears, revealed;
There saw into the depth of human souls,
Souls that appear to have no depth at all
To careless eyes.　And — now convinced at heart
How little those formalities, to which
With overweening trust alone we give　　　　　170
The name of Education, have to do
With real feeling and just sense; how vain
A correspondence with the talking world
Proves to the most; and called to make good search
If man's estate, by doom of Nature yoked
With toil, be therefore yoked with ignorance;
If virtue be indeed so hard to rear,
And intellectual strength so rare a boon —
I prized such walks still more, for there I found
Hope to my hope, and to my pleasure peace　　　　　180
And steadiness, and healing and repose
To every angry passion.　There I heard,
From mouths of men obscure and lowly, truths

Replete with honour; sounds in unison
With loftiest promises of good and fair.

There are who think that strong affection, love
Known by whatever name, is falsely deemed
A gift, to use a term which they would use,
Of vulgar nature; that its growth requires
Retirement, leisure, language purified   190
By manners studied and elaborate;
That whoso feels such passion in its strength
Must live within the very light and air
Of courteous usages refined by art.
True is it, where oppression worse than death
Salutes the being at his birth, where grace
Of culture hath been utterly unknown,
And poverty and labour in excess
From day to day pre-occupy the ground
Of the affections, and to Nature's self   200
Oppose a deeper nature; there, indeed,
Love cannot be; nor does it thrive with ease
Among the close and overcrowded haunts
Of cities, where the human heart is sick,
And the eye feeds it not, and cannot feed.
— Yes, in those wanderings deeply did I feel
How we mislead each other; above all,
How books mislead us, seeking their reward
From judgments of the wealthy Few, who see
By artificial lights; how they debase   210
The Many for the pleasure of those Few;
Effeminately level down the truth
To certain general notions, for the sake
Of being understood at once, or else
Through want of better knowledge in the heads
That framed them; flattering self-conceit with words,

That, while they most ambitiously set forth
Extrinsic differences, the outward marks
Whereby society has parted man
From man, neglect the universal heart.   220

Here, calling up to mind what then I saw,
A youthful traveller, and see daily now
In the familiar circuit of my home,
Here might I pause, and bend in reverence
To Nature, and the power of human minds,
To men as they are men within themselves.
How oft high service is performed within,
When all the external man is rude in show, —
Not like a temple rich with pomp and gold,
But a mere mountain chapel, that protects   230
Its simple worshippers from sun and shower.
Of these, said I, shall be my song; of these,
If future years mature me for the task,
Will I record the praises, making verse
Deal boldly with substantial things; in truth
And sanctity of passion, speak of these,
That justice may be done, obeisance paid
Where it is due: thus haply shall I teach,
Inspire; through unadulterated ears
Pour rapture, tenderness, and hope, — my theme   240
No other than the very heart of man,
As found among the best of those who live —
Not unexalted by religious faith,
Nor uninformed by books, good books, though few —
In Nature's presence: thence may I select
Sorrow, that is not sorrow, but delight;
And miserable love, that is not pain
To hear of, for the glory that redounds
Therefrom to human kind, and what we are.
Be mine to follow with no timid step   250

Where knowledge leads me: it shall be my pride
That I have dared to tread this holy ground,
Speaking no dream, but things oracular;
Matter not lightly to be heard by those
Who to the letter of the outward promise
Do read the invisible soul; by men adroit
In speech, and for communion with the world
Accomplished; minds whose faculties are then
Most active when they are most eloquent,
And elevated most when most admired.   260
Men may be found of other mould than these,
Who are their own upholders, to themselves
Encouragement, and energy, and will,
Expressing liveliest thoughts in lively words
As native passion dictates.   Others, too,
There are among the walks of homely life
Still higher, men for contemplation framed,
Shy, and unpractised in the strife of phrase;
Meek men, whose very souls perhaps would sink
Beneath them, summoned to such intercourse: 270
Theirs is the language of the heavens, the power,
The thought, the image, and the silent joy:
Words are but under-agents in their souls;
When they are grasping with their greatest strength,
They do not breathe among them: this I speak
In gratitude to God, Who feeds our hearts
For His own service; knoweth, loveth us,
When we are unregarded by the world.

   Also, about this time did I receive
Convictions still more strong than heretofore,   280
Not only that the inner frame is good,
And graciously composed, but that, no less,
Nature for all conditions wants not power
To consecrate, if we have eyes to see,

The outside of her creatures, and to breathe
Grandeur upon the very humblest face
Of human life. I felt that the array
Of act and circumstance, and visible form,
Is mainly to the pleasure of the mind
What passion makes them; that meanwhile the forms
Of Nature have a passion in themselves,   291
That intermingles with those works of man
To which she summons him; although the works
Be mean, have nothing lofty of their own;
And that the Genius of the Poet hence
May boldly take his way among mankind
Wherever Nature leads; that he hath stood
By Nature's side among the men of old,
And so shall stand for ever. Dearest Friend!
If thou partake the animating faith   300
That Poets, even as Prophets, each with each
Connected in a mighty scheme of truth,
Have each his own peculiar faculty,
Heaven's gift, a sense that fits him to perceive
Objects unseen before, thou wilt not blame
The humblest of this band who dares to hope
That unto him hath also been vouchsafed
An insight that in some sort he possesses,
A privilege whereby a work of his,
Proceeding from a source of untaught things,   310
Creative and enduring, may become
A power like one of Nature's. To a hope
Not less ambitious once among the wilds
Of Sarum's Plain, my youthful spirit was raised;
There, as I ranged at will the pastoral downs
Trackless and smooth, or paced the bare white roads
Lengthening in solitude their dreary line,
Time with his retinue of ages fled
Backwards, nor checked his flight until I saw

Our dim ancestral Past in vision clear;   320
Saw multitudes of men, and here and there,
A single Briton clothed in wolf-skin vest,
With shield and stone-axe, stride across the wold;
The voice of spears was heard, the rattling spear
Shaken by arms of mighty bone, in strength,
Long mouldered, of barbaric majesty.
I called on Darkness — but before the word
Was uttered, midnight darkness seemed to take
All objects from my sight; and lo! again
The Desert visible by dismal flames;   330
It is the sacrificial altar, fed
With living men — how deep the groans! the voice
Of those that crowd the giant wicker thrills
The monumental hillocks, and the pomp
Is for both worlds, the living and the dead.
At other moments — (for through that wide waste
Three summer days I roamed) where'er the Plain
Was figured o'er with circles, lines, or mounds,
That yet survive, a work, as some divine,
Shaped by the Druids, so to represent   340
Their knowledge of the heavens, and image forth
The constellations — gently was I charmed
Into a waking dream, a reverie
That, with believing eyes, where'er I turned,
Beheld long-bearded teachers, with white wands
Uplifted, pointing to the starry sky,
Alternately, and plain below, while breath
Of music swayed their motions, and the waste
Rejoiced with them and me in those sweet sounds.

   This for the past, and things that may be viewed   350
Or fancied in the obscurity of years
From monumental hints: and thou, O Friend!
Pleased with some unpremeditated strains

That served those wanderings to beguile, hast said
That then and there my mind had exercised
Upon the vulgar forms of present things,
The actual world of our familiar days,
Yet higher power; had caught from them a tone,
An image, and a character, by books
Not hitherto reflected. Call we this   360
A partial judgment — and yet why? for *then*
We were as strangers; and I may not speak
Thus wrongfully of verse, however rude,
Which on thy young imagination, trained
In the great City, broke like light from far.
Moreover, each man's Mind is to herself
Witness and judge; and I remember well
That in life's every-day appearances
I seemed about this time to gain clear sight
Of a new world — a world, too, that was fit   370
To be transmitted, and to other eyes
Made visible; as ruled by those fixed laws
Whence spiritual dignity originates,
Which do both give it being and maintain
A balance, an ennobling interchange
Of action from without and from within;
The excellence, pure function, and best power
Both of the objects seen, and eye that sees.

BOOK FOURTEENTH

CONCLUSION

In one of those excursions (may they ne'er
Fade from remembrance!) through the Northern tracts
Of Cambria ranging with a youthful friend,
I left Bethgelert's huts at couching-time,
And westward took my way, to see the sun

Rise, from the top of Snowdon.   To the door
Of a rude cottage at the mountain's base
We came, and roused the shepherd who attends
The adventurous stranger's steps, a trusty guide;
Then, cheered by short refreshment, sallied forth.   10

It was a close, warm, breezeless summer night,
Wan, dull, and glaring, with a dripping fog
Low-hung and thick that covered all the sky;
But, undiscouraged, we began to climb
The mountain-side.   The mist soon girt us round,
And, after ordinary travellers' talk
With our conductor, pensively we sank
Each into commerce with his private thoughts:
Thus did we breast the ascent, and by myself
Was nothing either seen or heard that checked   20
Those musings or diverted, save that once
The shepherd's lurcher, who, among the crags,
Had to his joy unearthed a hedgehog, teased
His coiled-up prey with barkings turbulent.
This small adventure, for even such it seemed
In that wild place and at the dead of night,
Being over and forgotten, on we wound
In silence as before.   With forehead bent
Earthward, as if in opposition set
Against an enemy, I panted up   30
With eager pace, and no less eager thoughts.
Thus might we wear a midnight hour away,
Ascending at loose distance each from each,
And I, as chanced, the foremost of the band;
When at my feet the ground appeared to brighten,
And with a step or two seemed brighter still;
Nor was time given to ask or learn the cause,
For instantly a light upon the turf
Fell like a flash, and lo! as I looked up

The Moon hung naked in a firmament   40
Of azure without cloud, and at my feet
Rested a silent sea of hoary mist.
A hundred hills their dusky backs upheaved
All over this still ocean; and beyond,
Far, far beyond, the solid vapours stretched,
In headlands, tongues, and promontory shapes,
Into the main Atlantic, that appeared
To dwindle, and give up his majesty,
Usurped upon far as the sight could reach.
Not so the ethereal vault; encroachment none   50
Was there, nor loss; only the inferior stars
Had disappeared, or shed a fainter light
In the clear presence of the full-orbed Moon,
Who, from her sovereign elevation, gazed
Upon the billowy ocean, as it lay
All meek and silent, save that through a rift —
Not distant from the shore whereon we stood,
A fixed abysmal, gloomy, breathing-place —
Mounted the roar of waters, torrents, streams
Innumerable, roaring with one voice!   60
Heard over earth and sea, and, in that hour,
For so it seemed, felt by the starry heavens.

When into air had partially dissolved
That vision, given to spirits of the night
And three chance human wanderers, in calm thought
Reflected, it appeared to me the type
Of a majestic intellect, its acts
And its possessions, what it has and craves,
What in itself it is, and would become.
There I beheld the emblem of a mind   70
That feeds upon infinity, that broods
Over the dark abyss, intent to hear
Its voices issuing forth to silent light

In one continuous stream; a mind sustained
By recognitions of transcendent power,
In sense conducting to ideal form,
In soul of more than mortal privilege.
One function, above all, of such a mind
Had Nature shadowed there, by putting forth,
'Mid circumstances awful and sublime,   80
That mutual domination which she loves
To exert upon the face of outward things,
So moulded, joined, abstracted, so endowed
With interchangeable supremacy,
That men, least sensitive, see, hear, perceive,
And cannot choose but feel.   The power, which all
Acknowledge when thus moved, which Nature thus
To bodily sense exhibits, is the express
Resemblance of that glorious faculty
That higher minds bear with them as their own.   90
This is the very spirit in which they deal
With the whole compass of the universe:
They from their native selves can send abroad
Kindred mutations; for themselves create
A like existence; and, whene'er it dawns
Created for them, catch it, or are caught
By its inevitable mastery,
Like angels stopped upon the wing by sound
Of harmony from Heaven's remotest spheres.
Them the enduring and the transient both   100
Serve to exalt; they build up greatest things
From least suggestions; ever on the watch,
Willing to work and to be wrought upon,
They need not extraordinary calls
To rouse them; in a world of life they live,
By sensible impressions not enthralled,
But by their quickening impulse made more prompt
To hold fit converse with the spiritual world,

And with the generations of mankind
Spread over time, past, present, and to come, 110
Age after age, till Time shall be no more.
Such minds are truly from the Deity,
For they are Powers; and hence the highest bliss
That flesh can know is theirs — the consciousness
Of Whom they are, habitually infused
Through every image and through every thought,
And all affections by communion raised
From earth to heaven, from human to divine;
Hence endless occupation for the Soul,
Whether discursive or intuitive; 120
Hence cheerfulness for acts of daily life,
Emotions which best foresight need not fear,
Most worthy then of trust when most intense.
Hence, amid ills that vex and wrongs that crush
Our hearts — if here the words of Holy Writ
May with fit reverence be applied — that peace
Which passeth understanding, that repose
In moral judgments which from this pure source
Must come, or will by man be sought in vain.

Oh! who is he that hath his whole life long 130
Preserved, enlarged, this freedom in himself?
For this alone is genuine liberty:
Where is the favoured being who hath held
That course unchecked, unerring, and untired,
In one perpetual progress smooth and bright? —
A humbler destiny have we retraced,
And told of lapse and hesitating choice,
And backward wanderings along thorny ways:
Yet — compassed round by mountain solitudes,
Within whose solemn temple I received 140
My earliest visitations, careless then
Of what was given me; and which now I range,

A meditative, oft a suffering, man —
Do I declare — in accents which, from truth
Deriving cheerful confidence, shall blend
Their modulation with these vocal streams —
That, whatsoever falls my better mind,
Revolving with the accidents of life,
May have sustained, that, howsoe'er misled,   150
Never did I, in quest of right and wrong,
Tamper with conscience from a private aim;
Nor was in any public hope the dupe
Of selfish passions; nor did ever yield
Wilfully to mean cares or low pursuits,
But shrunk with apprehensive jealousy
From every combination which might aid
The tendency, too potent in itself,
Of use and custom to bow down the soul
Under a growing weight of vulgar sense,   160
And substitute a universe of death
For that which moves with light and life informed,
Actual, divine, and true.   To fear and love,
To love as prime and chief, for there fear ends,
Be this ascribed; to early intercourse,
In presence of sublime or beautiful forms,
With the adverse principles of pain and joy — .
Evil as one is rashly named by men
Who know not what they speak.   By love subsists
All lasting grandeur, by pervading love;
That gone, we are as dust. — Behold the fields   170
In balmy spring-time full of rising flowers
And joyous creatures; see that pair, the lamb
And the lamb's mother, and their tender ways
Shall touch thee to the heart; thou callest this love,
And not inaptly so, for love it is,
Far as it carries thee.   In some green bower
Rest, and be not alone, but have thou there

The One who is thy choice of all the world:
There linger, listening, gazing, with delight
Impassioned, but delight how pitiable!   180
Unless this love by a still higher love
Be hallowed, love that breathes not without awe;
Love that adores, but on the knees of prayer,
By heaven inspired; that frees from chains the soul,
Lifted, in union with the purest, best,
Of earth-born passions, on the wings of praise
Bearing a tribute to the Almighty's Throne.

This spiritual Love acts not nor can exist
Without Imagination, which, in truth,
Is but another name for absolute power   190
And clearest insight, amplitude of mind,
And Reason in her most exalted mood.
This faculty hath been the feeding source
Of our long labour: we have traced the stream
From the blind cavern whence is faintly heard
Its natal murmur; followed it to light
And open day; accompanied its course
Among the ways of Nature, for a time
Lost sight of it bewildered and engulphed;
Then given it greeting as it rose once more   200
In strength, reflecting from its placid breast
The works of man and face of human life;
And lastly, from its progress have we drawn
Faith in life endless, the sustaining thought
Of human Being, Eternity, and God.

Imagination having been our theme,
So also hath that intellectual Love,
For they are each in each, and cannot stand
Dividually. — Here must thou be, O Man!
Power to thyself; no Helper hast thou here;   210

Here keepest thou in singleness thy state:
No other can divide with thee this work:
No secondary hand can intervene
To fashion this ability; 't is thine,
The prime and vital principle is thine
In the recesses of thy nature, far
From any reach of outward fellowship,
Else is not thine at all. But joy to him,
Oh, joy to him who here hath sown, hath laid
Here, the foundation of his future years!   220
For all that friendship, all that love can do,
All that a darling countenance can look
Or dear voice utter, to complete the man,
Perfect him, made imperfect in himself,
All shall be his: and he whose soul hath risen
Up to the height of feeling intellect
Shall want no humbler tenderness; his heart
Be tender as a nursing mother's heart;
Of female softness shall his life be full,
Of humble cares and delicate desires,   230
Mild interests and gentlest sympathies.

  Child of my parents! Sister of my soul!
Thanks in sincerest verse have been elsewhere
Poured out for all the early tenderness
Which I from thee imbibed: and 't is most true
That later seasons owed to thee no less;
For, spite of thy sweet influence and the touch
Of kindred hands that opened out the springs
Of genial thought in childhood, and in spite
Of all that unassisted I had marked   240
In life or nature of those charms minute
That win their way into the heart by stealth
(Still to the very going-out of youth)
I too exclusively esteemed *that* love,

And sought *that* beauty, which, as Milton sings,
Hath terror in it.　Thou didst soften down
This over-sternness; but for thee, dear Friend!
My soul, too reckless of mild grace, had stood
In her original self too confident,
Retained too long a countenance severe;　　　　　　250
A rock with torrents roaring, with the clouds
Familiar, and a favourite of the stars:
But thou didst plant its crevices with flowers,
Hang it with shrubs that twinkle in the breeze,
And teach the little birds to build their nests
And warble in its chambers.　At a time
When Nature, destined to remain so long
Foremost in my affections, had fallen back
Into a second place, pleased to become
A handmaid to a nobler than herself,　　　　　　260
When every day brought with it some new sense
Of exquisite regard for common things,
And all the earth was budding with these gifts
Of more refined humanity, thy breath,
Dear Sister! was a kind of gentler spring
That went before my steps.　Thereafter came
One whom with thee friendship had early paired;
She came, no more a phantom to adorn
A moment, but an inmate of the heart,
And yet a spirit, there for me enshrined　　　　　270
To penetrate the lofty and the low;
Even as one essence of pervading light
Shines, in the brightest of ten thousand stars
And the meek worm that feeds her lonely lamp
Couched in the dewy grass.
　　　　　　　　　　　With such a theme,
Coleridge! with this my argument, of thee
Shall I be silent?　O capacious Soul!
Placed on this earth to love and understand,

And from thy presence shed the light of love,
Shall I be mute, ere thou be spoken of ?   280
Thy kindred influence to my heart of hearts
Did also find its way.   Thus fear relaxed
Her overweening grasp; thus thoughts and things
In the self-haunting spirit learned to take
More rational proportions; mystery,
The incumbent mystery of sense and soul,
Of life and death, time and eternity,
Admitted more habitually a mild
Interposition — a serene delight
In closelier gathering cares, such as become   290
A human creature, howsoe'er endowed,
Poet, or destined for a humbler name;
And so the deep enthusiastic joy,
The rapture of the hallelujah sent
From all that breathes and is, was chastened, stemmed
And balanced by pathetic truth, by trust
In hopeful reason, leaning on the stay
Of Providence; and in reverence for duty,
Here, if need be, struggling with storms, and there
Strewing in peace life's humblest ground with herbs,
At every season green, sweet at all hours.   301

        And now, O Friend! this history is brought
To its appointed close: the discipline
And consummation of a Poet's mind,
In everything that stood most prominent,
Have faithfully been pictured; we have reached
The time (our guiding object from the first).
When we may, not presumptuously, I hope,
Suppose my powers so far confirmed, and such
My knowledge, as to make me capable   310
Of building up a Work that shall endure.
Yet much hath been omitted, as need was;

Of books how much! and even of the other wealth
That is collected among woods and fields,
Far more: for Nature's secondary grace
Hath hitherto been barely touched upon,
The charm more superficial that attends
Her works, as they present to Fancy's choice
Apt illustrations of the moral world,
Caught at a glance, or traced with curious pains.   320

Finally, and above all, O Friend! (I speak
With due regret) how much is overlooked
In human nature and her subtle ways,
As studied first in our own hearts, and then
In life among the passions of mankind,
Varying their composition and their hue,
Where'er we move, under the diverse shapes
That individual character presents
To an attentive eye.   For progress meet,
Along this intricate and difficult path,   330
Whate'er was wanting, something had I gained,
As one of many schoolfellows compelled,
In hardy independence, to stand up
Amid conflicting interests, and the shock
Of various tempers; to endure and note
What was not understood, though known to be;
Among the mysteries of love and hate,
Honour and shame, looking to right and left,
Unchecked by innocence too delicate,
And moral notions too intolerant,   340
Sympathies too contracted.   Hence, when called
To take a station among men, the step
Was easier, the transition more secure,
More profitable also; for, the mind
Learns from such timely exercise to keep

In wholesome separation the two natures,
The one that feels, the other that observes.

Yet one word more of personal concern; —
Since I withdrew unwillingly from France,
I led an undomestic wanderer's life   350
In London chiefly harboured, whence I roamed,
Tarrying at will in many a pleasant spot
Of rural England's cultivated vales
Or Cambrian solitudes.   A youth — (he bore
The name of Calvert — it shall live, if words
Of mine can give it life,) in firm belief
That by endowments not from me withheld
Good might be furthered — in his last decay
By a bequest sufficient for my needs
Enabled me to pause for choice, and walk   360
At large and unrestrained; nor damped too soon
By mortal cares.   Himself no Poet, yet
Far less a common follower of the world,
He deemed that my pursuits and labours lay
Apart from all that leads to wealth, or even
A necessary maintenance insures,
Without some hazard to the finer sense;
He cleared a passage for me, and the stream
Flowed in the bent of Nature.
                              Having now
Told what best merits mention, further pains   370
Our present purpose seems not to require,
And I have other tasks.   Recall to mind
The mood in which this labour was begun,
O Friend!   The termination of my course
Is nearer now, much nearer; yet even then,
In that distraction and intense desire,
I said unto the life which I had lived,
Where art thou?   Hear I not a voice from thee

Which 't is reproach to hear?   Anon I rose
As if on wings, and saw beneath me stretched   380
Vast prospect of the world which I had been
And was; and hence this Song, which, like a lark,
I have protracted, in the unwearied heavens
Singing, and often with more plaintive voice
To earth attempered and her deep-drawn sighs,
Yet centring all in love, and in the end
All gratulant, if rightly understood.

    Whether to me shall be allotted life,
And, with life, power to accomplish aught of worth,
That will be deemed no insufficient plea   390
For having given the story of myself,
Is all uncertain: but, beloved Friend!
When, looking back, thou seest, in clearer view
Than any liveliest sight of yesterday,
That summer, under whose indulgent skies,
Upon smooth Quantock's airy ridge we roved
Unchecked, or loitered 'mid her sylvan combs,
Thou in bewitching words, with happy heart,
Didst chaunt the vision of that Ancient Man,
The bright-eyed Mariner, and rueful woes   400
Didst utter of the Lady Christabel;
And I, associate with such labour, steeped
In soft forgetfulness the livelong hours,
Murmuring of him who, joyous hap, was found,
After the perils of his moonlight ride,
Near the loud waterfall; or her who sate
In misery near the miserable Thorn —
When thou dost to that summer turn thy thoughts,
And hast before thee all which then we were,   410
To thee, in memory of that happiness,
It will be known, by thee at least, my Friend!
Felt, that the history of a Poet's mind

Is labour not unworthy of regard;
To thee the work shall justify itself.

The last and later portions of this gift
Have been prepared, not with the buoyant spirits
That were our daily portion when we first
Together wantoned in wild Poesy,
But, under pressure of a private grief,
Keen and enduring, which the mind and heart,   420
That in this meditative history
Have been laid open, needs must make me feel
More deeply, yet enable me to bear
More firmly; and a comfort now hath risen
From hope that thou art near, and wilt be soon
Restored to us in renovated health;
When, after the first mingling of our tears,
'Mong other consolations, we may draw
Some pleasure from this offering of my love.

Oh! yet a few short years of useful life,   430
And all will be complete, thy race be run,
Thy monument of glory will be raised;
They, though (too weak to tread the ways of truth)
This age fall back to old idolatry,
Though men return to servitude as fast
As the tide ebbs, to ignominy and shame,
By nations, sink together, we shall still
Find solace — knowing what we have learnt to know,
Rich in true happiness if allowed to be
Faithful alike in forwarding a day   440
Of firmer trust, joint labourers in the work
(Should Providence such grace to us vouchsafe)
Of their deliverance, surely yet to come.
Prophets of Nature, we to them will speak
A lasting inspiration, sanctified

By reason, blest by faith: what we have loved,
Others will love, and we will teach them how;
Instruct them how the mind of man becomes
A thousand times more beautiful than the earth
On which he dwells, above this frame of things 450
(Which, 'mid all revolution in the hopes
And fears of men, doth still remain unchanged)
In beauty exalted, as it is itself
Of quality and fabric more divine.

1799–1805   *1850*

From THE EXCURSION

BOOK THIRD

DESPONDENCY

Argument

Images in the Valley. — Another Recess in it entered and described. — Wanderer's sensations. — Solitary's excited by the same objects. — Contrast between these. — Despondency of the Solitary gently reproved. — Conversation exhibiting the Solitary's past and present opinions and feelings, till he enters upon his own History at length. — His domestic felicity. — Afflictions. — Dejection. — Roused by the French Revolution. — Disappointment and disgust. — Voyage to America. — Disappointment and disgust pursue him. His return. — His languor and depression of mind, from want of faith in the great truths of Religion, and want of confidence in the virtue of Mankind.

.   .   .   .   .

"Is this," the grey-haired Wanderer mildly said,   225
"The voice, which we so lately overheard,
To that same child, addressing tenderly
The consolations of a hopeful mind?
'*His body is at rest, his soul in heaven.*'
These were your words; and, verily, methinks   230
Wisdom is ofttimes nearer when we stoop
Than when we soar." —
               The Other, not displeased,
Promptly replied — "My notion is the same.
And I, without reluctance, could decline
All act of inquisition whence we rise,
And what, when breath hath ceased, we may become.
Here are we, in a bright and breathing world.
Our origin, what matters it?   In lack
Of worthier explanation, say at once

With the American (a thought which suits   240
The place where now we stand) that certain men
Leapt out together from a rocky cave;
And these were the first parents of mankind:
Or, if a different image be recalled
By the warm sunshine, and the jocund voice
Of insects chirping out their careless lives
On these soft beds of thyme-besprinkled turf,
Choose, with the gay Athenian, a conceit
As sound — blithe race! whose mantles were bedecked
With golden grasshoppers, in sign that they   250
Had sprung, like those bright creatures, from the soil
Whereon their endless generations dwelt.
But stop! these theoretic fancies jar
On serious minds: then, as the Hindoos draw
Their holy Ganges from a skyey fount,
Even so deduce the stream of human life
From seats of power divine; and hope, or trust,
That our existence winds her stately course
Beneath the sun, like Ganges, to make part
Of a living ocean; or, to sink engulfed,   260
Like Niger, in impenetrable sands
And utter darkness: thought which may be faced,
Though comfortless! —
                    Not of myself I speak;
Such acquiescence neither doth imply,
In me, a meekly-bending spirit soothed
By natural piety; nor a lofty mind,
By philosophic discipline prepared
For calm subjection to acknowledged law;
Pleased to have been, contented not to be.
Such palms I boast not; — no! to me, who find,   270
Reviewing my past way, much to condemn,
Little to praise, and nothing to regret,
(Save some remembrances of dream-like joys

That scarcely seem to have belonged to me)
If I must take my choice between the pair
That rule alternately the weary hours,
Night is than day more acceptable; sleep
Doth, in my estimate of good, appear
A better state than waking; death than sleep:
Feelingly sweet is stillness after storm,   280
Though under covert of the wormy ground!

    "Yet be it said, in justice to myself,
That in more genial times, when I was free
To explore the destiny of human kind
(Not as an intellectual game pursued
With curious subtilty, from wish to cheat
Irksome sensations; but by love of truth
Urged on, or haply by intense delight
In feeding thought, wherever thought could feed)
I did not rank with those (too dull or nice,   290
For to my judgment such they then appeared,
Or too aspiring, thankless at the best)
Who, in this frame of human life, perceive
An object whereunto their souls are tied
In discontented wedlock; nor did e'er,
From me, those dark impervious shades, that hang
Upon the region whither we are bound,
Exclude a power to enjoy the vital beams
Of present sunshine. — Deities that float
On wings, angelic Spirits! I could muse   300
O'er what from eldest time we have been told
Of your bright forms and glorious faculties,
And with the imagination rest content,
Not wishing more; repining not to tread
The little sinuous path of earthly care,
By flowers embellished, and by springs refreshed.
— 'Blow winds of autumn! — let your chilling breath

Take the live herbage from the mead, and strip
The shady forest of its green attire, —
And let the bursting clouds to fury rouse   310
The gentle brooks! — Your desolating sway,
Sheds,' I exclaimed, 'no sadness upon me,
And no disorder in your rage I find.
What dignity, what beauty, in this change
From mild to angry, and from sad to gay,
Alternate and revolving! How benign,
How rich in animation and delight,
How bountiful these elements — compared
With aught, as more desirable and fair,
Devised by fancy for the golden age;   320
Or the perpetual warbling that prevails
In Arcady, beneath unaltered skies,
Through the long year in constant quiet bound,
Night hushed as night, and day serene as day!'
— But why this tedious record? — Age, we know,
Is garrulous; and solitude is apt
To anticipate the privilege of Age.
From far ye come; and surely with a hope
Of better entertainment: — let us hence!"

Loth to forsake the spot, and still more loth   330
To be diverted from our present theme,
I said, "My thoughts, agreeing, Sir, with yours,
Would push this censure farther; — for, if smiles
Of scornful pity be the just reward
Of Poesy thus courteously employed
In framing models to improve the scheme
Of Man's existence, and recast the world,
Why should not grave Philosophy be styled,
Herself, a dreamer of a kindred stock,
A dreamer yet more spiritless and dull?   340
Yes, shall the fine immunities she boasts

Establish sounder titles of esteem
For her, who (all too timid and reserved
For onset, for resistance too inert,
Too weak for suffering, and for hope too tame)
Placed, among flowery gardens curtained round
With world-excluding groves, the brotherhood
Of soft Epicureans, taught — if they
The ends of being would secure, and win
The crown of wisdom — to yield up their souls   350
To a voluptuous unconcern, preferring
Tranquillity to all things. Or is she,"
I cried, "more worthy of regard, the Power,
Who, for the sake of sterner quiet, closed
The Stoic's heart against the vain approach
Of admiration, and all sense of joy?"

   His countenance gave notice that my zeal
Accorded little with his present mind;
I ceased, and he resumed. — "Ah! gentle Sir,
Slight, if you will, the *means;* but spare to slight   360
The *end* of those, who did, by system, rank,
As the prime object of a wise man's aim,
Security from shock of accident,
Release from fear; and cherished peaceful days
For their own sakes, as mortal life's chief good,
And only reasonable felicity.
What motive drew, what impulse, I would ask,
Through a long course of later ages, drove,
The hermit to his cell in forest wide;
Or what detained him, till his closing eyes   370
Took their last farewell of the sun and stars,
Fast anchored in the desert? — Not alone
Dread of the persecuting sword, remorse,
Wrongs unredressed, or insults unavenged
And unavengeable, defeated pride,

Prosperity subverted, maddening want,
Friendship betrayed, affection unreturned,
Love with despair, or grief in agony; —
Not always from intolerable pangs
He fled; but, compassed round by pleasure, sighed   380
For independent happiness; craving peace,
The central feeling of all happiness,
Not as a refuge from distress or pain,
A breathing-time, vacation, or a truce,
But for its absolute self; a life of peace,
Stability without regret or fear;
That hath been, is, and shall be evermore! —
Such the reward he sought; and wore out life,
There, where on few external things his heart
Was set, and those his own; or, if not his,   390
Subsisting under nature's steadfast law.

"What other yearning was the master tie
Of the monastic brotherhood, upon rock
Aerial, or in green secluded vale,
One after one, collected from afar,
An undissolving fellowship? — What but this,
The universal instinct of repose,
The longing for confirmed tranquillity,
Inward and outward; humble, yet sublime:
The life where hope and memory are as one;   400
Where earth is quiet and her face unchanged
Save by the simplest toil of human hands
Or season's difference; the immortal Soul
Consistent in self-rule; and heaven revealed
To meditation in that quietness! —
Such was their scheme: and though the wished-for end
By multitudes was missed, perhaps attained
By none, they for the attempt, and pains employed,
Do, in my present censure, stand redeemed

From the unqualified disdain, that once 410
Would have been cast upon them by my voice
Delivering her decisions from the seat
Of forward youth — that scruples not to solve
Doubts, and determine questions, by the rules
Of inexperienced judgment, ever prone
To overweening faith; and is inflamed,
By courage, to demand from real life
The test of act and suffering, to provoke
Hostility — how dreadful when it comes,
Whether affliction be the foe, or guilt! 420

"A child of earth, I rested, in that stage
Of my past course to which these thoughts advert,
Upon earth's native energies; forgetting
That mine was a condition which required
Nor energy, nor fortitude — a calm
Without vicissitude; which, if the like
Had been presented to my view elsewhere,
I might have even been tempted to despise.
But no — for the serene was also bright;
Enlivened happiness with joy o'erflowing, 430
With joy, and — oh! that memory should survive
To speak the word — with rapture! Nature's boon,
Life's genuine inspiration, happiness
Above what rules can teach, or fancy feign;
Abused, as all possessions *are* abused
That are not prized according to their worth.
And yet, what worth? what good is given to men,
More solid than the gilded clouds of heaven?
What joy more lasting than a vernal flower? —
None! 'tis the general plaint of human kind 440
In solitude: and mutually addressed
From each to all, for wisdom's sake: — This truth
The priest announces from his holy seat:

And, crowned with garlands in the summer grove,
The poet fits it to his pensive lyre.
Yet, ere that final resting-place be gained,
Sharp contradictions may arise, by doom
Of this same life, compelling us to grieve
That the prosperities of love and joy
Should be permitted, ofttimes, to endure   450
So long, and be at once cast down for ever.
Oh! tremble, ye, to whom hath been assigned
A course of days composing happy months,
And they as happy years; the present still
So like the past, and both so firm a pledge
Of a congenial future, that the wheels
Of pleasure move without the aid of hope:
For Mutability is Nature's bane;
And slighted Hope *will* be avenged; and, when
Ye need her favours, ye shall find her not;   460
But in her stead — fear — doubt — and agony!"

This was the bitter language of the heart:
But, while he spake, look, gesture, tone of voice,
Though discomposed and vehement, were such
As skill and graceful nature might suggest
To a proficient of the tragic scene
Standing before the multitude, beset
With dark events. Desirous to divert
Or stem the current of the speaker's thoughts,
We signified a wish to leave that place   470
Of stillness and close privacy, a nook
That seemed for self-examination made;
Or, for confession, in the sinner's need,
Hidden from all men's view. To our attempt
He yielded not; but, pointing to a slope
Of mossy turf defended from the sun,
And on that couch inviting us to rest,

Full on that tender-hearted Man he turned
A serious eye, and his speech thus renewed.

"You never saw, your eyes did never look   480
On the bright form of Her whom once I loved: —
Her silver voice was heard upon the earth,
A sound unknown to you; else, honoured Friend!
Your heart had borne a pitiable share
Of what I suffered, when I wept that loss,
And suffer now, not seldom, from the thought
That I remember, and can weep no more. —
Stripped as I am of all the golden fruit
Of self-esteem; and by the cutting blasts
Of self-reproach familiarly assailed;   490
Yet would I not be of such wintry bareness
But that some leaf of your regard should hang
Upon my naked branches: — lively thoughts
Give birth, full often, to unguarded words;
I grieve that, in your presence, from my tongue
Too much of frailty hath already dropped;
But that too much demands still more.
                                        You know,
Revered Compatriot — and to you, kind Sir,
(Not to be deemed a stranger, as you come
Following the guidance of these welcome feet   500
To our secluded vale) it may be told —
That my demerits did not sue in vain
To One on whose mild radiance many gazed
With hope, and all with pleasure.   This fair Bride —
In the devotedness of youthful love,
Preferring me to parents, and the choir
Of gay companions, to the natal roof,
And all known places and familiar sights
(Resigned with sadness gently weighing down
Her trembling expectations, but no more   510

Than did to her due honour, and to me
Yielded, that day, a confidence sublime
In what I had to build upon) — this Bride,
Young, modest, meek, and beautiful, I led
To a low cottage in a sunny bay,
Where the salt sea innocuously breaks,
And the sea breeze as innocently breathes,
On Devon's leafy shores; — a sheltered hold,
In a soft clime encouraging the soil
To a luxuriant bounty! — As our steps   520
Approach the embowered abode — our chosen seat —
See, rooted in the earth, her kindly bed,
The unendangered myrtle, decked with flowers,
Before the threshold stands to welcome us!
While, in the flowering myrtle's neighbourhood,
Not overlooked but courting no regard,
Those native plants, the holly and the yew,
Gave modest intimation to the mind
How willingly their aid they would unite
With the green myrtle, to endear the hours   530
Of winter, and protect that pleasant place.
— Wild were the walks upon those lonely Downs,
Track leading into track; how marked, how worn
Into bright verdure, between fern and gorse,
Winding away its never-ending line
On their smooth surface, evidence was none:
But, there, lay open to our daily haunt,
A range of unappropriated earth,
Where youth's ambitious feet might move at large;
Whence, unmolested wanderers, we beheld   540
The shining giver of the day diffuse
His brightness o'er a tract of sea and land
Gay as our spirits, free as our desires;
As our enjoyments, boundless. — From those heights
We dropped, at pleasure, into sylvan combs;

Where arbours of impenetrable shade,
And mossy seats, detained us side by side,
With hearts at ease, and knowledge in our hearts
'That all the grove and all the day was ours.'

"O happy time! still happier was at hand;   550
For Nature called my Partner to resign
Her share in the pure freedom of that life,
Enjoyed by us in common. — To my hope,
To my heart's wish, my tender Mate became
The thankful captive of maternal bonds;
And those wild paths were left to me alone.
There could I meditate on follies past;
And, like a weary voyager escaped
From risk and hardship, inwardly retrace
A course of vain delights and thoughtless guilt,   560
And self-indulgence — without shame pursued.
There, undisturbed, could think of and could thank
Her whose submissive spirit was to me
Rule and restraint — my guardian — shall I say
That earthly Providence, whose guiding love
Within a port of rest had lodged me safe;
Safe from temptation, and from danger far?
Strains followed of acknowledgment addressed
To an Authority enthroned above
The reach of sight; from whom, as from their source,   570
Proceed all visible ministers of good
That walk the earth — Father of heaven and earth,
Father, and king, and judge, adored and feared!
These acts of mind, and memory, and heart,
And spirit — interrupted and relieved
By observations transient as the glance
Of flying sunbeams, or to the outward form
Cleaving with power inherent and intense,
As the mute insect fixed upon the plant

On whose soft leaves it hangs, and from whose cup   580
It draws its nourishment imperceptibly —
Endeared my wanderings; and the mother's kiss
And infant's smile awaited my return.

   "In privacy we dwelt, a wedded pair,
Companions daily, often all day long;
Not placed by fortune within easy reach
Of various intercourse, nor wishing aught
Beyond the allowance of our own fireside,
The twain within our happy cottage born,
Inmates, and heirs of our united love;   590
Graced mutually by difference of sex,
And with no wider interval of time
Between their several births than served for one
To establish something of a leader's sway;
Yet left them joined by sympathy in age;
Equals in pleasure, fellows in pursuit.
On these two pillars rested as in air
Our solitude.
        It soothes me to perceive,
Your courtesy withholds not from my words
Attentive audience. But, oh! gentle Friends,   600
As times of quiet and unbroken peace,
Though, for a nation, times of blessedness,
Give back faint echoes from the historian's page;
So, in the imperfect sounds of this discourse,
Depressed I hear, how faithless is the voice
Which those most blissful days reverberate.
What special record can, or need, be given
To rules and habits, whereby much was done,
But all within the sphere of little things;
Of humble, though, to us, important cares,   610
And precious interests? Smoothly did our life

Advance, swerving not from the path prescribed;
Her annual, her diurnal, round alike
Maintained with faithful care. And you divine
The worst effects that our condition saw
If you imagine changes slowly wrought,
And in their process unperceivable;
Not wished for; sometimes noticed with a sigh,
(Whate'er of good or lovely they might bring)
Sighs of regret, for the familiar good   620
And loveliness endeared which they removed.

"Seven years of occupation undisturbed
Established seemingly a right to hold
That happiness; and use and habit gave
To what an alien spirit had acquired
A patrimonial sanctity. And thus,
With thoughts and wishes bounded to this world,
I lived and breathed; most grateful — if to enjoy
Without repining or desire for more,
For different lot, or change to higher sphere,   630
(Only except some impulses of pride
With no determined object, though upheld
By theories with suitable support) —
Most grateful, if in such wise to enjoy
Be proof of gratitude for what we have;
Else, I allow, most thankless. — But, at once,
From some dark seat of fatal power was urged
A claim that shattered all. — Our blooming girl,
Caught in the gripe of death, with such brief time
To struggle in as scarcely would allow   640
Her cheek to change its colour, was conveyed
From us to inaccessible worlds, to regions
Where height, or depth, admits not the approach
Of living man, though longing to pursue.
— With even as brief a warning — and how soon,

With what short interval of time between,
I tremble yet to think of — our last prop,
Our happy life's only remaining stay —
The brother followed; and was seen no more!

"Calm as a frozen lake when ruthless winds   650
Blow fiercely, agitating earth and sky,
The Mother now remained; as if in her,
Who, to the lowest region of the soul.
Had been erewhile unsettled and disturbed,
This second visitation had no power
To shake; but only to bind up and seal;
And to establish thankfulness of heart
In Heaven's determinations, ever just.
The eminence whereon her spirit stood,
Mine was unable to attain.   Immense   660
The space that severed us! But, as the sight
Communicates with heaven's ethereal orbs
Incalculably distant; so, I felt
That consolation may descend from far
(And that is intercourse, and union, too,)
While, overcome with speechless gratitude,
And, with a holier love inspired, I looked
On her — at once superior to my woes
And partner of my loss. — O heavy change!
Dimness o'er this clear luminary crept   67v
Insensibly; — the immortal and divine
Yielded to mortal reflux; her pure glory,
As from the pinnacle of worldly state
Wretched ambition drops astounded, fell
Into a gulf obscure of silent grief,
And keen heart-anguish — of itself ashamed,
Yet obstinately cherishing itself:
And, so consumed, she melted from my arms;
And left me, on this earth, disconsolate!

"What followed cannot be reviewed in thought;   680
Much less, retraced in words. If she, of life
Blameless, so intimate with love and joy
And all the tender motions of the soul,
Had been supplanted, could I hope to stand —
Infirm, dependent, and now destitute?
I called on dreams and visions, to disclose
That which is veiled from waking thought; conjured
Eternity, as men constrain a ghost
To appear and answer; to the grave I spake
Imploringly; — looked up, and asked the Heavens   690
If Angels traversed their cerulean floors,
If fixed or wandering star could tidings yield
Of the departed spirit — what abode
It occupies — what consciousness retains
Of former loves and interests. Then my soul
Turned inward, — to examine of what stuff
Time's fetters are composed; and life was put
To inquisition, long and profitless!
By pain of heart — now checked — and now impelled —
The intellectual power, through words and things,   700
Went sounding on, a dim and perilous way!
And from those transports, and these toils abstruse,
Some trace am I enabled to retain
Of time, else lost; — existing unto me
Only by records in myself not found.

"From that abstraction I was roused, — and how?
Even as a thoughtful shepherd by a flash
Of lightning startled in a gloomy cave
Of these wild hills. For, lo! the dread Bastille,
With all the chambers in its horrid towers,   710
Fell to the ground: — by violence overthrown
Of indignation; and with shouts that drowned
The crash it made in falling! From the wreck

A golden palace rose, or seemed to rise,
The appointed seat of equitable law
And mild paternal sway. The potent shock
I felt: the transformation I perceived,
As marvellously seized as in that moment
When, from the blind mist issuing, I beheld
Glory — beyond all glory ever seen,   720
Confusion infinite of heaven and earth,
Dazzling the soul. Meanwhile, prophetic harps
In every grove were ringing, 'War shall cease;
Did ye not hear that conquest is abjured?
Bring garlands, bring forth choicest flowers, to deck
The tree of Liberty.' — My heart rebounded;
My melancholy voice the chorus joined;
— 'Be joyful all ye nations; in all lands,
Ye that are capable of joy be glad!
Henceforth, whate'er is wanting to yourselves   730
In others ye shall promptly find; — and all,
Enriched by mutual and reflected wealth,
Shall with one heart honour their common kind.'

"Thus was I reconverted to the world;
Society became my glittering bride,
And airy hopes my children. — From the depths
Of natural passion, seemingly escaped,
My soul diffused herself in wide embrace
Of institutions, and the forms of things;
As they exist, in mutable array,   740
Upon life's surface. What, though in my veins
There flowed no Gallic blood, nor had I breathed
The air of France, not less than Gallic zeal
Kindled and burnt among the sapless twigs
Of my exhausted heart. If busy men
In sober conclave met, to weave a web
Of amity, whose living threads should stretch

Beyond the seas, and to the farthest pole,
There did I sit, assisting. If, with noise
And acclamation, crowds in open air   750
Expressed the tumult of their minds, my voice
There mingled, heard or not. The powers of song
I left not uninvoked; and, in still groves,
Where mild enthusiasts tuned a pensive lay
Of thanks and expectation, in accord
With their belief, I sang Saturnian rule
Returned, — a progeny of golden years
Permitted to descend, and bless mankind.
— With promises the Hebrew Scriptures teem;
I felt their invitation; and resumed   760
A long-suspended office in the House
Of public worship, where, the glowing phrase
Of ancient inspiration serving me,
I promised also, — with undaunted trust
Foretold, and added prayer to prophecy;
The admiration winning of the crowd;
The help desiring of the pure devout.

"Scorn and contempt forbid me to proceed!
But History, time's slavish scribe, will tell
How rapidly the zealots of the cause   77(
Disbanded — or in hostile ranks appeared;
Some, tired of honest service; these, outdone,
Disgusted therefore, or appalled, by aims
Of fiercer zealots — so confusion reigned,
And the more faithful were compelled to exclaim,
As Brutus did to Virtue, 'Liberty,
I worshipped thee, and find thee but a Shade!'

"Such recantation had for me no charm,
Nor would I bend to it; who should have grieved
At aught, however fair, that bore the mien   780

Of a conclusion, or catastrophe.
Why then conceal, that, when the simply good
In timid selfishness withdrew, I sought
Other support, not scrupulous whence it came;
And, by what compromise it stood, not nice?
Enough if notions seemed to be high-pitched,
And qualities determined. — Among men
So charactered did I maintain a strife
Hopeless, and still more hopeless every hour;
But, in the process, I began to feel   790
That, if the emancipation of the world
Were missed, I should at least secure my own,
And be in part compensated. For rights,
Widely — inveterately usurped upon,
I spake with vehemence; and promptly seized
All that Abstraction furnished for my needs
Or purposes; nor scrupled to proclaim,
And propagate, by liberty of life,
Those new persuasions. Not that I rejoiced,
Or even found pleasure, in such vagrant course,   800
For its own sake; but farthest from the walk
Which I had trod in happiness and peace,
Was most inviting to a troubled mind;
That, in a struggling and distempered world,
Saw a seductive image of herself.
Yet, mark the contradictions of which Man
Is still the sport! Here Nature was my guide,
The Nature of the dissolute; but thee,
O fostering Nature! I rejected — smiled
At others' tears in pity; and in scorn   810
At those, which thy soft influence sometimes drew
From my unguarded heart. — The tranquil shores
Of Britain circumscribed me; else, perhaps
I might have been entangled among deeds,
Which, now, as infamous, I should abhor —

Despise, as senseless: for my spirit relished
Strangely the exasperation of that Land,
Which turned an angry beak against the down
Of her own breast; confounded into hope
Of disencumbering thus her fretful wings.   820

"But all was quieted by iron bonds
Of military sway. The shifting aims,
The moral interests, the creative might,
The varied functions and high attributes
Of civil action, yielded to a power
Formal, and odious, and contemptible.
— In Britain, ruled a panic dread of change;
The weak were praised, rewarded, and advanced;
And, from the impulse of a just disdain,
Once more did I retire into myself.   830
There feeling no contentment, I resolved
To fly, for safeguard, to some foreign shore,
Remote from Europe; from her blasted hopes;
Her fields of carnage, and polluted air.

"Fresh blew the wind, when o'er the Atlantic Main
The ship went gliding with her thoughtless crew;
And who among them but an Exile, freed
From discontent, indifferent, pleased to sit
Among the busily-employed, not more
With obligation charged, with service taxed,   840
Than the loose pendant — to the idle wind
Upon the tall mast streaming. But, ye Powers
Of soul and sense mysteriously allied,
O, never let the Wretched, if a choice
Be left him, trust the freight of his distress
To a long voyage on the silent deep!
For, like a plague, will memory break out;
And, in the blank and solitude of things,

Upon his spirit, with a fever's strength,
Will conscience prey. — Feebly must they have felt   850
Who, in old time, attired with snakes and whips
The vengeful Furies. *Beautiful* regards
Were turned on me — the face of her I loved;
The Wife and Mother pitifully fixing
Tender reproaches, insupportable!
Where now that boasted liberty? No welcome
From unknown objects I received; and those,
Known and familiar, which the vaulted sky
Did, in the placid clearness of the night,
Disclose, had accusations to prefer   860
Against my peace. Within the cabin stood
That volume — as a compass for the soul —
Revered among the nations. I implored
Its guidance; but the infallible support
Of faith was wanting. Tell me, why refused
To One by storms annoyed and adverse winds;
Perplexed with currents; of his weakness sick;
Of vain endeavours tired; and by his own,
And by his nature's ignorance, dismayed!

"Long wished-for sight, the Western World appeared;
And, when the ship was moored, I leaped ashore   871
Indignantly — resolved to be a man,
Who, having o'er the past no power, would live
No longer in subjection to the past,
With abject mind — from a tyrannic lord
Inviting penance, fruitlessly endured:
So, like a fugitive, whose feet have cleared
Some boundary, which his followers may not cross
In prosecution of their deadly chase,
Respiring I looked round. — How bright the sun,   880
The breeze how soft! Can any thing produced
In the old World compare, thought I, for power

And majesty with this gigantic stream,
Sprung from the desert? And behold a city
Fresh, youthful, and aspiring! What are these
To me, or I to them? As much, at least
As he desires that they should be, whom winds
And waves have wafted to this distant shore,
In the condition of a damaged seed,
Whose fibres cannot, if they would, take root.   890
Here may I roam at large; — my business is,
Roaming at large, to observe, and not to feel
And, therefore, not to act — convinced that all
Which bears the name of action, howsoe'er
Beginning, ends in servitude — still painful,
And mostly profitless. And, sooth to say,
On nearer view, a motley spectacle
Appeared, of high pretensions — unreproved
But by the obstreperous voice of higher still;
Big passions strutting on a petty stage;   900
Which a detached spectator may regard
Not unamused. — But ridicule demands
Quick change of objects; and, to laugh alone,
At a composing distance from the haunts
Of strife and folly, though it be a treat
As choice as musing Leisure can bestow;
Yet, in the very centre of the crowd,
To keep the secret of a poignant scorn,
Howe'er to airy Demons suitable,
Of all unsocial courses, is least fit   910
For the gross spirit of mankind, — the one
That soonest fails to please, and quickliest turns
Into vexation.
                    Let us, then, I said,
Leave this unknit Republic to the scourge
Of her own passions; and to regions haste,
Whose shades have never felt the encroaching axe,

Or soil endured a transfer in the mart
Of dire rapacity.   There, Man abides,
Primeval Nature's child.   A creature weak
In combination, (wherefore else driven back   920
So far, and of his old inheritance
So easily deprived?) but, for that cause,
More dignified, and stronger in himself;
Whether to act, judge, suffer, or enjoy.
True, the intelligence of social art
Hath overpowered his forefathers, and soon
Will sweep the remnant of his line away;
But contemplations, worthier, nobler far
Than her destructive energies, attend
His independence, when along the side   930
Of Mississippi, or that northern stream
That spreads into successive seas, he walks;
Pleased to perceive his own unshackled life,
And his innate capacities of soul,
There imaged: or when, having gained the top
Of some commanding eminence, which yet
Intruder ne'er beheld, he thence surveys
Regions of wood and wide savannah, vast
Expanse of unappropriated earth,
With mind that sheds a light on what he sees;   940
Free as the sun, and lonely as the sun,
Pouring above his head its radiance down
Upon a living and rejoicing world!

    "So, westward, tow'rd the unviolated woods
I bent my way; and, roaming far and wide,
Failed not to greet the merry Mocking-bird;
And, while the melancholy Muccawiss
(The sportive bird's companion in the grove)
Repeated o'er and o'er his plaintive cry,
I sympathised at leisure with the sound;   950

But that pure archetype of human greatness,
I found him not. There, in his stead, appeared
A creature, squalid, vengeful, and impure;
Remorseless, and submissive to no law
But supersititious fear, and abject sloth.

"Enough is told! Here am I — ye have heard
What evidence I seek, and vainly seek;
What from my fellow-beings I require,
And either they have not to give, or I
Lack virtue to receive; what I myself,   960
Too oft by wilful forfeiture, have lost
Nor can regain.   How languidly I look
Upon this visible fabric of the world,
May be divined — perhaps it hath been said: —
But spare your pity, if there be in me
Aught that deserves respect: for I exist,
Within myself, not comfortless. — The tenour
Which my life holds, he readily may conceive
Whoe'er hath stood to watch a mountain brook
In some still passage of its course, and seen,   970
Within the depths of its capacious breast,
Inverted trees, rocks, clouds, and azure sky;
And, on its glassy surface, specks of foam,
And conglobated bubbles undissolved,
Numerous as stars; that, by their onward lapse,
Betray to sight the motion of the stream,
Else imperceptible.   Meanwhile, is heard
A softened roar, or murmur; and the sound
Though soothing, and the little floating isles
Though beautiful, are both by Nature charged   980
With the same pensive office; and make known
Through what perplexing labyrinths, abrupt
Precipitations, and untoward straits,
The earth-born wanderer hath passed; and quickly,

That respite o'er, like traverses and toils
Must he again encounter. — Such a stream
Is human Life; and so the Spirit fares
In the best quiet to her course allowed;
And such is mine, — save only for a hope
That my particular current soon will reach   990
The unfathomable gulf, where all is still!"

BOOK FOURTH

DESPONDENCY CORRECTED

Argument

State of feeling produced by the foregoing Narrative. — A belief in a super-
intending Providence the only adequate support under affliction. — Wander-
er's ejaculation. — Acknowledges the difficulty of a lively faith. — Hence
immoderate sorrow. — Exhortations. — How received. — Wanderer applies
his discourse to that other cause of dejection in the Solitary's mind. — Disap-
pointment from the French Revolution. — States grounds of hope, and
insists on the necessity of patience and fortitude with respect to the course of
great revolutions. — Knowledge the source of tranquillity. — Rural Solitude
favourable to knowledge of the inferior Creatures; Study of their habits and
ways recommended; exhortation to bodily exertion and communion with
Nature. — Morbid Solitude pitiable. — Superstition better than apathy. —
Apathy and destitution unknown in the infancy of society. — The various
modes of Religion prevented it. — Illustrated in the Jewish, Persian, Baby-
lonian, Chaldean, and Grecian modes of belief. — Solitary interposes. —
Wanderer points out the influence of religious and imaginative feeling in the
humble ranks of society, illustrated from present and past times. — These
principles tend to recall exploded superstitions and Popery. — Wanderer
rebuts this charge, and contrasts the dignities of the Imagination with the
presumptuous littleness of certain modern Philosophers. — Recommends
other lights and guides. — Asserts the power of the Soul to regenerate herself;
Solitary asks how. — Reply. — Personal appeal. — Exhortation to activity
of body renewed. — How to commune with Nature. — Wanderer concludes
with a legitimate union of the imagination, affections, understanding, and
reason. — Effect of his discourse. — Evening; Return to the Cottage.

Here closed the Tenant of that lonely vale
His mournful narrative — commenced in pain,
In pain commenced, and ended without peace:
Yet tempered, not unfrequently, with strains
Of native feeling, grateful to our minds;
And yielding surely some relief to his,
While we sate listening with compassion due.
A pause of silence followed; then, with voice
That did not falter though the heart was moved,
The Wanderer said: —
                    "One adequate support   10
For the calamities of mortal life
Exists — one only; an assured belief
That the procession of our fate, howe'er
Sad or disturbed, is ordered by a Being
Of infinite benevolence and power;
Whose everlasting purposes embrace
All accidents, converting them to good.
— The darts of anguish *fix* not where the seat
Of suffering hath been thoroughly fortified
By acquiescence in the Will supreme   20
For time and for eternity; by faith,
Faith absolute in God, including hope,
And the defence that lies in boundless love
Of his perfections; with habitual dread
Of aught unworthily conceived, endured
Impatiently, ill-done, or left undone,
To the dishonour of his holy name.
Soul of our Souls, and safeguard of the world!
Sustain, thou only canst, the sick of heart;
Restore their languid spirits, and recall   30
Their lost affections unto thee and thine!"

Then, as we issued from that covert nook,
He thus continued, lifting up his eyes

To heaven: — "How beautiful this dome of sky;
And the vast hills, in fluctuation fixed
At thy command, how awful! Shall the Soul,
Human and rational, report of thee
Even less than these! — Be mute who will, who can,
Yet I will praise thee with impassioned voice:
My lips, that may forget thee in the crowd,   40
Cannot forget thee here; where thou hast built,
For thy own glory, in the wilderness!
Me didst thou constitute a priest of thine,
In such a temple as we now behold
Reared for thy presence: therefore am I bound
To worship, here, and everywhere — as one
Not doomed to ignorance, though forced to tread,
From childhood up, the ways of poverty;
From unreflecting ignorance preserved,
And from debasement rescued. — By thy grace   50
The particle divine remained unquenched;
And, 'mid the wild weeds of a rugged soil,
Thy bounty caused to flourish deathless flowers,
From paradise transplanted: wintry age
Impends; the frost will gather round my heart;
If the flowers wither, I am worse than dead!
— Come, labour, when the worn-out frame requires
Perpetual sabbath; come, disease and want;
And sad exclusion through decay of sense;
But leave me unabated trust in thee —   60
And let thy favour, to the end of life,
Inspire me with ability to seek
Repose and hope among eternal things —
Father of heaven and earth! and I am rich,
And will possess my portion in content!

   "And what are things eternal? — powers depart,"
The grey-haired Wanderer steadfastly replied,

Answering the question which himself had asked,
"Possessions vanish, and opinions change,
And passions hold a fluctuating seat: 70
But, by the storms of circumstance unshaken,
And subject neither to eclipse nor wane,
Duty exists; — immutably survive,
For our support, the measures and the forms,
Which an abstract intelligence supplies;
Whose kingdom is, where time and space are not.
Of other converse which mind, soul, and heart,
Do, with united urgency, require,
What more that may not perish? — Thou, dread source,
Prime, self-existing cause and end of all   80
That in the scale of being fill their place;
Above our human region, or below,
Set and sustained; — thou, who didst wrap the cloud
Of infancy around us, that thyself,
Therein, with our simplicity awhile
Might'st hold, on earth, communion undisturbed;
Who from the anarchy of dreaming sleep,
Or from its death-like void, with punctual care,
And touch as gentle as the morning light,
Restor'st us, daily, to the powers of sense   90
And reason's steadfast rule — thou, thou alone
Art everlasting, and the blessed Spirits,
Which thou includest, as the sea her waves:
For adoration thou endur'st; endure
For consciousness the motions of thy will;
For apprehension those transcendent truths
Of the pure intellect, that stand as laws
(Submission constituting strength and power)
Even to thy Being's infinite majesty!
This universe shall pass away — a work   100
Glorious! because the shadow of thy might,
A step, or link, for intercourse with thee.

Ah! if the time must come, in which my feet
No more shall stray where meditation leads,
By flowing stream, through wood, or craggy wild,
Loved haunts like these; the unimprisoned Mind
May yet have scope to range among her own,
Her thoughts, her images, her high desires.
If the dear faculty of sight should fail,
Still, it may be allowed me to remember   110
What visionary powers of eye and soul
In youth were mine; when, stationed on the top
Of some huge hill, expectant, I beheld
The sun rise up, from distant climes returned
Darkness to chase, and sleep; and bring the day
His bounteous gift! or saw him toward the deep
Sink, with a retinue of flaming clouds
Attended; then, my spirit was entranced
With joy exalted to beatitude;
The measure of my soul was filled with bliss,   120
And holiest love; as earth, sea, air, with light,
With pomp, with glory, with magnificence!

  "Those fervent raptures are for ever flown;
And, since their date, my soul hath undergone
Change manifold, for better or for worse:
Yet cease I not to struggle, and aspire
Heavenward; and chide the part of me that flags,
Through sinful choice; or dread necessity
On human nature from above imposed.
'Tis, by comparison, an easy task   130
Earth to despise; but, to converse with heaven —
This is not easy: — to relinquish all
We have, or hope, of happiness and joy,
And stand in freedom loosened from this world,
I deem not arduous; but must needs confess
That 'tis a thing impossible to frame

Conceptions equal to the soul's desires;
And the most difficult of tasks to *keep*
Heights which the soul is competent to gain.
— Man is of dust: ethereal hopes are his,   140
Which, when they should sustain themselves aloft,
Want due consistence; like a pillar of smoke,
That with majestic energy from earth
Rises; but, having reached the thinner air,
Melts, and dissolves, and is no longer seen.
From this infirmity of mortal kind
Sorrow proceeds, which else were not; at least,
If grief be something hallowed and ordained,
If, in proportion, it be just and meet,
Yet, through this weakness of the general heart,   150
Is it enabled to maintain its hold
In that excess which conscience disapproves.
For who could sink and settle to that point
Of selfishness; so senseless who could be
As long and perseveringly to mourn
For any object of his love, removed
From this unstable world, if he could fix
A satisfying view upon that state
Of pure, imperishable, blessedness,
Which reason promises, and holy writ   160
Ensures to all believers? — Yet mistrust
Is of such incapacity, methinks,
No natural branch; despondency far less;
And, least of all, is absolute despair.
— And, if there be whose tender frames have drooped
Even to the dust; apparently, through weight
Of anguish unrelieved, and lack of power
An agonizing sorrow to transmute;
Deem not that proof is here of hope withheld
When wanted most; a confidence impaired   170
So pitiably, that, having ceased to see

With bodily eyes, they are borne down by love
Of what is lost, and perish through regret.
Oh! no, the innocent Sufferer often sees
Too clearly; feels too vividly; and longs
To realize the vision, with intense
And over-constant yearning; there — there lies
The excess, by which the balance is destroyed.
Too, too contracted are these walls of flesh,
This vital warmth too cold, these visual orbs,   180
Though inconceivably endowed, too dim
For any passion of the soul that leads
To ecstasy; and all the crooked paths
Of time and change disdaining, takes its course
Along the line of limitless desires.
I, speaking now from such disorder free,
Nor rapt, nor craving, but in settled peace,
I cannot doubt that they whom you deplore
Are glorified; or, if they sleep, shall wake
From sleep, and dwell with God in endless love.   190
Hope, below this, consists not with belief
In mercy, carried infinite degrees
Beyond the tenderness of human hearts:
Hope, below this, consists not with belief
In perfect wisdom, guiding mightiest power,
That finds no limits but her own pure will.

   "Here then we rest; not fearing for our creed
The worst that human reasoning can achieve,
To unsettle or perplex it: yet with pain
Acknowledging, and grievous self-reproach,   200
That, though immovably convinced, we want
Zeal, and the virtue to exist by faith
As soldiers live by courage; as, by strength
Of heart, the sailor fights with roaring seas.
Alas! the endowment of immortal power

Is matched unequally with custom, time,
And domineering faculties of sense
In *all;* in most with superadded foes,
Idle temptations; open vanities,
Ephemeral offspring of the unblushing world;   210
And, in the private regions of the mind,
Ill-governed passions, ranklings of despite,
Immoderate wishes, pining discontent,
Distress and care. What then remains? — To seek
Those helps for his occasions ever near
Who lacks not will to use them; vows, renewed
On the first motion of a holy thought;
Vigils of contemplation; praise; and prayer —
A stream, which, from the fountain of the heart
Issuing, however feebly, nowhere flows   220
Without access of unexpected strength.
But, above all, the victory is most sure
For him, who, seeking faith by virtue, strives
To yield entire submission to the law
Of conscience — conscience reverenced and obeyed,
As God's most intimate presence in the soul,
And his most perfect image in the world.
— Endeavour thus to live; these rules regard;
These helps solicit; and a steadfast seat
Shall then be yours among the happy few   230
Who dwell on earth, yet breathe empyreal air,
Sons of the morning. For your nobler part,
Ere disencumbered of her mortal chains,
Doubt shall be quelled and trouble chased away;
With only such degree of sadness left
As may support longings of pure desire;
And strengthen love, rejoicing secretly
In the sublime attractions of the grave."

Stillness prevailed around us: and the voice
That spake was capable to lift the soul
Toward regions yet more tranquil. But, methought,
That he, whose fixed despondency had given
Impulse and motive to that strong discourse,   255
Was less upraised in spirit than abashed;
Shrinking from admonition, like a man
Who feels that to exhort is to reproach.
Yet not to be diverted from his aim,
The Sage continued: —

              "For that other loss,   260
The loss of confidence in social man,
By the unexpected transports of our age
Carried so high, that every thought, which looked
Beyond the temporal destiny of the Kind,
To many seemed superfluous — as, no cause
Could e'er for such exalted confidence
Exist; so, none is now for fixed despair:
The two extremes are equally disowned
By reason: if, with sharp recoil, from one
You have been driven far as its opposite,   270
Between them seek the point whereon to build
Sound expectations. So doth he advise
Who shared at first the illusion; but was soon
Cast from the pedestal of pride by shocks
Which Nature gently gave, in woods and fields;
Nor unreproved by Providence, thus speaking
To the inattentive children of the world:
'Vain-glorious Generation! what new powers
On you have been conferred? what gifts, withheld
From your progenitors, have ye received,   280
Fit recompense of new desert? what claim
Are ye prepared to urge, that my decrees
For you should undergo a sudden change;
And the weak functions of one busy day,

Reclaiming and extirpating, perform
What all the slowly-moving years of time,
With their united force, have left undone?
By nature's gradual processes be taught;
By story be confounded! Ye aspire
Rashly, to fall once more; and that false fruit,   290
Which, to your overweening spirits, yields
Hope of a flight celestial, will produce
Misery and shame. But Wisdom of her sons
Shall not the less, though late, be justified.'

  "Such timely warning," said the Wanderer, "gave
That visionary voice; and, at this day,
When a Tartarean darkness overspreads
The groaning nations; when the impious rule,
By will or by established ordinance,
Their own dire agents, and constrain the good   300
To acts which they abhor; though I bewail
This triumph, yet the pity of my heart
Prevents me not from owning, that the law,
By which mankind now suffers, is most just.
For by superior energies; more strict
Affiance in each other; faith more firm
In their unhallowed principles; the bad
Have fairly earned a victory o'er the weak,
The vacillating, inconsistent good.
Therefore, not unconsoled, I wait — in hope   310
To see the moment, when the righteous cause
Shall gain defenders zealous and devout
As they who have opposed her; in which Virtue
Will, to her efforts, tolerate no bounds
That are not lofty as her rights; aspiring
By impulse of her own ethereal zeal.
That spirit only can redeem mankind;
And when that sacred spirit shall appear,

Then shall *our* triumph be complete as theirs.
Yet, should this confidence prove vain, the wise   320
Have still the keeping of their proper peace;
Are guardians of their own tranquillity.
They act, or they recede, observe, and feel;
'Knowing the heart of man is set to be
The centre of this world, about the which
Those revolutions of disturbances
Still roll; where all the aspècts of misery
Predominate; whose strong effects are such
As he must bear, being powerless to redress;
And that unless above himself he can   330
Erect himself, how poor a thing is man!"

    .   .   .   .   .

  "O blest seclusion! when the mind admits   1035
The law of duty; and can therefore move
Through each vicissitude of loss and gain,
Linked in entire complacence with her choice;
When youth's presumptuousness is mellowed down,
And manhood's vain anxiety dismissed;   1040
When wisdom shows her seasonable fruit,
Upon the boughs of sheltering leisure hung
In sober plenty; when the spirit stoops
To drink with gratitude the crystal stream
Of unreproved enjoyment; and is pleased
To muse, and be saluted by the air
Of meek repentance, wafting wallflower scents
From out the crumbling ruins of fallen pride
And chambers of transgression, now forlorn.
O, calm contented days, and peaceful nights!   1050
Who, when such good can be obtained, would strive
To reconcile his manhood to a couch
Soft, as may seem, but, under that disguise,

Stuffed with the thorny substance of the past
For fixed annoyance; and full oft beset
With floating dreams, black and disconsolate,
The vapoury phantoms of futurity?

"Within the soul a faculty abides,
That with interpositions, which would hide
And darken, so can deal that they become   1060
Contingencies of pomp; and serve to exalt
Her native brightness. As the ample moon,
In the deep stillness of a summer even
Rising behind a thick and lofty grove,
Burns, like an unconsuming fire of light,
In the green trees; and, kindling on all sides
Their leafy umbrage, turns the dusky veil
Into a substance glorious as her own,
Yea, with her own incorporated, by power
Capacious and serene. Like power abides   1070
In man's celestial spirit; virtue thus
Sets forth and magnifies herself; thus feeds
A calm, a beautiful, and silent fire,
From the encumbrances of mortal life,
From error, disappointment — nay, from guilt;
And sometimes, so relenting justice wills,
From palpable oppressions of despair."

  The Solitary by these words was touched
With manifest emotion, and exclaimed;
"But how begin? and whence? — 'The Mind is free —
Resolve,' the haughty Moralist would say,   1081
'This single act is all that we demand.'
Alas! such wisdom bids a creature fly
Whose very sorrow is, that time hath shorn
His natural wings! — To friendship let him turn
For succour; but perhaps he sits alone

On stormy waters, tossed in a little boat
That holds but him, and can contain no more!
Religion tells of amity sublime
Which no condition can preclude; of One   1090
Who sees all suffering, comprehends all wants,
All weakness fathoms, can supply all needs:
But is that bounty absolute? — His gifts,
Are they not, still, in some degree, rewards
For acts of service?   Can his love extend
To hearts that own not him?   Will showers of grace,
When in the sky no promise may be seen,
Fall to refresh a parched and withered land?
Or shall the groaning Spirit cast her load
At the Redeemer's feet?"
                In rueful tone,   1100
With some impatience in his mien, he spake:
Back to my mind rushed all that had been urged
To calm the Sufferer when his story closed;
I looked for counsel as unbending now;
But a discriminating sympathy
Stooped to this apt reply: —
                "As men from men
Do, in the constitution of their souls,
Differ, by mystery not to be explained;
And as we fall by various ways, and sink
One deeper than another, self-condemned   1110
Through manifold degrees of guilt and shame;
So manifold and various are the ways
Of restoration, fashioned to the steps
Of all infirmity, and tending all
To the same point, attainable by all —
Peace in ourselves, and union with our God.
For you, assuredly, a hopeful road
Lies open: we have heard from you a voice

At every moment softened in its course
By tenderness of heart; have seen your eye,   1120
Even like an altar lit by fire from heaven,
Kindle before us. — Your discourse this day,
That, like the fabled Lethe, wished to flow
In creeping sadness, through oblivious shades
Of death and night, has caught at every turn
The colours of the sun. Access for you
Is yet preserved to principles of truth,
Which the imaginative Will upholds
In seats of wisdom, not to be approached
By the inferior Faculty that moulds,   1130
With her minute and speculative pains,
Opinion, ever changing!
                I have seen
A curious child, who dwelt upon a tract
Of inland ground, applying to his ear
The convolutions of a smooth-lipped shell;
To which, in silence hushed, his very soul
Listened intensely; and his countenance soon
Brightened with joy; for from within were heard
Murmurings, whereby the monitor expressed
Mysterious union with its native sea.   1140
Even such a shell the universe itself
Is to the ear of Faith; and there are times,
I doubt not, when to you it doth impart
Authentic tidings of invisible things;
Of ebb and flow, and ever-during power;
And central peace, subsisting at the heart
Of endless agitation. Here you stand,
Adore, and worship, when you know it not;
Pious beyond the intention of your thought;
Devout above the meaning of your will.   1150
— Yes, you have felt, and may not cease to feel.

The estate of man would be indeed forlorn
If false conclusions of the reasoning power
Made the eye blind, and closed the passages
Through which the ear converses with the heart.
Has not the soul, the being of your life,
Received a shock of awful consciousness,
In some calm season, when these lofty rocks
At night's approach bring down the unclouded sky,
To rest upon their circumambient walls;   1160
A temple framing of dimensions vast,
And yet not too enormous for the sound
Of human anthems, — choral song, or burst
Sublime of instrumental harmony,
To glorify the Eternal! What if these
Did never break the stillness that prevails
Here, — if the solemn nightingale be mute,
And the soft woodlark here did never chant
Her vespers, — Nature fails not to provide
Impulse and utterance. The whispering air   1170
Sends inspiration from the shadowy heights,
And blind recesses of the caverned rocks;
The little rills, and waters numberless,
Inaudible by daylight, blend their notes
With the loud streams: and often, at the hour
When issue forth the first pale stars, is heard,
Within the circuit of this fabric huge,
One voice — the solitary raven, flying
Athwart the concave of the dark blue dome,
Unseen, perchance above all power of sight —   1180
An iron knell! with echoes from afar
Faint — and still fainter — as the cry, with which
The wanderer accompanies her flight
Through the calm region, fades upon the ear,
Diminishing by distance till it seemed

To expire; yet from the abyss is caught again,
And yet again recovered!
            But descending
From these imaginative heights, that yield
Far-stretching views into eternity,
Acknowledge that to Nature's humbler power   1190
Your cherished sullenness is forced to bend
Even here, where her amenities are sown
With sparing hand. Then trust yourself abroad
To range her blooming bowers, and spacious fields,
Where on the labours of the happy throng
She smiles, including in her wide embrace
City, and town, and tower, — and sea with ships
Sprinkled; — be our Companion while we track
Her rivers populous with gliding life;
While, free as air, o'er printless sands we march,   1200
Or pierce the gloom of her majestic woods;
Roaming, or resting under grateful shade
In peace and meditative cheerfulness;
Where living things, and things inanimate,
Do speak, at Heaven's command, to eye and ear,
And speak to social reason's inner sense,
With inarticulate language.
            For, the Man —
Who, in this spirit, communes with the Forms
Of nature, who with understanding heart
Both knows and loves such objects as excite   1210
No morbid passions, no disquietude,
No vengeance, and no hatred — needs must feel
The joy of that pure principle of love
So deeply, that, unsatisfied with aught
Less pure and exquisite, he cannot choose
But seek for objects of a kindred love
In fellow-natures and a kindred joy.

Accordingly he by degrees perceives
His feelings of aversion softened down;
A holy tenderness pervade his frame.   1220
His sanity of reason not impaired,
Say rather, all his thoughts now flowing clear,
From a clear fountain flowing, he looks round
And seeks for good; and finds the good he seeks:
Until abhorrence and contempt are things
He only knows by name; and, if he hear,
From other mouths, the language which they speak,
He is compassionate; and has no thought,
No feeling, which can overcome his love.

"And further; by contemplating these Forms   1230
In the relations which they bear to man,
He shall discern, how, through the various means
Which silently they yield, are multiplied
The spiritual presences of absent things.
Trust me, that for the instructed, time will come
When they shall meet no object but may teach
Some acceptable lesson to their minds
Of human suffering, or of human joy.
So shall they learn, while all things speak of man,
Their duties from all forms; and general laws,   1240
And local accidents, shall tend alike
To rouse, to urge; and, with the will, confer
The ability to spread the blessings wide
Of true philanthropy. The light of love
Not failing, perseverance from their steps
Departing not, for them shall be confirmed
The glorious habit by which sense is made
Subservient still to moral purposes,
Auxiliar to divine. That change shall clothe
The naked spirit, ceasing to deplore   1250
The burthen of existence. Science then

Shall be a precious visitant; and then,
And only then, be worthy of her name:
For then her heart shall kindle; her dull eye,
Dull and inanimate, no more shall hang
Chained to its object in brute slavery;
But taught with patient interest to watch
The processes of things, and serve the cause
Of order and distinctness, not for this
Shall it forget that its most noble use,   1260
Its most illustrious province, must be found
In furnishing clear guidance, a support
Not treacherous, to the mind's *excursive* power.
— So build we up the Being that we are;
Thus deeply drinking-in the soul of things,
We shall be wise perforce; and, while inspired
By choice, and conscious that the Will is free,
Shall move unswerving, even as if impelled
By strict necessity, along the path
Of order and of good. Whate'er we see,   1270
Or feel, shall tend to quicken and refine;
Shall fix, in calmer seats of moral strength,
Earthly desires; and raise, to loftier heights
Of divine love, our intellectual soul."

   Here closed the Sage that eloquent harangue,
Poured forth with fervour in continuous stream,
Such as, remote, 'mid savage wilderness,
An Indian Chief discharges from his breast
Into the hearing of assembled tribes,
In open circle seated round, and hushed   1280
As the unbreathing air, when not a leaf
Stirs in the mighty woods. — So did he speak:
The words he uttered shall not pass away
Dispersed, like music that the wind takes up
By snatches, and lets fall, to be forgotten;

No — they sank into me, the bounteous gift
Of one whom time and nature had made wise.
Gracing his doctrine with authority
Which hostile spirits silently allow;
Of one accustomed to desires that feed   1290
On fruitage gathered from the tree of life;
To hopes on knowledge and experience built;
Of one in whom persuasion and belief
Had ripened into faith, and faith become
A passionate intuition; whence the Soul,
Though bound to earth by ties of pity and love,
From all injurious servitude was free.

1795–1814   *1814*

Rinehart Editions